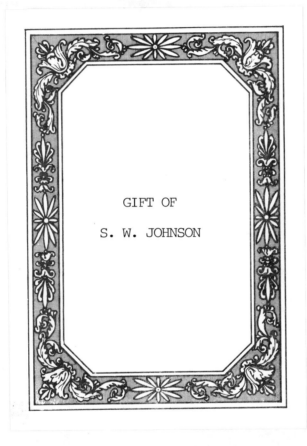

Key Ideas in Personality Theory

Key Ideas in Personality Theory

James R. Scroggs
Bridgewater State College

69-400

West Publishing Company
St. Paul   New York   Los Angeles   San Francisco

Copyediting: Stephen T. Conway
Design: Lucy Lesiak Design
Illustrations: Century Design
Cover art: Suzan Anson, Publishers' Graphics, Inc.
Composition: MGA Graphics

Library of Congress Cataloging in Publication Data

Scroggs, James R.
  Key ideas in personality theory.

  Bibliography: p.
  Includes index.
  1. Personality. I. Title.
BF698.S365   1985   155.2   84-20918
ISBN 0-314-85296-4

Acknowledgements

24 Figure 2–1, Reproduced by special permission of the publisher, Consulting Psychologists Press, Inc., from the Manual for the California Personality Inventory by Harrison G. Gough, copyright 1969; **123** From *Thematic Appreciation Test Manual* by Henry A. Murray *et. al..* Copyright 1943 by Harvard University Press. Reprinted by permission of the publisher; **150, 151, 152** From *Letters from Jenny* by Gordon W. Allport. Copyright 1965 by Harcourt Brace Jovanovich, Inc. Reprinted by permission of the publisher; **169** Table 8–2, From Raymond B. Cattell, *Personality and Learning Theory, Volume 1: The Structure of Personality in Its Environment,* pp. 61–72. Copyright © 1979 by Springer Publishing Company, Inc., New York. Used by permission; **194** Figure 9–1, From *The Behavior of Organisms: An Experimental Analysis* by B. F. Skinner. Copyright renewed 1966 by the author. Reprinted by permission of the author; **203** Figure 9–3, From "Effects of Teacher Attention on Study Behavior" by R. V. Hall, D. Lund, & D. Jackson, 1968, *Journal of Applied Behavior Analysis,* 1, p. 3. Copyright 1968 by Journal of Applied Behavior Analysis. Reprinted by permission of the Publisher; **275, 277, 278, 280** Specified excerpts from *Motivation and Personality,* Second Edition, by Abraham H. Maslow. Copyright © 1970 by Abraham H. Maslow. Reprinted by permission of Harper & Row, Publishers, Inc; **299-301** including Figure 13–1, Reprinted from *The Psychology of Personal Constructs, Volume 1, A Theory of Personality,* by George A. Kelly, by permission of W. W. Norton & Company, Inc. Copyright 1955 by George A. Kelly. Copyright renewed 1983 by Gladys Kelly.

(photo credits follow index)

To Emily

CONTENTS IN BRIEF

CONTENTS

PREFACE

This is a book about ideas, not a catalogue of facts. It is dedicated to those who resonate to the notion that tinkering with ideas, turning them over in your mind and playing with them is a supreme pleasure. Too many psychology texts seem to assume that learning about psychology means memorizing what a lot of psychologists have said, without doing any original, creative, or critical thinking of your own. This book, however, is designed to help you begin thinking and even theorizing about personality psychology.

It is gratuitous to assume that undergraduates cannot think about personality because they have not yet mastered a catalogue of facts. People develop their own personality theories without books; and the ideas of most of the theorists included here circulate widely in the popular culture, giving students a fund of ready knowledge to build upon.

Each of the ideas we will consider is associated with a great theorist of personality psychology. We will study the lives and theories of these personality psychologists, but we will pay just as much attention to the dozen or so great ideas these people produced. The ideas are enormously important and often controversial: Psychologists are not in complete agreement about them. The position you adopt in regard to each will reflect not only how you think about yourself, but how you relate to others. To stimulate your critical thinking about these ideas, I will present several pros and cons for each. Some of the pros and cons deal with the evidence for an idea's validity; others discuss the implications of accepting or rejecting an idea.

Arguments for each side, pro and con, are presented in a forceful, "no holds barred" manner that is intended to stimulate your thinking. I do not expect you passively to accept the pros and cons as established truth, or to embrace one side of the argument and reject the other—compromise positions are possible and even desirable. Instead, I would like to invite you to participate actively in a theoretical dialogue. My hope is that you will think your own way to whatever theoretical conclusions are most appropriate for you, given your own unique life history and future goals.

The introductory chapter examines a few of the basic issues that philosophers of science have raised concerning the nature of theorizing in personality psychology. Chapter two outlines the methods psychologists typically employ to study personality. The remaining chapters are devoted to the great ideas of personality theory presented in the forms developed by the master theorists who proposed them.

No one's list of the greatest personality psychologists can be absolutely definitive. I have based my "cast of characters" on several criteria. One of these criteria is the consensus of writers in the field: The theorists included here are the ones who appear most often in textbooks on personality psychology. Another criterion is balance: I have tried to give approximately equal exposure to each of the four major theoretical orientations— psychodynamic theories, trait theories, behavioral theories, and humanistic theories. But the criterion of the great idea itself was also an important consideration. Each theorist presented in this book represents a different "key idea." And whenever two or more candidates for inclusion represented substantially the same key idea, I selected only one as its spokesperson.

In other words, each theorist is presented as the champion of a key idea, an idea that is the *key* to his theory. Understand that idea, and you can reconstruct the main outlines of the whole theory. I have designed this book to encourage an understanding of the ideas, rather than memorization of every detail of the theories. In cases where a theorist is renowned for concepts that might not be readily deduced from his key idea, I discuss those concepts in separate boxes.

Because events in the theorists' lives often influence the direction of their thinking and allow deeper insight into their theories, I introduce each theorist with a brief biographical sketch. One astonishing fact that emerges from these life stories is that hardly any of our cast of personality psychologists started out with that career in mind. One wanted to be a writer, another an engineer, still another a chemist, and so on. Even during their undergraduate years, very few became psychologists, much less personality theorists.

The story of how each ultimately came to choose personality psychology is fascinating in and of itself. But it should especially interest readers of this book, who may be wrestling with the same career decision that preoccupied our theorists during their college years. With the potential benefits of that similarity in mind, I have focused the biographical sketches on the years between the late teens and the middle thirties, rather than offering a comprehensive life story for each theorist. This approach allows me to provide some depth of detail while remaining brief.

The concluding chapter compares and contrasts the key ideas of the various personality theories, emphasizing once again that they only suggest ways for you to think about human personality, and that in the last analysis it is up to you to choose the approach, or approaches, that seem right to you. Your evaluation of these ideas will depend on which questions you expect a theory to answer, what use you have for the theory, and which theoretical assumptions coincide with your personal values. The concluding chapter organizes the theories in light of these considerations. It might help to glance through this chapter first, especially if you already have some familiarity with personality theories.

A project of this kind cannot be completed without a good deal of help from other people. William G. T. Douglas deserves credit for the seed of the idea that grew, years later, into this book. He contributed further by reading the entire manuscript and offering countless helpful suggestions. Clark Baxter, my editor, offered superb guidance; his enthusiasm was a constant source of support. Carol Dolan, University of North Carolina at Greensboro, Judith Howard, Keene State College, and LeMaurice Gardner, Wayne State College read part or all of various drafts of the manuscript and offered valuable suggestions. I am indebted to all of these people for their assistance.

Credit is due also to the many students at Bridgewater State College who heard some of this material in lectures, and who generously shared their reactions. The cooperation of the staff of the Maxwell Library was a great help in locating books and references. Emily Scroggs also tracked down references, proofread, and contributed useful editorial comments. Thanks also to Elaine Fitzpatrick, who flawlessly typed the final manuscript.

James R. Scroggs

Key Ideas in Personality Theory

1/Introduction

You want to understand yourself, right? And you would like to be able to decipher the important people in your life. That is why you read a book on personality psychology, maybe even take a course on it. In short, you are shopping around for a personality theory. Not that you don't already have one, of course—everyone does. But you want to upgrade yours. It is like shopping for a new stereo system: You already have one, but you want something more powerful, something with better fidelity and the ability to accept a greater variety of inputs. You are perplexed by the number of brands on the market, bewildered by the seemingly endless combinations of features. You could cut through all this confusion by going to a store that sells just one brand, but only at the expense of closing your mind to everything else that is available.

This book introduces you to all of the major brands of personality theory. There are some books that, like the franchised stereo outlet, sell only one brand. These books are less confusing, but what sophisticated consumer would want to consider only one brand? Yet shopping in a dozen or so different stores, and exposing yourself to a succession of mindbending sales pitches, can make your head swim. Whether you are shopping for a personality theory or a stereo, you run up against the same problem—a glut of information. You are told more than you ever wanted to know. By the time you finish listening to the entire sales pitch on Brand B, you have forgotten most of what you learned about Brand A. And by the time the salespeople get to Brand H, they have you where they want you—so confused that you are ready to buy whatever they recommend.

There has to be some way to divide that glut of information into digestible portions; otherwise it will be impossible for you to make an informed choice. There has to be a way to hold the essential features of each major brand in front of your eyes, to present them—simultaneously or in rapid succession—so you can compare them and decide which ones you like best.

That is exactly what this book intends to be: a tool for easy comparison, a comsumer's guide to personality theories. The glut of information in personality psychology can choke you as easily as the vast array of stereo technology, but you can manage once you recognize that most theories are elaborations and embellishments of a single key idea. It may even be true, as one of my professors maintained, that most of the world's great thinkers had only one major idea. This is not to disparage them, as though they were too dull-witted to come up with more than one idea, but rather to underscore how scarce truly great ideas are in the history of human thought—and especially in personality theory. There are only a handful of key ideas; once you master them, each brand of theory will stand out in stark contrast to the others. This guide will give you those keys, by focusing on the big idea in each of the major brands of personality theory. It will also cut through all the technical jargon and translate each idea into plain English. How useful, after all, are expressions like "wow and flutter less than 1.03%" and "analog-to-digital conversion," or distinctions between "idiographic" and "nomothetic," "ergs" and "metaergs"? I am not sure all great ideas are essentially simple and—if they are true and not mere deceptions—capable of being understood by the average person. But I am ready to believe that that is the case in personality psychology. Why? Because each of the great theorists in this field seems to have taken one simple commonsense idea—often an idea that has been around since the first cave-dwellers acquired self-consciousness—and then embellished it, elaborated it, formalized it, perhaps even mathematicized it until its roots in folk wisdom are barely visible.

Consider the following examples of key ideas. George Kelly: If you understand how someone thinks (especially the mental categories used to organize the thinking process), then you know a lot about that individual's personality. Albert Bandura: Personality is largely the result of imitating what other people do, especially of children imitating their parents ("learning by observation"). Gordon Allport: There is no one else in the world exactly like you; personality is individual and unique. Henry Murray: Knowing the main themes of a person's life story provides the best possible understanding of that person, since the themes are the essence of the personality. Raymond Cattell: All people share certain characteristics, but the strength of these characteristics varies from person to person. (This, according to Cattell, is what we mean when we say that people have different personalities.) Erik Erikson: We all wrestle with the question "Who am I?" especially during adolescence; the answer we eventually arrive at is a reflection of our personality. Sigmund Freud: Human beings have a survival instinct that operates without their even having to think about it.

These ideas are not obscure or unfamiliar. They make sense because they correspond to what you already know from your own experience with people. And when they are stated in plain English as they are here, you have no difficulty understanding them. That is what this guide intends to give you: easily understood keys to the major theories of personality.

Once each theorist's key idea has been translated into plain English, you will be ready to make an informed choice among brands. Perhaps, as with buying a stereo system, you will prefer to assemble your own system using components from several different manufacturers. If so, you will have to make sure that the various brands are compatible. This turns out to be a greater problem with personality theories than with stereo components. In any case, in order to help you make your decision this guide indicates the advantages and disadvantages of the key feature of each brand of personality theory. The book presents pros and cons for each key idea. (As with stereos, there is no perfect system; each has its pros and cons.) It is up to you to decide which advantages you like best and which disadvantages you feel you can live with.

WHAT IS A KEY IDEA?

I have based this guidebook on the strategy of picking out the one key idea in each personality theory. To accomplish that, I established three principle criteria:

1. *The key idea must be one to which the theorist has devoted a major portion of his published writing.* It isn't necessary to count the number of times the idea is referred to, but it should be clear from the person's public pronouncements that the idea is one of his favorites—one that he argues fervently whenever he has the opportunity.

2. *The key idea must be distinctive.* It must be a concept uniquely associated with the theorist's name. This need not mean that nobody else uses it (other theorists may borrow it from him), nor that he originated it (he may have borrowed it from someone else). But he must be the one who has popularized and promoted it until it became his personal logo. Erikson's concept of identity is an obvious example.

3. *The idea must serve as a key to unlock the entire theory.* If you understand this idea, you should be able to understand, and reconstruct, the whole theory. By imagining all the implications of the idea, turning it around and examining it from different angles, and following its logical consequences, you should be able to build the theory yourself.

This is not unlike the task faced by inventors. Once they are given the idea of the wheel, it is not too difficult to build a wheelbarrow or a chariot. The real problem is coming up with the idea of the wheel in the first place. The strategy of the key idea is to identify the one idea that constitutes the "wheel" in each personality theory. Once you have the key idea, you do not have to memorize the structure of the entire theory, because you can reconstruct the theory at any time simply by reasoning logically from that starting point. More importantly if *you* have constructed the theory yourself, then you have gained an understanding of the theory. Anyone who puts something together from a kit, whether it be a dollhouse or an airplane model, understands that thing in a way that a person who sees only the finished product does not. The key idea should provide this kind of do-it-yourself understanding of a personality theory.

WHAT IS PERSONALITY?

There are as many definitions of personality as there are personality psychologists. Allport (1961, p. 28) says it is "the dynamic organization within the individual of those psychophysical systems that determines his characteristic behavior and thought." McClelland (1951, p. 69) says simply that it is "the most adequate conceptualization of a person's behavior in all its detail." For Guilford (1959, p. 5), it is "a person's unique pattern of traits."

Personality refers to whatever it is that makes a person a person—his or her *personness* or *personhood*. Perhaps we should use the hyphenated form *person-ality,* to remind ourselves that what we are talking about is the essence of what makes a person a person. In response to the difficulty of finding a word that unambiguously communicates the nature of this thing, Henry Murray suggested naming the whole discipline *personology*—the "ology," or science, of the person.

What does make a person a person? Even this question can be interpreted in a number of different ways. For instance, it could mean, what makes a person different from an orangutang or a brussels sprout? In that case, the question has to do with a person's nature as a member of the human race. The answer would have to be descriptive; It would have to try to describe the essence of human nature. But the question could also mean, what makes Tom Tom, and not Dick or even Harry—what makes any person different from any other person? Again the answer would be descriptive: It would try to describe the individual's unique characteristics. No matter how the question is interpreted, in other words, the answer relies on characteristics (human or individual); it is those characteristics that seem to make a person a person.

There is more to it than that, however. What makes persons persons is not only what they are, but also what they do, how they act, and even how they are likely to act. When a person does something out of character and we say, "Hey, Tom, it's not like you to act that way," we are basing our judgment on his personality. Hence another aspect of personality is the characteristic behavior of the individual. This characterization of behavior is not only descriptive, it is also predictive. To the extent that Tom's actions are consistent ("characteristic"), his behavior can be predicted by those around him. They see this consistent pattern of behavior as Tom's personality. And they are not the only ones who notice this consistency. Tom himself is aware of it. He knows that it is not like him to behave in certain ways. He recognizes that, once in a while, he just does not feel like himself. He has a subjective sense of his internal consistency, the thing that makes it possible for him to go to bed as Tom and wake up again as Tom, rather than

Dick or Harry. Tom takes this sense of internal consistency for granted, never noticing it except when it has been violated. He uses it not only to describe himself but to make predictions about himself. His sanity depends, in fact, on his conviction that his behavior is predictable and therefore under his control. He, too, considers that internal sense of consistency to be his personality.

Personality appears, then, to be what is enduring and unchanging about an individual. This does not mean that nothing about a person can change. But it does mean that if important changes occur, then we would have to say that the personality itself has changed.

Any adequate definition of personality therefore has to include some reference to consistency—consistency that renders the individual predictable to others, on the one hand, and that confers a feeling of being at one with yourself, on the other. It is this feeling of one-ness, of being integrated, organized, and stable, that breaks down in those pathological states we call psychoses.

The second feature that any adequate definition of personality must include is some reference to individual uniqueness, or if not uniqueness, at least distinctiveness. Personality is what distinguishes one individual from another.

WHAT IS A THEORY?

One of the peculiar ironies of personality is that while it is plain, it is also hidden. Personality is right out in the open for all to see, and yet we do not understand it—either in ourselves or in other people. How something that is in plain view can remain a mystery is a mystery in itself. Yet, so it is. And if the situation were different, there would be no need for personality theories. You do not need theory to explain something that is already apparent. The purpose of a theory is to explain what we do not understand.

A theory is a coherent set of principles (statements, assertions, propositions) that have been logically arranged for the purpose of explaining some phenomenon—in our case, personality. To explain something means to unlock its secrets by laying it out in the open. The Latin root of the word *explain* means *to lay out on a flat surface*—something like putting all your cards on the table. The function of an explanation is to render the phenomenon intelligible, understandable.

But there is more than one kind of understanding. The appliance technician who fixes your washing machine when it breaks down, who can take it apart and put it back together again, certainly understands washing machines. Yet we would also say that the portrait painter whose rendition captures every nuance of the model's character surely understands the model. The doctors who built an artificial heart had to have some kind of understanding of its natural, human counterpart. And what about the person who wins week after week in the football pools: Wouldn't you have to say that this person understands something about football?

Each of these people demonstrates a somewhat different kind of understanding, requiring a rather unique explanation. There are explanations of how things *are*, and there are explanations of how things *work*. Similarly, some theories of personality are designed to answer the question, *What is personality*, while others address the issue, *How does personality work?* Though the distinction is not always hard and fast in practice, trait and humanistic theories are generally more interested in the "what" question, while psychodynamic and behavioral theories are more concerned with the "how" question.

Explanations based on the "what" question are *descriptive*; they are able to describe large numbers of phenomena by classifying them within coherent systems. Examples of this type from the sciences are the periodic table of elements in chemistry, and the scheme of genuses and species in biology. These schemes aid our understanding by grouping many similar types into a manageable number of categories. They also serve a theoretical purpose by allowing us to infer the existence of things that have not been directly observed. Chemists, for instance, were able to predict the existence of several elements before these elements were actually discovered, simply by filling in gaps in the periodic table. And anthropologists have been able to posit a "missing link" in the evolutionary chain between apes and humans, although no truly convincing evidence for this link has been unearthed. Theories based on the "what" question serve at least two functions: (1) They organize previously unrelated observations in coherent systems of classification based on general themes or principles; and (2) they enable us to go beyond the thing we have actually observed and infer the existence of new things.

Explanations based on the "how" question are *functional* and often *causal*; that is, they explain subsequent events (effects) in light of previous events (causes). "If-then" statements predominate in such theories: *If* you push this button here, *then* that light goes on over there. This of course is the kind of understanding that is the stock-in-trade of the appliance repair technician, but it is also the kind of understanding of personality that is required for repairing broken and disintegrating personalities. Psychotherapists, rehabilitation counselors, and social workers all need causal theories to guide their professional activities. They need to know that *if* they perform a particular therapeutic manipulation, *then* a certain change in personality is going to follow. Causal explanations, you see, provide this kind of predictive understanding. They enable us to anticipate the consequences of our actions, rather than having to fumble around in the dark and leave the outcome to chance. The causal approach has certainly contributed to our understanding and gained wide acceptance: Most theories of personality today are aimed at predicting human behavior.

But to repair something, you need to understand how it works and the most awesome display of this type of understanding is certainly manifested by people who can build the thing themselves from scratch. The artificial heart is a case in point: The doctor who can keep a patient alive with an artificial heart dramatically demonstrates that he or she understands how the heart works. Models and simulations demonstrate the same kind of understanding in psychology. The most concrete example is the computer program that thinks, or mimics thinking, by playing chess, ordering a meal in a restaurant, or solving a variety of other cognitive problems. As a boy, I built a number of model airplanes. Some of them flew and some of them did not, but in the process I learned a great deal about what makes planes fly. In much the same way, psychologists build models of personality, test-fly them, and thus contribute to our understanding of how personality works.

Theories, like model airplanes, do not always fly. A theory, by definition, is to some extent conjectural. Facts and scientific laws are one thing; theories are another. This does not mean that theories are untrue, simply that they remain to be tested. It is generally agreed that the best theories are those that generate the most research, since research activity is most likely to increase our understanding of a phenomenon. But some theories are easier to test than others. The most testable theories are those whose statements are specific, rather than sweeping and general, and whose hypothetical constructs are clearly and concretely defined. Some theorists design their theories with these considerations in mind, so that the theories will be amenable to experimental testing. Others theorists feel compelled to follow wherever their curiosity leads them, even if this approach does not result in testable hypotheses. Yet even when theorists are careful to formulate their hypotheses in testable form, define their constructs properly, and so forth, it may still be impossible to test the ultimate truth of a theory, because the whole structure of the theory rests upon certain philosophical **assumptions.**

ALL THEORISTS MAKE ASSUMPTIONS

Philosophical assumptions (also called presuppositions) are the things a theorist takes for granted in constructing a theory; they are the foundation upon which the theory is built. Descartes' famous statement; "I think, therefore I am," is an example of a philosophical assumption. As the term implies, philosophical assumptions do not need to be proved, or even argued (if they could be proved, they would be facts, not assumptions). On the other hand, they are not entirely unfounded. Some assumptions are widely held among the members of a scientific discipline, others are less accepted.

SOME ASSUMPTIONS ABOUT REALITY

Orderliness.   The entire scientific enterprise rests upon the assumption that there is order in the universe. Things do not just happen by chance; they are governed by natural laws. But even before these natural laws were actually "discovered", it was assumed that they existed—otherwise no one would have bothered to look for them. And though some still question that assumption, it seems fairly safe in light of the available evidence.

Linear Time.   An assumption that forms another cornerstone of science is our linear view of time and history. We assume that "time marches on," that it does not stand still and does not roll backwards. Time has a beginning, proceeds along a straight line, and ultimately comes to an end. The theory of evolution is firmly rooted in this assumption, as is the theory of Karl Marx. But Hindu philosophy, with its doctrine of the endless cycle of reincarnation of souls, would not buy this idea at all. The linear concept of time and history is therefore an assumption, a fact that cannot be proved. It is part of the world view shared by most of western culture, another belief that we generally accept without thinking.

Causality.   Closely intertwined with the concept of linear time is the assumption of cause and effect, which is dear to science and to most of psychology, including personality theory. Causes come before their effects: When one event regularly precedes another in time, we call the former a cause and the latter an effect. But causality implies more than mere past coincidence; it implies that the first event *compels* the second event to follow, and that in the future the second event *must* inevitably follow from the first. This, inevitability can never be proved, however; it can only be inferred, since the future can never be known. Hence causality is an assumption. Once again, though, it is a pretty safe assumption (at least within the framework of western scientific thinking).

Determinism.   Moving from the assumption that some events are causally related, to the assumption that all events are causally related, is a short leap in logic. And though the latter assumption is just as impossible to prove, it too has produced one of the fundamental doctrines of science: *determinism*. According to determinism, everything that happens in the universe from this moment on is already decided by what happened before. Nothing can alter that course of events. And if we ever knew all the variables and all their causal relationships, we could predict the course of future events with absolute accuracy. While this goal may be utopian, science tries to gain as much causal knowledge as possible in order to make at least partial, short-term predictions. Without the assumption of determinism, such predictions would be impossible.

Determinism may be a safe assumption in the physical sciences, but it is less so in the psychology of personality. Human beings have free will—so most of us assume. Someone knowing all of the forces impinging upon me at the present moment, and all of my past history, still could not predict my behavior in the next moment, because I might freely decide to do just the opposite out of sheer contrariness. But free will is also an assumption. I cannot prove I have it, since my determinist adversaries can always argue that even my contrariness was determined by forces beyond my control and awareness. My alleged free choice, they would say, is just an illusion. (They cannot prove this, but neither can I disprove it.)

Still, if we are to have any kind of personality theory, we must assume one thing or the other—determinism or free will. You cannot say a single word about why people do the things that they do without making one or the other of these assumptions: either people are caused (compelled) to do what they do, or people freely choose to do what they do. We generally assume that events in the physical world are caused, hence predictable.

(We may not have enough knowledge yet to predict them all, but all are *in principle* predictable.) But if we assume that free will exists, we can no longer predict psychological events in the human personality. Theorists have to assume that human behavior is causally determined—that it is governed, like chemical reactions, by natural laws—otherwise the theorists' predictions would be nothing more than guesswork. The causal assumption of determinism predominated in psychology because most psychologists, and psychological theorists, want their science to predict and control human behavior.

WHY SO MANY DIFFERENT THEORIES?

Assumptions are therefore not optional equipment for personality theorists; they are part of the nature of theory. You cannot build a theory in a vacuum; you have to start with something, on some foundation or premise: If we assume that this is true, then that and that follow. But we can never prove that the assumption is true; we simply take it for granted for the sake of building the theory.

Most personality theories make perfect sense, once you accept the theorist's assumptions. Yet theories that are logically coherent, theories whose major hypotheses have been experimentally validated, may flatly contradict each other. How can this be? Why are there so many different personality theories? The answer is that personality theorists start with different assumptions. In the physical sciences, there is almost unanimous agreement on which assumptions are relatively safe; in personality theory, there is very little agreement in this area. That is why so many different brands of personality theory exist.

If you want to critique a personality theory, in other words, you must examine its assumptions. Unfortunately, not all theorists openly acknowledge their assumptions when presenting their theories. Some theorists make assumptions without realizing it. Often such assumptions are made unthinkingly because they are part of the worldview of the culture to which the theorist belongs. This guide to personality theories not only points out the basic assumptions of each personality theory and their consequences; it also teaches you how to ferret out hidden assumptions.

MORE ASSUMPTIONS ABOUT HUMAN NATURE

Rationality. All of the assumptions we have considered up to this point are of one type—they are **metaphysical** assumptions. Metaphysical assumptions are unexamined assertions about the nature of reality. They take it for granted that certain things exist: order in the universe, cause and effect, free will. To that list we might add a few other metaphysical assumptions that are common ingredients in most personality theories. According to Aristotle, for example, humans are rational animals. But that is a debatable, and ultimately unprovable, proposition. In fact, Freud, did his best to persuade us that that rationality is only an illusion, and that the essence of human personality is in the irrational, unconscious mind. Today some theories of personality assume that human nature is basically rational, while others assume that it is irrational.

Good and evil.   Closely related to rationality is the issue of whether human nature is basically good, or basically evil. This question really has to do with the perfectability of human nature: Can human beings some day learn to live together in peace and harmony, without wars and injustice, or is there some tragic flaw in the very core of our being that makes such a goal unattainable? Is it society that corrupts an otherwise innocent human nature, or is human nature itself guilty, and society only a reflection of that taint? Whatever answer we reach is bound to be arguable and ultimately unprovable. The personality theories we call humanistic are based on the assumption that human nature is good; at the opposite extreme are the theories of Freud and his followers.

Nurture or nature.   Finally, there is the proverbial nature/nurture controversy. Is human personality the result of innate (structural and genetic) factors, or is it a product of learning and social experience? Which is more important, heredity or environment? Behavioral theories assume that the answer is environment; Freudian theories and certain trait theories assume that heredity plays a larger role. But all of these theories rely on metaphysical assumptions, since they all make unproven and unprovable assertions about the nature of reality—more specifically, the aspect of reality we call personality.

ASSUMPTIONS ABOUT METHOD

In addition to metaphysical assumptions, there is a second type of assumption that we call *methodological*. Methodological assumptions are assertions concerning the right way to go about studying a phenomenon (in our case, personality). They are unexamined decisions about procedure. Theorists may have rationales for the methods they use; they may even get impressive results with those methods; but they still cannot prove that those methods are right and true, especially when other theorists produce equally impressive (but contradictory) results using different methodologies. Who has the truth? The procedural decisions cannot tell us because they are based not on facts, but on mere assumptions. An assumption is legitimate in relation to the result it produces. Only *after* the "hidden treasure" is discovered do we know that we were digging in the right place, using the right tool, and that digging itself was the appropriate activity to pursue. Yet every theory depends in this way on methodological assumptions. Without them, a theorist could not even begin to theorize.

Objectivity.   One methodological assumption that has played a crucial role in personality theory (though it is not unanimously accepted) is the matter of objectivity. If you assume that the right way to study personality is to be as objective as possible, then you are likely to use some of the following methods: observing subjects through one-way mirrors; measuring responses with objective instruments such as timers, polygraphs, chemical analyzers, or standardized personality tests; perhaps even using animals as subjects. The aim of objectivity is to detach psychologists as much as possible from what they are observing, so that they do not influence the responses of their subjects, or themselves become influenced by the subjects to interpret responses in certain ways. Objectivity is primarily a device for eliminating bias in the observer. It assumes that the most accurate picture of personality is from the perspective of the proverbial visitor from Mars.

Subjectivity.   Some personality theorists, however, contend that an unbiased perspective is not possible. Objectivity, they say, is a myth, a delusion. Psychologists cannot detach themselves from what they observe; and even if they could they would not acquire an accurate picture of personality by doing so. The subjective assumption says that to gain an accurate picture of personality, you need to *participate in* whatever you are trying to understand. In other words, you should listen to the person who has "been there," or "ask someone who owns one." Personality theorists who make this assumption use methods such as these: observing and analyzing their own subjective experience; trying to understand empathically the meaning of a person's dreams and fantasies; or examining the effects of hospitalization by voluntarily becoming a patient—a technique known as "participant observation."

Obviously, the subjective approach produces theoretical explanations very different from those arrived at with objective methods. In fact, the two sets of results may even contradict each other. Remember that neither assumption, objectivity or subjectivity, can be proven to be correct and true; they can only be shown to be useful, or not useful, in solving certain kinds of problems.

Atomism.   Another example of a methodological assumption—and one that no theory can avoid—has to do with whether things are best understood by taking them apart or by viewing them whole. The terms **atomism** and **elementalism** refer to the assumption that things need to be broken down into their constituent parts in order to be understood. Physics and chemistry have done just that, reducing all matter to atomic particles and chemical elements. **Analysis** is the word that denotes this process of taking things apart—the opposite of *synthesis*, which is putting things together. Thus *psychoanalysis* is the dissection of the mind, or psyche, for the purpose of observing its constituent parts. Psychoanalysts assume that analyzing the mind—reducing it to its most fundamental components, produces an understanding of the mind.

Holism.   "Not so!" object those personality theorists who champion the opposite assumption, which is called **holism.** Nearly all psychology students are familiar with their motto: The whole is more than the sum of its parts. That "extra something" is the pattern of relationships among the constituent parts. It does not help to know that the photo on the front page of your morning newspaper consists of specific numbers of black dots, dark grey dots, and light grey dots. These collections of dots do not convey a meaningful picture. The meaning is not in the elements themselves, but in the pattern they produce. Holistic psychologists assume that the same is true of personality—it makes sense only when you view it as a whole.

Choice of topic.   Assumptions about how to study a phenomenon are closely related to assumptions about which phenomenon to study. The very process of selecting a problem for research involves a methodological assumption. Behavioral theorists, for example, take it as perfectly self-evident that to understand personality you must discover the basic principles of human learning. Other brands of personality theorists say that the learning process is not the right place to start digging; these theorists spend their time investigating an entirely different region—psychopathology, for example, or **constitutional traits**.

If you are going to dig, you have to make assumptions about where to start. Wherever you dig you will find something, but what you find will depend much upon your starting point. The initial choice of topic—the questions theorists choose to address with their theories, or discard in advance—determines the character of those theories more powerfully than any subsequent discovery their research produces. And once again, the choice of topic relies on assumptions (or at the very least, value judgments).

Summary.   Why are there so many different personality theories? Why do personality theorists disagree and even contradict each other when they are all supposed to be studying the same thing—human personality? First because they ask different questions and therefore come up with different answers. Second, they use different methods to answer their questions; even if they all asked the same questions, the differences in their methods would lead them to different answers. Third, they begin with different views on the nature of human personality—is it free or determined, caused or uncaused?—and therefore dig in different places and discover different things. In short, personality theories differ because personality theorists make different assumptions, both metaphysical and methodological.

WHICH TOOL TO USE?

Since assumptions are unprovable, no personality theory has a corner on the truth. But you should not think of theories as right or wrong; you should think of them as tools, each one appropriate for a different job. (You would not use a screwdriver, for instance, to hammer nails; you could, but a hammer would work much better.) Of course we all have our preferences, our favorite tools. (I would rather work with my lathe than with my bandsaw, though I would not try to saw with the lathe or turn wood with the saw.) What you should do, first of all, is familiarize yourself with all of the "tools" for understanding personality, so that you know which tool to use for which job.

The *key idea* format used in this book explains which job each personality theory is designed to perform, which questions it can help answer. As you will see, each theory functions smoothy when used for the right job, but shows signs of stress and weakness when applied to any other job. Again, that is why it is important to learn which questions each personality theory is designed to answer. (Sometimes, of course, two or more theories "advertise" that they can do the same job, like aspirin and Tylenol.)

Not all disagreements among personality theories are the result of asking different questions. Sometimes theorists come up with different answers to one and the same question. In those cases, logic would seem to demand that you pronounce one right and the others wrong. But how are you to decide? Our earlier analogy offers a clue. Even when two different tools are able to do the same job, each tool has certain advantages and disadvantages. Aspirin and Tylenol will both provide relief from headache pain, for example, but aspirin is more effective for driving down fevers and reducing swelling in joints, while Tylenol is safer in that it does not cause bleeding or stomach irritation. Personality theories operate in much the same way: Each theory has its distinctive strengths, and by the same token, each certain drawbacks. The *pros and cons* section following the presentation of each *key idea* in this book elucidates these strengths and drawbacks, so that you may make an informed choice among competing brands and not be misled by "false advertising."

WHAT IS A PERSONALITY THEORY?

Although different personality theories attempt to answer different questions, there are certain questions about personality that *any* theory must answer if it intends to be comprehensive. Any comprehensive theory of personality must account for these three things: (1) the structure of personality; (2) the dynamics of personality; and (3) the development of personality.

STRUCTURE

A theory must explain personality structure—what the personality is made of. What are the building blocks of personality? What are its constituent units? And how are those units put together? Are they arranged according to some particular scheme? All of these are structural questions that a comprehensive theory of personality cannot evade.

To illustrate this point let us look at some familiar answers to the structural question. Both Allport and Cattell argue that the personality is made of traits. Allport's theory arranges these traits according to their relative strengths and the extent to which they pervade the whole personality. Freud, on the other hand, says that personality is comprised of three different mental processes: The **id** is the energy source, the instinctual part of the personality; the **ego** is the conscious self, the part that decides how to deal with the world; and the **superego** corresponds to what most of us think of as our conscience. Our final explanation of personality structure comes from Carl Rogers, who believes that the basic unit of personality is the self, and who refuses, because of his holistic orientation, to break that unit down into smaller elements. As these examples show, the nature of personality structure can be explained in any number of ways.

DYNAMICS

To ask about the dynamics of personality is to ask what sets the personality in motion. Why do people do what they do? Why do they do anything at all? What motivates them? What is the "fuel," the energy sources, that makes them go? (if we must conceive of this process in physicalistic terms!) In short, the question of dynamics is the question of motivation.

One of the broad, sweeping issues that cuts across the whole question of dynamics and divides personality theorists, is whether personality is moved primarily by being pushed, or by being pulled. Are we driven by instincts and childhood traumas, as Freud says, or are we attracted by the pull of future goals and aspirations, as the humanistic psychologists argue? Another issue central to dynamics is the question of free will–versus–determination, the question of whether human behavior is controlled, or merely influenced, by environmental stimuli. In a classic debate that was published (1956) and reprinted many times, B. F. Skinner defended the determinist position and Carl Rogers argued on behalf of free will.

Where personality dynamics are concerned, the answers are as varied as the questions. Here are some of the answers given by the standard brands of personality theory. According to Freud, instincts are the personality's energy source; they operate on the basis of the **pleasure principle**, which says that a person will do whatever maximizes pleasure and minimizes pain. Both Murray and Maslow theorize, however, that we are motivated by a variety of needs, such as achievement, power, love, and a sense of belongingness. Rogers' notion that we need to be accepted as persons, and Kelly's assumption that we need to make cognitive sense of our experience, are also dynamic constructs. Behaviorists generally avoid using the word, *dynamics*, but they certainly do address the issues connected with that word. Their solution is summed up in the concept of **reinforcement.** People will do anything that gives them positive reinforcement; furthermore, any behavior that is not reinforced, dies out—it ceases to be performed.

DEVELOPMENT

Personality development is the last question that any comprehensive theory of personality must answer. How does the personality reach its present form? How does the personality grow? How does it change with the passage of time? There are more specific questions as well. Are there, for instance, critical periods in personality development, periods during which a person is especially adept at learning things that may be difficult, or even impossible, to learn later on.

Another specific developmental question concerns the possibility of **remediation**. How permanently damaging are developmental defects? Are they reversible? If so, by what means? Obviously, the possibilities for disagreement, and for conflicting theories, are legion.

Psychologists have tended to answer structural and dynamic questions borrowing concepts from physics and chemistry, although they have found biology more relevant to the developmental question. Bodily growth seems conspicuously analogous to personality growth; and Freud, for instance, tied his theory of personality development to the timetable of bodily maturation. Most developmental theorists have followed suit.

The most common answer to the developmental question is the one proposed by Freud, namely, that personality development occurs in phases, or stages. There are certain phases we all pass through on our way from infancy to adulthood. These phases, or stages, occur in the same sequence for everyone—there is no skipping stages. Some people progress through these stages faster than others, and some never complete the whole course. Furthermore, some of us spend a long time in certain stages but zip through others. Most theories of developmental stages also consider it possible to slip back a rung or two on the ladder of development—something Freud called *regression*. Most of these theories also argue that at each stage of personality development, there is some problem to be resolved or some lesson to be learned. In Erikson's scheme of development, each stage is characterized by a specific crisis, beginning with the crisis of basic trust–versus–basic mistrust, and ending with the crisis of integrity–versus–despair.

A comprehensive theory of personality answers all three questions: structure, dynamics, and development. But relatively few personality theorists make a serious attempt to be comprehensive; most are satisfied to concentrate on only one or two of the three questions. Among the theorists presented in this book, the developmental question is the one that is most frequently ignored or given short shrift. By contrast, the question of dynamics is the most popular one among personality theorists. In fact, more than a few personality theories are nothing more than theories of dynamics. A personality theory does not have to be comprehensive to be worthwhile; but all other things being equal, comprehensiveness is to be preferred.

CHAPTER SUMMARY

1. One of the main problems in choosing among personality theories is the glut of information. This book is designed to help you handle that information glut, by concentrating on one key idea from each theorist, and by avoiding the use of unnecessary technical jargon. The book also discusses the pros and cons of each key idea, so that you can decide which features you feel are most important.

2. Each theorist's key idea has been selected according to the following criteria: (1) it must be an idea to which the theorist has devoted the major portion of his writing; (2) it must be distinctive; (3) it must provide the key to the entire theory.

3. There are innumerable definitions of personality. An adequate definition must (1) refer to consistency—consistency that renders you predictable to others and that confers upon you an internal feeling of coherence; and (2) account for individual uniqueness, or at least distinctiveness.

4. Theories are built to explain. Some explain *what*, and some explain *how*. Those that explain *what* are descriptive; the ones that explain *how* are functional and causal.

5. Philosophical assumptions are the things a theorist takes for granted when laying the foundation of a theory. Assumptions cannot be proved. Metaphysical assumptions concern the nature of reality; methodological assumptions have to do with proper procedures for studying personality. Some of the most common metaphysical assumptions in personality theory are that human behavior is lawful; that time is linear; and that behavior is causally determined.

6. The idea that objectivity is the only basis for studying personality is a methodological assumption; so is the choice between an atomistic and holistic approach. Even a theorist's decision to investigate certain aspects of personality, rather than others, involves a methodological assumption. In fact, it is impossible to theorize without making assumptions. One reason why there are so many personality theories is that theorists make different assumptions.

7. No one theory has a corner on the truth. Each theory is a tool that is appropriate for a specific job.

8. A comprehensive personality theory must explain (1) structure; (2) dynamics; and (3) development. The question of structure concerns what the personality is made of. Dynamics has to do with what moves the personality (theories of motivation are theories about dynamics). Development is the way in which the personality grows and changes with the passage of time. Few personality theorists deal equally with all three of these areas, and many concentrate on just one (dynamics is the most popular).

REFERENCES

Allport, G.W. (1961). *Pattern and growth in personality.* New York: Holt, Rinehart & Winston.

Guilford, J.P. (1959). *Personality.* New York: McGraw-Hill.

McClelland, D. (1951). *Personality.* New York: Holt, Rinehart & Winston.

Rogers, C., & Skinner, B.F. (1956). Some issues concerning the control of human behavior: A symposium. *Science, 124,* 1057–1066.

2/How Are Theories Built?

METHODS IN PERSONALITY PSYCHOLOGY

Lack of agreement about methodological assumptions is one of the major reasons why there are so many different personality theories. It is now time to describe and evaluate the unique strengths and weaknesses of each assumption, each method. How does the personality theorist go about collecting data and constructing a theory? How is the theory tested once it is formulated? There are four principle methods: (1) philosophical speculation; (2) clinical observation; (3) measurement of individual differences; and (4) experiment. Some theorists maintain a doctrinaire allegiance to a single method, while others use any combination that seems to work.

PHILOSOPHICAL SPECULATION

Philosophical speculation is just a fancy name for sitting down and thinking about something. The primary tool here is **inductive reasoning**: Observing specific things, then generalizing from those observations to form universal laws or principles. The observations come from either **introspection** or naturalistic observation. To introspect is, literally, "to look inside." Introspection involves observing your own subjective experience. Of course, it is difficult *not* to observe your own subjective experience, and hence we may wonder what is so special about this method. Alas, that is a difficult question to answer. Serious personality theorists certainly try to introspect more carefully and systematically than the casual mental sightseer, and they ordinarily prepare for this task by steeping themselves in the relevant literature; yet beyond that, it is hard to say what they do that the rest of us do not do all the time. The crucial difference seems to have more to do with the product than with the method of producing it. Some individuals have such a rare gift for observing and describing their inner experience that we find their reports extraordinarily sensitive and insightful. Still, their methods are a mystery.

Naturalistic observation is the practice of looking "outside," rather than "inside." Again, the observation must be systematic if it is to be anything other than haphazard, but what it boils down to is "people-watching." **Ethologists** such as Jane Goodall, who studied apes in their natural habitat, have developed very respectable scientific methods of naturalistic observation. Social psychologists, and also some personality theorists, have adapted ethological field methods to "people-watching."

In brief, philosophical speculation involves watching yourself or other people, and applying your rational faculties, and coming up with a coherent set of generalizations that constitutes a theory. The stress is clearly on the rational faculties: The whole process depends on the observer's ability to conceive principles and relationships the rest of us would never think of.

All personality theorists begin with philosophical speculation, at least in order to form their initial hypotheses. But no major American personality theorist would be satisfied with philosophical speculation alone. That would be too . . . well, too philosophical! Great contributions to psychology have been made by thinkers who employed nothing more than philosophical speculation—people such as René Descartes or John Locke—and yet these thinkers are considered philosophers, not psychologists. Even the psychological writings of the late French existentialist, Jean-Paul Sartre, are considered by American psychologists to belong to philosophy, because they are based solely on speculation and rational argument. Most psychologists (including personality theorists) are suspicious of philosophical speculation when it is used exclusively.

PROS

It worked for Einstein. Is it possible to make a case for philosophical speculation? Yes. First of all, this method seems entirely adequate when used by a great genius. Albert Einstein, for example, extracted the theory of relativity almost entirely from his own brain. He did not take measurements or conduct experiments; he just thought the whole thing out. There is no precise parallel in psychology, though William James, the first great American psychologist, comes to mind in this context. James' methods really did not go much beyond philosophical speculation; yet his theories about the nature of the self, the role of habit, and the triggering of emotion have been immensely influential.

No artificial ingredients. In the second place, philosophical speculation is the least artificial of the methods available to personality theorists. The example of ethology is relevant here. Ethologists urge us to study animals in their natural habitats, because animals do not act naturally in zoos and laboratories. The same thing applies, of course, to human beings. When people are given silly multiple-choice tests, when they are so near the end of their ropes that they present themselves at a clinic or mental hospital, or when they play the role of guinea pig in a psychological laboratory, they just do not act naturally! Neither, incidentally, do psychologists who observe people under these circumstances. But when theorists engage in philosophical speculation, they act in very much the same way that all of us do. They behave very naturally, and the behavior they are observing is also very natural. At least they have the option of observing natural behavior (if they wanted, they could also swallow a psychedelic drug and introspect about some unnatural behavior), an option that, strictly speaking, is not open to those who use clinical observation, mental measurement, or experiment.

CONS

There is no generally accepted way to verify theories based solely on philosophical speculation.   As a result they are often greeted with some suspicion: How can you check on their claims of truth? You cannot **replicate** the observations that provided the data: Introspections are by nature private, not open to public scrutiny. Even naturalistic observation — "people-watching"—is uncontrolled; here too, it is impossible to reproduce and review the original sequence of events. Because no recording devices or measuring apparatus were used, we are forced to accept the theorists' claims that their observations were accurate and undistorted. But even if we could check their observations, we might find that we disagreed with the logic by which they arrived at their theoretical conclusions. There are no courts to arbitrate these disputes. What is logic to one person may be nonsense to another. Psychologists therefore prefer to rely on methods that permit verification by objective tests, rather than methods that require subjective evaluations of the plausibility of competing "logical" arguments.

CLINICAL OBSERVATION

Clinical observation is what most of us think of as the *case study method*. The model comes from medicine: The psychologist sees the patient in a private office, a mental hospital, or clinic; gives an examination and diagnosis; then prescribes, and in most cases personally administers, a treatment program. The examination may include various psychological tests, or it may be nothing more than a series of questions. In either case, the psychologist aims to acquire the fullest possible understanding of the patient and the problem, so that appropriate therapy can begin. As the therapy progresses, the psychologist continues to listen and watch closely, learning more and more about the patient, revising or fine-tuning the diagnosis, and adjusting the "dosage" of the therapeutic intervention. The psychologist makes a record of all observations, traditionally by jotting down notes, though nowadays often with the help of technological innovations such as tape-recording or filming. As the number and variety of the cases he or she has seen increases, the psychologist acquires a sufficient data base to begin building a personality theory.

Sigmund Freud is responsible for pioneering and popularizing this method; and though it is often condemned by academic psychologists for being too unscientific, it is arguably still the most popular method used in personality psychology. A survey of contemporary college textbooks on personality theories reveals that approximately half of the theories discussed are based on clinical observation. Similarly, about half of the cast of characters of this book prefer the method of clinical observation. Of course, the ones who belonged to Freud's circle—Jung and Erikson—use substantially the same methods as their master. But two of the non-Freudian superstars of personality theory also base their theories on clinical observation: Carl Rogers and George Kelly. In all, five of our cast of characters (Freud, Jung, Erikson, Rogers, and Kelly) base their personality theories on clinical observation of patients who came to them for help with psychological problems.

But why wait till people come to you with their problems? There is no reason why you cannot use the same methods to study "normal" people, people who have no special problems. All you need is some way of getting them to consent to having their cases studied. Henry Murray, who pioneered the use of clinical observation in the study of normal personality while working at the Harvard Psychological Clinic in the 1930s, found that paying people to serve as subjects worked perfectly well. His colleague, Gordon Allport, also championed the case-study approach to exploring normal (as opposed to psychologically ill) personalities. Allport favored the idea of obtaining some of the individual's personal documents—diaries, memoires, letters—and studying them just as you would study an individual in the clinic. That is exactly what Allport himself did, in his book *Letters from Jenny* (Allport, 1965). Perhaps it is stretching things a bit to call this clinical observation, since Allport is not exactly a clinician, but his approach is more akin to clinical observation than to any other methods. In any case, if we include Murray and Allport as clinical observers (Murray fits the bill more clearly), then clinical observation emerges as the foundation of the majority of the most popular, and influential, personality theories.

PROS

Depth.   Undoubtedly the foremost strength of the clinical observation method is its great depth. The sheer amount of time clinical observation devotes to each case might account for this advantage. No test administrator or experimenter spends anything like the several hundred hours a psychoanalyst typically devotes to studying a single personality. It stands to reason that the longer you watch someone, the better you get to know that person.

Furthermore, the great depth of clinical observation is brought about by more than just the duration of the period of observation. In clinical observation, the relationship between the psychologist and the subject is typically one of unique intimacy. In a psychotherapeutic relationship, patients may tell their doctors things they would never divulge to anyone else; things they may not even have admitted previously to themselves. The same holds true for personal documents: People often entrust private, intimate revelations to diaries, and very personal letters to confidantes. These documents reveal data that would never show up in an experiment or personality test.

Finally, clinical observation may achieve its greater depth by studying abnormal personalities. Some psychologists think that studying abnormal, distorted, personalities produces distorted personality theories; others believe that this kind of study is advantageous. Those who claim that it is advantageous usually do so on the basis of the belief that abnormal personality processes are simply magnifications of normal personality functions. Hence the abnormal personality serves the same purpose in psychology as the microscope does in biology: magnifying things so that they can be more readily studied. In other words, personality theorists who use clinical observation may be gaining deeper insight into personality precisely *because* their subjects are distraught. But no matter how it comes about, depth appears to be a desirable property in a personality theory, and those who use clinical observation seem most likely to gain that depth.

Realism.   A second advantage of the clinical observation method is its realism, its lack of artificiality. In contrast to a test-taking situation or a contrived laboratory experiment, clinical observation deals with real lives as they are lived. This is especially true when the subjects are normal personalities, or when the data are personal documents. The psychotherapeutic situation is a bit more artificial, although less so than the laboratory setting. Some would argue, however, that, far from being artificial, psychotherapy is super-real, "larger than life." These people would say that the problems and issues patients struggle with in therapy are the most real things in the world to them. How dare we call psychotherapy "artificial"?

CONS

Possibility of observer bias.   Despite its widespread popularity, clinical observation has its disadvantages. As with philosophical speculation, first of all, there is no check on the observer's bias. We see everything through the eyes of the clinical observer; if that observer is cross-eyed or near-sighted, our picture of the personality is distorted accordingly. If the clinician films the interviews or conducts them with a team of other psychologists, then we have a means for checking bias. Unfortunately, however, these are not standard practices.

No possibility of replication.   With clinical observation, there is no chance for taking a second look either. The great advantage of the experimental method is the possibility of replication—you can do the experiment over and over again to see if it comes out the same way. Not so with clinical observation, where the psychologist typically sees an event happen only once, and often unexpectedly. The same set of circumstances can never be exactly reproduced to provide a second look. There is no one else around to ask: "Did you see what I saw?" or "Did I remember that correctly?"

As we have already seen, even when two psychologists agree on what they observed, they may still come up with different explanations of it. Using as data nothing more than letters from the boy's father, Freud analyzed the case of little Hans, a five-year-old who suddenly became so afraid of horses that he dared not venture out of the house. The root of the problem, Freud believed, was in the child's unconscious **castration anxiety:** the fear that his father would mutilate him sexually, in retribution for the child's romantic attachment to his mother (part of what Freud called the **Oedipus complex**). Two behaviorally oriented clinicians, Wolpe and Rachman (1960), looked at the very same letters some years later and offered a contradictory explanation: Hans' phobia was caused by **sensitization** and conditioning. The method of clinical observation provides no way of testing the validity of such alternative explanations of the same observations.

Possibility of sample bias.   Finally, there is the problem of sample bias. Some of Freud's harsher critics have suggested that it is because he saw only sick people that he came up with such a sick theory. Whether this is a fair criticism or not, it does serve to point out that by observing something less than a representative sample of humanity, a theorist runs the risk of developing an unbalanced perception of personality. And it cannot be denied that clinicians tend to see a high proportion of disturbed individuals. Murray and Allport attempted to avoid such bias by studying normal people. Maslow went all the way to the opposite extreme by basing his theory exclusively on the study of specimens of superior mental health. But whatever sample one employs, the fact that the method of clinical observation restricts one to the study of a relatively small number of cases means almost inevitably that it will be difficult to draw universally valid conclusions about human personality.

THE MEASUREMENT OF INDIVIDUAL DIFFERENCES

Psychologists who use the method of measuring **individual differences** operate on the basis of a kind of mental chemistry. Here personality is viewed as akin to a chemical compound that is composed of certain universal elements. The strategy is first to discover what these elements are, and, second, to devise methods for measuring how much of each element is present in a given individual.

These psychologists generally call the constituent elements of personality *traits*—characteristics such as shyness, pugnacity, theatricality, or perseverance. Individuals have different amounts of these traits. Psychologists can measure how much of each trait you possess by having you (or someone who knows you well) rate yourself on a scale of one to ten for that trait. For greater accuracy, they could have several people rate you, then average the ratings. And if they wanted something even fancier, they could construct a test composed of statements that people having the trait in question tend to agree with. To measure your shyness, for example, they might ask for your reaction to the following statement: "It is hard for me to go up and introduce myself to strangers at a party." In short, we can measure as many traits as we like, and obtain the numerical scores of as many individuals as we like. We can then summarize these scores in the familiar form of a test profile (see Figure 2–1). The profile not only provides a capsule description of the individual's personality; it also graphically demonstrates how that personality differs from another's.

Yet none of this insures that the traits we measure are the most fundamental and irreducible elements of the personality. Some of the traits we chose to measure might overlap. Suppose we had chosen both sub-

FIGURE 2-1

A Sample Test Profile for the California Psychological Inventory

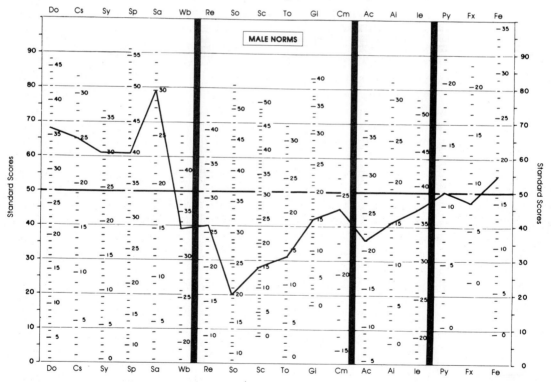

AUTHOR'S NOTE: This subject is very strong in traits Sa and Do, but weak in So. He is above average in the first five and the last trait measured and below average in all the rest. Abbreviations refer to traits, e.g., Do = dominance.

Reproduced by special permission of the publisher, Consulting Psychologists Press, Inc. From *The Manual for the California Personality Inventory*, by Harrison G. Gough. Copyright 1969.

missiveness and shyness, for example. We would probably find that most of the individuals who rated high in shyness also rated high in submissiveness: These two traits overlap. But they do not overlap entirely, since some people who are shy are not submissive, and some submissive individuals are not shy. The extent to which the traits overlap can be calculated by taking the scores of a number of individuals and subjecting them to a statistical procedure known as *correlation* (the "coefficient of correlation" indicates the extent of the overlap). Traits that are truly elements do not overlap at all; their correlation with each other is nil. In effect, the process of determining which traits are fundamental involves calculating the coefficients of correlation for all possible combinations of traits, and designating as elements those that are not correlated with any others. This procedure is called **factor analysis,** the favorite statistical tool of personality theorists who employ the method of measuring individual differences.

Once these psychologists are satisfied that they have identified the elemental traits of personality, they work to refine their personality tests so that the tests will measure those, and only those, traits as reliably and as validly as possible. One way to confirm the validity of a test is to see how well it works as a predictive device. Suppose some company wanted to recruit and train a new sales force. We might use our test to assess candidates and to predict, for instance, that those who scored high in shyness would do poorly in sales work, while those who scored low in shyness would do far better. We might then monitor the sales crew's performance in the training program and examine their sales records for the first few months of work. If our test for shyness is valid, its predictions should be consistent with the sales crew's actual performance. In practice, of course, we would need to conduct a validation test for each of the traits we wanted to measure.

Among our cast of characters, Raymond Cattell is most noted for using the methods outlined above. He was able to reduce personality to some fifteen or twenty elemental traits, and to develop a widely used test for measuring them. Henry Murray employed similar techniques in his personnel selection for the Office of Strategic Services and in some of his research at the Harvard Psychological Clinic, although this was only one of several methods—and not the primary one—he used to construct his theory. Gordon Allport also employed a variety of methods, including measuring traits with tests he devised himself. Even Carl Jung tried his hand at test construction. Thanks to his efforts to conceptualize and measure traits, **introvert** and **extrovert** have become household words. Measuring individual differences was not Jung's characteristic method, however, and very little of his theory is based on it.

As this brief list of practitioners indicates, the method of measuring individual differences has been very popular in personality psychology. Few theorists have used it exclusively, but almost every personality theorist has at least experimented with it at one time or other.

PROS

Quantification of observations.   Theorists who base their theories on the measurement of individual differences typically espouse the belief that psychology is (or should be) a science. Naturalistic observation has been the cornerstone of science ever since Aristotle decreed that this was so. But measurement refines naturalistic observation by making it more precise and more objective. Of course, a measurement is still an observation; but it is a particular kind of observation: A measurement is a quantified observation. Measurements are more exact than observations made with the naked eye. The radar gun a police officer uses to measure your car's speed is more than a minor improvement on the officer's own judgement ("slow"–"fast"–"faster"); it can actually detect the difference between speeds of fifty-five and fifty-six miles per hour. What is more, the officer's subjective bias does not influence the gun's readout. Insofar as personality tests operate in this way, they provide precise, objective, and discriminating naturalistic observations for constructing personality theories. Since these observations are in a quantified form, it is easy to compare them with each other, and—using statistical procedures—with the probability of chance occurrences. All of these things add scientific credibility to a theory; and for most psychologists, this is a pro.

Discovery of universals.   Measuring individual differences is scientific in still another way: It reveals the *universal* ingredients of personality. Science, as we normally define it, is less interested in the individual case, the particular, than in the universal. A personality theory can focus on the uniqueness of individual human beings, or it can focus on the things all human beings have in common. Logic dictates that the things people have in common, the universal traits of humanity, constitute the essence of human nature. The unique traits of individuals may be interesting, but they do not permit generalization, and generalization is the aim of science. The vast majority of theorists who use personality measurement set out to discover the universal elements of personality. Their work is therefore scientific.

CONS

Too impersonal.   Discovering the universal elements of human personality may be very scientific, but it lacks the richness and depth that we get in a good case study of individual personality. A test profile may be precise and objective, but it is also sterile and lifeless. By focusing on what all human beings have in common, theorists who use this method may reach such a high level of abstraction that they ignore the little quirks and idiosyncrasies that make us human. This con (impersonalness) is the flip side of the last pro (universality). But deciding whether this is a pro or a con entails a value judgment: If you think personality theories should reveal the elements all human beings have in common, it is a pro; if you think personality theory should provide an in-depth view of individual character, it is a con.

Too abstract.   A second criticism of personality theories based on the factor analysis is that the so-called "elements" of personality that are discovered may not exist; they may be nothing more than abstractions conjured up by the theorist. The elements of chemistry are "real" and tangible: You can hold iron or sulfur in your hand. But applying that analogy to personality may be misleading. The elements of personality are much more like biological classifications. It is not absolutely clear, for instance, that "crustaceans" really exist. Individual crabs, lobsters, and shrimp exist, of course, but "crustacean" is just a shorthand name zoologists use when referring to a set of characteristics that certain individual animals have in common. There are no individual crustaceans, in reality, since every individual animal has unique characteristics, beyond the minimal ones that define this classification. The same may be true of human personality. The psychologist's "elements" may not capture the essence of personality; they may be no more than convenient—and rather arbitrary—classifications.

In still another sense, the elemental traits revealed by personality measurement may not exist. Walter Mischel (1968) stirred up a hornet's nest in personality psychology more than a decade ago when he argued persuasively that traits are situation-specific. He meant that no person, for example, is shy "across-the-board", only shier in some situations and less shy in others. Shyness (or any other trait) depends on the situation, not on some stable internal disposition. We all know that a child may act quite shy in front of his parents' friends, yet be anything but bashful with his own peers. If you want to predict behavior, then, you are better off knowing the nature of the situation in which it occurs than the subject's trait score on a personality test. And in fact, Mischel gathered dozens of examples demonstrating that situational factors predict behavior much more powerfully than do trait scores. Most psychologists believe that the situation–versus–trait controversy has been resolved. A compromise position known as **interactionism** has evolved, recognizing the roles of both situational influences and traits in determining behavior. But though Mischel and most other experimental personality psychologists are now willing to acknowledge that traits exist, they still tend to regard the influence of traits on behavior—and hence their usefullness in predicting it—as relatively inconsequential.

Too arbitrary.   The third con concerns the arbitrary nature of this classification system. Factor analysis—the tool that reveals the alleged elements of personality—is vaunted by its advocates for its objectivity. Established mathematical procedures supposedly preclude bias. But in reality, these mathematical procedures are not universally accepted; the rationale for using one procedure rather than another is based on mere assumptions. How else can we explain the awkward fact that factor analysts "discover" different universal elements in human personality? This disagreement among the experts certainly doesn't inspire our confidence.

Causes not found.   Psychologists who employ experimental methods offer a final criticism of the measurement approach. It's chief defect, they say, is that its correlational techniques do not demonstrate cause-and-effect relationships. Showing that two variables are correlated is not the same as proving that one causes the other. Both may be caused by a third factor, for example. The incidence of narcotics addiction is significantly higher in urban areas than elsewhere, but this does not prove that living in the city causes people to use narcotics, or even that using narcotics causes one to live in the city. There is a correlation, but not necessarily a causal relationship. The experimentalists define science, however, as a discipline that discovers causes.

EXPERIMENT

The experimental method involves changing one condition while keeping all others constant, then seeing whether that one change affects the outcome. If you have a lamp that does not light, first you change the bulb. If it still does not work, perhaps you fiddle with the plug. Next, you might plug it in somewhere else. But you do not do all three at once if you want to isolate the cause of its faulty behavior. The experimental method operates by manipulating potential causes until it discovers one that makes a difference. The process is not hit-or-miss; it is guided by carefully formulated hypotheses. You would not, for example, try changing the lampshade.

Situational variables can be manipulated much more conveniently than traits can. Suppose you were interested in finding out what makes people willing to help others who are in distress. If you thought this behavior was caused by a trait, such as generosity or kindness, you might try to find (or devise) a test that would measure individual differences with respect to that trait. You might give your test to a large class taking the psychology of personality, then find some way to measure their willingness to help someone in trouble. One of the standard ploys for measuring willingness to help is telephoning each subject, saying your car has broken down, and that you just used your last dime to phone the garage for help, but dialed the subject's number by mistake. You ask whether the subject would mind calling the garage for you and you give out the phone number. Of course, the number you give is not that of the garage; it is the number of a confederate, who has agreed to record how many subjects demonstrate their willingness to help by actually making the call. To prove your hypothesis, all you have to do is to see whether the subjects who scored high on the test for generosity make significantly more calls than those who scored low. Unfortunately, this kind of research has usually failed to show that traits powerfully affect behavior, perhaps because the tests have not provided accurate measurements, or perhaps because traits are really situation-specific.

Experiments manipulating situational variables, on the other hand, often show situational variables powerfully affecting behavior. Isen, Clark and Schwartz (1976), hypothesized, for instance, that people would be more willing to help others if they were feeling good themselves. The experimenters manipulated the moods of one group of subjects by giving them small gifts just before someone else asked them for help. After answering the doorbells of their suburban homes, the subjects were confronted with a young woman who gave them complimentary packets of note cards and envelopes, worth less than half a dollar. Moments later, the subjects' telephones rang. The caller, claiming that she had been given the wrong number by the operator and had used her last dime, asked the subjects to look up the number for her and make the call. The caller did not say there was any real emergency, just that her brother was expecting her to pick him up at a friend's house. Clearly, the social pressure put on the subjects was not very strong, nor was the inexpensive gift a very powerful incentive; yet after receiving the stationery, over 80 percent of the subjects volunteered to help by making the phone call. Among the **control group**, those who did not receive any gift, only 12 percent agreed to help. The difference between 80 percent and 12 percent is enormous; in other words, the rather weak manipulation of a situational variable has a powerful effect on subsequent behavior. Differences of this magnitude are rarely found among groups selected on the basis of trait scores, but they are not unusual when subjects are randomly selected for exposure to situational influences.

The experimental method, which manipulates situational variables, is both a more convenient method and a more powerful predictor, because it makes extraneous influences on behavior easier to control. If you were to use the trait-measuring approach to research on helping behavior, you would have to make certain that subjects who scored high on your generosity test did not differ in any systematic (non-random) way from those who scored low; otherwise,you could never tell whether the differences in helpfulness were caused by their varying levels of generosity, by another trait, or by some uncontrolled situational variables. To demonstrate a specific cause, you must be able to rule out all other causes. Research using trait scores to establish subject groups for comparison usually attempts to accomplish this by matching subjects on such obvious traits as age, sex, social status, and intelligence. Not only is this method laborious; it leaves a great deal of room for extraneous variables to creep in.

The experimental method resolves this dilemma by placing subjects in experimental conditions at random. If you choose all the residents of a given street as the subjects for your experiment on helpfulness, you might draw half the names out of a hat and allow this group to receive the gifts. The other half serves as the control group, receiving the call for help without first getting a gift from the young woman at the door. Of course, subjects chosen in this manner will differ from each other in important ways, but it is safe to assume that the random selection will counteract those differences. In other words, the same differences should exist in both the first group and in the control group. The researchers can ignore these other differences and conclude that any difference in the groups' responses to the pleas for help has been caused by the situational variable that was manipulated: gift–vs.–no gift. Again, the experimental method demonstrates causal relationships by manipulating one variable at a time, and by ruling out the influence of all other variables.

The most vocal exponents of the experimental method in personality psychology are the behaviorally oriented personality theorists. The experimental method is the stock and trade of Albert Bandura, for example. Walter Mischel, already mentioned as the arch-situationalist, is of course also an avid experimentalist. B. F. Skinner and his followers are also strictly experimental. The experimental method is perhaps less exclusively adhered to in personality psychology than in psychology as a whole, yet even in the narrower field of personality theory it has its champions.

PROS

Prediction.   The primary advantage of the experimental method is that it works! Rather than just explaining behavior after it occurs, the experimental method predicts behavior—especially in the laboratory, but often in real life as well. And it predicts better than any other method. Any young psychologist who wants conclusive, publishable results from an anticipated research project would be well advised to employ an experimental design. Some historians of psychology have even suggested that the experimental method has risen to prominence in general psychology precisely because it produces more tangible and applicable results than philosophical speculation or naturalistic observation.

Causes.   A second advantage is that the experimental method discovers causes. Discovering causes is not only intellectually satisfying; it is also immensely useful. Without a knowledge of causal relationships, you might approach a psychological problem in the wrong way, like trying to fix a burned-out light bulb by changing the lampshade. But if you can find out what causes **agoraphobic** behavior, or **anorectic** behavior, or hyperactive behavior, then perhaps you can resolve the problem by removing its underlying cause. If you know what causes something, you can begin to control that thing (witness the desperate quest for the cause of cancer!). The experimental method is aimed specifically at finding causes, for with the discovery of causes comes the promise of control.

Objectivity.   The third advantage of the experimental method is its objectivity. Experimentation is far more successful than either philosophical speculation or clinical observation in eliminating possible sources of observer bias. Though it has been demonstrated that they sometimes influence the outcome of their experiments in subtle ways, experimenters are nevertheless more detached from what they observe than practitioners of any other method. And we have already seen that experimentation is more objective than the method of measuring individual differences, because the experimental method permits greater control over extraneous variables. In short, if objectivity is your goal, you cannot beat the experimental method.

Applicability.   Finally (and perhaps redundantly), the experimental method has the advantage of being readily applicable to therapy. In fact, behavior modification techniques are often employed for both experimental and therapeutic purposes. Malamid and Siegel (1975), for example, studied how the anxiety level of children who were about to undergo surgery was affected by having these children watch other children calmly go through the whole operation on film. Young patients awaiting surgery were randomly assigned to either the experimental group—who saw the filmed account of a seven-year-old boy being admitted to the hospital, entering surgery, then returning safely home—or to a control group—who saw a film of equal length, about a boy who took a trip to the country to look at nature. The children who saw the film about the operation were much less anxious on the night before their own surgery than the children from the control group. Furthermore, the first group remained less anxious even weeks after the operation; they did not show the increase in behavioral problems that was characteristic of the control group after they returned home. This experiment not only revealed something about the causes of anxiety in children; it had a merciful, therapeutic effect on those youngsters who were fortunate enough to be assigned to the experimental treatment. This immediate applicability is characteristic of psychology experiments that manipulate situational variables.

CONS

If the experimental method is so great, why doesn't everyone use it? For one thing, it is not always possible, or appropriate, to experiment during the earliest stages of theorizing. Scientists must engage in some naturalistic observation and speculation before they can produce an hypothesis that can be tested by experimentation. Some personality theorists have nothing against the experimental method, but feel that personality psychology is not yet ready to be an experimental science (though they see that as a desirable goal). Other personality theorists contend that the experimental method itself is flawed, either intrinsically or in the way it has been practiced.

Artificiality.   One criticism of the experimental method is that it employs artificial situations and deceptive tactics. The charge of artificiality was leveled against one of the experiments we will discuss later. In this experiment by Bandura (1966), children watched violent films in the laboratory and later exhibited aggressive behavior toward a Bobo doll. Critics point out that the laboratory situation was too different from real life to allow us to conclude that children who watch violent TV shows at home will inevitably become more aggressive toward real people. Field experiments, such as the one involving the telephone call for help, or the children facing surgery, are designed to avoid the artificiality of laboratory experiments; yet they sometimes suffer from similar problems. Besides questioning the ethics of deceiving subjects for experimental purposes, we need to ask whether the deceptions were successful. In the experiment in which subjects were telephoned for help, for example, isn't it possible that some of them refused to return the call because they were not sure the appeal was genuine? If subjects suspect that they are being manipulated, they may respond just as artificially in field experiments as they do in the laboratory. Despite much recent criticism of experiments involving deception, thousands of these experiments are still conducted. The validity of their conclusions depends entirely upon the premise that the subjects have been successfully deceived.

Triviality.   A second criticism of the experimental method is that the constraints it imposes—controlling extraneous variables; matching control groups; observing only repeatable behaviors; and accepting only measurable outcomes (**dependent variables**)—limit the phenomena it studies to trivial and irrelevant matters. While this criticism does not apply to the experiments we have considered so far, a brief review of even the best journals in the field is enough to show that many experiments simply confirm things that are already apparent to common sense, things so trivial that they deserve one of Senator Proxmire's famous "golden fleece" awards.

Loss of person.   A third criticism of the experimental method is that by concentrating so heavily on the role of situational factors in determining behavior, it risks losing sight of the person in personality. Everyone may be generous in some situations and uncharitable in others, but unless people have stable traits and dispositions—unless some people are fundamentally more generous than others—it makes no sense to talk about individual *personality*. Personality is whatever is consistent and distinctive about a person, the thing that makes the person recognizable and predictable as an individual. Experiments that manipulate situational variables may yield very interesting and valid psychological data, but these data may be more appropriate to social psychology than to the psychology of personality. When a psychology of situations represents itself as a psychology of personality, it encourages the kind of "double-think" that is already dangerously widespread. Any psychology of personality that ignores what makes a person a person is not really a psychology of personality.

Only prediction.   The final criticism of the experimental method has to do with the nature of its goals. No one would deny that all of the methods we have discussed aim toward knowledge and understanding; but as we have seen, the definitions of knowledge and understanding are always based on specific philosophical assumptions. Experimentalists assume, for instance, that being able to predict a phenomenon with a certain degree of accuracy is the same thing as understanding that phenomenon. It is not all that clear, however, that prediction equals understanding. Predictive ability does confer one kind of understanding, a practical understanding that can be put to use. But when lumberjacks accurately predict that the tree trunks they are sawing through will fall to the ground instead of floating off into space, do they really understand the phenomenon of gravity? In a limited sense they understand how gravity works, but do they understand what gravity *is*? The answer, of course, is no.

Where gravity is concerned, the larger question may not be so important; it is usually enough to know how the phenomenon works. But some students of human nature do not feel that it is enough merely to know how personality works; they want to know what personality is. More than that, they want to understand what it *means* to be human. The ability to predict behavior does not confer this kind of understanding. The proponents of prediction readily admit this, saying that such understanding is outside the purview of psychology. But because I believe that this type of understanding is an important and legitimate goal for psychology, I am counting the fact that the experimental method ignores it as a con.

CHAPTER SUMMARY

Personality psychologists employ four distinct methods for collecting data, and constructing and testing theories.

1. The first method is philosophical speculation. This involves observing yourself or other people, thoroughly studying relevant literature, using your rational faculties, to produce a coherent set of generalizations that constitutes a theory.

Pros. Philophical speculation is the least artificial of all methods; when used by a genius, it is often the only method needed.

Con. The main disadvantage of this method is that there is no generally accepted way to verify theories based on philosophical speculation.

2. The second method, clinical observation, is what most of us associate with the case study method. Here psychotherapists reflect upon their observations of patients and develop theories to guide their practice. Freud, Jung, Erikson, Rogers, and Kelly based their theories on this method. Murray and Allport used essentially the same technique, even though they did not treat their subjects as patients.

Pros. The strengths of this approach are its great depth and its relative lack of artificiality.

Cons. In clinical observation, ordinarily there are no safeguards against observer bias; no possibility of replication; and, especially when the subjects are patients, no representative sample of humanity to prevent the theory from becoming unbalanced.

3. The third method, measurement of individual differences, assumes that personality consists of a finite number of traits ("elements") that can be measured with psychological tests. Theorists who use this approach spend a lot of time constructing tests, and their analyses typically use correlational techniques, especially factor analysis. Cattell is the purest example of this kind of theorist, although Murray, Allport, and even Jung sometimes use this method.

Pros.   The main advantage of this method is that it is scientific. Measurement is precise, objective, and replicable. By quantifying observations, you make them available for statistical analysis. This method is also scientific because it reveals the *universal* ingredients of personality.

Cons.   These universal elements of personality may be too abstract, too sterile and lifeless. They may lack the richness and depth of a good case study. In fact, these elements may not even exist except as mathematical abstractions; and if they do exist, they may change with each new situation. Moreover, it is disconcerting to find that theorists have "discovered" entirely different sets of personality elements with this method. Finally, the correlational techniques of this method fail to demonstrate causal relationships.

4.   Fourthly and last, there is the experimental method, which entails changing one condition while keeping all others constant, then seeing whether that one change affects the outcome. Using psychological jargon, we would say that the independent variable is manipulated, and changes in the dependent variable are then observed. The variables manipulated in experiments are usually situational variables, because these factors are easy to manipulate and often have powerful effects. Bandura and Skinner are the most avid exponents of this method.

Pros.   The experimental method works. It predicts behavior, and predicts it better than any other method. What is more, it discovers causes and therefore provides very useful suggestions for changing behavior. Finally, it is objective.

Cons.   Personality psychology is a very young discipline. Some critics say that experimentation is premature, and it should wait until more theorizing based on speculation and naturalistic observation has been done. Other critics argue that experimentation will never be appropriate, because it always employs artificial situations and deceptive tactics. In addition, the constraints imposed by the experimental method practically guarantee that only trivial phenomena will be studied. Then, too, by concentrating almost exclusively on situational variables, experimental personality psychologists risk losing sight of the person in personality. Finally, it is questionable whether predicting behavior is the same thing as understanding personality.

REFERENCES

Allport, G. W. (1965). *Letters from Jenny.* New York: Harcourt, Brace & World.

Bandura, A., Grusec, J. E., & Menlove, F.L. (1966). Observational learning as a function of symbolization and incentive set. *Child Development, 37,* 499–506.

Isen, A. M., Clark, M., & Schwartz, M. F. (1976). Duration of the effect of good mood on helping: "Footprints on the sands of time." *Journal of Personality and Social Psychology, 34,* 385–393.

Melamed, B. G., & Siegel, L. J. (1975). Reduction of anxiety in children facing hospitalization and surgery by use of filmed modeling. *Journal of Consulting and Clinical Psychology, 43,* 511–521.

Mischel, W. (1968). *Personality and assessment.* New York: Wiley.

Wolpe, J., & Rachman, S. J. (1960). Psychoanalytic "evidence," a critique based on Freud's case of Little Hans. *Journal of Nervous and Mental Disease, 131,* 135–147.

PART ONE

Psychodynamic Theories

Psychodynamic theories of personality all have one thing in common—the notion that the contents of the mind are active, rather than passive. To understand what that means, let us use the analogy of a tape recorder. Perhaps ideas are stored in your mind in much the same way that a song is recorded on tape. In that case, the mind contains the ideas in the same way that the tape contains the song. The song is there on the tape, whether you recorded it yourself or bought it pre-recorded. And it will stay there on the "tape" as long as you do not erase it (forget the idea). Whenever you want to hear the song again (remember the idea), you can get out the tape and play it. The tape, of course, will always play the same song; it never edits the song or decides to play some other song. The song recorded on the tape is passive, not active. It cannot do anything by itself. It does not have a will and cannot make decisions: It does not have a mind of its own. It is only a tape, an inanimate thing.

That is just the point, say the psychodynamic personality theorists. The mind and its ideas are not inanimate, they are alive. The mind is not a tape recorder. To understand the psychodynamic perspective, we need to put the tape recorder analogy aside for the moment. The analogy may be fine for much of the recent research relating computer functioning to human thought processes, but it does nothing to illuminate the psychodynamic model of the mind; unless, that is, you can visualize a tape that records one thing today and plays back something entirely different tomorrow.

We will have to look for another analogy to illustrate psychodynamic theories. Suppose you want to remind yourself of a dentist appointment at 4:30 on Friday afternoon. You write yourself a note, which stores the memory for you. When you want to remember the appointment, all you have to do is to look at the note. But this is still a passive storage system. It is not really very different from the tape recorder analogy. The ink on the notepaper cannot erase itself, or rearrange itself into new words. If the contents of the mind are truly active, rather than passive, then the mind cannot be just some huge container where we store all the notes we have written to ourselves over a lifetime, no matter how much that image may appeal to common sense.

But there is another strategy we all use to remember dates and appointments, and this strategy represents the psychodynamic view of the mind very nicely. I am referring to the simple device of asking somebody else to remind you. Instead of writing yourself a note, you say to your roommate, "Don't let me forget to go to the dentist on Friday at 4:30." Under these circumstances you would not be surprised, when Friday rolls around, to hear the message played back to you in a form like this: "Didn't you have an appointment with the eye doctor this morning?" It does not amaze you that the message has been changed, because the storage medium was not something dead, like ink on paper, but something alive and growing, always changing—namely, another mind. According to the psychodynamic theorists, then, storing memories in your mind is not like writing notes to yourself, or even making tape recordings; it is like asking another person to remember something for you. Memories, ideas—whatever we call the contents of the mind—have a "mind" of their own. They are living, growing, changing, organic things.

But all of this activity within the contents of the mind involves more than just growth and change. Ideas and memories can actually come into conflict with each other. A strong idea may block a weaker one, or several weak ideas may team up to push down a stronger one. There is a perfectly good analogy for this, too, in our everyday behavior. Suppose that instead of telling just one other person to remind you of your dentist appointment, you tell a whole group of people—your family, or all of your roommates. When the time comes for retrieving the message, it not only contains changes, but exists in several contradictory versions that generate arguments. One person thinks the appointment was at 9:30; another says it was at 4:30. One argues it was with an eye doctor, while another insists it was an appointment for a hair cut. Just as your friends may fight over whose version is correct, conflicting ideas battle, according to psychodynamic theorists, to decide which one will enter your conscious mind when you seek to recollect something.

In short, the contents of the mind are active. They do not just lie there in the storehouse of your mind, like so many notes on a tablet. They are dynamic, not static. They form alliances, clash, and when the battle is over, form new alliances. In the process they are changed: Some become stronger, while others are pushed farther and farther into the background. The essence of the psychodynamic theory is that ideas stored in your mind have lives of their own. The task of psychodynamic psychology is to investigate the nature of those lives.

Almost all psychodynamic theories of personality are psychoanalytic, or at least derived from *psychoanalysis*—the "brand name" for Sigmund Freud's theory of personality. There have been a few non-Freudian psychodynamic theories, but none of these has been very popular. For most practical purposes, therefore, the terms *psychodynamic, psychoanalytic,* and *Freudian* are interchangeable.

3/Sigmund Freud

A Biographical Sketch

Sigmund Freud was born in 1856 in the city of Freiberg, which is now in Czechoslovakia. His father, a wool merchant, moved the family to Vienna when Sigmund was four years old, in search of better markets.

Young Sigmund, the first born and favorite of his mother (the second wife of his much older father), was an outstanding student almost from the moment he learned to read. He was awarded a room of his own in the family's Vienna apartment, so that he could pursue his studies without interruption. It was the only room equipped with an oil lamp, rather than candles. At one point, the ten- or eleven-year-old Sigmund complained that his sister's piano practice disturbed his studies, though great care had been taken to locate the piano at the far end of the apartment. The piano was quickly removed from the premises.

Despite his great scholarship, or perhaps because of it, Freud did not find it easy to choose a career. In fact, he did not settle on the profession of personality theorist until sometime between the ages of thirty and thirty-five. Throughout his high school years, he seems to have had a vague intention to pursue a career in law. He got this idea from several sources: the influence of an older school friend; the effect, on him and his parents, of a fortune-teller's casual prophecy that he would grow up to be a government minister; and undoubtedly also the fact that, for the first time, there were a few Jews who had become government ministers. (As a Jew, Freud was restricted, for all practical purposes, to a career in business, law, or medicine.)

Freud tells us that he never intended to become a doctor. Yet his growing fascination with the new and controversial theories of Charles Darwin, and the effect a public reading of Goethe's *Ode to Nature* had on him, nudged him in the direction of medical school, where he enrolled at the age of seventeen. He still had no plans to become a doctor; he considered himself more what we would nowadays call an undergraduate biology major.

Freud took seven-and-a half years to graduate, at least three years longer than the norm. At least part of this procrastination was due to uncertainty about the direction his life should take. Though he attended all the required lectures and labs in chemistry, physiology, and anatomy, he also took elective courses in philosophy and, at one point, considered taking a degree in philosophy after finishing his medical studies.

It was Ernst Brücke, the world-famous physiologist, who finally captured young Freud's attention and gave him his first sense of professional identity. Under Brücke's influence, Freud decided to become a research physiologist. Brücke, incidentally, was one of a group of physiologists who crusaded in favor of absolute **mechanistic** determinism in the biological sciences. This ideology struck a responsive chord in Freud and continued to guide his thinking, even when he constructed his theory of personality years later. Freud published a number of well-received papers on his research at the Brücke Institute, most of them having to do with the histology of the nervous system of fish and other lower animals.

Only after he had finally graduated and received his M.D. did Freud discover the sad truth that it would be unrealistic for him to aspire to a career in pure research. Such careers were the prerogative of men of independent means. Freud was poor, still dependent on his father for financial assistance. What is more, he had fallen in love with the woman who was to become his wife, and he needed to make financial provisions to marry. This was undoubtedly one of the critical moments in Freud's life.

Reluctantly, he abandoned the laboratory and began working in a hospital. Neurology was the logical choice of specialization for someone with his background. During the next three years, Freud served as house physician at the General Hospital. He kept his research interests alive by working at the Institute of Cerebral Anatomy, where he traced the tracts in the medulla oblongata. He became so proficient in this area that he could diagnose the site of a lesion in the medulla with astounding accuracy. Physicians came from as far away as America to learn his methods.

Economic reality once again directed him to specialize more narrowly in the treatment of nervous diseases. In the Vienna of that era, there were very few specialists in this branch of medicine. Of course, that also meant that there were few experts with whom Freud could study. If he were to become properly qualified as a doctor of nervous disorders, Freud would have to go to Paris and study with the famous Jean Martin Charcot. After a series of maneuvers, including obtaining an appointment as University Lecturer on Nervous Diseases in Vienna, Freud won a fellowship to study with Charcot. The year was 1885, and Freud was twenty-nine years old.

The education Freud received at Charcot's clinic was another important turning point in his life. Charcot's specialty was hysteria, a "nervous disorder" that had no apparent neurological cause, but many intriguing psychological dimensions, as we will see very shortly. From Charcot, Freud learned many things about hysteria and its treatment, and about hypnosis. These things were unknown in Vienna.

When Freud returned to Vienna to set up his own private practice as a specialist in nervous diseases, he was one of the few doctors there who welcomed hysterical, and other neurotic, patients. Yet even in this endeavor he did not succeed immediately. At first he tried to make a living by treating cases of organic neurological pathology. Only when it became clear that there were too few

cases to support all of the doctors in his specialty did Freud begin actively seeking out the more psychologically disturbed clientele that would turn his thinking in the direction of personality theory. By then he was well into his thirties; in fact, he did not entirely abandon his dream of becoming a great research neurologist until sometime in the 1890s, when he finally accepted the idea of being a mere psychologist.

That decision sparked a tremendous burst of creative activity, including book publications at the rate of almost one a year, and carried Freud into a larger, global arena. As early as 1909, he was asked to lecture at Clark University's twentieth anniversary celebration in Worcester, Massachusetts. He continued to be immensely productive for thirty more years, although he never again visited America. He left Vienna in 1938, when the Nazi storm troopers were literally on his doorstep. He fled to England, where he died on September 23, 1939.

FREUD'S THREE KEY IDEAS

Every book about personality theories begins with Sigmund Freud, and with good reason. He was not only the first to write extensively on personality, but probably wrote more than anyone else on the subject. His collected works fill twenty-three volumes, or about two feet of library shelf-space. There is almost no question about personality that Freud did not think about and try to answer. He is undoubtedly the most influential figure in the entire history of psychology—despite the fact that he was not a professor of psychology but a medical doctor. Some people even argue that Freud was one of the two or three greatest shapers of Western thought in the last hundred years, along with Karl Marx and Charles Darwin.

Freud was so prolific that I will have to abandon, or at least modify, my key idea format right at the outset. There is simply no way to argue convincingly that Freud had only one key idea. At the very least, he had three: (1) the idea of unconscious motivation; (2) the idea of **pansexualism,** (i.e., that all behavior is sexually motivated); and (3) the idea of stages of development. If you grasp these three key ideas, you will have the key to the contents of all twenty-three volumes of Freud's thought.

KEY IDEA #1
UNCONSCIOUS MOTIVATION

The *idea of unconscious motivation* assumes that people can be compelled to do things without knowing the reasons for their actions, and perhaps without having any control over those actions. Freud tells us that he became absolutely convinved that this idea was valid after witnessing a demonstration of posthypnotic suggestion in 1889, at the clinic of Hippolyte Bernheim in Nancy, France (Freud, 1940/1964).

SOURCES OF FREUD'S IDEA OF UNCONSCIOUS MOTIVATION

HYPNOTISM

The Nancy clinic was famous for its work with hypnotism, and Freud had gone there as a young doctor to study with Bernheim. One rainy day, while following Dr. Bernheim on his rounds, Freud watched as the doctor hypnotized a patient on one of the wards. While the patient was under hypnosis, Berheim instructed him that when he, the doctor, returned later that day, the patient would greet him by picking up an umbrella Bernheim had left standing in the corner of the ward, and opening it above the doctor's head. Bernheim told the patient that he would remember nothing that had taken place while he had been hypnotized, then woke the patient from his trance and walked out of the ward, leaving the umbrella behind. When Bernheim and Freud returned some hours later, the patient, somewhat perplexed, carried out the doctor's suggestion. When Bernheim asked him why he was opening an umbrella indoors, the embarrassed patient mumbled that the doctor needed to open his umbrella inside the room before going out into the rain. Freud interpreted this explanation as a spur-of-the-moment dodge to mask the patient's ignorance of the real motive: namely, the doctor's posthypnotic suggestion, which the patient did not remember. To those who might doubt that "mental acts which are unconscious do exist," Freud replied that anyone "who has witnessed such an experiment will receive an unforgettable impression and a conviction that can never be shaken" (Freud, 1940/1964, p. 285).

Clearly, the phenomenon of posthypnotic suggestion provided the model for Freud's idea of unconscious motivation, which has several salient features. When an action is unconsciously motivated, (1) there is a motive, a reason, for the action; (2) the person performing the action does not know what that motive is; and (3) the person is compelled to perform the action even though it is "irrational."

HYSTERIA

Very likely, the type of patient Freud dealt with also influenced him to think about unconscious motivation and, for that matter, to pursue the study of hypnotism. Many of Freud's patients were women suffering from a **neurotic** reaction called conversion hysteria. In conversion hysteria, patients develop the symptoms of some real physical disease, though medical examination fails to reveal anything physically wrong with them. The illness is "all in their heads"; in fact, you can achieve the same effect by hypnotizing normal people and telling them that they are paralyzed. The hypnotic command does not damage the nerves in their legs—a few words do not produce an organic disease—yet these hypnotized people will be unable to walk. Futhermore, if a posthypnotic suggestion tells them they will remain paralyzed even after being awakened from the trance, their subsequent symptoms will be indistinguishable from the symptoms of people suffering from hysterical paralysis. In both cases—posthypnotic suggestion and hysteria—the people are not faking; they genuinely believe that they are paralyzed, even though there is nothing physically wrong with them. And no amount of urging or coaxing, no well reasoned arguments, no bribes or even dire threats will succeed in curing them. They cannot, by force of conscious effort, overcome their paralysis. The hypnotized subject can, of course, have the paralysis removed by a simple command to that effect from the hypnotist; but, then, so can the hysteric! The most dramatic proof that hysteria is purely mental is the capacity for removing its symptoms through hypnosis. Hysterical paralysis can be cured, for instance, by hypnotizing the patients and telling them they will be able to move their dead limbs and will no longer be paralyzed. In fact, Bernheim's Nancy clinic built its reputation on exactly this kind of cure.

Had Freud not been confronted with so many baffling cases of conversion hysteria, he would probably not have become interested in hypnosis, and he would probably never have travelled to Nancy. But, even if he had not gone to Nancy, his work with hysterical patients would have led him to hypothesize unconscious mental processes to account for what he saw. An hysterical patient seems to be of two minds. Witness the following case.

> Miss M. was referred to the university psychology department for a determination of auditory thresholds by a local otologist. She had complained of a persistent buzzing and ringing in her ears for the past five months. The symptoms had progressed to the point where they interferred with her work as a stenographer, since often she could not accurately hear dictation. Tests of pitch and loudness thresholds, however, showed no real loss of acuity. A Rorschach test showed a personality structure consistent with hysteria. A series of interviews, aimed at tracing the psychological situation in which the symptoms developed, disclosed the following pertinent information. Approximately six months previous she had gone to a party at a friend's mountain cabin, and while more or less under the influence of alcohol and a moonlit night had engaged in a rather abortive attempt at sexual intercourse. The next day she experienced a

panicky fear that she was pregnant and, after hurried consultation with some of her intimate girl friends, began to take large doses of quinine sulphate.

She continued this medication for two weeks, remaining in a state of fearful agitation. The quinine produced unpleasant symptoms of nausea and ringing in her ears. Her regular menstrual period then occurred, and she gradually recovered her normal spirits. Unfortunately the man who was a party to the original incident was an office associate and a frequent escort to dances, shows, and other parties. A mild "petting" experience with this man about a month after the original incident was followed by feelings of nausea and a return of her auditory symptoms, which became chronic and persistently annoying enough to prompt her to seek medical advice. A diagnosis of hysterical akoasm was made and she was referred to a psychiatrist for treatment. (O'Kelly, 1949, pp. 180–181)

This patient seems to be "of two minds" because of her relationship with the man who is described in the story as "an office associate and frequent escort to dances, shows, and other parties." Part of the patient— one of her "minds"—seems to want this relationship to progress to greater and greater intimacy, while a second "mind" seems to want to stop, or at least slow down, the relationship. The first mind regards the ringing and buzzing in the ears as an affliction, something that interferes with her work. This mind wants to be cured and motivates the patient to come to the doctor. But the second mind has its reasons for wanting the ringing in the ears (or any other symptom) to continue, and is sometimes surprisingly indifferent to what must strike the rest of the world as a personal catastrophe.

The ringing in her ears prevents Miss M. from taking dictation. If she cannot take dictation, she cannot work in the office; and if she does not go to the office, she will not encounter the gentleman with whom—we may infer—she fears that she will tumble into bed. The second mind puts up with the ringing in the ears because the ringing offers a solution to Miss M's problem. It would be fair to say, in fact, that the second mind has caused the ringing in the ears.

Miss M's first mind—her normal waking mind, the one that holds conversations with other people—is totally unaware that the second mind exists. If Miss M. were told that she wanted her ears to ring so that she would not have to deal with her feelings about Mr. X., she would deny any knowledge of that motive. And her denial would be based not on deceit, but genuine ignorance: She honestly does not know that she has a second mind, nor can anyone else contact this mind through conversation or any other normal channel of communication. Yet logic may force us to infer the existence of the second mind, even though we cannot directly observe it. After all, the ringing in Miss M's ears must originate somewhere in her mind, since there is nothing physically wrong with her. Faced with case after case of this sort, Freud was driven to the conclusion that hysterical symptoms are produced by the operation of a second mind in the patient, a mind he referred to as the unconscious.

HARTMANN

It may surprise you to learn that the idea of an unconscious mind is not very old. In fact, Freud himself is often credited with the discovery of the unconscious. Whether he discovered it, or as some of his critics contend, invented it, the idea was not very popular before his time.

For a better perspective on the development of the idea of the unconscious, you should keep in mind that hypnosis was virtually unknown before 1775, and it was not accepted by the medical profession as a therapeutic tool until the middle of the nineteenth century.

Conversion hysteria, which also has the potential to suggest unconscious mental activity, did not become faddishly popular until the second half of the nineteenth century. During the Victorian age, it was one of the favorite complaints of idle bourgeois women who were only then beginning to adopt the fashion of visiting doctors.

Perhaps the greatest impetus for the idea of the unconscious came from the book *Philosophy of the Unconscious*, written by the German philosopher Eduard von Hartmann in 1868. Freud did not begin writing about the unconscious until the 1890s. Therefore, if anyone discovered the unconscious, it was Hartmann, not Freud. Many people think Freud got his ideas about the unconscious directly from Hartmann, and Freud was certainly familiar with Hartmann's work. But if the idea of the unconscious was already in the air when Freud began writing about it, it is probably pointless to argue whether he borrowed it from Hartmann or not. In any case, Freud made unconscious motivation the main idea in his personality theory, and that theory became one of the most influential representations of human nature in the twentieth century.

WHAT UNCONSCIOUS MOTIVATION EXPLAINS

NEUROTIC SYMPTOMS

Freud found an endless number of applications for his new concept. Unconscious motivaton was able to explain an astounding range of human experiences, both normal and abnormal. We have already seen how conversion hysteria was traced to an unconscious wish to avoid some unpleasant urge. In other cases of hysteria, some overwhelming fear is "repressed," that is, pushed down into the unconscious, where it is converted into a set of physical symptoms. **Phobias, obsessions,** and **compulsions** Freud also explained in much the same way. These symptoms—an irrational fear of feathers, a nagging conviction that you are going to drive your car into a pole, or the desperate urge to wash your hands every ten minutes, for example—are merely the outward manifestations of some conflict among motives buried in your unconscious.

Freud demonstrated that the idea of unconscious motivation was equally useful for explaining normal, everyday "symptoms." In *Psychopathology of Everyday Life* (1901/1960), he explained how a variety of very common accidents and blunders—slips-of-the-tongue or pen (ever since referred to as "Freudian slips"); forgetting names and appointments; losing or misplacing things; getting out the wrong key to open a door—were produced by similar conflicts among unconscious motives. He referred to these everyday blunders as examples of psychopathology, implying that the mental processes involved in them were no different from the ones he saw operating in neurosis.

DREAMS

Freud was always looking for new ways to peer into the unconscious. Neurotic symptoms provide one route, but this route is indirect, almost entirely dependent on inference. In the *Interpretation of Dreams* (1900/1953), Freud argued that dreams provide windows to the unconscious. Unfortunately, even these windows aren't completely transparent: Unconscious forces are hard at work, trying to hide the true meaning of the dream from the dreamer. One of these unconscious processes which Freud calls "the censor", cuts certain portions of your dreams out of your waking recollection, in much the same way that an X-rated movie is edited for prime-time TV. Furthermore, dreams are symbolically coded to prevent the dreamer from understanding their true, unconscious significance. In the *Interpretation of Dreams*, Freud reveals how he cracked this code and deciphered what he called the "latent content" of dreams—that is, their unconscious meanings. Once again, Freud's idea of unconscious motivation provided the key to understanding a common human experience: dreams.

CAREER CHOICES AND OTHER PERSONAL PREFERENCES

In *Leonardo da Vinci: A Study in Psychosexuality* (1910/1957), Freud attemped to demonstrate that unconscious motivation was also the key to understanding the creative drive of great geniuses. According to Freud, Leonardo's creativity was the product of an unconscious mental process called **sublimation.** What goes on in sublimation is not very different from what happens in dreams. In both cases, your unconscious motives are hidden from you by being disguised. In dreams they are disguised by being shown to you in a secret symbolic code; in sublimation, an unacceptable unconscious motive disguises itself by finding a more acceptable way to get what it wants. A simple example: *You want to suck your thumb, so you smoke a cigarette.* According to Freud, the desire for a smoke is nothing more than infantile urge in disguise. Leonardo's paintings were also disguises for unacceptable unconscious motives. Freud says that Leonardo was basically a mamma's boy who was frustrated by being separated from his mother at a rather young age. The unconscious desire to be with his mother is what caused him to paint so many pictures of the Madonna. In other words, Leonardo's true motive camouflaged itself by finding an outlet that seemed to Leonardo and everyone else (except Freud), artistic and religious.

Leonardo's sublimation was by no means unique. Just as we all dream, we all sublimate. And though some of us do not paint masterpieces, we all do some kind of work and plan careers. If you had the time and money to undertake a lengthy psychoanalysis, you would probably discover that you have chosen your career in order to satisfy some infantile craving: The plumber, deep down, is a kid who likes to play in toilets; the doctor is someone who still wants to "play doctor"—examine peoople with their clothes off. In fact, Freud argues that all adult curiosity is nothing but a sublimated version of our infantile curiosity about the kinds of genital organs other people have. In that regard, the jungle explorer is no different from the medical doctor; his disguise is simply better. Or consider the astronomer who gazes at heavenly *bodies*. We could go on and on; but suffice it to say that any career you choose, any hobby you pursue, any sport you play represents a specific unconscious motive in disguised form. Freud's first key idea covers a lot of ground.

SOCIAL INSTITUTIONS

But Freud did not stop there. He went on to say that unconscious motives, disguised by sublimation, accounted for the nature and existence of entire social institutions. In *Totem and Taboo* (1913/1955), Freud argued that the institution of religion (especially the rite of sacrifice) is a gigantic sub-limation of the **Oedipus complex.** According to the Oedipus complex, at the age of four or five boys typically fall in love with their mothers, want the mothers all to themselves, and want to do away with their fathers. It is no accident, Freud says, that religions cast God in the role of father and priests in the role of sons. In the rite of sacrifice the priests, or sons, ritually kill the Father—precisely what little boys do in their fantasies. This analogy may sound a bit fantastic when it is stated so baldly, but Freud makes a very convincing argument for it.

For Freud, all civilization, all of what sociologists call culture, is the product of sublimated unconscious motives. The arts, the sciences, ex-ploration and invention, government, business, education, the military— all are disguised expressions of unconscious, infantile motives. Freud isn't trying to say that this is bad. Quite the contrary: If those motives were allowed to express themselves in a direct, undisguised fashion, human beings would be no different from any other animals. We would still be swinging by our tails in the primeval forest.

Unconscious motivation was a spectacular idea. Freud used it to explain something like ninety percent of our entire psychic life. He said that the mind is like an iceberg, nine-tenths submerged. And the idea of uncon-scious motivation is the master key that unlocks all the secret chambers below the surface. In its explanatory power, unconscious motivation is comparable to Darwin's idea of evolution, or Einstein's theory of relativity. Keys that can be made to fit so many locks are extremely rare; no more than a handful have been found throughout all of human history. Freud's idea of unconscious motivation is one of that handful.

The very fact that an idea opens so many doors makes it very attractive and persuasive. Any idea that works this well must be true, we say. Yet some people think that Freud's first key idea is false, and that unconscious motivation was not a Freudian discovery, but a Freudian invention. Let us take a look now at the pros and cons of this idea, examining not only the arguments for and against its validity, but also the consequences of accepting it as a true picture of human nature.

PROS and CONS

Pro #1: This key idea appeals to common sense.   The most obvious advantage of Freud's idea of unconscious motivation is that it appeals very strongly to our common sense and everyday experience. All of us have suffered the embarrassment of forgetting someone's name, then realized upon reflection that we really disliked that person. I cannot begin to count the number of times I have arrived at my office door in the morning and attempted to jam my house key into the lock. Then the flash of truth strikes me: I would rather still be home in bed. Even a five-year-old child seems to know that when you make a slip-of-the-tongue, you inadvertently say what you are really thinking, although you meant to say something else. And we have certainly all forgotten appointments that promised to be unpleasant. Freud's examples from everyday life make his argument very persuasive, since everyone knows from experience that your own mind can play tricks on you.

Pro #2: This key idea is supported by many experiments.   Numerous experiments have been performed in an effort to prove the validity of Freud's idea of unconscious motivation. Freud did not conduct any of these experiments himself, of course. His methods were exclusively clinical and observational. The business of trying to establish whether or not unconscious motives operate in the manner described by Freud was left to other researchers, some hostile and some friendly. Regrettably, their results have been inconclusive. Many of the experiments have been methodologically flawed. Others have suffered from problems of definition—what the experimenter studied was not exactly the same thing Freud was talking about. In others, the data are subject to interpretations other than those presented by the experimenter.

The earliest experiments simply demonstrated that people's recollections of their childhoods contained more pleasant than unpleasant memories (Jersild, 1931). The scarcity of unpleasant memories was interpreted as evidence of repression, the unconscious motive to forget events that are unpleasant or threatening.

Another classic experiment flashed words at the subjects, beginning with exposure times too brief for the words to be read, and then gradually lengthening exposures until the subjects correctly identified the words

(McGinnies, 1949). The trick here was that some of the words were dirty. The results—subjects required longer exposure times to identify dirty words than inoffensive words—were interpreted as proof that the unconscious tries to prevent us from becoming aware of anxiety-provoking stimuli.

Nowhere, according to Freud, is the unconscious permitted such free reign as in the production of dreams. Hall and Van de Castle (1965) collected written reports of dreams from 120 male and female college students. They asked a board of independent judges to examine the dreams, using criteria developed by the experimenters, for evidence of three Freudian themes: (1) **castration anxiety,** the fear of being castrated; (2) **castration wish,** the desire to see someone else castrated; and (3) **penis envy,** the desire to have a penis, or in men, to have a better penis.

If unconscious motives affect dreams as Freud claimed, Hall and Van de Castle predicted that the theme of castration anxiety would be paramount in the dreams of male subjects, whereas penis envy would show up most frequently in the female subjects' dreams. That is exactly what happened. The men dreamed more castration-anxiety dreams, and the women dreamed more penis-envy dreams. Assuming that these student subjects were not consciously aware of harboring such primitive fears and jealousies—and that seems a fairly safe assumption—then what we have here is another experimental demonstration that unconscious motives influence behavior.

These are only a few examples of the hundreds of experiments that have been done to test various aspects of Freudian theory having to do with unconscious motivation. I have chosen to discuss these experiments because the experimenters were not prejudiced against Freud; the results support Freud's idea, and because each of these experiments was regarded by many as a significant gain for Freud when it was first published. Freud's enemies were not so easily persuaded, however, and I would be remiss if I did not point out that each of these experiments has been criticized on some, or all, of the grounds mentioned earlier—methodological flaws, problems of definition, interpretation of results. But the same thing is true of almost any sampling of other experiments on this topic.

What then is the status of experimental evidence for the existence of unconscious motivation? Walter Mischel (1981) devotes an entire chapter of his *Introduction to Personality* to this question. And while it is clear that Mischel is no great friend of Freud, he does acknowledge that the question is still open. The evidence, on balance, is inconclusive. No crucial experiment has been devised. In fact, it may very well be impossible, given the nature of the concept, to design a single experiment that will once and for all settle the issue. Mischel (1981) concludes that "consequently one has to seriously question not merely the methods of studying the unconsious but also the nature of the phenomenon itself, while remaining fully open to the possibility that better methods and studies will bring new understanding" (p. 445).

Pro #3: This key idea is the basis for effective psychotherapy.   For Freud, of course, the existence of unconscious motivation was proved by the fact that his therapy, which was founded squarely on that notion, cured his patients. The therapeutic method of psychoanalysis consists of making conscious that which was unconscious. To that end the psychoanalyst uses dream analysis, **free association, transference,** and interpretation of the patient's symptoms, **resistances,** slips of the tongue, and so forth. Psycho-analysts continue to cure people today in great numbers. Some psycho-analysts now work with modified versions of their mentor's theories. Yet even today, the cornerstone of all psychoanalytic theory is that idea of unconscious motivation. Freud developed his personality theory so that he would have some basis for curing the neurotic patients who consulted him. In other words, the therapy grew directly out of the theory. And the therapy works—there is no question about it. That is where Freud rests his case.

Con #1: This key idea is a contradiction in terms.   The first criticism of Freud's idea of unconscious motivation—first historically and in terms of logical priority—is that it is a contradiction in terms, because it confuses what is mental, or psychic, with what is bodily, or physical.

Unconscious, but not mental.   Suppose that as I sit here writing, the thought occurs to me that I would love to have a nice cold drink. That thought conflicts with another thought I have at the same time, namely, that I want to finish writing this chapter. A little debate takes place on the screen of my consciousness, and the desire for a drink is defeated. That thought vanishes from the screen—in fact, both thoughts vanish from the screen—as I turn my attention back to writing. The thoughts are not lost, since I may recollect an hour from now that I wanted a drink but decided to keep writing instead. So the thoughts must have been recorded in my memory. When they left my consciousness they were transformed into some sort of neurological change in the cells of my brain.

The question is, What do these thoughts do while they lie there in storage outside of consciousness? Freud said that they do exactly the same thing that they did when they were conscious: They continue their debate. They argue and they conflict in the same way that they did when they were on the screen, except that now they are not on the screen and I am not conscious of the debate. In short, they behave according to the laws that govern all *mental* processes. What goes on in Freud's model of the uncon-scious mind is not something physiological—not some rearrangement of neural pathways, for example—but a thought process very similar to ordi-nary conscious thinking, except that in this case the thinkers do not, indeed cannot, know that they are thinking. That, say Freud's critics, is ridiculous.

These critics say that sharp distinctions should be made between neu-rological processes and thought processes. Neurological processes are *physical* (electrochemical) activities; they are not mental debates and argu-ments. The critics agree that memories may sometimes distort our original recordings of experiences, but insist that such distortions are brought about by physiological processes. And physiological processes follow a set of laws entirely different from those that may be deduced for mental debates appearing on the screen of consciousness. Consciousness follows one set of rules; what is "out of consciousness" follows another set of rules. Freud's idea of the unconscious mind contends, however, that both consciousness and what is out of consciousness follow a similar set of rules.

Critics insist that Freud's unconscious mind is either not mind, or not really unconscious. It cannot be both, they say. They do not deny that we may process information without being aware of it; they simply say that when that happens, one of the following two things must be true: (1) either the processes involved are physiological, and not mental; or (2) the processes involved are not totally outside of consciousness. These are really two separate criticisms. The first says: "True, there are unconscious processes, but they are not mental." The second says: "True, there are mental processes that appear to be unconscious, but in fact they are not." We have already discussed the first criticism. Let us turn to the second.

Mental, but not unconscious.   There are mental processes going on that Freud said were unconscious, but that in fact are conscious—that is what this criticism boils down to. According to Freud's explanation of neurotic anxiety, people are anxious because they are afraid that their unconscious instincts will break through the lid of **repression** and be revealed to them in consciousness. Consider the characteristically Freudian case of

> a young man [who] developed a violent dislike of ballet after having attended a performance during which he was thrown into a panic. His heart pounded, he had difficulty breathing, and he broke into a cold sweat. As soon as he left the theater, his symptoms subsided. Later, events revealed that this man had strong unconscious homosexual tendencies which he was struggling to keep from becoming conscious. He was unconsciously attracted to the male ballet dancers. His panic was a reaction to the threat that his defenses might break down and that he might reveal the homosexual component of his personality to himself or to others (Kisher, 1964, p. 267).

Right here, at the heart of Freud's theory, is where we find the most glaring contradiction. The young man in this case either knows that he is attracted to members of his own sex, or he does not know it. If he does know it, then there is nothing further to explain, since, given our society's attitude toward homosexuals (especially until very recently), any young man would be frightened to find himself possessed of such tendencies and would try to deny them. His homosexual tendencies would not need to be unconscious to cause such a panic attack at the ballet. Nor should we find it surprising that he denies knowing what caused him to panic—even today, homosexuals do not step out of the closet without some fear of social disapproval. The young man does not need to be unconscious of his homosexuality in order to develop anxiety in connection with it. And if this is true, then Freud's idea of unconscious motivation is superfluous.

But let us consider the other possibility. Let us assume that the young man really does not know that he has homosexual tendencies, and that those tendencies are truly unconscious. But if they are truly unconscious and, if he is absolutely unaware of them, then how can he know that coming face to face with them will be a devastating experience? If you are faced with opening a locked closet whose contents are unknown, you might be a little apprehensive; but you will not be thrown into complete and utter panic unless you have already been given a clue that something terrifying is inside. That is exactly what happens in Freud's model of the psyche: the unconscious mind gives the conscious mind little hints and clues about what is hidden away in the closet. Without these hints, the conscious mind would not know that it had anything to be afraid of.

But a secret that provides clues to its own discovery is no longer completely secret. An unconscious mind that leaks news (even in coded or ambiguous form) to the conscious mind is no longer totally unconscious. And to talk about an unconscious mind that is not totally unconscious makes about as much sense as talking about being a little bit dead. To avoid meaningless contradictions, we must assume that a motive is either conscious or unconscious. It cannot be "a little bit unconscious." Wouldn't it make more sense to say that the young man at the ballet was conscious of his homosexual tendencies but was trying not to think about them—trying, but in this case not quite succeeding?

Con #2: This key idea is only one of several plausible explanations.   Virtually all of the phenomena that Freud ascribes to the operation of unconscious motivation can be explained with equal plausibility by other theories—if indeed they are so mysterious as to require an explanation. Behavioral theory, for example, explains neurotic anxiety much more simply. Suppose little Tommy is caught beating up his kid brother after this brother has stolen one of Tommy's toys. Tommy's parents punish him very severely: Let's say that Tommy's father, who is pretty drunk at the time, beats him so badly that he requires medical attention. Now, whenever he gets angry at people and feels the impulse to punch them, Tommy becomes very anxious and apprehensive. Later, after he has grown up, he may or may not remember the beating his father gave him, but in either case he will become very confused and emotionally distraught whenever anyone angers him. Obviously, this does not need to involve anything more than Tommy's learning to associate the welling up of angry impulses inside himself with being savagely punished. Whenever he gets angry, he expects to get punished again. Conditioning had occurred, say the learning theorists, and there is no need to drag in any mysterious unconscious motivation.

Remembering and forgetting have been exhaustively studied and explained by **cognitive** psychologists. They claim, for example, that most instances of forgetting (including slips-of-the-tongue) are caused by *interference effects*, the jamming of your information channels. Your memory obviously uses some kind of filing system to organize the millions of bits of information it holds, these psychologists say. When you are trying to recall a person's name, it may be especially difficult if that name is very similar to other names you know, or if the name sounds as though it might be spelled in several ways. Any number of problems can disrupt the rational processing of information, and none of these problems has anything at all to do with whether or not you happen to like the person whose name you cannot recall. In speaking too, of course, you are pulling out a string of words from your memory file. Sometimes you pull out the wrong word. That is what we call a slip-of-the-tongue. Many slips-of-the-tongue occur when something is pulled by mistake from the file folder next to the one you wanted. The embarrassed moderator who announces that after the business meeting, everyone will retire to the lounge for a little sexual intercourse, may not be revealing lascivious motives at all; he may merely be showing that the terms *sexual intercourse* and *social intercourse* are filed side by side in his memory.

In certain other instances of slips-of-the-tongue, it is clear that what the person was planning to say a split second in the future interferes with what is actually said at the moment (Norman, 1980). The radio announcer's classic blooper, advertising "Hand's Hind Cream," is a case in point. Note also that these two examples, and most of those chosen to support Freud's theory, have some sexual connotations. But what of the thousands of less spicy slips-of-the-tongue we all make, sometimes many per day? Doesn't it make more sense to regard them as accidents of information processing, rather than an disguised motives? And is it not likely that Freud picked as examples those things that fit his preconceived theory?

Since the early 1960s, there has been a resurgence of research on the topic of sleep and dreams. Hundreds of experimental subjects have dreamed thousands of dreams while they slept in laboratories, hooked up to all kinds of electronic monitoring equipment and carefully observed by scientists from a variety of disciplines. By and large, the data from these experiments have not supported Freud's intuitions concerning dreams. The unconsciously motivated censoring process, for example, has not be found. Quite the contrary: If subjects are awakened during the time that they are actively dreaming, they invariably remember their dreams and are able to relate them. Whether or not you remember your dreams when you wake up in the morning seems to depend on what stage of sleep you awaken from, rather than any alleged process of unconscious repression. Nor is there much evidence that dreams are messages disguised by obscure symbolism. Dreaming, it seems, can be quite plausibly explained as the product of the dreamer's need to process information, most of it acquired during the preceding day: to organize that information and file it away so that it will be more, not less, accessible in the future (Kiester, 1980; Greenberg & Fisher, 1977).

What Freud called repression is, according to modern-day behavioral and cognitive theorists, nothing more than purposely not thinking about something. Most people, if something is bothering them, are able to put it out of their minds for a while. We can make a conscious decision not to think about something until tomorrow. And many therapists today are finding that, with a little coaching, their clients can improve their skills in finding constructive solutions to problems, and ignoring worrisome feelings that have immobilized them in the past.

In a very similar way, Jean-Paul Sartre (1956) argued that all of the phenomena Freud ascribes to unconscious motivation can be much more simply understood on the basis of the observation that we just plain lie to ourselves. We kid ourselves; we deceive ourselves about our true motives and intentions whenever those motives and intentions contradict the comfortable, self-righteous picture we have of ourselves. Admittedly, we use a lot of the techniques Freud called **defense mechanisms** (unconsciously motivated distortions of reality that serve to protect us against experiencing anxiety). We blame others for our mistakes (projection); we take out our frustrations on somebody else (displacement); we insist that we are not angry, even when everyone around us can see the smoke coming out of our ears (denial).

Yet, any of these so-called defense mechanisms can be easily understood without resorting to a concept like unconscious motivation. All that is required to explain these defense mechanisms is the commonplace observation that people often purposely deceive themselves. And they know that they are deceiving themselves. Liars know when they are lying. Freud's unconscious is ridiculous, from Sartre's point of view, because it requires a lie without a liar. If there is a lie, there must be a liar. Liars, by definition, are people who know that they are not telling the truth. If people make false statements that they believe to be true, they are not liars, but ignoramuses. A lie requires conscious knowledge of its untruthfulness. Defense mechanisms are therefore not unconscious; they are simply cases of the self lying to itself.

Con #3: This key idea denies free will.   Sartre feels that Freud, with his concept of the unconscious as a lie without a liar, has absolved human beings of all responsiblity for their actions. Con #3 says that Freud's idea of unconscious motivation denies human beings free will. Unconscious motives—instincts of which you have no knowledge and over which you have no control—can make you do anything at all, whether you want to or not, and no matter how irrational, self-destructive, or socially unacceptable the action is. You are the slave, and your unconscious is the master. The situation is something like being carried along on the back of a galloping horse, but having no reins or other means for stopping, or even steering, the beast. Freud himself proposed this analogy. The horse represents the unconscious motivating instincts, and the helpless rider being carried blindly to his or her fate is the conscious self.

If our unconscious motives can cause us to do things over which we have absolutely no control, then clearly we cannot be held responsible for our actions. We can always excuse ourseles by saying that our unconscious must have made us do it. The dangers of relieving people of responsibility for their actions are all too vivid in the minds of Sartre and his generation, who remember with horror the Nazi holocaust for which so many of the exterminators excused themselves by pleading that they were only following orders—rather like hypnotized subjects, actually.

To accept Freud's deterministic theory of unconscious motivation is to view human nature as something victimized by hidden forces. This is not an entirely pessimistic view, since some of these forces may be uncovered and brought under control through psychoanalytic therapy. Yet Freud acknowledged that psychoanalysis never succeeds in making the whole of the unconscious conscious. And after all, how many people can afford the time and money to be psychoanalyzed to that extent (or at all)? Those who can may become an elite of free citizens, but the rest of us will remain psychic puppets whose strings are pulled by an invisible master.

Con #4: The success of the therapy does not make the theory true.   Freud's psychoanalytic therapy is based squarely on his idea of unconscious motivation, and psychoanalytic therapy works. Yet therapies based on other theories work equally well. Joseph Wolpe's studies (1958), for example, show that **systematic desensitization**, a behavioral technique combining conditioning and relaxation training, is much more effective than psychoanalysis in treating neurotic phobic disorders. Patients are cured more quickly by systematic desensitization. Patients are not screened for systematic desensitization therapy, Wolpe claims, whereas psychoanalysts typically turn away as unable to profit from therapy a substantial proportion of those patients who apply to them. Wolpe parenthetically adds that it takes less time and money to train a behavioral therapist than a psychoanalyst.

There are innumerable other studies of a similar sort, the most damaging being Eysenck's research (1952), which showed that, at least in certain diagnostic categories, patients recover just as often without any psychotherapy at all as they do with psychoanalysis.

In fairness to Freud and his followers, I should point out that Wolpe and Eysenck's studies, and most other studies producing similar results, were conducted by psychologists who started out with strong prejudices against Freud's theory. I should also add that studies on the effectiveness of psychotherapy are notorious quagmires. It is nearly impossible to design studies that have no methodological flaws. The thorniest problem is just defining to everyone's satisfaction what constitutes a cure. Perhaps the real reason why psychoanalysis appears less successful and takes longer is that it attempts to do more than other therapies.

Still, we should keep in mind that the validity of a theory is not proved by the success of the therapy that is based upon that theory; otherwise we would have a hard time explaining how two therapies based on mutually contradictory theories could be equally successful in curing patients. Do not be misled: Whatever effectiveness psychoanalysis has as a method of therapy does not prove the existence of unconscious motivation.

KEY IDEA #2
PANSEXUALISM

Pansexualism is the idea that sexual instincts motivate all of human behavior. The emphasis here is on the *all*. Sex is everywhere. There is absolutely nothing we think or do that cannot ultimately be traced back to our sexual instincts. Small wonder that this theory got Freud ostracized from the medical circles of Victorian Vienna. Much later in his career, Freud modified his theory by adding aggressive instincts as well, but his early insistence that sex is the single and master motive made the term *Freudian* almost synonymous with the adjective *smutty*.

SOURCES OF FREUD'S IDEA OF PANSEXUALISM

But Freud was more than an erudite pornographer who aimed to titillate. He was led to the idea of pansexualism not by prurient interest, but under the powerful influence of Darwin's theory of evolution. The theory of evolution emphasized, first of all, that *instincts* account for the behavior of all species of animals. The theory went on to demonstrate that human beings are themselves animals—the highest form yet evolved, but animals nonetheless. Psychologists and philosophers began compiling lists of human instincts, some of these lists running to as many as several hundred. But Freud was searching for just one, the basic instinct from which all the others were derived. He found the key in Darwin's theory.

DARWIN'S THEORY OF EVOLUTION

"Survival of the fittest" is the concept we all remember from Darwin's theory, if we remember anything. This concept might lead us to postulate that aggression is the key motive in the universal struggle for survival. But we should look beyond the fighting itself and see what animals (and humans) are really fighting for: the privilege of mating with the most desirable female members of the "herd."

Oddly enough, **sociobiology,** a theory of human social behavior recently advanced by biologists, offers the best insight into the Darwin-Freud connection. Sociobiologists maintain that, from an evolutionary perspective, the primary instinct of every organism is sexual—namely, to get as many of its genes into the next generation as possible, and at the lowest cost to itself. Darwin's concept of sexual selection said that species reproducing the most offspring are most likely to survive. The idea Freud added, and passed on to sociobiologists, is that the drive to reproduce is an instinct that is built into every animal. The will to live, the struggle to survive, should not be seen as an individual urge. Individual animals are not driven to save their own skins for selfish reasons; their instincts are designed to insure the survival of their race by passing their genes on to the next generation.

But, for any animal's genes to survive, the animal must reproduce. And in order to reproduce, it must have sexual relations. Hence, sex has evolved as an instinct that is favored by the process of natural selection. The more offspring a species produces, the more likely that species is to survive. To encourage animals to engage in sexual relations—thus increasing the odds that their genes will survive—the sexual activity needed for reproduction is designed to give the animals pleasure; if it were not, the animals would not engage in it and would not transmit their genes. Any species that derived little pleasure from sex is presumably no longer around. In other words, sex is fun for us because the human race would have died out long ago if it were not.

This is nothing more than what Freud called the **pleasure principle.** All human behavior, he said, is motivated by the desire to maximize pleasure and minimize pain. That simple idea, he argued, is adequate to explain everything we do.

Freud was forced to broaden his concept of sexuality beyond sexual intercourse for the purpose of reproduction. When he talks about the sexual motives of a two-year-old, for example, he certainly does not mean that children of that age are looking for others to have intercourse with. He simply means that these children are seeking pleasant physical sensations. In fact, this is what Freud meant when he used the term *sexual*: anything that feels good. Stroking one's genital organs is pleasurable, and according to Freud, sexual. Very often, in fact, Freud's use of the word *sexual* seems much closer to what we would call *sensual*. Savouring a gourmet meal would be, from Freud's perspective, a sexual experience. Holding or rubbing your hand against your cheek is also sexual behavior, as is sunbathing in the summer, or warming yourself by the fire in winter. In short, any sensual pleasure felt through the tissues of the body is sexual, according to Freud. Once you understand that, the idea that everything we do is motivated by sexual instincts may seem a little less incredible.

Why did Freud use the word *sexual* if he really meant *sensual*, especially where children were concerned? His theory of infantile sexuality shocked his contemporaries. He aroused considerable antagonism against his theories by publishing in professional papers what every nursemaid already knew: Little children love to play with themselves; infants delight in finger painting with their feces; children of three and four explore each other's genitals under the pretext of playing doctor; and children of both sexes spontaneously adopt the theory that all human beings originally come off the production line as males, and that the female model was created by castrating a male original. Since bourgeois Victorian families typically had their children cared for by nursemaids, the parents seldom witnessed these things. But Freud knew about them; he saw all of these infantile sensual pleasures as the prototypes of adult genital and sexual desires.

For the purpose of evolution—survival of the species—reproductive activity must be pleasurable. And although prepubescent human beings cannot reproduce, they can certainly warm up for it. They can learn things that will make it easier for them to reproduce when they grow up. Infants who are breast-fed by their mothers learn, for example, how pleasurable it is to be in intimate physical contact with another soft, warm body. They also learn what love is; a tender, caring, emotional attachment to another human being. Hence love develops out of the sensual/sexual pleasure of the infantile feeding situation. And it develops because it is valuable for survival. True, individuals can reproduce without sharing tender feelings; but the species could not have survived without the tenderness that allowed parents to form stable families and to care for their offspring. Even something as simple as an infant's delight in being cuddled and fondled is a design feature built into our species over millions of years of evolution, to insure that we will reproduce and survive. Because the final *aim* of this feature is reproduction, Freud calls it sexual, rather than sensual.

PATIENTS WITH HYSTERICAL NEUROSES

Freud developed the notion of infantile sexuality by listening to his adult patients recall their childhood experiences, under hypnosis or by using free association. Once again, the type of patient Freud tended to see was a significant factor in leading him in this direction. Many of Freud's patients, as we know, were hysterics. Even in ancient times, people suspected that hysteria was rooted in a sexual disturbance. The word itself suggests a connection of this kind: "Hysteria" comes from the Greek word for uterus. (The same root appears in "hysterectomy," for example.) The ancient Greek physicians, who had already identified the symptoms of hysteria, believed that it occurred when a woman's uterus became "dislocated" and began wandering around in her body. Freud knew about this ancient belief. But he also discovered a fact that male psychotherapists regard as commonplace today; namely, that female hysterics may be sexually provocative while pretending to be pure and innocent. Freud would say that their seductive behavior is unconsciously motivated. In any case, they often talk a great deal about sex, and their behavior seems to invite sexual advances from the therapist. In fact Joseph Breuer, an older doctor who took Freud in as a partner, got out of the hypnotherapy business when he found this kind of patient too hot to handle. Freud was apparently made of sterner stuff, and not so easily scared off.

Early in his career, Freud was so impressed by the reports of his hysterical patients, he concluded that childhood sexual abuse was the root cause of all hysteria. After lengthy probing into long-forgotten childhood memories, almost every hysterical patient finally confronted some shameful, terrifying recollection of being seduced, or even raped, by her father, uncle, or older brother. It was the emotions associated with this premature sexual experience, emotions which were subsequently repressed and bottled up, that produced physical symptoms without any physical basis— hysteria.

This "seduction theory" was one of Freud's earliest explanations for hysteria. It isn't hard to understand why. Freud did not need to "read" sex into these situations; it was already there. He did not have to be a dirty old man looking for sexual innuendos in every one of his patients' statements; the patients themselves made the sexual content explicit. Freud did not start out looking for sexual motives in everything. He was led in that direction primarily because he chose to concentrate on the treatment of hysterical, neurotic reactions. But even that choice was to some extent an historical accident: Freud concentrated on hysterical reactions because they were very common during his era, especially among the clients who were likely to seek his services. Hysteria was a characteristically Victorian neurosis. It thrived on the sexual repression within that physically and mentally corseted society. If Freud had lived in a different era, he would not have found such a predominance of hysterics among his patients. And if he had concentrated less on hysteria and more on some other syndrome, he might never have developed one of his most important ideas—pansexualism.

PROS and CONS

Pro #1: This key idea provides a most parsimonious explanation. Single-cause explanations are highly attractive. What is causing the widespread energy shortage today? The greedy oil companies! If someone says, "Wait a minute, it's more complicated than that," we refuse to listen. People prefer simple, one-cause explanations, because people want to believe that they can understand problems completely and do something to control them. But it is not just the Archie Bunkers of the world who prefer simple explanations. Science itself decrees that all theories must obey the **law of parsimony.** This law merely says that the best theory is the simplest theory, or at least the simplest theory that accounts for all the relevant data.

Freud's key idea, pansexualism, does just that: It is a simple, one-cause theory, and it accounts for all the relevant data. Broadened into the pleasure principle, pansexualism is none but the ancient doctrine of **psychological hedonism,** the prototype of all single-cause theories of motivation. Psychological hedonism says that people seek out whatever gives them pleasure, and try their best to avoid whatever leads to pain. What could be simpler than this principle? It easily disposes of apparent contradictions: The suicide is a person who has decided that death will be less painful than the continuing misery of life; the masochist is someone who cannot achieve sexual pleasure without enduring physical pain, and who decides that the pleasure is worth the pain; the altruist, the hero who enters a burning building to save a child, calculates that any pain he may feel is far less than the pain of the guilty conscience, and worth risking for the pleasure of being praised and admired if his rescue attempt succeeds. Anything an individual does can be explained on the basis of the pleasure principle. One cause fits all.

Behaviorist notions of reinforcement are cut from the same cloth. What gives pleasure is reinforcing; what gives pain is not. Consequently, people will continue doing things that are reinforcing and stop doing things that are not. Some behaviorists add the concept of **primary reinforcement** (reinforcement that satisfies physical, bodily needs), producing a theory that's surprisingly similar to Freud's. This theory, too, is appealing because it is simple, parsimonious, and accounts for all the relevant data.

In short, why have a more complex explanation when a simple one will do just as well? The business of science is to make numerous observations of phenomena, then deduce principles that are as elementary and simple as possible. Freud's key idea of pansexualism does this, and I consider that a pro.

Pro #2: This key idea appeals to common sense.   When Freud associates pansexualism with the *life instinct*, the innate will to survive, he appeals strongly to our common sense. We take it for granted that all living things have an instinct for survival. Try to swat even so much as a fly, and it struggles instinctively to preseve its tiny life. Human beings are no different. Whether they are shipwrecked or afflicted with some incurable disease, they instinctively struggle to survive. Life is precious to us. No one doubts that; it is simply common sense.

And when people engage in sexual activity, we say that they are only "doing what comes naturally." *Eros*, the name Freud gave to the life instinct, the vital principle, not only tries to preserve life, but to procreate it. We do not need Darwin or the sociobiologists to tell us that, if our ancestors didn't have a strong, healthy interest in sex, none of us would be here today to argue the question.

Even common sense dictates that our sexual instincts, broadly viewed as a kind of vital principle, are both innate and fundamental; the human race simply would not have survived without them.

Con #1: Which came first, the chicken or the egg?   The idea of pansexualism, like any single-cause theory, lacks flexibility. Applying it to a wide range of phenomena it is like trying to use one tool to do many different jobs. You could use a screwdriver to drive nails, for example, but it would be pretty awkward. You could also use it to scrape paint, but you might have to perform some odd contortions. A screwdriver, in other words, is somewhat flexible; it will do more than one job. But using it for anything other than its intended purpose—driving screws—requires some stretching and straining. The same is true of the "tool" of pansexualism. Freud's idea that sexual instincts motivate behavior works well to explain why people marry and have children, why prostitution is called the world's oldest profession, why people enjoy dirty jokes, why people masturbate, why pornography is popular, and so on. But trying to use that theory to

◀◀ ID, EGO, AND SUPEREGO

Mental activity, according to Freud, is comprised of three different processes: the id, the ego, and the superego. The id corresponds to what we have been calling the instincts. The sexual instincts, or life instincts—the instincts we have been considering under the rubric of pansexualism—are id processes. So too, of course, are the aggressive or death instincts. These id instincts constitute the ultimate motive force behind everything that we do or think.

The id instincts are mental processes, but they are unconscious. True, we are aware of sexual urges and angry feelings, but these are surface ripples that only hint at the "seething cauldron" Freud calls the id. The idea of unconscious motivation is therefore indispensable to Freud's concept of id.

These three mental processes unfold according to a developmental schedule. From birth through infancy, only id processes exist. In fact, the word Freud used was not *id* but the ordinary German word meaning *it*. In German, as in English, people often refer to animals and infants not as "she" or "he," but "it": Don't touch the baby, it's asleep. Freud's English translators, perhaps fearing that *the it* would be awkward, translated Freud's term as *the id*.

Similarly, the word translated into English as *ego* is simply the German word for *I*. This also makes perfect sense, because the ego comes into existence when a child begins to develop a sense of self. Ego processes are therefore largely conscious; they involve the self and its dealings with the world of external reality. Freud

explain why people write poems, build rockets to fly to the moon, or fight wars requires contortions that stretch and strain one's credulity.

To increase the flexibility of this idea and make it applicable to more than just explicitly sexual behavior, Freud postulates all kinds of rechannelings, transformations, or as he called them, sublimations of the sexual instincts. And even if we accept the one-cause explanation—even if we agree, for instance, that it is easier to see the desire for power as a disguised sexual instinct than to invent a separate instinct for power—we still need to ask how we can be sure that power is disguised sex, instead of sex being disguised power.

Alfred Adler raised that very question with Freud. Adler was one of Freud's earliest, and most trusted, collaborators. But he eventually concluded that power was the one and only original instinct, from which all the others were derived. Freud, never one to tolerate dissent, told Adler he could change his mind or get out of the club. Adler left and started a movement of his own.

Let's think about that for a moment. Say we take something as ostensibly sexual as prostitution and play Freud's game in reverse. We can develop a convincing argument that men who use prostitutes are not motivated by sexual instincts, but by a need to exercise power over women. Even Casanovas, who are sufficiently skilled in the art of seduction not to require the services of prostitutes, refer to the women who succumb to their charms as *conquests. Scoring*, making conquests, seems a lot more like a power trip than a sexual orgy. Our argument makes just as much sense for other areas of behavior: Isn't it more reasonable to assume that the saw ego processes as a kind of mediator be-tween the id instincts and the outside world. The ego's job, he said, is to negotiate for as much instinctual gratification as social reality will per-mit. Social reality demands that the id instincts be sublimated; the ego appraises these de-mands for the id, then strikes the best possible bargain.

The supergo (*over-I* in German) develops last—not until about three years of age. Super-ego processes include what most of us think of as conscience. That includes the small voice that punishes you and makes you feel guilty when you do something the superego con-siders wrong; it also includes your ego ideal—

the idealized picture of the self you would like to be. The superego is partly conscious and partly unconscious. Consequently, you feel guilty without knowing why.

These three concepts form the basis of Freud's theory of personality structure. They are also developmental concepts. In fact, all three of Freud's key ideas are closely connected to the concept of id, ego, and superego. The id and part of the superego are unconscious. The sexual instincts of the id conflict with the ego's appraisal of reality and the superego's moral demands, resulting in sublimation. And id, ego, and superego evolve according to a schedule of developmental stages.

---

president of General Motors attained that position because of his drive for power, rather than because he was oversexed?

Single-cause theories are hard to justify in the face of the hundreds of motives that seem, at least superficially, to direct human behavior. If there is only one original cause, we need to demonstrate how all of the others are derived from it. And even if it is conceded that there may be a single original cause from which all of the others are derived, it is difficult to prove which is derived from which and so arrive at the original.

Con #2: Freud later modified the idea. This second criticism of Freud's idea of pansexualism is closely related to the first (Con #1). It has to do with deriving all motives from the sexual instincts. The tool analogy applies here as well: There are some jobs you just cannot do with a screw-driver. So, too, there are some behaviors that just cannot be explained on the basis of sexual motives. Freud acknowledged this and modified his theory accordingly.

How, for example, do you explain masochism, suicide, and other self-destructive behavior on the basis of the life instincts, or the pleasure principle? For a long while, Freud thought he could do this: He found that there is usually a strong sexual element in masochism; he argued that for those who commit suicide, the pain of living is greater than the pain of killing oneself; he explained other self-destructive behaviors, such as alco-holism and drug addiction in a similar way, as escape mechanisms designed to avoid pain. But once again, his theory had to be stretched and strained to cover these instances.

After World War I, when Freud encountered soldiers who relived harrowing battlefield experiences in their dreams, he abandoned his theory of pansexualism. He was still convinced that dreams expressed instinctual wishes, but he could not conceive of these nightmares as expressions of pleasurable sexual instincts. He concluded (1920/1955) that there must be another basic instinct, which he called *thanatos*, the death instinct. Thanatos was an aggressive, destructive instinct that could either be directed outward toward other people or objects, or inward upon the self. Now there were two instincts to explain human behavior, and the role of the sexual instincts was decreased by half. Pansexualism, in other words, became *demisexualism*.

KEY IDEA #3
STAGES OF DEVELOPMENT

According to Freud's third key idea, in the process of growing up a person passes through an orderly series of stages, or phases. Everyone passes through these stages in the same order, though some people may spend more time than others in a particular stage. It is possible, nevertheless, to specify an average (normal) duration for each stage.

Some people get stuck in one stage and never move beyond it—a dilemma Freud called **fixation.** When that happens, a twenty-five-year-old may have the body of an adult, but the emotional maturity of a three-year-old. Other people slide back into an earlier stage; Freud calls this situation **regression.**

The model of developmental stages, including the notions of fixation and regression, has been tremendously influential in psychology. Other psychoanalysts, such as Erik Erikson (1950), used this model extensively; Jean Piaget (1954) built his entire psychology of cognitive development around it. In addition, Kohlberg (1969) discovered that moral development could be described as a series of stages; and Robert Havighurst (1953) taught fellow educational psychologists that in the process of growing up, children encounter a series of developmental tasks, like a set of stairs to be climbed. Gail Sheehy's 1976 bestseller, *Passages*, told us about later life what Dr. Spock (1946) had told us about earlier life, namely, that it has its seasons.

SOURCES OF FREUD'S IDEA OF STAGES OF DEVELOPMENT

ARCHEOLOGY AND EVOLUTION

Once again, Freud may not have originated this idea, but he made it popular by applying it in a brilliant, illuminating fashion. The idea of stages of development is Darwinian, and more specifically, evolutionary. The developmental stages Freud discovered in children are analogous to the developmental stages geologists and archeologists revealed by digging into the earth's history, stratum by stratum. In fact, the theory of evolution, really began with the discovery of fossils buried under many layers of soil. Geologists soon recognized that these layers represented periods of the earth's development: the archeozoic, proterozoic, paleozoic, mesozoic, and cenozoic eras.

Closer to Freud's own lifetime, archeologists discovered tools, human skeletons, and entire buried cities from the ancient world. All were dated by examining the earth's strata. By digging beneath the earth's surface, peeling away layer after layer, one could expose the secrets of earth's past and see why its history developed as it did.

THE NATURE OF THE PSYCHE AS FREUD DISCOVERED IT

In more than just a metaphorical sense, Freud was a psychic archeologist. He dug into the unconscious, first with hypnosis and later with free association, to uncover buried conflicts and lost memories. And as he dug further into the psyche he noticed, as the geologists and archeologists had noticed while digging into the earth, that the thing consisted of layers. There was a series of strata, each with its own distinctive character, and rather clear boundary lines between them.

Freud's stroke of genius was to combine the notion of psychic strata with the concept of infant sexuality, to produce the idea of psychosexual stages of development. (See Table 3-1). Each psychic layer corresponded to a specific era of childhood development, and in each era the child focused its sexual instincts on a specific area of the body: first the mouth, then the anus, then the genitals. As the instincts changed their focus, the child progressed from one stage to the next. It is a mark of Freud's powerful intellect that he was able to combine his three major ideas—unconscious motivation, pansexualism, and stages of develoment—in one tightly wrapped package.

Child psychology is inconceivable without Freud. He was one of the first to take an interest in the developmental psychology of children. Yet, to my knowledge, Freud never worked much with children directly. He obtained his data primarily by asking adult patients to recall their childhood memories through free association, and while under hypnosis. It might be more accurate to say that Freud was interested in childhood, rather than children. But the end result is the same: Freud focused attention on the child-rearing practices and childhood experiences that created adult personalilty patterns. In brief, Freud's third key idea pioneered the developmental approach to the study of personality.

TABLE 3-1
The Psychosexual Stages of Development

Age	Stage Name	Focus of Sexual Instincts	Gratifying Behaviors	Gratification Results In:	Frustration Results In:
0–1½	**ORAL**	Mouth	Sucking swallowing; biting.	Trust, independence.	Passivity; gullibility, immaturity; unrealistic optimism; manipulative personality.
1½–3	**ANAL**	Anal Region	Retention and expulsion of feces.	Self-control, mastery.	Obstinacy; stinginess; conscientiousness; orderliness; punctuality; cleanliness or messiness.
3–6	**PHALLIC**	Genital Organs	Examining genitals; self-manipulation; sexual curiosity.	Sexual identity (through identification with same-sex parent); healthy conscience.	Men: ambition; recklessness; vanity; exhibitionism; Don Juanism; Women: striving for superiority over men; flirtationsness; seductiveness; promiscuity.
6–12	**LATENCY**	None (instincts are sublimated)			
puberty onward	**GENITAL**	Genital Organs and Sublimation	Intercourse; intimacy; loving and being loved; sublimation of instincts in creative work.	Ability to love unselfishly; ability to find fulfillment in work; responsibility; ability to delay gratification.	Narcissism; aimlessness; lack of ego integration; stagnation.

PROS and CONS

Pro #1: This key idea focuses on development. The first thing to be said in favor of Freud's idea of developmental stages is that it focuses attention on development. It underscores the fact that personality is a living, growing, ever-changing thing. Personality is viewed as a process, not just the sum total of a person's traits. The developmental approach places greater emphasis on how we grow, than on what we are. It says (to use another analogy) that you cannot capture personality with a snapshot;

you have to make a movie. Freud took the idea that personality is dynamic very seriously.

The developmental approach in psychology is currently enjoying a resurgence of popularity. This comeback began about a decade ago, when American psychologists discovered Piaget's cognitive developmental psychology. Erikson also reached the pinnacle of his productivity and popularity during that period. Perhaps even more important, the ideal of **self-actualization,** championed by the human potential movement in the 1960s, encountered the phenomenon of an aging American population in the 1970s. The flower children of the '60s were then approaching their thirtieth birthdays, anxious about whether they would find new learning experiences and feel themselves still growing as they approached middle age. At the same time the Black Panthers were being replaced by the Grey Panthers, and the AARP (American Association of Retired Persons) assured us that there is growing to be done even after retirement. Courses in the psychology of aging are now commonplace in college catalogues. What used to be child psychology has now become life-span psychology. The developmental approach that Freud pioneered is finally being applied in a comprehensive manner to the entire span of life. Because the developmental approach to the study of personality seems so obviously correct to so many people at this moment in history, I consider it a plus for Freud's idea of developmental stages.

Freud's developmental ideas had a more direct influence during his lifetime. The idea of developmental stages had a great impact on child-rearing practices. One example may suffice to make the point. Everyone has heard of Dr. Spock. Benjamin Spock's *Infant and Child Care* is one of the best selling books of all times, second only to the Bible in number of copies printed. And like the Bible, it has been translated into innumerable foreign languages. Well, Spock's recipe for raising children is taken almost straight from Freud. The fundamental Freudian assumption Spock adopts is that the experiences a child has as it passes through the psychosexual stages of development determine its adult personality. Parents, Spock taught us, must be careful how they raise their children, because the way in which they gratify (or frustrate) the child's needs sets the stage for either a healthy, or a neurotic, adult.

A whole generation of American children was raised on Dr. Spock's advice. American parents and educators bought the gospel of Freud according to Spock. And though Spock has recently recanted some of his ideas and American educators have become disenchanted with certain methods based on his principles, the core idea that child-rearing practices affect adult personality is still as widely held today as it was a generation ago. All in all, it speaks well for Freud that so many psychologists, and educators, and parents still consider developmental stages a compelling notion.

Pro #2: This key idea provides a convenient system of notation.   Freud's scheme of psychosexual stages organizes and structures personality growth in a very neat, clear, and coherent manner. His **oral stage–anal stage–phallic stage–latency stage–genital stage** framework serves the same purpose for students of personality that the lines of longitude and latitude on the globe serve for geographers. Both schemes divide something complex into manageable, digestable chunks. That seems to be a natural, human way of understanding things. When musicians study a symphony, they do it movement by movement. In that sense, Freud's stages are like the movements of a symphony.

The scheme of psychosexual stages, like the lines on the globe or the measures in music, serves as a set of benchmarks. The boundaries between stages are handy reference points for measuring; they provide a convenient system of notation. Just as you can say 48 degrees west longitude, 37 degrees north latitude to a geographer and be immediately understood, you can say three months into the phallic stage to psychoanalysts and they will know right away what kind of personality you are trying to describe. Much of science is regarded as valid for no other reason than that it is useful in much this same manner.

Con #1: This key idea is an arbitrary abstraction.   The lines on the globe are not really there: If you fly over the equator, you do not see a line painted on the earth. These lines are only imaginary abstractions, and their placement totally arbitrary. Zero degrees longitude, for example, runs through Greenwich, England, only because that is where the people who first drew the lines were based.

The same thing may be true of personality. Perhaps there are no actual boundary lines in personality development. The growth of the personality may actually be continuous, like a gradually rising ramp rather than a flight of stairs. In that case, the developmental stages, or steps, are also arbitrary abstractions. They do not really exist. And, even if stages did exist, the boundaries separating them might not lie where Freud arbitrarily placed them. We divide world history, for instance, into two major stages: before Christ and after Christ. And within each of those two major stages, we place more stages. But the Chinese see things in a different way. For them, this is the year five thousand and something. Why? Because the events that we consider important enough to mark the boundary of a new stage are irrelevant to their history. Perhaps the events Freud used to fix the boundaries of our individual histories—shifts in the focus of the sexual instincts—were no less culturally prejudiced.

Most people do not experience sudden radical changes in personality. Most of us feel that we grew up in a smooth, gradual fashion—no big jumps, no big bumps. After all, our bodies do not suddenly change size and shape overnight as we advance from one stage to another. Why should our personalities? After extensively studying the case histories of hundreds of Harvard students, Stanley King (1973) concluded that personality development is more like a ramp than a flight of stairs. Perhaps sudden, "steplike" changes in personality are more typical of the neurotic personalities Freud studied. At any rate, King proposed what he calls a *continuity theory* of personality development. In essence, this theory says that there are no stages of the kind Freud, and particularly Erikson, proposed, in the development of most normal personalities. Like all living things, personality grows in a smooth, gradual, continuous fashion.

The trouble with this continuity theory is that once you have pointed out that personality grows in a smooth, gradual, continuous fashion, little else can be said. On the other hand, if you contend that personality develops in stages, you can write volume after volume on the nature of the stages; the events that mark the boundaries between stages; how people progress from one stage to another; why some progress faster than others; why some become fixated and others regress; what helps or hinders a person at each stage; and so on. In short, if you are a developmental personality theorist who believes that development is continuous, you practically put yourself out of a job. Perhaps stage theories are more popular merely because they, at least, can be talked about.

CHAPTER SUMMARY

Freud was such a prolific thinker that his theory contains not one, but three big ideas: *unconscious motivation, pansexualism,* and *stages of development.*

UNCONSCIOUS MOTIVATION

According to Freud's first key idea, when an action is *unconsciously motivated*: (a) there is a motive, or reason, for that action; (b) the person is not aware—not *conscious*—of that motive; (c) still, the person feels compelled to perform the action.

1. Freud was led to this idea by observing post-hypnotic suggestion, by treating patients suffering from conversion hysteria, and by reading Hartmann's *Philosophy of the Unconscious* (1868). These sources convinced Freud of the existence of unconscious motives.

2. With this idea, Freud was able to explain an astounding range of human experiences. He said that neuroses and everyday blunders (slips-of-the-tongue, missed appointments) are often caused by a conflict of unconscious motives. Dreams present unconscious motives in disguised forms. Career choices depend on unconscious motives that have been made socially acceptable by a process called *sublimation*. Even large social institutions result from the sublimation of unconscious motives; according to Freud, for instance, religion is s sublimated form of the Oedipus complex.

3. Pros and Cons—the Idea of Unconscious Motivation.

Pro #1: It appeals to our common sense. We all make slips-of-the-tongue that expose what we were secretly thinking.

Pro #2: It is supported by many experiments. Even opponents of psychoanalysis have been unable to disprove this idea.

Pro #3: It is the basis of an effective psychotherapy. Freudian techniques for revealing unconsciuos motives (dream analysis, free association, interpretation of slips-of-the-tongue) have cured many people and are still widely used.

Con #1: It is a contradiction in terms. It assumes that there is a mind at work outside our normal conscious mind—an unconscious consciousness. That is logically absurd. What is outside the mind is physical not mental. Or it is not outside!

Con #2: It is only one of several plausible explanations. Behavioral theories, information theory, and the approaches of people like Sartre offer equally valid explanations for such things as slips-of-the-tongue, dreams, defense mechanisms, and neurotic anxiety.

Con #3: It denies the existence of free will. If we are mere slaves of the unconscious, we have no free will and cannot be held responsible for our actions.

Con #4: Even though therapy based on this idea works, the theory may not be true. Therapies based on other theories work just as well.

PANSEXUALISM

Freud's second key idea, *pansexualism*, argues that all human behavior is motivated by sexual instincts.

1. Freud was influenced by Darwin, who said that every species (including humans) tries to survive by reproducing itself, and that we are motivated to reproduce by the pleasure that comes from satisfying our sexual instincts. Freud extended the concept of sex to include all forms of pleasant bodily sensations, because these are the basis not only of sex but of the tenderness that binds families together and so contributes to the survival of our species. Generalizing further, he argued that we act in accordance with the *pleasure principle*, meaning that we strive to maximize pleasure and minimize pain.

2. Freud also adopted the idea of pansexualism because so many of his patients were women afflicted with hysterical neuroses. These patients seemed preoccupied with sex, leading Freud to believe that all neurotic disturbances are caused by buried sexual conflicts and traumas. His patients' recollections of childhood sexual desires formed the basis for Freud's theory of infantile sexuality.

3. Pros and Cons—the Idea of Pansexualism.

Pro #1: It is a very parsimonious explanation. One simple cause, the pleasure principle, accounts for every phenomenon.

Pro #2: It appeals to common sense. It doesn't surprise us to hear that we prefer pleasure to pain, and survival to non-survival.

Con #1: It raises the "chicken-or-egg" question. Is our drive for power a sublimated form of a deeper sexual drive, for example; or, as Alfred Adler argued, is it the other way around?

Con #2: It was later modified by Freud himself. After thinking about the recurring nightmares of war veterans, Freud no longer believed that human behavior is exclusively motivated by sexual instincts and the pleasure principle. He postulated equally powerful destructive instincts.

STAGES OF DEVELOPMENT

Freud's third key idea is that all human beings pass through the same *stages of development*. In each of these stages, the person's sexual instincts focus on a different area of the body: first the mouth, then the anus, then the genitals.

1. Some people pass through stages more quickly than others; some get stuck in a particular stage (fixation). Some even slide back into an earlier stage (regression).

2. For Freud, the stages of human development are like the stages of the earth's history. Freudian psychoanalysis is a kind of archeology of the mind. The mind, like the earth, is stratified. Uncovering the past casts light upon present problems. Freud's real stroke of genuis was combining this archeological approach with his idea of infantile sexuality, then defining specific psychosexual stages of development: oral, anal, and genital.

3. Pros and Cons—the Idea of Stages of Development.

Pro #1: It accounts for personality changes. By looking at personality as a living, growing, changing thing, Freud revolutionized our view of human development and laid the groundwork for the science of child psychology. The developmental approach that Freud pioneered is making a strong comeback in psychology today.

Pro #2: If offers a convenient system of notation. Freud's stages of development provide a clear framework for mapping personality growth, much like the lines of latitude and longitude on the earth.

Con #1: It is abstract and arbitrary. There are no real lines of latitude and longitude on the earth's surface, and there may be no real divisions in personality growth either. Human development may actually be a smooth and gradual process, a slowly rising ramp instead of a series of abrupt steps.

REFERENCES

Erikson, E. H. (1950). *Childhood and society.* New York: W. W. Norton.

Eysenck, H. J. (1952). The effects of psychotherapy: An evaluation. *Journal of Consulting Psychology, 16,* 319–324.

Freud, S. (1953). The interpretation of dreams. In J. Strachey (Ed. and Trans.), *The standard edition of the complete psychological works of Sigmund Freud* (Vol. 4 & Vol. 5, 339–627). London: Hogarth Press. (Original work published 1900.)

Freud, S. (1955). Beyond the pleasure principle. In J. Strachey (Ed. and Trans.), *The standard edition of the complete psychological works of Sigmund Freud* (Vol. 18, 3–64). London: Hogarth Press. (Original work published 1920.)

Freud, S. (1955). Totem and Taboo. In J. Strachey (Ed. and Trans.), *The standard edition of the complete psychological works of Sigmund Freud* (Vol. 13, ix–162). London: Hogarth Press. (Original work published 1913.)

Freud, S. (1957). Leonardo DaVinci and a memory of his childhood. In J. Strachey (Ed. and Trans.), *The standard edition of the complete psychological works of Sigmund Freud* (Vol. 11, 59–137). London: Hogarth Press. (Original work published 1910.)

Freud, S. (1960). The psychopathology of everyday life. In J. Strachey (Ed. and Trans.), *The standard edition of the complete psychological works of Sigmund Freud* (Vol. 6). London: Hogarth Press. (Original work published 1901.)

Freud, S. (1964). Some elementary lessons in psycho-analysis. In J. Strachey (Ed. and Trans.), *The standard edition of the complete psychological works of Sigmund Freud* (Vol. 23, 279–286). London: Hogarth Press. (Original work published 1940 [1938].)

Greenberg, R. P., & Fisher, S. (1977). *The scientific credibility of Freud's theories and therapy.* New York: Basic Books.

Hall, C. S., & Van de Castle, R. L. (1965). An empirical investigation of the castration complex in dreams. *Journal of Personality, 33,* 20–29.

Hartmann, E. V. (1869). *Philosopie des unbewussten* [The Philosophy of the unconscious]. Berlin: Duncker.

Havighurst, R. J. (1953) *Human development and education.* New York: Longmans.

Jersild, A. (1931). Memory for the pleasant as compared with the unpleasant. *Journal of Experimental Psychology, 14,* 284–288.

Kiester, E. (1980, May/June). Images of the night: The physiological roots of dreaming. *Science 80.*

King, S. H. (1973). *Five lives at Harvard: Personality change during college.* Cambridge, MA: Harvard University Press.

Kisker, G. W. (1964). *The disorganized personality.* New York: McGraw-Hill.

Kohlberg, L. (1969). Stage and sequence: The cognitive-developmental approach to socialization. In D.A. Goslin (Ed.), *Handbook of socialization theory and research.* Chicago: Rand McNally, 347–480.

McGinnies, E. (1949). Emotionality and perceptual defense. *Psychological Review, 56,* 244–251.

Mischel, W. (1981). *Introduction to personality* (3rd ed.). New York: Holt, Rinehart & Winston.

Norman, D. A. (1980, April). Post-Freudian slips. *Psychology Today,* 41–44.

O'Kelly, L. I. (1949). *Introduction to psychopathology.* New York: Prentice-Hall.

Piaget, J. P. (1954). *The construction of reality in the child.* New York: Basic Books.

Sartre, J. P. (1956). *Being and nothingness* (H. E. Barnes, Trans.). New York: Philosophical Library.

Sheehy, G. (1976). *Passages: Predictable crises of adult life.* New York: E. P. Dutton.

Spock, B. (1946). *The pocket book of baby and child care.* New York: Pocket Books.

Wolpe, J. (1958). *Psychotherapy by reciprocal inhibition.* Stanford: Stanford University Press.

4/Carl Gustav Jung

A Biographical Sketch

Accounts of the life of Carl Gustav Jung are almost as contradictory as interpretations of his theory. Everyone agrees that he was born in 1875 in Kesswil, a village on Lake Constance in Switzerland. He was the first surviving child of his parents (an older brother died a few days after birth). His father was a pastor in the Swiss Reformed Church. Carl grew up in the parsonage on the outskirts of Basel, where the family moved shortly after he was born. Carl's mother was herself the daughter of a clergyman. Some of the myth and mystery surrounding Jung's origins begins long before his birth, in the person of his namesake grandfather, Carl Gustav Jung, an illustrious doctor and professor at the University of Basel Medical School who was rumored to be an illegitimate son of the great German poet Goethe. The rumor was improbable, but young Carl seems to have accepted it at face value.

Even as a child, Carl Jung seems to have been a dreamer, a rather isolated child who spent a good deal of time daydreaming and conjuring up an elaborate internal fantasy world. When he was only three, his mother was hospitalized for several months. Nevertheless, she was the stronger of his parents, both physically and through the force of her personality. Carl's father was apparently consumed by a spiritual malaise, trapped in a vocation he could not put his heart into. The father died when Carl was in his early twenties, but the mother lived on until Carl was almost fifty, and even then seemed capable of exercising almost occult powers over him. Ever since childhood, Jung regarded his mother as something of a witch, a seer, a prophetess who could see right through him and control his actions by threatening to send him terrifying nightmares. It is hard to say how much of this was fact, and how much was the product of Jung's fertile imagination. His mother may have been mentally unstable; but then again, Jung himself may have had a nervous breakdown. In any case, Jung had his mother all to himself until he was nine years old, when his first sibling, a sister, was born.

In the following year, he was "exiled" to a high school in Basel, where he was apparently regarded as a kind of poor country bumpkin. In early adolescence, Jung suffered a series of fits following an episode in which he was pushed down and struck his head. Later in life he referred to this illness as a neurosis, but at the time his baffled doctors tentatively diagnosed it as epilepsy. The spells were associated with school matters and came on whenever he opened a textbook, though Carl loved books as much as he hated his outsider status at school. If we believe Jung's account of events, after several months of brooding at home, he eventually cured himself through the force of his own will power. He returned to school and worked hard enough at his studies to rise to the top of his class in mathematics. He did lose a year (although being reassigned to a new peer group might have been beneficial).

How could a dreamer pick a vocation, except by obeying his dreams? The introspective, bookish teenager was uncertain whether he should become a philosopher, an historian, an anthropologist, or a natural scientist. Apparently he considered archeology and classical philology as well. A dream that came to him just before he graduated from high school seemed to suggest that he should delve as deeply as possible into the secrets of nature by studying zoology. Considering his lack of funds, the humiliation his poverty had caused him in high school, and the need to acquire a paying occupation, he compromised by enrolling in the Medical School at Basel. It is tempting to think that Carl's grandfather, though he died before his namesake was born, exerted some influence on this decision.

In 1895, when Jung was twenty, he began medical school. A chance encounter with a book on spiritualism turned his interests in that direction, and before the end of his medical studies he managed to parley this new interest into a dissertation topic. How do spiritualism and medical studies fit together?—under the rubric of psychiatry, of course! Whether Jung specialized in psychiatry simply to indulge his fascination with spiritualism, or would have become a psychiatrist anyway, is unclear. What is clear is that he began attending seances conducted by Helene Preiswerk, a cousin of his who was a medium. Under the direction of Professor Eugen Bleuler, who later became world famous for his studies on schizophrenia, Jung completed a case study of Preiswerk for his doctoral thesis. Helene Preiswerk was undoubtedly affected with hysteria, perhaps even **multiple personality**, and that is how Jung diagnosed her in his thesis. Two years after he graduated from medical school, in 1902, Jung went to Paris to increase his knowledge of hysteria by studying with Pierre Janet, Charcot's successor and the reigning authority on hysteria and the **paranormal**.

But in 1900, immediately after medical school, Jung set out to do his internship at the Burghölzli, the psychiatric hospital of the

University of Zurich, where Bleuler was the director. In his early years there, Jung discovered that the word-association test could be used to delve into the unconscious just as effectively as hypnosis, or Freud's technique of free association. In fact, Jung invented the **projective personality test** before Rorschach. Using a stop watch and devices for measuring his subjects' rates of breathing and perspiration, Jung recorded not only the words with which his subjects responded to stimulus words, but the time it took them to respond and their accompanying emotional states.

In 1906, soon after a book on his research with the word association test was published, Jung initiated what was to be one of the most important relationships of his life by sending a copy to Sigmund Freud. A year later he went to visit Freud in Vienna. Each man seemed to fulfill a deep need in the other: Freud wanted a son and heir to carry on his work; Jung wanted a father-mentor to replace his own spiritually inadequate father. They got on famously, although in retrospect one can see potential points of stress early on. In 1909, Jung accompanied Freud on his visit to America, where both men lectured and received honorary degrees at Clark University. In the following year, over the sometimes rancorous objections of his Viennese colleagues, Freud managed to get Jung elected as the first president of the newly founded International Psychoanalytic Association. Paradoxically, the relationship began to deteriorate very soon afterward. More and more, Jung began to deviate publicly from Freud's positions, especially the idea of pansexualism, and Freud in turn found such insubordination intolerable. By 1913 the split was final. Both men seem to have been deeply shaken by the experience. In the same year, Jung gave up the lectureship he had held at the University of Zurich since 1905. He withdrew from everything except his private practice. Some historians claim that he was wrestling with a breakdown of some sort.

It was really not until after World War I that Jung emerged from his dark night of the soul to become his own person. Only then do we see the beginnings of his own unique theory of personality; only then did he find his true vocation. Though he was already in his mid-forties, fortunately he would live almost another forty years before dying in 1961. It was during the latter half of his life that he developed his concept of the collective unconscious and its archetypes; undertook various anthropological expeditions to study African primitives and American Indians; and developed his expertise in a range of other arcane topics, from ancient Tibetan religious texts to medieval alchemy. In all, Jung's collected works fill twenty volumes.

THE KEY IDEA
THE COLLECTIVE UNCONSCIOUS

The name Carl Jung is uniquely associated with the idea of the collective unconsious. Freud had argued that the unconscious mind was individual and personal. Jung, one of Freud's closest disciples until they split in 1913, stressed the motivating force of an unconscious mind that was shared, in some sense, by all members of the human race. Jung did not deny the existence of Freud's individual unconscious; he simply felt the collective unconscious exerted a much more powerful influence on people's thoughts and behavior.

Jung did for the idea of the collective unconscious what Freud did for the idea of the individual unconscious: He made it, if not a household word, at least popular enough to be seen in newspapers and heard on television soap operas. Almost all of us have heard of the term *collective unconscious*. But like Freud, Jung did not invent the idea himself. There were others who toyed with it beforehand, and perhaps it will become a bit clearer if we see what some of them had to say.

THE HISTORY OF THE IDEA

VICO'S NEW SCIENCE

Giambattista Vico, whose famous book on political philosophy (*Principles of New Science of Giambattista Vico Concerning the Common Nature of the Nations*), appeared in Italy in 1725, is generally regarded as the modern inventor of the idea of the collective unconscious. In his *New Science*, Vico asked himself why human societies, widely separated by time and geography, and without any means to communicate with each other, all develop the same fundamental institutions. All societies have religions, governments, families, and military institutions. The forms of these institutions may vary—one society may practice monogamy and another polygamy—but all have the basic institutions of marriage and the family. Why are the same institutions found in all societies? Why should even isolated societies spontaneously and independently create these institutions?

Did they all use the same blueprint? In a sense, yes. Similar institutions developed, Vico reasoned, because all human beings face the same fundamental problems. The blueprint, the thing that never varies from one society to the other, is human nature. Take the family, for example. It is the nature of human beings to be helpless for an extended period following birth. Many other animals can fend for themselves as soon as they are born—but not humans. Humans must be taken care of for long years before they can go it alone. All human beings therefore face the problem of designing a social structure to care for their offspring during this period of helplessness. Various solutions have been devised, but they all fit into the general category of *family*. Of course, early societies did not sit down and deliberately plan a family structure to solve this problem; the solution came automatically, without the need for rational planning. Other human institutions developed in the same way, as solutions to universal problems created by the interaction between human nature and certain aspects of the human environment. No conscious consideration or rational forethought was needed; the unconscious, irrational, automatic forces that shaped our social institutions were shared by all humans.

Vico also believed that by carefully examining the mythology of a culture, you could see how the culture approached, and began to solve, common human problems. The unconscious forces that shaped institutions were revealed in the mythological accounts a culture developed to sanctify its practices. Perhaps the culture began when the gods annointed its first tribal chieftan. Or perhaps in some battle celebrated in legend and song, one tribe defeated another tribe, and that is why the second tribe has been condemned to serve as slaves for the first.

COLLECTIVE REPRESENTATIONS

The same fascination with mythology as a representation of common human concerns is evident, in fact conspicuous, in the writings of Emile Durkheim (1858–1917), the famous French sociologist. To designate these common human concerns—ideas unknowingly shared by all humans, but surfacing only in myths—Durkheim invented the term *collective representations*. That is precisely what they are: representations, symbols that represent, or stand for, ideas and concerns that are held collectively by the entire culture. We act on these representations without being consciously aware of them, just as we may speak English perfectly well without consciously considering the rules of English grammar. What intrigued Durkheim was the power of these collective representations. There is an irrational force residing in them. People will die, for example, for their flag; for a painted piece of cloth they will brave endless perils. Surely, that is not rational; but just as surely, the flag has great power. It is the power of an idea, not a piece of cloth. And the idea is not an individual, but a collective, one. Furthermore, the average person, especially in a primitive society, would not be able to articulate that idea, because it is unconscious.

"Out of the interplay of minds come symbol-products which are mutually owned and mutually proclaimed. These collective symbolizations have force because they are collectively created and developed" (Bogardus, 1947, p.419). That force is the power to motivate behavior and to move emotionally. People not only die for their flag; they tingle with emotion whenever the flag is raised, or the national anthem played. Pilgrims still travel to Rome, some at great personal expense, to receive the Pope's blessing, and many are moved to tears by the experience. Examples of collective representations are endless, even in our allegedly sophisticated, non-superstitious society. The legends of our own society's heroes and the myths of their exploits—from George Washington's chopping down the cherry tree to Babe Ruth's pointing to where he would hit his home run—are stories that stay alive because they forcefully capture the imagination. According to Durkeim, the individual responds powerfully, irresistably, to these symbols precisely because they are *collectively* produced.

Durkheim contends that because the social values embodied in these symbols and myths are products of collective, rather than individual, behavior, these values develop a kind of independent, objective existence. They become moral imperatives commanding the allegiance of every individual in the society. In other words, these representations take on a life of their own, a life apart from the lives of individuals. That is what Durkheim meant when he said that collective representations are objective.

Following in Durkheim's footsteps, Lucien Lévy-Bruhl (1857-1939), an almost exact contemporary of Freud, studied collective representations within the "primitive mind." Collective representations, he said, "are common to the members of a given social group; they are transmitted from one generation to another; they impress themselves upon its individual members, and awaken in them sentiments of respect, fear, adoration, and so on" (Lévy-Bruhl, 1910/1966, p. 3). As we will soon see, one of the key issues surrounding Jung's theory is the question of how these collective ideas are transmitted from one generation to the next. Their transmission is, of course, crucial to Jung's theory. In any case, Lévy-Bruhl wrestled with this question before Jung did, and Jung acknowledges that Lévy-Bruhl's concept of collective representations corresponds to his idea of the collective unconscious (Jung, 1954/1968c).

THE NATURE OF SYMBOLS

What we have been talking about here, and what forms the essence of Jung's idea of the collective unconscious, are symbols. It may be helpful to clarify that term. Signs and symbols both point beyond themselves to something else, something they "stand for." A zigzag line on a road sign stands for a reverse curve up ahead on the highway. We call that zigzag line a sign, rather than a symbol, because it means little in and of itself. It does not inspire adoration, nor would we march off to war using it as a banner. A symbol has another dimension, an affective dimension. The flag is also a kind of sign, pointing beyond itself to represent the nation. But it is a symbol too: It "participates" in the thing it points to. The flag embodies all of the values, all of the emotions, all of the things patriots treasure about their country. A symbol means something in and of itself. A sign is simply a convenience, a conscious, deliberate shorthand that can easily be changed whenever something more convenient is found. But try to change a nation's flag and you might have a revolution on your hands. Symbols have a kind of autonomous existence; they are not deliberately invented. That does not mean they never change, because they do. But once again, they are not changed by conscious intent. They are living things, and when they cease to evoke a response from people, they die. But you cannot kill them by force, as so many tyrants have learned to their dismay.

Myths are elaborated symbols; they are symbolic stories. In order to understand myths, you must forget the popular belief that myths are untrue. That misunderstanding results from interpreting myths as signs. But myths are not signs, they are symbols. They can either be true or untrue, depending on your evaluation of the values they symbolize. In short, everything we have said about symbols applies equally to myths.

THE COLLECTIVE UNCONSCIOUS

The source of symbols and myths, according to Carl Jung, is what he called the collective unconscious. Jung's idea of the collective unconscious can be best understood as a combination of Durkheim's idea of collective representations, and Freud's idea of the individual unconscious mind. Jung was fascinated to find the same (or very similar) symbolic motifs occurring over and over again in widely separated times and places. The mythologies of ancient peoples and modern-day primitives; all religions; medieval alchemy; art, literature, drama; people's dreams; and even the delusions and hallucinations of psychotic patients—all employ symbols that seemed strikingly similar. If a patient of Jung's came in one day, perplexed about the meaning of a dream he had had the previous night, Jung might find that the dream's plot was identical to that of some ancient Persian myth the patient could not possibly have known about. Or a schizophrenic patient, recording his hallucinations on paper with crayons, might draw a design identical to some medieval alchemical symbol, one that only a very few scholars were familiar with.

THE ARCHETYPES

Behind every tangible symbol lies some intangible collective idea, image, or concept. The symbol itself may be conscious, of course, but the idea standing behind it is unconscious: we are not aware that it is in our minds. Jung calls these unconscious, collective ideas **archetypes.** Again, the symbols and myths that we consciously see are not the archetypes themselves; they are just concrete representations of the archetypes. The archetypes are mental, existing only as ideas, or images, in the unconscious realm of our minds. And the very same archetypes, the very same ideas and images, are in everyone's mind, whether they were born today or five thousand years ago, in New York City or in New Guinea.

Like Freud's unconscious sexual instincts, Jung's archetypes determine behavior—they make you do what you do. They influence your attitudes and beliefs, your likes and dislikes. They affect all the major decisions of your life: the choice of your career, your mate, your whole life style. And when these archetypes somehow "get out of whack," they can make you neurotic or even psychotic. Your entire character and personality are shaped by the relative strengths of different archetypes in your unconscious. The archetypes often act against your own conscious will and critical reasoning. They can make you do things against your better judgment. Just like Freud's individual unconscious, the archetypes of the collective unconscious constitute an irrational force that motivates thought, feeling, and action.

SOURCES OF THE ARCHETYPES

Where do they come from, these archetypes of the collective unconscious? If they are not animal instincts in the Freudian sense, what is their source? Jung's answer (1937/1958, p. 50) is that

> The archetypal motifs presumably derive from patterns of the human mind that are transmitted not only by tradition and migration but also by heredity. This latter hypothesis is indispensable, since even complicated archetypal images can be reproduced spontaneously without there being any possibility of direct tradition.

Does Jung really mean to say that we inherit *ideas* through our genes? That is certainly a pretty far-fetched notion. No wonder many scientific psychologists dismiss him as a mystic and a quack. Actually, I do not think that Jung intends to imply that the genes transmit ideas from one generation to the next (Jung, 1948/1960 p. 53). Surely, Jung knows better than that. And it does him a disservice to interpret his perhaps careless use of the term *inherit* literally.

THE MOTHER ARCHETYPE

The archetypes are transmitted from one generation to the next in two ways. First of all, all people, in all ages, have certain experiences in common. These similar experiences give rise to similar ideas. Take, for example, what Jung (1954/1968d) calls the mother archetype. The idea of motherhood, of the great mother, or earth mother, is found all over the world, from prehistoric times onward. Venus, Isis, Astarte are some of the names given to her in the ancient world; in India, she is called Kali. Today we westerners know her as the Blessed Virgin Mary in Christianity, or in her debased secular role as Mother Nature, hawker of oleomargarine ("You can't fool Mother Nature"). These symbols of motherhood appear in almost all cultures and in all historical eras. Why should that be? The answer is actually rather simple: The experience of having a mother and being nurtured by her is common to all human beings, wherever and whenever they live. New life is born from the mother. If mothers did not bear children, the human tribe would not survive; if mothers of other animals did not bear young, the human tribe would not eat meat; if the Mother Earth did not bear fruit, the human tribe would not eat at all. Even the most primitive humanoids know this—small wonder, then, that the idea of perfect, ideal motherhood is impressed upon their minds. Archetypes, like this are inherited, in other words, only in the sense that the human condition itself—having mothers, needing to eat, and so on—is inherited.

The second way that archetypes are transmitted from one generation to the next is closer to genetic inheritance, but still does not require ideas themselves to be inherited. Note that in the quotation above, Jung does not say that ideas are transmitted by heredity; he says there are "patterns of the human mind that are transmitted." "Patterns of the human mind"—what does he mean by that?

The mind is built in a certain way. We do not know exactly how it is built, but does have some kind of structure, some pattern. In the realm of sensation, for example, we are built to detect certain light waves and sound waves, but not radio waves. And even within the sound spectrum, we are built to hear only frequencies between 20 and 20,000 cycles per second, whereas dogs can hear frequencies as high as 40,000 cycles. The same thing is true of the mind. Because of the way the mind is built, human beings tend to think in certain ways and not in other ways. The structure, or pattern, of human thinking is clearly related, in some sense, to the structure of the brain. And the structure of the brain—its "wiring diagram"—is inherited.

THE ARCHETYPE OF THE WAY

The archetype of the way, or journey, as it is sometimes called, is one that arises out of the structure of the human mind. Symbols of this archetype represent life as a trip, a journey, a voyage. Getting from here to there is their essential feature, and the "there" is often some state of paradise. In Buddhism, "the way" includes eight steps that lead to nirvana; in Christianity, Jesus said, "I am the *way*." Pilgrimages to holy places have been a prominent feature of human behavior since the dawn of history. The pilgrimage is an acted-out symbol of the archetype of the way. Legends resembling the search for the holy grail turn up again and again, in many different cultures. And, of course, drug *trips* are nothing new in human experience.

Why does the metaphor of life as a trip along a certain pathway arise so naturally, and spontaneously, in the human mind? The most fundamental reason is that we experience things sequentially. The mind is like a movie, advancing frame by frame. Just as we walk step by step, we think from moment to moment. It is possible for us to imagine a mind that does not experience things sequentially—in fact, that is one of the characteristics theologians attribute to God. God, they say, sees not only each individual life, but all of history at the same time—including the future. But we humans have to march through time step by step. We do not experience it all at once. The archetype of the way is a reflection of our step-by-step experience. If we experienced everything at once, as God is supposed to do, this archetype would not exist. But since we are built to experience things one after another, like steps along a pathway, it is only natural that we should conceive of life as a trip.

THE ARCHETYPE OF THE SELF

The archetype of the self also develops from the innate, inherited structure of the mind. The raw materials the mind works with are events, happenings. For the newborn infant these happenings are, as William James observed, a booming, buzzing confusion. But as the infant's mind grows and matures, it begins to make some sense and order of that chaos and confusion. The human mind is, in fact, a sense-making gadget. It takes the chaos of experience and harmonizes it, balances it, unifies it, and puts it into some kind of order. Why? Because that is what the mind is built to do, what its structure and pattern are meant to accomplish.

We call the aspect of the mind that unifies and orders experience the self. What ties together yesterday's events and today's events is that they both happened to me, to the very same self. This sense of ownership makes a meaningful, sensible whole out of all my experiences, all the things that happen in the theater of my mind. That wholeness explains why symbols for the archetype of the self are always variations of the circle. The circle of the zodiac, with its twelve familiar signs, is just one example of what are technically called **mandalas** (Jung, 1950/1968a). Hundreds of different mandalas, symbols of the archtype of the self, are depicted in Jung's works. The zodiac, and other mandalas, are symbols of the universe; but this concept of the universe is a precise reflection of the mind's orderly, unifying, holistic processes. The idea of the self occurs to human beings in all eras and locales, because the human mind is designed to organize its experience around a stable center.

ANIMA AND ANIMUS

Closely associated with the archetype of the self are the archetypes of anima and animus, the female and the male principles. These ideas, too, arise very naturally from the way we are built. We have genders—human beings come in two basic models. If there were three sexes instead of two, or none at all, we would not have this archetype. But because all human beings are constructed according to one of these two basic patterns, the archetypes of anima and animus are present in everyone's collective unconscious.

Perhaps the most familiar symbol of the union of anima and animus is a letter "S" inscribed in a circle, with the "S" dividing the circle in half (see Figure 4-1). This is the ancient Chinese symbol for yin and yang, the female and male principles. Enclosing both within one circle signifies that female and male qualities are found in every self; and the "S"-shaped dividing line suggests that those qualities are closely intertwined. The yin-yang symbol continues to be used today by people who have no idea at all of its origins or significance, proving Jung would say, that its power is unconscious and still very much alive.

FIGURE 4-1

A Mandala Representing Anima and Animus

THE ARCHETYPE OF REBIRTH

Another archetype we can easily trace back to the inherited structure of the human mind is the archetype of rebirth, or resurrection (Jung, 1950/1968b). Many people raised in a nominally Christian society are not aware how common this theme is in the mythology of other cultures. Jesus Christ is by no means the only God or hero whose legendary exploits include rising from the dead. The theme has been popular throughout the world, and throughout history. Rituals such as baptism, through which initiates are "born again," were a common practice among the pre-Christian mystery cults of ancient Greece. The recent popularity of born-again Christianity demonstrates that the archetype has not yet exhausted its power.

Why does the archetype of rebirth occur to the human mind? Because we all die, and we know that we will die. That is the way we are built. There is almost no one who would not like another chance at this life. Who among us has not thought "If I had only known then what I know now?" Because we experience life as a series of steps along a pathway that only goes forward, a movie that cannot be shown in reverse, we cannot help wondering what it would be like to start at the beginning again. Unfortunately, our inherited structure does not give us that option. Small wonder, then, that the doctrine of reincarnation, another manifestation of the archetype of rebirth, captures the minds of so many.

The archetypes of the collective unconscious are not inherited in the same way that blue eyes and blond hair are inherited, but they are nevertheless passed on from one generation to the next without having to be taught. Every human being inherits a body whose mental processes automatically follow certain lines, the lines they were built to follow. Though it isn't strictly correct to say that the archetypes are inherited, the end result is the same: They have been passed on in an unbroken succession, from our cave-dwelling ancestors right up to the present without the need for comment or awareness.

In all, some thirty or forty archetypes have been identified and studied by Jung and his followers. A brief look at a few more of these archetypes may help to delineate Jung's idea of the collective unconscious even further.

PERSONA AND SHADOW

It is possible to place Jung's thirty or forty archetypes into categories. One category, for example, is archetypes that have to do with the person. We have already mentioned the archetype of the self, and that of anima and animus. To the same category, we can add the archetype of the *persona*. The word **persona** literally means "mask." Our persona, or mask, is the front we put on for other people. It is not our real self, but our social self—the self we show to others. It is a role we play, not because we are dishonest or deceitful, but because the role is prescribed for us by society as a collective whole. Playing our role, wearing our mask, acts as a social lubricant. Supermarket clerks do not have time to know your real self, so you present them with a mask, they show you their masks, and your groceries are rung up with dispatch. Each society may have its own masks, of course; but the idea of displaying a mask to all but your most intimate kinfolk is universal.

The *shadow* is another archetypal aspect of the person. It is the dark side of your personality, Jung's name for the old idea that there is an evil side to everyone's character. Most of the time this shadow is repressed and unconscious; but it is always lurking inside, ready to break out at any time. Demons, devils, and evil spirits are all symbols of the archetype of the shadow.

HERO, TRICKSTER, SAGE

Stock characters are a second category of archetypes. These are dramatic roles that appear over and over again in folktales, like the "good guys" wearing white hats in Western movies. If you have seen one of these characters, you have seen them all. The men in the white hats are examples of what Jung calls the archetype of the *hero*. The hero's essential role is to vanquish evil and rescue the downtrodden. This archetype is so powerful, examples of it are found everywhere: David and Goliath; St. George and the dragon; Superman; the Lone Ranger; Hercules; Robin Hood. Military and political figures often try to enhance their influence by investing themselves with this archetype. The rise to political prominence of a George Washington or an Adolf Hitler may not depend so much on the conscious, rational judgment of their constituents, as on the leaders' ability to embody archetypes in the collective unconscious of their supporters. People seem to hunger for heroes and create new ones every day. You need only consult the sports pages of your daily newspaper to see this. The collective unconscious is the fertile seedbed of the human imagination, unrelentingly pressing for concrete symbols.

The *trickster,* or *magician,* is another "stock character" archetype (Jung, 1954/1968e). The essence of this role is playing pranks and practical jokes sometimes with the aid of magic spells, potions, and so forth. Puck and his fairy friends, have this function in Shakespeare's *A Midsummer Night's Dream,* Merlin the Magician in the tales of King Arthur. Till Eulenspiegel is a legendary German prankster depicted in Richard Strauss's famous symphonic poem, *Till Eulenspiegel's Merry Pranks.* The tale of the sorcerer's apprentice, set to music by Paul Ducas and popularized by the Walt Disney movie *Fantasia,* is still another example. In fact, that brings to mind Bugs Bunny, an even more contemporary symbol of the trickster archetype. Whole hosts of less famous gremlins, elves, and leprechauns pay further tribute to the pervasiveness of the trickster archetype.

The essential nature of the *wise old man* archetype is self-evident. He astonishes everyone by solving some conundrum with his consummate sagacity. You may recall the story of King Solomon, the epitome of this archetype, who, when confronted by two women both claiming to be the mother of the same child, ruled that the baby should be cut in two and half given to each, whereupon the real mother relinquished her claim. Though sages are a rarity nowadays, society still hungers for them. The oriental gurus and maharishis, so popular in recent years, demonstrate that this archetype is far from extinct.

POWER AND NUMBER

A third category of archetypes consists of words denoting abstract qualities. The archetype of *power* is one example. The eagle, the lion, the sword, and various other weapons; the clenched fist, the lightning bolt, goose-stepping soldiers, and martial music are all symbols of the archetype of power. The Black Power salute, with the clenched fist held defiantly aloft, caught on quickly after being internationally televised at the Mexico City Olympic Games in 1964. Hitler's Nazis, of course, manipulated the symbols of power with masterful skill. Jung contends that the entire Nazi success in Germany can be attributed to the fact that the German people were unconsciously enchanted by the archetype of power.

Jung also found that certain numbers have archetypal qualities. The numbers 3, 4, 5, 7, 10, and 12 occur throughout history and throughout the world in sacred contexts, or as lucky numbers, much more frequently than 2, 6, 8, 9, and 11. The number three is sacred to Christians, who worship a trinity: Father, Son, and Holy Ghost. Four is the number of directions—

north, south, east, and west—or winds, if you prefer, that most cultures recognize. (A reminder: Those four directions were not originally marked on the earth itself, waiting only for some early geographer to discover them.) Four is also sacred to Christians; although there are additional gospels, the Church officially recognizes only four. There are seven deadly sins, and seven days in the week. The seven-day week, we are taught, was ordained by God when the world was created. Ten is the number of commandments God gave to Moses, five on each tablet. Ten is also the basis of all decimal and metric systems. There are twelve months, which can be divided into four seasons of three months each. This, too, is a common, but not universal, arrangement (there have been ten-month calendars). There were twelve tribes of Israel, but ten were lost when taken into captivity by Sargon II. And who can explain the survival of such a cumbersome measure as the dozen, or stranger still, the gross, comprised of a dozen dozen?

Almost all of these numbers have been more or less arbitrarily selected by human beings. The directions—north, south, east, and west—did not exist until human beings invented them. Why did they come up with four, rather than three, six, or some other number? The answer probably lies where we found it earlier—in the human structure, the inherited patterns Jung spoke of. When a human being lies flat on the ground, the head points in one direction, the feet in another, and the hands in two more. In fact, the symbol of the cross, those nasty X-and Y-axes of mathematics, and the four points of the compass all are abstracted from the pattern of the human body. The source of the popularity of the numbers five and ten is even more clearly structural: There are five fingers on each hand, ten in all.

If archetypes are not derived from the pattern on which human beings are built, they are derived from aspects of experience that are common to all people. For example, the popularity of the number twelve is probably due to the fact that, as anyone can see (especially people living closer to nature than we do), the moon goes through twelve cycles while the sun goes through one; that is, there are approximately twelve lunar months in each solar year.

These numbers, then, are no different from the other archetypes of the collective unconscious. They derive either from the way human beings are built, or from impressive features of the environment, features that are observable in all times and places. Numeric archetypes appear as concrete symbols, such as the cross and the zodiac, or as elements in mythology, such as the three wise men or Snow White's seven dwarfs. The irrational power of these numbers is evident even today, in people who have lucky numbers (whether they play them in lotteries or wear them on the backs of their athletic uniforms), and in the taboo against thirteenth floors in hotels.

Jung does not say how many archetypes constitute the collective unconscious, only that he has studied thirty or forty. The few examples we have discussed should help to define Jung's notion of the archetype and his key idea of the collective unconscious, since the collective unconscious is the sum total of the archetypes.

◄ PSYCHOLOGICAL TYPES

Jung's terms *introvert* and *extrovert* have become household words. Far more people are familiar with these ideas than with the notion of the collective unconscious. But the introvert–extrovert dichotomy is only part of an elaborate scheme of personality types devised by Jung (1921/1971).

Introvert and extrovert are called *attitudinal types*. The two are polar opposites: the introvert is oriented toward the inner, subjective world, and the extrovert toward the external, objective world. Introverts tend to be somewhat inhibited, retiring individuals who prefer solitude and mental reflection. They may even appear defensive and mistrustful as they shy away from social interaction. Extroverts, on the other hand, are outgoing and make new friends readily. They appear more open, less guarded, and possessed of more careless confidence. Extreme, or pure, types exist only in theory, of course. Most of us fall somewhere between the extremes of 100% introvert and 100% extrovert. And even if you are pegged as a moderate extrovert, you still have some introverted moments. In visualizing personality types, we should avoid the pitfall of rigidly pigeonholing people.

Jung saw four *functional types* interacting with his two attitudinal types. The functions in question are ways of relating to the world. We relate to the world, Jung observed, by thinking, feeling, sensing, and intuiting. *Thinking* is an intellectual process that involves ideas. The aim (intentional or unintentional) of thinking is comprehensive or understanding. By thinking about something, you figure out what that thing is: its name, the category it belongs to, and so on.

Feeling is an evaluative function; it allows you to gauge the value, or worth, of something. Do you like, or dislike the thing? Does it give you pleasure or pain? Do you "value" it or not. You may desire something intensely, or be repelled by it. A thing can anger or frighten you. In fact, feeling can trigger any of hundreds of emotions; but no matter which emotion it triggers, the essential function of feeling is to let you know whether you value, or do not value, the thing in question.

Sensing tells you what exists. Without evaluating or categorizing, sensing presents the concrete reality of the world to your mind. It tells you that something exists, without saying what it is, or whether it is good or bad.

Intuiting goes beyond facts, and even feelings, to provide you with premonitions, creative inspirations, mystical experiences, and eerie feelings of unease. It is concerned with what is going to happen, or with things that have already happened but have not been perceived by any of the other functions.

Jung called thinking and feeling *rational functions*. He meant by this that they both make use of reason and judgment. They employ abstract mental processes in an effort to discover some lawful order in experience. He called sensing and intuiting *irrational functions*. The processes involved here are beyond language and reason; they are directly tied to the concrete, physical world: Concrete particulars present themselves without the intervention of reason or judgment.

Jung thought of these four functions as two pairs of opposites, two sets of poles: thinking–feeling, and sensing–intuiting. The line connecting the poles of thinking and feeling was intersected at right angles by the line connecting sensing and intuiting:

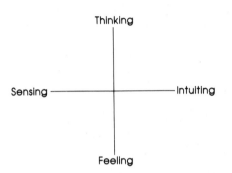

Just as individual differences exist along the introvert-extrovert spectrum, they exist between the poles of these functional types. Some of us are more thinking types than feeling types, others are more sensing than intuiting, and so on. Adding all possible combinations of the attitudinal typology (two types) and the functional typology (four types) produces eight personality types. A person may tend more or less strongly toward any of these eight types, each of which has its unique set of characteristics.

The *extroverted thinking type,* for example, perceives everything as an intellectual problem to be solved by getting the facts, and reasoning to a logical conclusion, These people make very good executives.

Introverted thinking types follow their ideas inward, rather than outward. Their thinking may be so thoroughly preoccupied with subjective reality that they are incomprehensible to others—"eggheads" or mad scientists.

The *extroverted feeling type* loves being with people, loves to talk, and flourishes in work involving face-to-face contact. These people are particularly attuned to the approval of others.

Introverted feeling types are the ones we describe with the phrase, "Still waters run deep." Their lives are governed by strong con-

victions and loyalties, but these feelings hardly show until you penetrate their mask of reserve, or even banality.

In the category of *extroverted sensing type,* Jung includes people who relish concrete sensory experience: the gourmet, the aesthete, even the baseball afficionado who knows every player's batting average. These people notice and remember more concrete details than any other type.

Introverted sensing types are practical people who also have great memories for detail. Since they are quiet and introverted, it is not immediately apparent that their perception of reality can be a bit peculiar.

In the *extroverted intuiting type,* we find people who perpetually hatch plans for new projects, which they promote with infectious enthusiasm and carry out with impulsive energy. Tycoons, theatrical agents, and politicians often are of this type. They hate routine and find attention to detail dreadfully boring.

Finally, the *introverted intuiting type* is a person committed to an inner vision—mystical, artistic, scientific, etc. Such a person may be genuinely creative, or a crank. Even the genuinely creative ones are often misunderstood by their peers and must struggle to get their work accepted.

The extent to which an individual personality resembles any of these ideal types can be measured by the Myers-Briggs Type Indicator, a 166-item paper-and-pencil test that produces a score on each of these bipolar dimensions (Myers, 1962).

PROS and CONS

Pro #1: This key idea is based on much scholarly research. The first thing that strikes a reader of Jung's works is that the man's scholarship is prodigious. In studying a single archetype, for instance, he seems to have combed the most obscure libraries of the world for folktales and illuminated manuscripts. Jung must have been an habitué of museums and archeological digs. He seems to have read all of ancient history, not only for Europe and Africa, but the Far East as well. He also knew philosophy and medicine. By the time he died in 1961, Jung seemed to have become the incarnation of his wise old man archetype. The sheer amount of evidence he marshalled for each of his archetypes is formidable. It is hard to remain skeptical as he trots out one example after another. He has found the most astoundingly similar graphic designs and story plots in cultures so widely separated in time and place that they can hardly have had contact with each other; and he has found them, in some cases, by the hundreds. On one topic that caught his fancy, medieval alchemy, he became the acknowledged authority in the world. Experimental verification may be the yardstick in psychology today, but perhaps there is still a little room for wisdom.

Pro #2: This key idea has wide relevance. A second thing that can be said in favor of Jung's key idea of the collective unconscious is that it (and all that he has written about it) is very relevant and useful in the study of art, literature, drama, cinema, religion, anthropology, mythology, folklore and linguistics, just to name a few areas. Many scholars in these disciplines have accepted Jung's idea of the collective unconscious and have applied it to their subject matter. Herbert Read, for example, is an art critic and aesthetician whose interpretations of works of art are strongly Jungian.

Pro #3: This key idea is fascinating. Jung's idea of the collective unconscious and its archetypes is intrinsically fascinating. That is admittedly a highly subjective judgment, but I invite you to thumb through any of Jung's works yourself. Most are filled with illustrations and even photographs that make them fun to look at. I often pass them around in my classes, and students pore over them. Jung's works on this subject provoke questions and arouse curiosity. We might have said the same things about Freud's key idea of pansexualism, since sex is undoubtedly fascinating too. But the fascination Jung's idea holds for us is somehow deeper and more complex.

Pro #4: This key idea explains many things. Jung's theory of the collective unconscious unifies a astounding range of observations. In a sense, Jung's theory, like Freud's, is a single-cause explanation. Freud's explanation says that behavior is determined by the instincts; Jung's explanation says that all behavior is caused by the collective unconscious. One major difference between the two theories is that Freud's individual unconscious contains only one or two instincts, while Jung's collective unconscious embodies many, many archetypes. Jung retains the advantage of single-cause theories: attributing many kinds of psychic phenomena to one cause, the collective unconscious; he also avoids some of the disadvantages of single-cause theories, by having that single cause composed of many different elements, the archetypes. But, like Freud's theory, Jung's explains just about everything a person does or thinks; and it does this with just one key idea—the collective unconscious.

Con #1: This key idea is not clearly presented. Con #1 is closely tied to Pro #1. Although Jung's scholarship is prodigious, and perhaps because of this, his writing is hard to understand. Jung is not only difficult for the beginning psychology student, he is opaque even to many highly trained psychologists. In fact, Jung is probably the most frequently misunderstood of the personality theorists we will consider. If you peruse the standard textbooks on personality theory, you find more contradictory interpretations of Jung's theory—especially the idea of the collective unconscious—than of any other personality theory. This is an unfortunate state of affairs; but that is simply the way it is with Jung.

Con #2: This key idea smacks of mysticism. The word *unconscious* was perhaps an unfortunate choice of terms on Jung's part, since it implies something mysterious, unscientific, or even occult. People who would not object to the notion of collective *representations* balk at the idea of the collective *unconscious*. In assessing Freud's idea of unconscious motivation, we enumerated some of the objections to the term "unconscious." Freud postulated a second mind, distinct from the conscious mind, *within* the individual. Jung seems to postulate a second mind, distinct from the individual conscious mind, *outside* the individual. Jung's idea of the collective unconscious has been interpreted by some as a kind of cosmic mind or oversoul, a psychic entity that exists independently and apart from individual human minds. This idea is common in oriental philosophies, but it is not welcomed by Western scientists. Jung's preoccupation with the subjects of magic, religion, and the occult only serves to reforce that interpretation. In the end, however, the idea of the collective unconscious as a cosmic mind is not essential to Jung's theory, and I do not think that he intended it to be viewed in that way. Still, he has certainly left himself open to that interpretation.

Con #3: This key idea postulates innate ideas. The issue of innate ideas has been around since the beginning of philosophy. One school of thought holds that at birth, the mind is a blank slate. The behaviorists are heirs to this tradition; they hold that everything that a person does or thinks is the result of learning, and that all ideas derive from experience. The other school of thought holds that certain ideas occur to the mind without needing to be learned from experience. These ideas are innate; you get them as part of your original equipment, at no extra cost. They may not be apparent at birth, but, like your ability to walk, they are there in potential form, waiting to emerge at the proper time. The question of how these ideas get into the mind has been answered in a number of different ways by thinkers in the innate-ideas camp. Which specific ideas are innate, and which ones are not, is another question that causes disagreement among "innatists." This disagreement is largely due to the fact that theorists apply the notion of innate ideas to different problems. The **Gestalt psychologists** applied it to perception, for example. They found that apparent movement was an innate idea. When people watch films, they see, without having to learn how, *moving* pictures, despite the fact that they are really looking at nothing but a series of still pictures shown in rapid succession. In the area of **cognitive** development, Jean Piaget found that the orderly succession of modes of thinking is innate. What he calls the concrete operational mode of thinking, for example, does not have to be learned—in fact, it cannot be taught before the child reaches a certain critical age—but simply occurs one day in very much the same way as walking. The linguist Noam Chomsky discovered that certain grammatical arrangements are innate. And of course Jung himself, working with dreams, symbols, and myths, found that the archetypes of the collective unconscious are innate.

Nevertheless, the innate-ideas position is not the majority position in American psychology. Despite the prestige of people like Piaget, and despite the warm welcome given to Gestalt psychology in this country, most American psychologists still consider the innate-ideas concept unscientific, mere philosophical speculation. The fact that Jung's key idea of the collective unconscious is a version of the discredited and disparaged innate-ideas concept is a distinct disadvantage, a con rather that a pro (though if you like the innate-ideas notion, as I do, it ceases to be a con).

CHAPTER SUMMARY

The collective unconscious is the key idea in the **analytic psychology** of Carl Gustav Jung, one of the early defectors from Freud's Vienna circle. According to Jung, human beings are motivated by an unconscious mind shared by all members of the race.

1. The idea of the collective unconscious goes back at least to 1725, when Giambattista Vico wondered why all human societies develop the same institutions, even in widely separated circumstances where imitation is impossible. Vico explained that because human beings in all eras and locations face the same fundamental problems (e.g., caring for their helpless offspring), they inevitably develop the same, or similar, institutions (e.g., the family). Vico also noted that societies develop myths to sanctify their institutional practices.

2. Emile Durkheim developed the idea further, using the term *collective representations*. This term refers to ideas that are automatically (but unconsciously) shared by every member of the human race, ideas that appear in myths and symbols. In their mythological and symbolic forms, these ideas exert a powerful irrational force: People will die for their country's flag, for example. Collective representations, precisely because they belong to the whole human race, have a kind of objective existence beyond the individual; and they are transmitted from one generation to the next without conscious awareness.

3. Jung's idea of the collective unconscious seems to combine Durkheim's idea of collective representations with Freud's idea of unconscious motivation. The question Jung asked was similar to Vico's: Why do the same symbols and myths appear again and again, in the mythology of ancient peoples and modern day primitives, in all religions, in medieval alchemy, in art, in literature and drama, in people's dreams, and even in the delusions and hallucinations of psychotic persons?

4. *Archetype* is the word Jung used to refer to the collective, unconscious idea that lies behind the tangible symbol. The flag, for example, is the tangible symbol of an idea, something mental rather than material; the idea of the motherland or fatherland. The same archetypes inhabit the minds of all human beings, no matter when or where they are born; and although archetypes have enormous motivating force, they remain largely unconscious.

5. Where do these archetypes, which together make up the collective unconscious, come from? Jung generated great controversy by maintaining that they are inherited. This position is actually very similar to Vico's. Consider the mother archetype, for example. All its numerous manifestations—from the fertility goddesses and earth mothers of antiquity, through the Blessed Virgin Mary of Christianity, up to the secularized Mother Nature of television commercials—can clearly be traced to a single, common source: the experience of having a mother and being nurtured by her, which all humans share no matter where or when they live. Jung's explanation is structural; certain ideas are inevitably impressed upon human minds because of the way humans are built. And it is this structure, (e.g., we are built to have mothers) that is inherited. The archetype of the way exists because our experience is structured in a temporal sequence. The archetype of the self comes from the fact that our experience is structured around a unifying core, or central agency. The archetypes of anima and animus exist because humans come in two models, female and male.

6. A second category of archetypes are the stock characters. Heroes, tricksters, and sages, for example, seem to be a staple of every human society. You need only consult the sports pages of your daily newspaper to see that we hunger for heroes and create them in abundance.

7. A third category of archetypes consists of words denoting abstract qualities—power, for example. Jung found that certain numbers also have archetypal qualities. These numbers also derive their archetypal qualities from structural features of human beings (we have *10* fingers), or impressive features of the environment (there are approximately 12 lunar months in one solar year).

8. Pro #1:   The sheer mass of scholarly research Jung presents to support his key idea is prodigious. Though his evidence is not the kind psychologists typically respect, it is difficult to refute, because few psychologists are as well versed as Jung was in most of these matters.

Pro #2: The idea of the collective unconscious is useful not only in psychology and psychiatry, but in the study of art, literature, drama, cinema, religion, anthropology, mythology, folklore, and linguistics.

Pro #3: The idea of the collective unconscious and its archetypes is intrinsically fascinating to a great many people.

Pro #4: Jung's key idea is capable of explaining nearly everything human beings think or do. If you like grand theories, ones that trace everything back to a single cause, you'll be as happy with this one as with Freud's.

Con #1: Jung's writings are hard to understand, sometimes even opaque. There is more controversy about the correct interpretation of Jung than about any of the other theorists we will study.

Con #2: Jung seems to posit a mystical oversoul, or cosmic mind—a second mind existing outside of the individual, and separate from the individual's conscious mind. Jung's preoccupation with the occult makes this interpretation plausible, and perhaps valid.

Con #3: This key idea postulates the existence of innate ideas. Because the opposite position—the notion that the mind at birth is a blank slate, and that all its contents are the result of learning—is the majority opinion in psychology, Jung's dependence on innate ideas is listed as a con. (It is only fair to point out, however, that the innate ideas position is supported by all of Gestalt psychology, by Piaget, and by Chomsky.)

REFERENCES

Bogardus, E. S. (1947). *The development of social thought* (2nd ed.). New York: Longmans, Green.

Durkheim, E. (1915). *The elementary forms of the religious life* (J. W. Swain, Trans.). New York: Macmillan. (Original work published 1912)

Jung, C. G. (1958). Psychology and religion. In H. Read, M. Fordham, & G. Adler (Eds.), *Psychology and religion: East and west.* In *The collected works of C. G. Jung* (Vol. 11, pp. 3–105). New York: Pantheon Books. (Original work published 1937)

Jung, C. G. (1960). On psychic energy. In H. Read, M. Fordham, & G. Adler (Eds.), R. F. C. Hull (Trans.), *The structure and dynamics of the psyche.* In *The collected works of C. G. Jung* (Vol. 8, pp. 3–66). New York: Pantheon Books. (Original work published 1948)

Jung, C. G. (1968a). Concerning mandala symbolism. In H. Read, M. Fordham, G. Adler, & W. McGuire (Eds.), R. F. C. Hull (Trans.), *The archetypes and the collective unconscious* (2nd ed.). In *The collected works of C. G. Jung* (Vol. 9, Pt. 1, pp. 355–384). Princeton, NJ: Princeton University Press. (Original work published 1950)

Jung, C. G. (1968b). Concerning rebirth. In H. Read, M. Fordham, G. Adler, & W. McGuire (Eds.), R. F. C. Hull (Trans.), *The archetypes and the collective unconscious* (2nd ed.). In *The collected works of C. G. Jung* (Vol. 9, Pt. 1, pp. 113–147). Princeton, NJ: Princeton University Press. (Original work published 1950)

Jung, C. G. (1968c). The concept of the collective unconscious. In H. Read, M. Fordham, G. Adler, & W. McGuire (Eds.), *The archetypes and the collective unconscious* (2nd ed.). In *The collected works of C. G. Jung* (Vol. 9, Pt. 1, pp. 42–53). Princeton, NJ: Princeton University Press. (Original work published 1954)

Jung, C. G. (1968d). Psychological aspects of the mother archetype. In H. Read, M. Fordham, G. Adler, & W. McGuire (Eds.), R. F. C. Hull (Trans.), *The archetypes and the collective unconscious* (2nd ed.). In *The collected works of C. G. Jung* (Vol. 9, Pt. 1, pp. 75–110). Princeton, NJ: Princeton University Press. (Original work published 1954)

Jung, C. G. (1968e). On the psychology of the trickster-figure. In H. Read, M. Fordham, G. Adler, & W. McGuire (Eds.), R. F. C. Hull (Trans.), *The archetypes and the collective unconscious* (2nd ed.). In *The collected works of C. G. Jung* (Vol. 9, Pt. 1, pp. 255–272). Princeton, NJ: Princeton University Press. (Original work published 1954)

Jung, C. G. (1971). *Psychological types* (H. Read, M. Fordham, G. Adler, & W. McGuire, Eds.; Revision by R. F. C. Hull of Trans. by H. G. Baynes). In *The collected works of C. G. Jung* (Vol. 6). Princeton, NJ: Princeton University Press. (Original work published 1921)

Lévy-Bruhl, L. (1966). *How natives think* (L. A. Clare, Trans.). New York: Washington Square Press. (Original work published 1910)

Myers, I. B. (1962). *The Myers-Briggs type indicator.* Princeton, NJ: Educational Testing Service.

5/Erik Erikson

A Biographical Sketch

The man we know as Erik Erikson grew up as Erik Homburger, unaware that his father, a pediatrician in Karlsruhe, Germany had married his artist mother and adopted him while Erik was still very young. In 1902, when Erik was born in Frankfort, his biological father had already abandoned his mother. Because Erik inherited the blond, blue-eyed, Aryan looks of his Danish natural father, but was raised in anti-semitic Karls-ruhe as a Jew by a Jewish mother and stepfather, he early on experienced conflicts concerning his identity. We will return to this topic very shortly.

Erik's secondary education took place at a high school in Karlsruhe that emphasized a liberal arts, rather than a scientific or technical, curriculum. His academic performance was mediocre, except in the subjects of art and history. Against his father's wish that he enroll in medical school, after graduation from high school Erik entered an art academy. He had already spent a year away from home, sketching and ruminating. Later in his life, Erikson would look back on these years as a valuable moratorium, the kind of interim period many young people need for testing out various options. Before long he transferred to the art academy in Munich, then took up residence in Florence, Italy, a very appropriate site for an art education. He spent much of his time in Italy visiting museums and galleries.

As with so many of our theorists, a chance occurrence proved to be the turning point in Erikson's life. In 1927, when Erik was twenty-five years old, one of his high-school friends invited him to come to Vienna and join him on the teaching staff of the Bur-lingham School, a progressive institution founded by Anna Freud, Sigmund's daughter. The student body consisted of children who were being psychoanalyzed, or whose parents were in analysis. When he left Vienna six years later, in 1933, Erikson had a wife who would be his lifelong companion and professional collaborator; a mentor and mythical father-figure in Sigmund Freud; his credentials as a psychoanalyst; and, of course, a new identity.

At the Burlingham School, Erikson discovered that he loved working with children. He became so interested in the education of children, in fact, that he had himself certified by the Montessori Association of Vienna to teach the Montessori method, an approach that allows children to follow the dictates of their own curiosity.

Through Anna Freud, Erikson not only learned about the psychoanalytic study of children, but was introduced to Sigmund Freud and the other members of the Vienna Psychoanalytic Institute. Though he had no medical training, Erikson was eventually accepted as a candidate at the Institute, completing the course of training—including being psychoanalyzed by Anna Freud—in 1933.

In that year he and his wife Joan Serson, a fellow teacher at the Burlingham School, moved to Copenhagen to set up the first psychoanalytic center in Denmark. When that venture failed, they left Europe and came to the United States.

Settling in Boston in 1933, Erikson established a practice as the first child psychoanalyst in the city, secured an appointment on the staff of the Harvard Medical School, and did research with Henry Murray at the Harvard Psychological Clinic. In 1936, Erikson accepted an appointment at Yale University's Institute of Human Relations, which included an instructorship in the medical school. He spent part of 1938 studying child-rearing customs on a Sioux reservation in South Dakota, an experience that further fueled his strong interest in anthropological methods, and in the effects of culture on personality development.

He remained Erik Homburger until 1939, the year in which he was granted his United States citizenship. On his naturalization papers he had his name inscribed as Erik Homburger Erikson. In the same year, he accepted a post at the University of California at Berkeley. There he did research, continued his clinical work, and studied the Yurok Indians of Northern California. In 1942 he became professor of psychology at Berkeley. He remained there until 1950, when, amid the witch hunts of the McCarthy era, he was forced to resign his professorship after refusing to sign a loyalty oath. Ironically, *Childhood and Society*, the book that would assure Erikson's fame, was published in the same year. He was not a subversive, Erikson said, but he objected to the oath on principle.

Throughout the 1950s, Erikson was on the staff of the Austen Riggs Center, a treatment facility in Western Massachusetts for young people with emotional problems. From 1960 until 1975, when he retired, Erikson taught at Harvard, where his lectures drew standing-room-only crowds. Since his retirement, Erikson has continued to work and write, especially on the developmental aspects of aging. Appropriately enough, in 1982 he published a book entitled *The Life Cycle Completed.*

◥◣ THE KEY IDEA
IDENTITY AND THE RELATIONSHIP
BETWEEN IDENTITY AND IDEOLOGY

Among our cast of characters, Erik Erikson rates near the top in the category of name recognition. It was clear that Erikson had achieved superstar status when his face appeared on the cover of Time Magazine some years ago. To my knowledge, only one other living psychologist had been accorded that honor: B. F. Skinner. It is ironic that Erikson achieved such fame in psychology, considering that he entered the field almost by chance. What if he had pursued an artist's life? What if he had not had a friend at the Burlingham School? Or suppose he had been summoned to some other school, in some other city, a school that had no ties to Freud and his movement.

When we examine the biographies of these theorists, we are struck with how easily a great idea might have been lost—particularly Erikson's, because it seems highly unlikely that anyone else would have formulated his key idea when he did, or in quite the same way. I am not referring to his idea that developmental stages extend beyond puberty, well into middle age. That in itself is a major idea (see Box: Eight Stages of the Life Cycle), but someone else might have divided the life cycle into eight, or some other number of, stages. No, the key idea that bears the unique stamp of Erik Erikson is the idea of *identity,* and especially, the relationship between *identity and ideology.*

IDENTITY: SAMENESS AND CONTINUITY

The idea of identity is simply an extension of the notion of ego, or self. Freud wrote extensively about the ego, and philosophers had used the concept of self for centuries beforehand. What Erikson did was to focus on a particular aspect of the self, or ego: the internal sense of sameness and continuity that we all have, and that we all take for granted most of the time. I feel that the experiences shown on the screen of my mind belong to me. They are my private movie and nobody else's. Futhermore, I am convinced that the "I" who watches that movie screen today is the same "I" who watched it yesterday, and who will watch it again tomorrow. I have a sense of continuity. I went to bed Jim Scroggs yesterday, and I woke up Jim Scroggs today. Not terribly surprising? Of course not! We all feel this way if we have a sense of identity.

And yet, that is exactly what is lost in amnesia, dissociative neurotic states, and in many cases of schizophrenia. People suffering from these disorders have the bizarre feeling that their experience does not belong to them. Ideas pop into their minds that seem to belong to someone else; feelings well up in them that they do not own. They may even view themselves from the outside, as though they were independent observers watching themselves act in a play. Needless to say, they may be utterly confused about who they really are, which self is their true self, and whether this true self ever existed.

While working during World War II on cases of "battle neurosis," Erikson encountered patients with these symptoms and many similar ones. The patients were soldiers who "did not know any more who they were" (Erikson, 1968, p. 67). To describe this condition, Erikson coined the term *identity crisis*. Eventually he would turn this phrase into a household word.

PERSONAL SOURCES OF THE IDEA

A clue to Erikson's fondness for the idea of identity comes from his personal life. He seems to have had more than the usual difficulties in discovering his own identity. His problem began before he was even born (Erikson, 1975, p. 27). Erikson's biological father abandoned his mother before Erik was born. She remarried soon thereafter. But Erik was never told about this. His mother and his stepfather, whom Erik naturally considered to be his father, were both Jews. His mother was Danish by nationality; his stepfather, German. They lived in Karlsruhe in southern Germany. Erik turned out to be blond and blue-eyed, a perfect Nordic, "Aryan" type. He looked different from his parents and relatives, and he felt conspicuously different. At the temple the other boys teased him, calling him "goy"—a derogatory term for non-Jews—yet at school other Aryan types derided him and called him "Jew." No wonder he was confused about who he was.

Theodor Homburger, the stepfather Erik assumed to be his biological father, was a medical doctor who pressed young Erik to pursue that vocation. True to form, Erik rebelled against his stepfather's wishes, rejecting the medical profession for the life of an artist and going off to lead the Bohemian existence expected of aspiring artists. Not that Dr. Homburger was cruel to his stepson—quite the opposite; Erik simply had to pass through what he would later call an identity crisis before the air could be cleared between him and his stepfather. When it was cleared and the smoke had settled, Erik had become a doctor of sorts. True, he had maintained his own integrity by not going to medical school and never earning a doctoral degree. Yet he entered the role his parents had hoped he would: "my son, the doctor." He worked as a doctor, but he did it on his own terms. He later acknowledged his gratitude to his stepfather by keeping Homburger, as his middle name; but he also forged his own identity by choosing his own last name, Erikson.

When Erikson went to Vienna, he discovered in Sigmund Freud exactly what he needed. Freud provided just the right balance of firmness and permissiveness as a father figure. And Freudian psychoanalysis offered just the right balance between cultural and historical concerns, including the arts, and the individual psychic conflicts Erikson himself was experiencing. With Freud's help, Erikson worked out his identity and found

⧉ EIGHT STAGES OF THE LIFE CYCLE

Erikson took over Freud's idea of developmental stages and modified it by (1) adding three more stages to Freud's scheme, thereby extending personality development to cover the entire span of life; (2) redefining the stages as a series of crises that challenge the developing ego to acquire particular strengths, rather than focusing on how the id discharges its instinctual energies; and (3) paying more attention to social and cultural influences on personality development. But Erikson's basic view of development—that people pass through the stages in a fixed order; that some people develop more quickly than others; that some people become fixated in a particular stage and others regress from an advanced to an earlier stage—remained essentially Freudian.

BASIC TRUST VERSUS BASIC MISTRUST
Erikson's description of the first stage reflects his interest in the developing ego. He says that developing a sense of basic trust is the first challenge that confronts an infant. Infants whose expressed needs are consistently gratified learn to trust the world as a dependable provider of support, and to trust their own urges and instincts as reliable guides to behavior. Failure to receive consistent support engenders a sense of basic mistrust in an infant, not only blocking progress toward the next stage but also giving the person a tendency to withdraw socially. The child-rearing practices of a culture may make basic trust relatively easy, or rather difficult, to develop. For Freud, this childhood drama focuses on the mouth; Erikson broadened Freud's oral concept to include all *incorporative* modes of relating. He said that infants *take in* everything. Not only do they put things into their mouths, they take things in with their eyes and pick up things with their fingers. If this taking-in process is consistently gratifying, the infant develops a sense of basic trust.

AUTONOMY VERSUS SHAME AND DOUBT
Somewhere around the age of two, children begin responding to parental commands with a "No, I won't." Sometimes this budding defiance occurs in connection with toilet training, but Erikson observes that it may be expressed through spitting out food or dropping things on the floor. Depending partly on cultural prescriptions, parents may respond by crushing the child's will with physical force, or threatening to withdraw affection. Or they may try to shame children into compliance by making them feel guilty for their lack of respect for legitimate authority, especially in connection with toilet-training accidents. Parents may also support and affirm their children's autonomy, perhaps by channeling the child's wilfullness into games and activities where persistence, effort, and the exercise of will power result in accomplishments in which the child can take pride. The later approach engenders a healthy sense of autonomy, whereas punitive responses encourage the development of personalities that are compulsive, crippled by obsessive self-doubts, and prone to masochistic and even sadistic behavior.

INITIATIVE VERSUS GUILT
Around three years of age, children not only discover sex, as Freud observed, but become much more mobile. They run and jump and climb everywhere—often where they are not supposed to! Erikson characterizes this mode of behavior as *intrusive*. At this stage, children often interrupt adult conversations. They jump into adult's laps, tug at their legs, bat their newspapers away. At the same time, their inter-

est in finding out what kind of genitals other people have may lead them to invade adults' bathroom privacy, or to play doctor with their playmates. Society's need to control such behavior causes the child to develop a superego: The parental commandments become internalized as the "voice of conscience." An overly harsh conscience creates a personality that is inhibited and guilt-ridden; more flexible parental treatment endows a child with a sense of purpose and personal initiative.

INDUSTRY VERSUS INFERIORITY

During the elementary-school years, children are primarily occupied with producing things. They learn to work, and the work they do is constantly evaluated. They are graded in school; they bring home papers and projects to show their parents; they are subject to being chosen first or last for teams made up of their playmates. Children who receive good evaluations for what they do develop a sense of industry. They discover an intrinsic satisfaction in working, and a feeling of self-worth. Children whose work is not praised learn to devalue themselves and are left with an abiding sense of inferiority. Instead of acquiring a feeling of competence, they sink into inertia, trying less and less and doing less and less.

IDENTITY VERSUS IDENTITY CONFUSION

Challenged by the sudden bodily changes accompanying puberty, and by society's demands that they accept more adult responsibilities, adolescents must reconsider the question of who they are. Successful resolution of this crisis provides an individual with a strong sense of identity, which is the basis for commitment and fidelity to personal values and interpersonal relationships. Failure to meet this challenge results in lack of a personal center and repudiation of any philosophy of life.

INTIMACY VERSUS ISOLATION

In early adulthood, individuals are faced with a need to build more lasting, and more intimate, personal relationships. Intimacy includes, but is not limited to, sexuality. Intimacy demands a degree of openness and honesty that is not possible without a secure sense of identity. Personal rejection is the great risk at this stage. People who successfully negotiate this crisis discover a sense of intimacy and learn to love. Those who fail tend to exclude themselves from future relationships and to withdraw into isolation.

GENERATIVITY VERSUS STAGNATION

The task of adulthood is to create something that will contribute to the maintenance of the world. Many people accomplish this by raising children. Others leave their mark in business or public life. Still others plant gardens, build bridges or birdhouses. There are many outlets, but the end result is always the same: The generative person learns to care, both in the sense of *taking care of* and in the sense of *caring for*. But the person who fails to create stagnates, rejecting others and refusing to care for them.

INTEGRITY VERSUS DESPAIR

Reviewing your life from the perspective of old age, you cannot help asking whether you would live it the same way if you had another chance. The challenge is to survey your life, declare it satisfactory, and so achieve integrity. Failing that—if you cannot emotionally "own" your life when it is too late to change it—you will fall into despair. With the sense of integrity comes wisdom; despair brings only disdain.

his vocation. But more than that he found a theme that would occupy him for the remainder of his life. His opinions on this theme would strike a sympathetic chord in thousands of readers, especially young Americans in the 1960s—the identity crisis.

CHALLENGES TO IDENTITY

Identity is the sense of self that begins to form during the very first year of life—probably when the child learns to respond to its own name. The sense of identity continues to grow throughout childhood, but this early sense of identity is shaken by the traumatic events of adolescence, such as sudden bodily changes and new demands made by society.

Adolescence gives you a different body to live in, a body that has gender in a way it never had before. The sex roles that were established at the conclusion of the Oedipus complex, at age six or seven, are called into question. Being male or female now means something more than just playing soldiers, or playing with dolls. The child has to find out what that something more means and come to terms with it. Society adds to the pressure by demanding that the adolescent at least begin practicing for the task of choosing a mate.

Though adults jokingly ask children what they want to be when they grow up, it is not until adolescence that society seriously pressures young people to make vocational choices. By the time adolescents reach high school, they must decide whether to take the college course, the business or "general" course, or head toward a vocational school. Of course, the choice you make determines your identity. In our society, *you are what you do.*

These are the major challenges to the adolescent's sense of identity, challenges that can precipitate an identity crisis.

RESOURCES TO MEET THE CHALLENGE

CLOTHING AS IDENTITY: YOU ARE WHAT YOU WEAR

What resources are available to meet this challenge? How can an adolescent in the midst of an identity crisis find out who he, or she, is? One way is by paying attention to clothes—*you are what you wear.* Clothes, whether they are uniforms or a stenciled T-shirt, provide a kind of ready-made identity. The clothes you wear tell you, and the rest of the world, who you are. Children have reached adolescence when they begin refusing to wear the clothes their mothers buy for them. Adolescents are fanactical about clothes, because adolescents are confused about their identities and clothes confer identity. Quasi-military uniforms—Boy Scouts and Girl Scouts, Cub Scouts and Brownies—proclaim the adolescents's worth, her or his rank, just as military uniforms do later on. Not only do these uniforms indicate your individual rank, they let it be known that you belong to some larger organization. And that is important, too, because *you are also who or what you belong to.* (Ask any Marine!) Adolescents also wear band uniforms and drum-and-bugle-corps uniforms. But in recent years, athletic uniforms have become more popular than any other kind. The Boy Scout uniform has lost out to the Little League baseball suit. The function is the same; only the cut of the clothes has changed. The sports uniform not only tells which group you belong to, but proclaims your own unique identity—your number. Football jerseys and baseball caps are often worn off the field as well as on. Teams have such a desperate need to buy uniforms, that they are not afraid to go out and "beg" for the money on streetcorners. And as the age at which adolescence begins has steadily declined in recent years, the age of children engaged in uniformed team sports has declined accordingly. Our society provides a long, protracted period of adolescence during which personal identity may be elusive. But it also allows young people to try on ready-made identities along the way, from peewee hockey player to college athlete.

But you do not have to be an athlete to enjoy the identity-conferring benefits of clothing. Nor must you belong to a formal organization. There is an everyday adolescent uniform, one that changes often. Some fads catch on more than others, and many fashions lose their identity-conferring powers when they are taken over by the adult establishment. Blue jeans, long hair and beards was the uniform of young people in the sixties, but when Wall Street brokers began sporting beards and the President donned jeans, that was the end of that. A few years ago, "jock chic" was in vogue. Track shorts, tank tops (in cooler climates, warm-up suits), and jogging shoes suddenly adorned many an adolescent shape, no matter how svelte or corpulent. More recently, the T-shirt and sweatshirt craze erupted. You can have anything you want written on the front of a T-shirt: "Led Zeppelin"; "Adidas"; "I'm a Virgin—This is an old T-shirt"; "Keep off the grass"; "Property of Arizona State A.A." Each one tells something about who the wearers think they are as individuals, but it also announces their membership in a certain generation of young people. The stenciled T-shirt epitomizes clothing as a conferrer of identity.

IDENTIFICATION AND IDENTITY

But clothing is not the only resource available in the quest for identity. There are live models too, some encountered in personal acquaintance, some known only through the media. These are people who embody ready-made identities that you can copy or imitate. Psychologists call such people role models, and they call the process *identification.* You may decide that one of your teachers, or a summer-camp counselor, has just about everything you admire. So you hang around that person as much as you can, talking and trying to get him or her to notice and like you. You dress like this person, walk like this person, try to become an expert on whatever this person is interested in. In short, you borrow this person's identity and try it on for size. Adolescent crushes are another form of shopping around for an identity.

If you cannot find the right role models among your acquaintances, you can find a vast selection of them in the media. The "people" magazines—rock and roll magazines, movie magazines, sports magazines—offer a veritable Sears catalogue of ready-made identities. Of course, you can also find role models on TV, in the movies, or on stages and playing fields. And you can become a fan—you can follow your idols everywhere, never missing any of their public appearances. You can collect memorabilia: autographs, posters, bits of their clothing or hair. You can use the same brands and models they use and endorse. You can adopt their style: dress like them, talk like them, walk like them. You may even be lucky enough to enter a look-alike contest, where you can get an objective evaluation of the success of your **identification**. And if you feel alone in all this, there are fan clubs to offer you the sense of belonging we talked about earlier.

Fan phenomena are typically, and almost exclusively, adolescent. The reason is simple: Adolescents are shopping around for an identity. They are at the age when identity is shaken and called into question. Being a fan gives them an individual identity; it also allows them to belong to something or someone.

IDEOLOGY AND IDENTITY

The word *fan* is a shortened form of the word *fanatic*. That brings us to the final resource for meeting the challenge of the identity crisis. Not only is being a fan a typically adolescent thing; being a fanatic is also largely confined to that age group—there are very few middle-aged revolutionaries. Adolescence is the prime time for ideological conversions. And whether those conversions are to Maoism or the Moonies, the basic motive is the same: Ideologies offer ready-made identities. Religions and political-action groups—the Church of Scientology, Students for a Democratic Society, the Southern Christian Leadership Conference—provide ready-made identities in the form of belief systems that can be tried on in much the same way that you might try on outfits in a clothing store, posing before the mirror to see how you like yourself in each guise. In other words, *you are also what you believe in*, what you care about, what you are committed to. Ideologies are identities. That is why adolescents are so fascinated by them, and why adolescents become so fanatically committed to them.

Ideologies also unify. They allow adolescents to "get their heads together." How? By taking all the apparent contradictions, all the disjointed pieces of information, and shaping them into a coherent, comprehensive philosophy of life. In this way, ideologies give meaning to life. They give life purpose and direction, making sense out of the otherwise senseless world. An ideology is something to live for, even to die for. It is a faith—something to have faith in, and be faithful to. Fidelity (the ability to be faithful), Erikson says, is the basic strength acquired from the successful resolution of the identity crisis.

Erikson applied his ideas about identity and ideology to the lives of a number of historical persons. *Young Man Luther,* published in 1958, is undoubtedly the best of these studies. One could hardly find a better example of Erikson's theme, ideology as identity, than Martin Luther. Erikson's book is now a classic in a field that has come to be called psycho-history, largely due to Erikson's lead. Erikson borrowed the idea of analyzing historical figures from Freud, who had already done a fair amount of this sort of thing. But there is a subtle difference between Freud's treatment of Leonardo DaVinci (1910/1957), for example, and Erikson's portrait of Martin Luther. In *Young Man Luther,* the author conveys warmth and sympathy for his character. Erikson has a fondness for Luther that makes his story more than just a detached, clinical dissection of Luther's psyche, or a supercilious explaining-away of his unique contributions.

In the next decade, Erikson traveled to India to gather material for another piece of psychohistory. The subject this time was Mahatma Gandhi, again someone with whom Erikson himself may have identified to a considerable extent. The result was *Gandi's Truth,* published in 1969. Erikson was then in his late sixties and would soon retire. For most of his very productive lifetime, he had focused his attention on a single key idea: identity, and especially, ideology as a form of identity.

IDEOLOGY AND IDENTITY
IN THE LIFE OF MAHATMA GANDHI

Perhaps by taking a closer look at Erikson's portrait of Gandhi, we can see how Erikson used his key idea to enhance our understanding of the life of the Mahatma. Actually, the theme of identity appears in *Gandhi's Truth* in connection with three interrelated persons and groups. Naturally, Erikson explores the way in which Gandhi forged his own identity. But he also devotes considerable attention to Gandhi's cadre of disciples, and to the way in which Gandhi and his philosophy provided them with a solution to their quest for identity. This was a logical approach for Erikson to take; during his stay in India, he lived with some of these disciples and was able to interview a number of others. But there was more: Gandhi not only developed identity and bequeathed it to the handful of followers; Mahatma Gandi created a new identity for India itself. Perhaps he would have preferred to say that he assisted at the rebirth of India's age-old identity. Whatever the case, though, Erikson illuminates the process by considering it in the light of his key idea.

Gandhi and his followers built their identities by using the resources we have already examined. Clothing played a particularly significant part in Gandhi's struggle to form his own identity, and it became the basis for the identity he passed along not only to his disciples but to all of the Indians who followed him. The image of a bald and wizened little brown man in white cotton loincloth was universally associated with the Mahatma; but like so many oppressed and colonial peoples, Gandhi began his search for identity by trying to identify with his oppressors. While studying law in London as a young man, he did his best to cultivate the image of the perfect English gentleman. He describes himself on one occasion as wearing a silk hat and black coat, asking where he could get dancing lessons (Erikson, 1969, pp. 146–147); and on another occasion he appears in a photo of the Vegetarian Society, a white handkerchief cascading over the rim of his breast pocket (Erikson, 1969, p. 152). Several years later, after a two-year stay in India, Gandhi accepted a plea to handle a lawsuit on behalf of some Indian merchants in the Transvaal of South Africa. He "arrived dressed in a frock coat, shining boots, and a turban, which the Mahatma describes as an imitation of the 'Bengali pugree' " (Erikson, 1969, p. 164). Much as hippies "freaked out" the "straights" just a few years ago, Gandhi produced consternation when he appeared in the courtroom in this attire. The judge requested him to remove his turban; Gandhi refused; the judge insisted; and Gandhi walked out. He did offer to put on the high hat worn by English barristers, and to follow the European custom of removing it indoors. But in South Africa this was not permitted. Only Indians who were Christians were expected to wear European clothes, and most of these people were clerks or waiters. If Gandhi had been a Moslem, he would have been allowed to wear a turban in the courtroom. He would have been classified as an "Arab," rather than an "Asiatic." Remember, we are talking about the land of apartheid. "Arabs" were not considered "colored;" "Asiatics" were. Gandhi was a "colored," or "coolie," barrister.

South African racism hastened the resolution of Gandhi's identity crisis. Within a week of being ejected from the courtroom, Gandhi was thrown off a train when he refused to surrender his first-class compartment to a white man who objected to spending the night in the company of a coolie. Worse still, Gandhi's bags were confiscated, and he was left to spend a cold night without his coat, shivering and humiliated in a small-town railway station. By morning he had determined his vocation and, by extension, his identity: He would become the leader of the thousands of Indians in South Africa, directing the struggle to end these intolerable, discriminatory practices. This momentous decision, according to Erikson, marks the "solution" of Gandhi's identity crisis (Erikson, 1969, p. 47). He was then twenty-three years of age. Of course, the coolie barrister was not instantly transformed into the Mahatma; the unique content of that identity would be assembled, one feature at a time, over the next several decades. One of those features, appropriately enough, would be his clothing.

When Gandhi returned to his native India twenty years later, he was extravagantly received by resident dignitaries fitted out in their finest formal attire. Gandhi walked down the gangplank dressed in the shawl and loincloth that was to become the trademark of his mature identity. Gandhi learned the hard way that you are what you wear; but once he had learned this lesson, he applied it with great effectiveness.

Identifying with role models also helped Gandhi to discover who he was. When he returned to India after finishing law school in England (before he first went to South Africa), Gandhi met a young philosopher-poet who came as close to being his guru as anyone in his life (Erikson, 1969, p. 158). Rajchandra was a saintly, other-wordly seeker of truth. To Gandhi, he embodied the notion of non-violence. Rajchandra was a member of the Jains, a small religious sect that broke away from orthodox Hinduism thousands of years ago. Jains ardently believe in the value of rigid asceticism and fasting; celibacy (for monks); nudity or simple white clothing; and doing everything possible to avoid endangering any form of animal life. You may have seen pictures of Jain temples, with the monks wearing mosquito-net masks to avoid inadvertently breathing in, and killing, insects, or carefully sweeping paths lest someone sin by crushing a worm. None of these ideas were brand-new to Gandhi. There were many Jains in the part of India where Gandhi grew up; in fact, his mother's sect of Hinduism was strongly influenced by Jainism. Nevertheless, Gandhi cites Rajchandra as one of the three mentors who inspired him most (Erikson, 1969, p. 162). The four major tenets of Jainism were to become fundamental features of Gandhi's identity, leaving little doubt about Rajchrandra's influence.

John Ruskin and Leo Tolstoy are the two others Gandhi ranks with Rajchandra. Gandhi encountered these men through their writings. He incorporated several of Ruskin's ideas into his identity, including the notion that modern industry is ugly and spawns disease and social corruption, and the companion idea that workers ought to organize to protest against their exploitation by the factory system. Once the Mahatma's mature identity was established, not a day went by when he did not spend a prescribed amount of time spinning cotton. He spearheaded a drive to revitalize spinning as a cottage industry in India and admonished all his followers to spin, and to wear homespun cloth, as he did. Erikson organized his book around the event he considered most crucial for Gandhi's identity: the 1918 millworkers' strike in Ahmedabad. Gandhi led this strike, his first major public act since concluding his work in South Africa. He may have been a saint, but he was also a labor organizer.

"Tolstoy Farm" was the name Gandhi gave to a community he founded in 1904, while still in South Africa. The name expresses his intellectual and emotional debt to the famous Russian nobleman. Tolstoy's life like Gandhi's was a continual struggle between an earthy sensuality and a rather strict puritanical streak. In his late forties, Tolstoy underwent a religious conversion, after which he committed himself to a life of Christian love and to non-resistance of evil. ("But I say unto you, That ye resist not evil: but whosoever shall smite thee on thy right cheek, turn to him the other also." Matthew 5:39.) In fact, Tolstoy felt that using force in any context was morally wrong. Gandhi not only incorporated these precepts into his identity, he also organized the farm in South Africa (and later, his *ashrams* in India) according to the principles Tolstoy had advocated and used to improve the lot of serfs on Russian estates.

The contributions of Gandhi's mentors to his identity were primarily ideological. For Gandhi, identity was ideology, especially because Gandhi acted out his ideology. He did not bury it in musty tomes, like some pedantic dogma; he lived it, adopting it as a progam of action.

Gandhi called his ideology *satyagraha* —"truth force," or "holding or grasping of the truth." The term suggests not a static condition, but truth in action. ("Ethical integrity" and "the opposite of hypocrisy" are some of its other connotations.) In effect, *satyagraha* meant passive resistance to the evils of racism, colonialism, and industrialism. But "passive resistance," as Erikson observes, is too bland a description; it seems rather inadequate for the courage, commitment, and self-discipline needed to march unarmed into the ranks of military troops who have just smashed the skulls of a previous wave of marchers. "Militant non-violence more nearly captures the flavor of *satyagraha*."

Gandhi himself was a fanatic. He was commited to his ideology to the death. Seventeen times during his life, he solemnly vowed to fast until he died, if necessary. Time and again he was arrested for civil disobedience, spending a total of over six years in prison. Though wealthy as a young man, he later lived in self-imposed poverty, literally sleeping on a board, dressing as a peasant, engaging in manual labor, taking a vow of celibacy, and limiting himself to a strict vegetarian diet. Gandhi lived his truth, and lived it aggressively, not passively.

Erikson remarks that Gandhi had a penchant for ritual (Erikson, 1969, p. 157), and that ritual is ideology acted out. You can ideologically indoctrinate prospective converts by prescribing rituals for them to perform. For an intellectual with strong academic credentials, for example, Gandhi might prescribe cleaning latrines, a task that was all the more repugnant to Hindus because the caste system assigned it to untouchables. Before the Ahmedabad strike, Gandhi recruited Shankerlal Banker to take charge of the program aimed at reintroducing the spinning wheel and loom into Indian villages. In an interview with Erikson, Banker said that the Mahatma prescribed a vegetarian diet and a cotton loincloth for him. Gandhi's keen insight into human nature quickly told him how proudly attached Banker was to his English gentleman's wardrobe, and how shamefully fond he was of eating meat. In fact, every individual who joined Gandhi at one of his various ashrams—the monastic communities that he set up in India on the model of his Tolstoy Farm—had to take the ashram pledge. Pledges and vows are ritual promises, and ever since Gandhi's mother made him vow not to eat meat while he was studying law in England, he had found profound meaning in this ritual. Later, he inaugurated his celibate life with a vow, and his fasts always began with a vow that he would not eat again until the wrong he was protesting had been corrected. For his ashramites, he prescribed vows of celibacy, vegetarianism, non-violence, and manual labor. This ideology-in-action provided a completely new identity, one specifically tailored to the needs of young Indians who were just becoming conscious of the extent to which British colonialism had debased and distorted their former identity, by driving out their native language, replacing native crafts with manufacturing, and making them ashamed of their traditional dress.

What Gandhi accomplished, in the end, was to restore India's identity with the philosophy of *satyagraha* (Erikson, 1969, p. 265). And Erikson could not have found a better person than Gandhi to illustrate his theme of ideology-as-identity, because Gandhi expressed his ideology more in the way he lived than in his speeches and writings. Gandhi's identity—the person he was—coincided with his ideology, his belief system. In Gandhi these two things were inseparable, opposite sides of the same coin.

PROS and CONS

Pro #1: This key idea is humanistic. Erikson's sympathetic psychohistorical treatments of Gandhi and Luther show, perhaps, that his overall orientation is more humanistic than that of his mentor, Freud. Erikson's image of human nature seems less derogatory than Freud's. To Freud, human beings are nothing more than animals selfishly driven by primitive instincts; Erikson's view seems to allow the possibility of something more noble in human nature. The difference is also evident in a more technical sense: Erikson is an exponent of **ego psychology**. Ego psychologists are neo-Freudians, Freudian revisionists, who hold that the ego is autonomous. They do not accept Freud's view that the ego is enslaved to the id, that the id instincts directly control all human thought and action. They leave some room for free will. In that sense, Erikson is less deterministic than Freud.

Erikson also places less emphasis than Freud on biological determinants of behavior, and more on social learning. The different emphases are undoubtedly connected to the differing amounts of medical training the two men had. But Erikson's anthropological field studies of American Indians really convinced him that cultural conditioning can cause great variations in human behavior. His emphasis on the role of socio-cultural (as opposed to biological) factors in forming personalities is optimistic and democratic. Take the matter of criminality: Are criminals born, or are they made? A biological, instinctual theory (not necessarily Freud's) might argue that criminality is an instinct some people are born with. But if people are born with criminal instincts, there is very little you can do to change their behavior. The problem of criminality could be combatted only with a broad, national campaign that included compulsory genetic counseling, sterilization of people with criminal genes, and abortion of criminal fetuses. On the other hand, if criminals are products of certain kinds of social conditioning, the prospects seem much brighter—criminality is potentially preventable, and proven criminals are potentially curable. The only trick is to identify the social conditions that contribute to criminality—poverty, parental rejection, broken homes, failure in school—and alleviate them.

The same kind of analysis holds true for any other undesirable trait of personality, from mere shyness to full-blown schizophrenia. If socio-cultural factors cause these problems, then rearranging socio-cultural factors should enable us to prevent them. This process leaves a lot more room for individual free will than rearranging people's genes does. Erikson's theory is much closer than Freud's to the ideas of humanistic psychologists, such as Maslow and Rogers, because his view of human nature is more optimistic and less deterministic.

Pro #2: This key idea is relevant. Erikson's key idea of identity, especially identity as ideology, was strikingly relevant for the generation of the 1960s, the era when Erikson reached the pinnacle of both his professional career and his popularity. His humanistic sentiments were fervently shared by the "flower children," who were certain that adverse social conditions were the root of all evil. Human nature, they assured themselves, is basically good. They "dropped out" and went off to live in communes, to prove that, once free of the warping influences of their sick society, they would blossom as human beings. A whole generation of adolescents rebelled in unison against their parents, but more particularly against their parents' values. This was an ideological revolution. **Charismatic** ideological leaders arose on every side to serve as role models. Young people adopted distinctive modes of dress to identify their ideological position. They joined communes, marched and demonstrated, went to teach-ins, sit-ins, and went to Woodstock. The sense of belonging to a group who shared the same values was electrifying. The 1960s, more than any other time in recent memory, was an era in which your ideology was your identity. What you believed in really seemed to matter. In fact, you were what you believed in. Erikson understood this, and young people felt that Erikson also understood them in a way that perhaps their parents and other elders did not. Erikson even helped these young people to understand themselves (although they did not want it known that there was anything they did not understand). He also helped parents to understand their children. In short, Erikson was relevant at precisely the moment when the cry for relevance was first voiced—in the 1960s.

Con #1: This key idea, though relevant, is not practical. Relevant though Erikson was to the ideological soul-searching of young people in the 1960s, his ideas about identity and ideology, and in fact his entire theory, are not particularly practical for the treatment of individual cases. To put it another way, there is no school of Eriksonian therapists. Erikson himself spent years offering therapy to adolescents at the Austen Riggs Foundation. Some of his insights into identity crises must have been formed during that period. But though other **neo-Freudian** therapists have trained groups of disciples to practice their brands of therapy and founded organizations to promote their methods—The William Alanson White Foundation, which promotes Harry Stack Sullivan's interpersonal theory of psychiatry, is a case in point—Erikson has done nothing of that sort. He has trained a number of individual therapists, of course, but there is no school of Eriksonian identity-and-ideology therapy. Perhaps this is because Erikson was never very interested in organizing and founding things. The more likely reason, however, is that what Erikson thought and wrote about proved more useful to psychohistorians and social policy makers than to therapists. Erikson's theories are just that—theories. And, unlike Freud's, they may be destined to remain theories, mere academic exercises with little or no practical application. Perhaps Erikson envisions his work as basic research, whose concrete applications will have to be figured out later by someone else. But what if that someone else never comes along? In any case, so far Erikson has not written any "cookbook" with his recipes for treating patients in the throes of an identity crisis. His theories about identity and ideology remain an academic exercise—spectacular, captivating, and even persuasive, but an academic exercise nonetheless.

Con #2: This key idea is essentially deterministic.   Despite his humanistic sympathies, Erikson is still a Freudian. As a neo-Freudian and an ego psychologist, he is a lot closer to his mentor than a great many others are. Erikson's first five crises in the life cycle nicely parallel Freud's first five psychosexual stages, with the identity crisis corresponding to Freud's genital stage. Erikson does not contradict anything Freud said about these stages; he merely shifts the emphasis a bit. Where Freud emphasized the role of the sexual instincts almost exclusively, Erikson slightly de-emphasizes these instincts in favor of socio-cultural factors. Yet the instincts remain powerful in Erikson's theory; in fact, since Erikson remains fundamentally Freudian, he is susceptible to all the criticisms that are leveled against the Master. While less deterministic than Freud, Erikson is still far more deterministic than the humanistic psychologists whose views he is often regarded as sharing. His commitment to instinctual sexual motivation becomes evident when he classifies Martin Luther as an anal character. Erikson says that Luther's famous "revelation in the tower," which produced the doctrine of justification-by-faith-alone, occurred in the midst of a particularly gratifying bowel movement (Erikson, 1958).

Con #3: This key idea rests upon little empirical research.   Finally, Erikson's ideas about identity and ideology are derived solely from naturalistic and clinical observation, and from philosophical speculation. His theories are supported by very little of what most psychologists would consider "hard" data. Inspired by Erikson's theory, half a dozen psychologists have constructed paper-and-pencil tests or interview formats to measure where people stand between the poles of identity and identity diffusion. By administering such tests to a wide range of subjects, from grade-schoolers to adults, these psychologists established rather conclusively that identity concerns first arise during adolescence and peak during the college years. After college, people tend to consolidate whatever identity they have committed themselves to, rather than continuing to explore alternatives (Waterman, 1982). Hence there is some empirical evidence for the existence of the adolescent identity crisis. Most of this research assumes, though, that identity is a matter of choosing a vocation and wrestling with questions of religious and political ideology. The relationship between identity and ideology has more often been taken for granted than tested through research.

Perhaps the closest researchers have come to establishing a link between identity and ideology was a series of three studies on college students. These studies found a positive correlation between moral development and progress toward ego identity. Students who had passed through an identity crisis and committed themselves to a specific identity tended strongly to reach the highest stage on Kohlberg's scale of moral development (Waterman, 1982). Unfortunately, because the research method was not developmental—the tests were given at only one point in time—it was impossible to tell whether moral development facilitates the establishment of identity, or vice versa. This fault was overcome by a **longitudinal** study of college students, which demonstrated that freshmen who scored higher than their peers on "The Cultural Sophistication Scale" were more likely to achieve identity by the time they became seniors (Waterman, 1982). The Cultural Sophistication Scale measures a person's interest in art, music, literature, foreign films, and related areas—not ideology per se, but as close as any of this research comes to defining it! Waterman speculates that the connection between cultural interests and identity formation may not be direct. Instead, some underlying factor, such as greater curiosity or a stronger drive to explore, might promote both diverse cultural interests and consideration of alternative identities (Waterman, 1982). Perhaps so, but bear in mind that even this longitudinal research has not produced any empirical evidence for a causal relationship between cultural interests and identity formation. (The connection between cultural interests and identity, and especially the correlation of moral development with identity formation, once again brings Mahatma Gandhi to mind. When his identity finally crystallized, Gandhi undoubtedly had reached the very highest level of moral development.)

In sum, there is a body of empirical research that is at least obliquely related to Erikson's key idea, but (1) none of it has been done by Erikson himself; (2) none of it directly tests the validity of the key idea as Erikson defined it; and (3) most of it employs methodology that is far from ideal. This failure to support Erikson's theory with empirical research must be counted as a con for his key idea of identity, and the relationship between identity and ideology.

CHAPTER SUMMARY

Erikson's key idea is the concept of identity, including the relationship between ideology and identity. Identity refers to the internal sense of sameness and continuity we have. This is closely related to our sense of self, or ego; but it refers specifically to that feeling that we have an internal core that provides continuity throughout the hours and days and years of our lives, and that remains our true selves despite all of our outward changes and varying roles. This core is precisely what is lost in neurotic amnesia.

1.   Erikson's obsession with the topic of identity derives from his personal experience. As a child, Erikson often felt that he did not belong. He did not look anything like the rest of his family: He was a Jew in anti-semitic Germany, yet looked like the ideal Nordic type. This perplexing situation came about because Erikson's mother hid the fact that his biological father had deserted her, and that the man Erikson considered his father was really his stepfather. Small wonder that Erik was confused about who he was. Meeting Freud helped Erikson resolve his identity crisis and discover his vocation.

2.   The sense of identity begins to develop very early in childhood, but it is confronted at adolescence with a number of formidable challenges: sudden changes in the body's outward appearance and its inner "feel" (the emergence of adult sexuality); pressures from society to prepare for choosing a mate; and pressures from society to choose and prepare for a vocation.

3.   Fortunately, society also provides some resources to meet these challenges. One of these resources is clothing. You are what you wear. Clothes announce your identity and also indicate who, or what, you belong to. By trying on different clothes, you can try out different identities.

4.   Another resource is role models. You can identify with, and appropriate, the identities of people you know, public figures you encounter through the media, and even historical or fictional characters. Fan clubs are a conspicuous example of this process.

5.   Ideologies are still another resource. You are what you believe in. Ideologies are identities: They give purpose and direction to life; provide something to have faith in, and to be faithful to; and confer a sense that you belong to a group of like-minded believers. Adolescence is the prime time for ideological conversions.

6.   Erikson produced extensive studies of the role of identity and ideology in the lives of a number of historical figures, almost singlehandedly launching the modern discipline of psychohistory. *Gandhi's Truth* (1969) demonstrates all of Erikson's themes. Erikson shows that Gandhi not only forged his own identity with his ideology of satyagraha, but held up this ideological identity as a model for his associates, and indeed for all of India. Gandhi demonstrated the link between clothing and identity when he abandoned European dress and donned his famous shawl and loincloth. He illustrated the theme of identification with role models when he appropriated aspects of the identity of his personal guru, Rajchandra, and of two writers who influenced his thinking, John Ruskin and Leo Tolstoy. The theme of identity as ideology is pervasive in Erikson's treatment of Gandhi. This is because Gandhi's ideology of *satyagraha*—militant non-violence—

was an acted out ideology. Gandhi did not just preach it, he lived it. And he demonstrated his unswerving commitment to this ideology again and again, by willingly enduring long imprisonment, undertaking seventeen fasts-to-the-death, and repeatedly risking personal injury and death in other contexts as well. Ideology is also acted out in ritual, and Gandhi had a penchant for ritual: celibacy, vegetarianism, non-violence, manual labor, spinning and wearing of homespun garments. Gandhi *was* his ideology.

7. Pro #1:   Erikson's key idea is part of a humanistic theory of personality. His image of human nature is less derogatory than Freud's. As an ego psychologist, Erikson seems to leave room for free will, and he places less emphasis than Freud on biological determinants of behavior, stressing instead social and cultural factors. Hence Erikson's viewpoint is less fatalistic; it is optimistic about the chances for improving the human condition.

Pro #2: Erikson's key idea of identity, and the relationship between identity and ideology, was strikingly relevant during the 1960s and early 1970s, when his career reached its zenith. That era more than any other in recent memory was a time when it mattered desperately what you believed, because your ideology was thought to be your identity.

Con #1: Though Erikson's key idea is relevant, it is not practical. He has not developed a system of psychotherapy based on this idea, nor has he trained a body of disciples to carry on his work. Erikson's work is for the most part an academic exercise, theoretical and with only the vaguest practical applicability.

Con #2: Humanistic sentiments notwithstanding, Erikson is a Freudian through and through; his theory is essentially deterministic, with very little room for free will.

Con #3: Erikson's ideas about identity and ideology depend exclusively upon philosophical speculation, and clinical and naturalistic observation. He has conducted no empirical research on the topic. Other psychologists have compiled a small body of research on identity in recent years, but none of this research bears directly on the role of ideology in identity formation. Hence there is no empirical support for Erikson's key idea, which therefore remains speculative at best.

REFERENCES

Erikson, E. H. (1958). *Young man Luther: A study in psychoanalysis and history.* New York: W. W. Norton.

Erikson, E. H. (1968). *Identity: Youth and crisis.* New York: W. W. Norton.

Erikson, E. H. (1969). *Gandhi's truth: On the origins of militant non-violence.* New York: W. W. Norton.

Erikson, E. H. (1975). *Life history and the historical moment.* New York: W. W. Norton

Erikson, E. H. (1982). *The life cycle completed.* New York: W. W. Norton.

Freud, S. (1957). Leonardo DaVinci and a memory of his childhood. In J. Strachey (Ed. and Trans.), *The standard edition of the complete psychological works of Sigmund Freud* (Vol. 11, 59–137). London: Hogarth Press. (Original work published 1910)

Waterman, A. S. (1982). Identity development from adolescence to adulthood: An extension of theory and a review of research. *Developmental Psychology, 18,* 341–358.

6/Henry A. Murray

A Biographical Sketch

Henry Murray was born in New York City in 1893, the middle child in a very well-to-do family. He had an older sister and a younger brother. He seems to have enjoyed all the cultural advantages of his privileged position: During his childhood and adolescence, he was taken four times on extensive tours of Europe; the family summered regularly at the seaside on Long Island; and when it came time for him to go to school, he was sent off to Groton, one of the elite New England prep schools.

It was a short step from Groton to Harvard. As an undergraduate at Harvard, Murray majored in history. He not only showed no interest in psychology but earned below-average grades in college. He later attributed his poor academic performance to his preoccupation with athletics—he played football, rowed, and boxed. He described this love of sport, in turn, as an effort to compensate for a visual handicap acquired early in childhood, when an operation to correct his crossed eyes left him slightly wall-eyed. Murray's visual handicap also affected his self-confidence, causing him to stutter, and disrupted his eye-hand coordination.

Despite his low grade-point average and an undergraduate major in history, after graduating from Harvard, Murray was admitted to the Columbia College of Physicians and Surgeons. That admissions decision proved prophetic when Murray graduated first in his class in 1919. He was twenty-six and apparently committed to his vocational choice. He spent the next year completing an M.A. in biology at Columbia, after which he returned to Harvard as an instructor in physiology. After a short while, however, he bounced back to New York to do a two-year surgical internship at Presbyterian Hospital.

His only dilemma at this point seems to have been choosing between research and practice. He had already practiced in the hospital, and now he secured an appointment as a research assistant at the Rockefeller Institute for Medical Research. Here he performed embryological research on chicken eggs, signalling the beginnings of a lifelong interest in the processes of growth and development. During this same period, Murray took a leave of absence to study at Cambridge University in England, where he received a Ph.D. in biochemistry in 1927. He was now thirty-three years old and had two doctoral degrees, neither one in psychology or any of the other behavioral sciences.

Murray's serious interest in psychology actually began in 1923, when he came across a copy of Jung's just published book, *Psychological Types*. (Murray had registered for a psychology course during his undergraduate days at Harvard, but had walked out in boredom before the end of the second lecture). Now the time was more auspicious. He was becoming bored with chicken embryos, and Jung's book set him thinking about the great variations in human personality, and prepared the way for the momentous meeting of the two men several years later.

While studying in England, Murray took advantage of the Easter vacation to travel to Switzerland and spend three weeks with Jung in Zurich. The result was something akin to a religious conversion. Murray, the

laboratory scientist, was not conquered by abstract scientific data, but by the insight gained into his own personality. From Jung, Murray learned how his visual handicap and his stuttering were related. He also encountered the unconscious, which would become a prominent feature in his own personality theory. Jung was, he said, "the first full blooded, spherical—and Goethian, I would say—Intelligence I had ever met" (Murray, 1940, p. 153). For Murray "The great floodgates of the wonder-world swung open, and I saw things that my philosophy had never dreamt of" (Murray, 1940, p. 153) He left Zurich as a convert to depth psychology.

Murray had to spend a little more time "staring at chicken embryos," as he put it, but in 1927 he found the opportunity that would determine the path of his subsequent life. Once again, a shrewd judge of character saw potential in Henry Murray that was not evident from his professional credentials. Morton Prince, a renowned psychiatrist and founder of the *Journal of Abnormal Psychology*, invited Murray to become his assistant at the newly founded Harvard Psychological Clinic. At the age of thirty-three, without taking a single psychology course, Murray was suddenly a personality psychologist. A year later, Prince left the clinic and Murray became its director.

We will run through Murray's accomplishments at the Harvard Psychological Clinic later in this chapter. He remained there until World War II interrupted his work, producing the classic *Explorations in Personality* in 1938. In the mid 1930's he was instrumental in founding the Boston Psycho-analytic Society, where he himself was psychoanalyzed. During the War he worked for the Office of Strategic Services, directing a program for the selection and training of candidates for espionage and other secret and dangerous missions. After the War he returned to Harvard, set up the Harvard Psychological Clinic Annex, and continued to

teach and do personality research until 1962, when he officially retired. It was a retirement in name only, and he has continued to write and do research. At the time of this writing, Henry Murray still lives in Cambridge, Massachusetts, just a short walk from the Clinic he built, the place where he was finally able to practice his true vocation.

A PSYCHODYNAMIC THEORIST UNLIKE ALL OTHER PSYCHODYNAMIC THEORISTS

Henry Murray belongs in a class by himself. Perhaps he realized that himself when he coined the word *personologist* to refer to his profession. Most other psychologists who do what he does refer to themselves as personality theorists. Actually, Murray invented the term *personology* to designate the entire field of personality psychology, but somehow it never caught on widely. Murray is one of the very few who still call themselves personologists.

The TAT, or Thematic Apperception Test, is the thing that comes first to mind in connection with the name Henry Murray. If you know anything at all about Murray, it is probably that he devised the TAT. Actually, the TAT is a good illustration of Murray's unique and far-ranging concerns. Murray is a psychodynamic theorist: His personology is a theory of dynamics, that is to say, motivation. His famous list of **needs** and **press** (plural form) is a list of motives. *Press* are enviromental pressures that aid or hinder the gratification of people's needs. The TAT is designed to find out what needs and press are operating in the personality of the subject taking the test, and in what magnitude they are operating.

The TAT is a **projective test,** like the **Rorschach** inkblot test. You look at a series of ambiguous pictures, and you make up a story about each one. From your stories, the psychologist infers the presence of certain motives. But why doesn't he just ask you how strong your aggressive need is, instead of showing you, say, a picture of two people who might be interpreted either as wrestling or hugging? The answer is simple: He does not think you know this information. He does not think you are consciously aware of your true motives. In short, he thinks that the important motivational foundations of personality are unconscious. Only personality theorists who are strong believers in the importance of unconscious motivation use projective personality tests. Murray not only invented one of the most popular projective tests ever designed, but based much of his theory on data collected from it. This strong emphasis on unconscious motivation certainly places him in the psychodynamic camp.

Yet Murray's emphasis on personality assessment, on measuring personality with tests, is far more typical of the trait theorists. In fact, Murray became famous among psychologists for the work he did on psychological assessment for the Office of Strategic Services during World War II. Certainly, none of the other psychodynamic theorists we have considered devoted anything like the energy Murray did to the objective measurement of personality variables.

In some ways, Henry Murray is a very typical psychodynamic personality theorist. First, while traveling in Europe in 1927, he stopped into Jung's clinic and was captivated by what he learned there. Second, like Freud and most of his disciples, Murray had been to medical school and earned an M.D. Third, Murray was a charter member of the Boston Psychoanalytic Institute, one of many such organizations founded by loyal disciples of Freud in cities around the world, for the express purpose of training more loyal disciples and spreading the gospel according to Freud. To become a psychoanalyst, you must be psychoanalyzed yourself. Murray underwent a training analysis with Franz Alexander and Hans Sachs, both of whom were trained by Freud himself. Fourth, Murray uses Freud's concepts of id, ego, and superego in his own personality theory. (Murray's personality theory is more a theory of dynamics than a comprehensive theory. He is original when discussing dynamics; but when it comes to discussing structure and development, he relies heavily on Freud's concepts.) Finally, Murray is a typical psychodynamic personality theorist because he has always focused his attention on dynamics, especially unconscious dynamics.

But in other respects, Henry Murray is not at all a typical psychodynamic personality theorist. First of all, he was an academic researcher having only a limited clinical practice for a part of his career. The vast majority of psychodynamic theorists are primarily engaged in the private practice of psychotherapy; they sit in their offices all day, every day, talking to patients. Their life style is modeled on the physician's. They are not ordinarily associated with a college or university, but Murray is a professor. He has spent most of his life behind a lectern or in a psychological laboratory. Only for a few years, back in the 1930s, did he play the role of doctor by seeing patients. And even then, he saw them for only a few hours a week. Murray is also atypical for devoting some of his most productive efforts to the field of psychological assessment. Jung may have tinkered with a test for introversion-extroversion, and Hermann Rorschach may have tipped over his ink bottle, but no psychodynamic theorist has made research on personality assessment his trademark in the way that Murray has. Most of the psychodynamic theorists, taking their cue from Freud, have nothing to do with measuring and quantifying personality variables. Finally, Murray is often grouped not with psychodynamic theorists, but with humanistic psychologists. A recent book by Salvador Maddi and Paul Costa, entitled *Humanism in Personology* (1972), turns out to be about Allport, Maslow, and Murray.

The apparent contradictions in Murray's background, and in his personality theory, can be traced largely to one (according to him, fortuitous) event: an invitation from Morton Prince to join the staff of the newly founded Harvard Psychological Clinic. That was in 1926. When Prince left the clinic in 1929, Murray became director. By 1938 he and his staff had completed their monumental study of fifty individual men, publishing their findings in a work entitled, *Explorations in Personality.*

There had never been anything like the Harvard Psychological Clinic before. Because it was connected with an academic psychology department rather than a hospital, the clinic inevitably emphasized research. Though the clinic was obligated to provide therapy for its clients, its chief mission was to discover fundamental facts about personality. While Doctor Murray maintained his medical identity as a clinician, he created an entirely new identity in the field of psychology: the clinical research psychologist.

For most of the decade of the 1930s, Murray straddled the Charles River, with one foot in the academic world of Cambridge's Harvard University, and the other in the medical world of Boston's Psychoanalytic Institute. This formidable stunt largely accounts for the unique flavor of Murray's personology. His emphasis on dynamics, especially unconscious dynamics, reflects the influence of the psychoanalytic theories of Freud and Jung, although Murray also credits academic psychologists such as Harvard instinct theorist William McDougall, and Kurt Lewin, the dynamic field theorist. Murray's emphasis on development is also characteristically psychoanalytic, though even before he joined the Boston Psychoanalytic Institute he was convinced that Freud was correct in emphasizing developmental history as essential for understanding adult personality. This conviction was based on several years of research at the Rockefeller Institute, where Murray studied the growth of chicken embryos (just before he went to Harvard). In fact, before he became a psychologist, Henry Murray had published twenty-one articles on embryology and medicine. But it was from academic psychologists at Harvard that Murray first learned the techniques of personality testing and the methodology of experimental psychological research. The early work of Gordon Allport—his *Studies in Expressive Movement* (1933); the tests he devised for assessing personality in *A Study of Values* (1931), and for measuring the traits of ascendance and submission in *The A-S Reaction Study* (1928)—served as a model for Murray's explorations in personality at the Harvard Psychological Clinic.

By straddling the Charles River, Murray managed to synthesize the views of two traditional adversaries. Today we take that synthesis for granted; but if it had not been for Henry Murray and the Harvard Psychological Clinic, that synthesis might have been much slower in coming about—and, if it had not been for the Harvard Psychological Clinic, Henry Murray's personology might not exist for us today.

THE STUDY OF LIVES

In 1979, forty years after the publication of *Explorations in Personality,* Radcliffe College honored him by establishing the Henry A. Murray Research Center for the Study of Lives. The center's name was highly appropriate, since the *study of lives* was Henry Murray's chief concern. He did not study stimuli and responses, isolated personality traits, or disembodied psyches. Henry Murray studied lives—whole, real lives in the process of being lived.

One of the first decisions psychologists at the Harvard Psychological Clinic made was to study the whole person. That meant chronicling the person's life history, since "the history of the personality *is* the personality" (Murray, 1938, p.604). Every subject who entered the clinic was required, as one of his first tasks, to write an autobiographical statement. Subsequent interviews probed further into recollections of important events in the subject's life. In fact, a whole battery of tests was administered to reactivate memories of early childhood—for example, the TAT pictures most subjects interpreted as representing children interacting with parents. When the clinic team had compiled all its data on a particular subject, one psychologist was appointed the subject's biographer and charged with the task of writing the subject's "psychograph," a kind of psychological biography.

Personology ideally aims to produce a type of abstract biography. Murray uses the analogy of a musical score to explain this. Personologists, he says, hope to develop a system of shorthand notation—not musical notes on a staff, of course, but some system of abstract symbols to designate the events in a person's life. Murray imagines that such a notational system for the study of lives might even include multiple staffs, or lines. The top line, for example, might contain appropriate symbols for the significant environmental forces in the person's life history. A second line might depict the individual's subjective impressions of important environmental events. A third line could be used to chart overt behavior or action; a fourth, emotions and sentiments; and a fifth, thoughts and fantasies. The objective would be to reduce lives to some manageable number of data (while maintaining a view of the whole life), so that lives could be more easily compared with each other in an effort to discover some universal principles.

Explorations in Personality contains some symbols and abbreviations—the rudiments of a system of a life-history notation—but Murray knew even then that human personality is too complex ever to be reduced to such an abstract form. Perhaps this *could* be done if present technological limitations were overcome. But even then, Murray feels something would inevitably be lost. Not that personologists should not aim for this goal—they should, because even if their efforts fall short, the exercise itself will focus their attention on significant events and variables in individual lives.

At the same time, however, Murray urges personologists to sharpen their literary skills and learn to write biographies that communicate what an abstract system of notation cannot: the essence of a unique flesh-and-blood character. Murray observes that even in the physical sciences, the greatest theorists usually have a flair for writing well and are consequently able to transmit their ideas persuasively. Personologists, he advises, can profit greatly by observing how a competent novelist goes about constructing a character sketch and, as an antidote for professional conceit, by trying themselves to duplicate the piece.

This is advice born of experience: Henry Murray has had a lifelong avocation as a literary critic, especially on the writings of Herman Melville. *Endeavors in Psychology: Selections from the Personology of Henry A. Murray* (1981), edited by Edwin Shneidman, is presumably intended as a representative sample of Murray's writings. The book contains about 600 pages, of which more than 100 are devoted to Murray's literary criticism. There is "In Nomine Diaboli," Murray's archetypal analysis of Captain Ahab, the tragic hero of *Moby Dick*. Murray's lengthy introduction to the 1949 edition of *Pierre*, "the most openly psychological" of Melville's novels, is reprinted in its entirety. Then, too, we are offered his short piece on Melville's *Bartleby the Scrivener*, as well as his analysis of the life of Melville himself ("Dead to the World: The Passions of Herman Melville"). No other personality theorist has devoted so much energy to studying the lives of fictional characters and their authors.

Thanks to Murray, the study of lives has become a tradition at Harvard. Robert White—one of Murray's graduate students, a collaborator on *Explorations in Personality*, and Murray's successor as director of the Harvard Psychological Clinic—has carried on this tradition with great distinction. White's engagingly written book, *Lives in Progress*, fulfills one of the most precious aims of Murray's research program: It assesses subjects over a long period of time, in each of the seasons of their lives.

When it first appeared in 1952, *Lives in Progress* simply chronicled the lives of three Harvard students from birth through their early twenties (college graduation). The span of life it studied was no larger than in the fifty cases that provided the data for *Explorations*, although White's book is much less technical, and far more readable, than Murray's. The longitudinal dimension was not introduced until White invited his three subjects back to the clinic years later, when they were approaching middle age. They were once again interviewed and tested with the same procedures (well-established by then), and the new results were incorporated in an updated, second edition of *Lives in Progress*. More recently, a third edition followed our familiar friends through their fiftieth birthdays (White, 1975).

We should not be surprised to learn that Robert White, like Henry Murray, was an undergraduate major in history. In fact, White taught history at the University of Maine before he studied with Murray. Both men's background in history proved extremely useful: The Harvard Psychological Clinic's approach to the study of lives emphasized the historical dimension of personality development.

In sum, Henry Murray and his colleagues approached the study of lives by taking a long look at a few cases. The fifty subjects referred to in

Explorations were each seen for about thirty-five hours at the clinic — not as long as the several hundred hours required for a complete psychoanalysis, but much longer than the hour or two of group testing that forms the data base of most trait theories. The ideal aim of Murray's approach is to re-examine subjects at regular intervals throughout their lives, in order to produce a comprehensive developmental case history of each individual from the moment of birth right up to the present day.

Because it is desirable to examine each life so thoroughly, only a limited number of lives can be studied. This raises the possibility of sample bias. (You will recall that Freud's theory has been accused of being biased because his patients were almost exclusively bourgeois female hysterics.) While Murray recognizes the danger of bias in studying a relatively few cases, he has adopted at least two strategies for counteracting bias. One of these strategies is the diagnostic council—those few life studies are examined not only by one observer, but by a whole diagnostic team using an arsenal of diagnostic instruments. At the very least, this should compensate for any bias within individual observers, especially if, as Murray suggests, the diagnostic team represents a variety of theoretical viewpoints. But beyond that, the team approach increases the chance of detecting sample bias. In short, Murray's strategy for the study of lives requires that a diagnostic team take a long look at a few cases.

Murray's second strategy for avoiding a biased sample in his few cases is to select ordinary, "normal" people as subjects. *Explorations* is based on the study of fifty young men who applied not to the clinic (for psychological help), but to the student employment office for part-time work. They were paid subjects, not patients. And though White's *Lives in Progress* studies three students who originally came to the clinic as patients needing help with their problems, we never think of them as anything other than normal young people, struggling with many of the same problems of growing up that most of us have. More specifically, then, Murray's strategy for the study of lives requires that a diagnostic team take a long look at a few *normal* cases.

There is one more salient feature in Murray's approach to the study of lives. That long look at a few cases, if it is worth anything, must also be a *deep* look, a look beneath the surface. One reason for seeing subjects for so many hours, and over a long period of time, is to allow them to feel comfortable at the clinic and to develop a rapport with the staff. Only then can they be expected to volunteer the intimate details of their life histories. Another way in which the clinic pursued its goal of taking "a deep look" was by using at least half a dozen projective assessment techniques, including, of course, the newly devised TAT. The deep look, as Murray conceives it, includes studying unconscious motives and past events whose memory has been repressed. The resulting case histories include a liberal dose of interpretation in the psychoanalytic tradition. Yet Murray's brand of psychoanalysis is **eclectic,** borrowing almost as readily from Jung as from Freud, and occasionally applying the insights of Alfred Adler. All in all, though,

Murray's approach involves less interpretation in terms of unconscious dynamics, and more attention to the manifest personality, than one finds in the typical psychoanalytic case history. The result, he says, is a much more "imaginable social animal" (Murray, 1938, p. 32). He admits that psychoanalysis achieves more depth than his approach; but he seems to feel that if you must choose between a long look and a deep look, the long look is preferable. The ideal, however, is a balance between the two.

The tradition Henry Murray established for the study of lives, therefore, involves assembling a multidisciplinary team of behavioral scientists to take a long and deep look at a small number of ordinary people. No other approach, according to Murray, promises to contribute as much to our understanding of human personality.

THE KEY IDEA
THEMES IN YOUR LIFE STORY

Most personality textbooks leave the impression that Henry Murray's key idea was his need-press theory of motivation, especially his list of fifteen or twenty needs. That is certainly one of his principle ideas, and it has been highly influential (see Box: The Need-Press Theory of Motivation). Yet the notion that we have aggressive urges, or desires for achievement, and that these are either gratified or frustrated by circumstances in the environment, is not Murray's most distinctive idea. In fact, Murray's thinking here is in line with the majority of personality theorists, which may explain why this part of his personology has been so readily appropriated by other personality psychologists, who blithely ignore the rest of his system. The concepts of need and press are not the most comprehensive key to Murray's personological system either. The real key to Murray's personality theory, the idea that bears his unique stamp, is the notion that your personality *is* the themes running through your life story. The reason for studying lives, then, is to analyze the plot and extract the dominant themes.

Murray's notion of personality as the themes running through your life story reminds us that the word *personality* was originally borrowed from the theater. The *persona* was the mask actors wore in Greek plays to indicate which role they were playing. Hence the concept of role is implicit in our notion of personality. "All the world's a stage," as Shakespeare so aptly observed, "and all the men and women merely players." Playing roles is not confined to the theater. We all play roles, but we do not play the same role all of the time. We switch masks, playing different roles in different situations. You may play child to your parents, sympathetic confidant to your friend, and knowledgeable expert when you are trying to sell merchandise to a customer—all in the same day. Yet, through all these different roles that you play, there runs some unifying theme. This under-lying theme, which remains constant no matter how many masks are worn over it, is your true personality.

Murray's key idea says that the personologist's job is to take a long, deep look at an individual's life story in order to discover the most basic themes in that story—like a literary critic who looks at a novel and tries to extract the main features of its plot.

No wonder Murray studied personalities by having people tell him stories. He shows you twenty TAT pictures, for example, and you tell him twenty stories. What does he look for in these stories? Themes! That is why his test is called the *Thematic* Apperception Test, and that is why he wants twenty stories—so there will be an opportunity for recurrent themes to stand out. Though Murray typically scores TAT stories by estimating the intensity of the needs and environmental press experienced by the stories' heroes, that is not his ultimate goal. It may be interesting, he says, "to know that a given subject's heroes manifest, let us say, an unusual amount of anxiety, passivity and abasement, or that their environments are peopled with many threatening, domineering figures" (Murray, 1943, p. 13); but at some time, the interpreter must

> put reality together again; and he does this by taking each unusually high need in turn and noting the press with which it is most commonly combined in the stories; after which he observes with which needs and emotions the unusually high press most often interact. In this way the interpreter will obtain a list of the most prevalent themas (need-press combinations), to which he will add any other themas, which, though not frequent enough to result in a high total score for the need or press involved, seem significant for one reason or another—uniqueness, vividness, intensity, explanatory value (Murray, 1943. p. 13).

The secondary role of the needs and press is evident from the fact that a TAT interpreter can omit scoring them altogether.

> It is also possible to make an over-all thematic analysis without scoring the separate variables. Here it is a matter of viewing each story as a whole and picking out the major and minor themes, the plot and sub-plots. The question is: what issues, conflicts or dilemmas are of the greatest concern to the author? There are common themes, for example, centering round problems of achievement, rivalry, love, deprivation, coercion and restraint, offense and punishment, conflict of desires, exploration, war and so forth (Murray, 1943, p. 13).

Since Murray believes that personality consists essentially of the themes running through an individual's life story, it makes sense to study the personality by eliciting a few short stories from the "Author" and examining the themes in them. The Thematic Apperception Test is the method-

ℤ THE NEED-PRESS THEORY OF MOTIVATION

Murray's theory of motivation is truly inter-actional, because it views behavior as the product of internal needs interacting with external press. "A need is a construct (a convenient fiction or hypothetical concept) which stands for a force . . . in the brain region, a force which organizes perception, apperception, intellection, conation and action in such a way as to transform in a certain direction an existing unsatisfying situation" (Murray, 1938, pp. 123–124). *Press* refers to the power that objects (including persons) in the environment have to harm or benefit a person. *Alpha press* refers to the objective potential for harm or benefit; *beta press* refers to that potential as subjectively perceived by the person. Behavior may be instigated by needs—hunger (need for food) initiates a trip to the refrigerator—but press may block gratification: the refrigerator is empty. Or press may precipitate behavior by triggering a need: a cold blast of air triggers your need for cold avoidance and you proceed to close the window.

Needs can be classified as viscerogenic or psychogenic. Viscerogenic needs include those for air, water, food, sensory stimulation, sex, excretion, and avoidance of heat, cold, noxious stimuli, and physical harm. More famous, although not necessarily more important in directing behavior, is Murray's list of psychogenic needs (Murray, 1938, pp. 80–83, 746–750):

n Abasement: to surrender; to comply and accept punishment.
n Achievement: to overcome obstacles.
n Affiliation: to form friendships and associations.
n Aggression: to assault or injure; to belittle a person.
n Autonomy: to resist influence; to strive for independence.
n Counteraction: proudly to overcome defeat by restriving.
n Deference: to admire and willingly follow a leader.
n Defendance: to defend oneself against blame or belittlement.
n Dominance: to influence or control others.
n Exhibition: to attract attention to one's person.

ological consequence of Murray's key idea that personality is the themes running through one's life story.

This key idea has an important theoretical consequence. If personality is the themes running through one's life story, then the units of personality must be *events*, not static structures such as traits or stimulus-response *repertoires*, or even drives. In answer to the structural question; What is the personality made of, Murray would answer: *events*. This means that personality is not something fixed and static, but a series of happenings.

The difference between Murray's model of personality and the models of most other theorists is like the difference between painting and music. A painting exists outside of time and change, in the sense that it communicates its message to the viewer all at once. Its various levels of mean-n Harmavoidance: to avoid pain, physical injury, illness, death.

n Infavoidance: to avoid failure, shame, humiliation, ridicule.

n Nurturance: to nourish, aid or protect a helpless other.

n Order: to arrange, organize, put away objects; to be tidy.

n Play: to relax; amuse oneself; seek diversion and entertainment.

n Rejection: to snub, ignore or exclude another.

n Sentience: to seek and enjoy sensuous impressions.

n Sex: to form and further an erotic relationship; to have sex.

n Succorance: to seek aid, protection or sympathy.

n Understanding: to analyze experience; to synthesize ideas.

Even though this list of needs is not intended to be exhaustive, it is far more difficult to come up with a similar list of press because environmental situations can vary so widely. Consequently, the following list of press (Murray, 1938, pp. 299–314) is only a sampling of the many possibilities:

p Danger: physical dangers arising from natural causes.

p Lack: not having something one wants.

p Rejection: being spurned and treated with emotional unconcern.

p Rival: the presence of someone who competes for affection, goods, recognition.

p Aggression: verbal or physical abuse; punishment.

p Nurturance: cherishing affection; sympathy; leniency; gifts.

p Deference: praise; recognition; honors.

p Affiliation: friendship; companionship.

p Illness: any kind of sickness, brief or prolonged.

p Inferiority: being below average physically, socially, or intellectually.

Needs and press interact to produce behavioral episodes. A *thema* is precisely such a need-press combination.

---

ing are all present at the same time. When you look at a painting, you see "the whole picture" in one instant. Not so with a piece of music, because music exists in time. According to Murray, music, like personality, has "duration." "Time is an integral element, not only of every pattern of processes, but of every single process in every pattern. Thus everything with which the psychologist deals has *duration*" (Murray & Kluckhohn, 1953/1981, p. 210). True, music has synchronous (occurring at the same time) features such as the harmony of its chords—what musicians call "vertical structure"—but you cannot really experience music unless you hear these chords played as part of some organized sequence or progression. Music is a series of acoustical events: Things happen in music; there is change and development. You cannot hear a symphony all at once,

in a single instant; you must take time to listen to it. You can only apprehend its meaning as its melodic themes unfold, develop and interact.
Human personality is no different. While the aim of most personality
theorists is to paint a portrait of human nature, the goal of Murray's personology is to study lives in much the same manner that a musicologist
studies a symphony.

Musicologists, of course, have developed a special vocabulary for referring to the things that happen in a symphony: movements, transpositions,
melodic inversions, and so forth. Because few other personality theorists
have taken the temporal, historical nature of personality so seriously,
Murray has had to invent a whole new set of concepts to refer to aspects of
events. This helps to explain why Murray's personality theory contains so
many unfamiliar terms, terms that no other theory employs. Though events
are fleeting and insubstantial by nature, they are not necessarily difficult to
conceptualize. The problem is that we are not used to hearing psychologists
speak about such things.

Yet describing events is part of our ordinary experience. Consider
Murray's use of the term **serial**. A serial, in the language of Murray's
theory, refers to a sequence of biographical events that are separated in
time, but still belong together because they are directed toward the same
goal. Our lives are full of ongoing serials: taking guitar lessons; working
weekends at the supermarket; being involved in a romantic relationship.
These events may not occur in an unbroken sequence, but they make the most
sense when viewed as elements in a single, related series. That explains
why a television sitcom can show you just one aspect of its hero's life—
Barney Miller at the station house; Lucy in her apartment—and still give
you the impression of a real, three-dimensional character. What you are
seeing is one serial in that character's life, which is why we call this kind of
program a television *series*, or *serial*. In fact, when Murray talks about
"serials," "*serial programs*," and "schedules," we are tempted to think of
"As the World Turns," "Days of Our Lives," or some other televison or
radio soap opera. It may seem trite to say that personality is like a soap
opera, but it is not far from the truth.

A serial conveys a plausible impression of a character's personality
because the serial has a certain unity and consistency—it is held together
by a single theme—(which is what makes it a serial in the first place). The
simplest, shortest events, which Murray calls **episodes**, and the somewhat
longer transactions that he calls **proceedings** combine over time to form a
serial, precisely because the same theme runs through all these events. The
result is what Murray calls a **serial thema.**

Murray views human beings as **proactive,** not just reactive. By this he
means that events do not just happen to people; people have something to
do with making them happen. His term **serial program,** for example, refers
to the planning activity that largely determines the direction of events in
our lives. A series of guitar lessons does not just happen to us; we arrange
that serial with a certain goal in mind. To accomplish that goal, we have to

organize our time, perhaps foregoing some of the other things we would like to do. Murray calls this planning activity **scheduling.**

The proactive and reactive causes of events correspond to Murray's concepts of *need* and *press.* Turning on the TV again, we can follow the serial of Hawkeye Pierce, Chief Surgeon of M.A.S.H. 4077. Hawkeye seems to be a mixture of knight in shining armor and merry prankster. He ends up in the operating room partly because he wants to, and partly because he has to—partly out of need, and partly as a result of press. He wanted to be a doctor and repair broken bodies; he had a *need* for that. But he did not want to do it in Korea in the middle of a war; that was a consequence of the draft, a particularly intrusive environmental pressure, or *press,* as Murray would call it. Episodes unfold as they do because of the interaction between personal needs and environmental press. Sometimes the roll of personal needs is paramount; on other occasions environmental press seem to be the major influence. But in every event, both things interact.

Themes may be thought of as recurrent interactions of needs and press. The theme of Hawkeye's serial is the interaction between his need to use his medical skills to save lives, and the press of the environment to aid him in that mission (as when a local peddler constructs a desperately needed vascular clamp) or to frustrate his aims (as when a patient he has saved is taken away to be interrogated as a spy and presumably shot). According to Murray (1938, p. 42),

> the simplest formula for a period of complex behavior is a particular press-need combination. Such a combination may be called a *thema.* A *thema* may be defined as the dynamical structure of a simple *episode,* a single creature-environment interaction. In other words, the endurance of a certain kind of *press* in conjunction with a certain kind of *need* defines the duration of a single *episode,* the latter being a convenient molar unit for psychology to handle. Simple episodes (each with a simple thema) may relatedly succeed each other to constitute a *complex episode* (with its *complex thema*). The biography of a man may be portrayed abstractly as an historic route of themas (*cf.* a musical score).

If we pull this all together, and try, appropriately enough to identify the theme running through all of Murray's writings—his key idea—here is what we find. The history of the personality *is* the personality. That history is a sequence of events. The personologist may choose to observe events of very short duration (episodes), events of longer duration (proceedings), or sequences of related events (serials). The latter are likely to be most revealing, because what holds the serial together and makes it a serial is the common theme running through it. This theme is a series of interactions between a persistent and recurring need in the individual, and a repeated press in the environment. When personologists examine a person's entire life history, they find that certain types of need-press interactions (themas) happen again and again. To check the validity of themas they identify, personologists employ a number of methods. They can check their impressions against the impressions of colleagues who have also studied the subject. They can give the subject various projective tests and see if the same themes emerge. Dreams, too, may reveal the same themes. Or they can try to infer the occurrence of certain childhood experiences and then check with the subject to see if these events did in fact occur. Using the same method, they can predict future events in the subject's life—much as one anticipates the ending of a story—and see how things really turn out. If the data from all these methods point in the same direction, the personologist can safely conclude that the major themes in the subject's life story have been correctly identified. Furthermore, the personologist can safely conclude that these themes, taken together, constitute an abstract representation of the subject's personality. The basic assumption, once again, is that the personality *is* major themes running through a person's life story.

PROS and CONS

Pro #1: This key idea is developmental.   The idea that your personality consists of the major themes that run through your life story results in a personality theory that is strongly developmental in its emphasis. The theory relies on methods that are longitudinal, rather than cross-sectional. The developmental emphasis of the theory is a pro, for several reasons. In the first place, developmental approaches have become enormously popular in the whole field of psychology (not just in personality psychology) during the last decade or so. If anything, that popularity seems to be increasing. The popularity of this approach among psychologists has been transmitted to psychology students and the lay public. It all began with the popular "discovery" of Piaget in the late 1960s, a claim you can easily verify for yourself. Look through the most widely used introductory psychology textbooks from the middle 1960s. In most cases, Jean Piaget is not mentioned at all in these books—despite the fact that Piaget himself had been turning out books at the rate of almost one a year since about 1930. His name does not even appear in the indexes of some of these books. Today Piaget rates a full chapter in some introductory textbooks, and at least half a chapter in most others. Piaget's name has become synonymous with developmental psychology. As Piaget's fame has spread, so has the developmental, longitudinal approach to psychological questions. More and more psychologists have come to recognize that many of their questions can best be answered by studying individuals as they grow and change throughout the entire span of life. Murray and his colleagues at the Harvard Psychological Clinic knew this forty or fifty years ago. In fact, Murray's 1938 *Explorations in Personality* cites Jean Piaget. In short, Murray's key idea—that personality consists of the themes running through your life—fits in with the current emphasis on developmental approaches. That is a definite plus.

Another advantage of this idea is the strong appeal it makes to our common sense. The idea may be fairly new to psychologists, but the average person has always known that the people you understand best are the ones you have known all their lives. It is plain common sense that the longer you know a person, the better you know that person. True, it also helps to know the person intimately, in depth—to hear the person's deepest secrets, hopes, dreams and fears—but nothing can replace knowing a person from birth for giving you an understanding of the person's personality.

Pro #2: This key idea is truly dynamic.   Murray's theory is dynamic in the most fundamental sense. Freud's, Jung's, and Erikson's theories are all *called* dynamic because they place such great emphasis on unconscious motivation—they regard the contents of the mind as active. But when Freud and his followers analyze those unconscious dynamics they produce something analogous to the freeze-frame or stop-action on your video recorder, rather than the flow of action we see in a movie. Freud stops that action because he wants to take a closer look at the forces that contribute to it. Murray does this, too, when he begins measuring needs and press; the difference between the two is not absolute, but rather one of emphasis. Nevertheless, reading Freud is like watching a succession of still pictures from a movie, while reading Murray is more like watching the film roll. This is because Murray, in the final analysis, is interested in extracting actual themes from a life story, whereas Freud is more concerned with uncovering the hidden, internal psychic forces (needs, drives, instincts) behind actions that are already completed. Freud describes permanent entities that cause change, while Murray describes the process of change itself. Murray seriously believes that personality is dynamic, always changing and growing. If personality is a story, then it must be described with concepts that convey the change and flow of events, dynamic concepts such as thema.

Pro #3: This key idea produces an interactional theory.   The concept of thema as a need-press combination, a creature-environment interaction, produces a theory in which behavior is equally influenced by internal dispositions and external, situational circumstances. Social stimuli are as important in guiding our actions as are instinctual urges. The resulting personality theory is more balanced than that of Freud, who has been justifiably criticized for not paying sufficient attention to the social and cultural determinants of behavior.

But even more relevant today, Murray's concept of themas as need-press interactions offers a solution to the trait-versus-situational-variables controversy that plagued personality psychologists during the 1970s. Perhaps that is why the recent revival of interest in the personology of Henry Murray has coincided with the "discovery" of interactionism by such trend setters in personality psychology as Walter Mischel. Murray himself discovered interactionism—the new buzz-word of the 1980s—fifty years ago. At that time Murray was probably out to modify Freud's one-sided emphasis on internal dynamics, but Murray's theory is relevant today as an alternative to the behaviorists' preoccupation with environmental stimuli in recent decades. Seymour Epstein (1979) offers this analysis of what he calls "the dark ages" of personality psychology—the years between the publication of *Explorations in Personality* and the present:

> Instead of following Murray's example of studying individuals in breadth and depth, we have pursued a narrow vision of science, one in which method had become more important than substance. As a result, our journals are filled with studies describing laboratory manipulations of variables of little significance to the people in the experiments. Not surprisingly, the yield has been low, and, as a result, it has become scientifically fashionable to be nihilistic, to doubt the existence of stability in personality, and by inference of personality itself.

Fortunately, Murray's interactional concept of thema provides a key for putting the *person* back into *person*ality; while at the same time, it preserves the behaviorists' insights into the role of situational variables.

Pro #4: This key idea relies on very few assumptions.

If you limit yourself to describing events that recur in a person's life story (i.e., highlight themes), you do not need to make philosophical assumptions. True, there may be some bias in your choice of themes, but still no assumptions need to be made. You are simply describing something, like a biologist who sketches a specimen seen under a microscope. You are revealing something that was always there, but was never seen before. You are not inferring anything about what *cannot* be seen; that is, you are not making any assumptions. Scientists can make perfectly valid contributions to knowledge by applying their special training and technical equipment to show us things we could not otherwise see. The TAT is a good example of this kind of "technical equipment." When Murray characterizes the TAT as the personologist's x-ray machine, he implies that it is a device that reveals things that are really there (rather than simply assumed), but that we would never see otherwise.

Making few or no philosophical assumptions is an advantage, a pro, for a theory. And as long as Murray thinks of themes as series of similar events recurring in a life story, and as long as he sticks to describing those events, he does not need to make any assumptions. His key idea of finding themes in life stories does not infer the existence of any hypothetical forces or structures. That is a pro.

Con #1: This key idea does not discover causes, or else it makes assumptions.

While avoiding assumptions is clearly desirable, it has rather serious consequences. If you avoid assumptions by sticking to pure description, you cannot discover causes. You can describe how iron filings line up on a piece of paper when you hold a magnet under it; you can even sketch this process: but that does not explain what *caused* the filings to assume that configuration. To explain that phenomenon, you would have to infer the existence of invisible forces from the orderliness of the event, from the fact that iron filings always line up that way in the presence of a magnet. You cannot have a causal theory without making assumptions. In this game, you cannot have your cake and eat it too. But if you are unwilling to make assumptions, you cannot deal with causes. And without a knowledge of causes it is difficult to decide which factors must be manipulated to bring about changes in personality—to cure mental illness or to rehabilitate criminals, for example.

Though it is possible to use the idea of thematic analysis in a purely descriptive manner, Murray did opt for causal explanations. By defining themes as need-press interactions, he moved beyond the realm of the visible and into the domain of inference; in short, he made certain assumptions. He did this not so much with press as with need. Press are objectively observable in most cases; behaviorists cherish these environmental stimuli for precisely that reason. But needs are not objectively observable; they must be inferred. In Murray's own words, "A need is a hypothetical process the occurrence of which is *imagined* [italics added] in order to account for certain objective and subjective facts" (1938, p. 54). You may see individuals strive for excellence in their school work or in athletic competition, and they may tell you they always try to do their best in these endeavors; yet, as in the case of the magnet that lines up the iron filings, you do not actually observe the force that causes these events, only the effects. You then infer that these effects were caused by a magnetic force, or an achievement need. The achievement need is invented in order to account for the observed events. It is a mere assumption; it says as much about the observer's need to think she or he understands the causes of events as it says about the events themselves.

This, in a nutshell, is the dilemma confronting all psychological theories of motivation. Murray is not the only one struggling with this problem; hence this con should not be directed solely against his theory. In fact, Murray is more honest and open about the dilemma than most. It sometimes seems that he himself cannot decide whether personology should be more like literary criticism, psychoanalysis, or mental testing. The larger question, though, is whether to avoid assumptions by describing themes, or to assume the existence of needs in order to explain causes. Whichever course he chooses, Murray cannot avoid some con or other.

Con #2: This key idea leaves room for bias.   What stands out as a theme for one reader of a story may not seem at all thematic to another. When a theme does stand out, it is because the reader perceives some similarity among a series of events, some common thread running through them. But again, one reader may see similarities where another sees none. Do you see any similarity, for example, in the following events: (1) the subject had embarrassing instances of **enuresis** (wetting his pants), sometimes in school, until the age of eleven; (2) even today, as a college student, he gets a thrill by lighting fires in his wastebasket; and (3) he tries very hard to be the center of attention and loves to be showered with applause and adulation. Are these all aspects of a single theme? I doubt that most people would say so. Yet to Henry Murray (1955/1981, p. 548), the common thread running through these apparently unrelated events, the underlying theme, is as plain as day: **urethral eroticism.**

When Henry Murray applies his technique of thematic analysis of life stories, the themes he finds are overwhelmingly psychoanalytic. Despite his promise to show us a much more "imaginable social animal" than the psychoanalysts do (Murray, 1938, p. 32), Murray finds themes that often seem as farfetched as many of Freud's interpretations.

The theme of urethral eroticism, for example, appears in Murray's article, "American Icarus" (1955/1981). Here Murray analyzes the life of Grope, a student seen at the Harvard clinic. As a boy, Grope was embarrassed not only by his enuresis, but by the awkwardness of getting erections prior to urination. Furthermore, he shared the childish misconception that the sex act consists of the male peeing into the rectum of the female. Murray attributed Grope's fascination with fire and his "burning" ambition to the fact the Grope associated the burning sensation in his penis (produced by the need to urinate) with the erotic excitement of penile erection. Grope's exhibitionism, and especially his Icarus fantasy of rising into the air to fly like a bird, grew out of his proud fascination with the wondrous swelling of his member.

Many of Murray's other analyses unearth similar psychoanalytic themes. He concluded that Captain Ahab, hero of Melville's *Moby Dick*, was suffering from a castration complex (Murray, 1951/1981). The white whale, you will remember, had bitten off Ahab's leg. In fact, Herman Melville's own life can be interpreted, according to Murray, on the basis of an oral fixation theme. Young Herman's

> first consequential trauma was that of weaning (at the age of twelve months) or its equivalent, a virtual expulsion from the paradise of this mother's embracing arms, up until then monopolized, this deprivation being dynamically related to an impatient, howling impulse to bite his mother's preferred apple-breast and eat of it with "cannibal delight." This hypothesis is supported by our knowledge that Herman had three teeth at the unusually early age of three months (Murray, 1967/1981b, p. 507).

A similar trauma, Murray tells us, had profound repercussions in his own life. In his contribution to *A History of Psychology in Autobiography*, Murray confesses that he was abruptly weaned at the age of two months, because his mother feared he would suffocate and was annoyed by his continual batting of her breasts with his hands. Murray says that he was attracted twenty-seven years later to the writings of Herman Melville, with their tragic themes of paradise lost, precisely because he himself had been prematurely cast out. What is more, this infantile experience paved the way for at least three handicaps that were to plague Henry Murray for years to come: He was cross-eyed, he stuttered and he had a hard time hitting a baseball. "Today I am partial," he says, "to the notion that a primary suffocation experience which, as mentioned earlier, involves a panicky incoordination of sucking, breathing, an inturned eye, and hands lunging at the breast could have established a predisposition to all three of the disabilities I have mentioned" (Murray, 1967/1981a, p. 69). Interestingly enough, the only full-length case included in *Explorations in Personality* has the fundamental theme of **oral deprivation** (Murray, 1938, pp. 604–702).

Murray is well aware that many readers will find such interpretations far-fetched. "We expect most readers to be skeptical of our reconstructions of infancy" (Murray, 1938, p. 611). He is resolute, however, in maintaining that "there are critical occurrences in every life—and one is usually taxed to state just why they are critical—which register in the brain and thenceforth are ever ready to be revived by an appropriate press" (Murray, 1938, p. 611).

This con, then, has to do not so much with Murray's key idea itself as with the way in which he applied it. The predominantly psychoanalytic nature of the themes he extracts from the study of lives is a con for most psychologists who are not partisans of psychoanalysis. It would be unfortunate, however, if anti-psychoanalytic prejudice blinded them (as it seems to have done) to the *virtues* of Murray's key idea of thematic analysis.

Con #3: This key idea may be little more than verbal sleight of hand.

Murray makes use of jargon. Beginning with the term "personology" itself, Murray's writings contain an unusually large number of terms that he has coined to describe his concepts—terms no one else uses in the way he does, and whose meaning is not evident without a definition from Murray (*Explorations* has an eight-page glossary). The words he coined in connection with his key idea of thematic analysis—episode, thema, serial, serial program, schedule, proceeding, **prospection, ordination**—are only a small sample. Although this terminology lends an air of scientism to the theory, it seems unnecessary. True, almost all personality theorists invent some new terms, though few as many as Murray. In some instances there are good reasons for doing this; but when the jargon is removed from Murray's writings, what remains is little more than ordinary verbal descriptions of events. And when Murray analyzes the "themas" and "schedules" behind a "proceeding," he does not seem very different from the top-notch news reporter who gives us an "up-close" biographical segment on Jackie O. or Liberace—except, of course, for the psychoanalytic baggage. Perhaps we may even be excused for cynically concluding that the only difference is that one writes in language we cannot understand, while the other writes in language anyone can understand.

CHAPTER SUMMARY

Henry Murray belongs in a class by himself, a fact he may have recognized when he coined the term *personology* to refer to his work. He is a typical psychodynamic theorist in these respects: (1) visiting Jung turned him on to psychology; (2) he was an MD; (3) he was a charter member of the Boston Psychoanalytic Institute; (4) he uses Freud's structural and developmental concepts in his personality theory; and (5) his personality theory focuses on dynamics, especially unconscious dynamics. Yet he is not at all like most psychodynamic theorists in other ways: (1) he was a professor and an academic researcher, rather than a practicing clinician; (2) he was an acknowledged expert on psychological assessment and spent a large part of his career in that field; and (3) he is often grouped with the humanistic psychologists.

1. As director of the newly founded Harvard Psychological Clinic during the decade of the 1930s, Murray undertook a new approach on a series of cases, an approach he referred to simply as *the study of lives*. The study of lives consisted of assembling a multidisciplinary team of behavioral scientists to take a long and deep look at a small number of ordinary people. Fifty normal Harvard students volunteered, as paid subjects, to be tested and interviewed over a period of years by Murray and his team. Murray's longitudinal, developmental emphasis required that each subject write a detailed autobiography, and that one staff member be assigned to prepare an extensive psychological biography—a psychograph—for each subject. The emphasis on depth was evident in the number of hours (35) that each subject was studied at the Clinic; in the vast arsenal of diagnostic instruments, including half a dozen projective devices, used to study each subject; and in the predominantly psychoanalytic interpretation of many cases. These studies culminated in the publication of *Explorations in Personality* in 1938.

2. Murray has had an abiding interest in literature and literary criticism. He is a recognized authority on the works of Herman Melville. A recent book, presumably intended as a representative sampling of Murray's professional writing, devotes 100 of its 600 pages to examples of Murray's literary criticism.

3. Though Murray is justifiably famous for his need-press theory of motivation, his more distinctive contribution—worthy of being designated as his key idea—is the notion that your personality *is* the themes running through your life story. The object in studying lives is to analyze their plots and extract their dominant themes; the object in collecting stories (told in response to a series of twenty TAT pictures) is to see if recurrent themes emerge.

4. Because personality is the themes running through one's life story, the units of personality must be *events*, not static structures such as traits or stimulus-response repertoires, or even drives. Consequently, Murray has had to invent a whole new vocabulary to describe aspects of events. He uses, for example, the concept of *serial*: a sequence of biographical events that are separated in time and belong together because they are directed toward the same goal. Serials can be broken down into *episodes*, the shortest event-unit, and *proceedings*, somewhat longer transactions. What binds all of these events together is a common theme, the *serial thema*. The concepts of need and press are also incorporated into this system; Murray regards themes as recurrent interactions between the same needs and press. When personologists examine a person's entire life history, they find that certain need-press interactions (themas) happen again and again. This information provides the best possible basis for predicting future events in a person's life.

5. Pro #1:   Murray's key idea, with its emphasis on longitudinal rather than cross-sectional methods, is strongly developmental. Developmental approaches have become tremendously popular in psychology during the past decade. But even if psychologists rejected this approach, our own common sense tells us that the people we understand best are the ones we have known all their lives.

Pro #2: With its emphasis on events, Murray's key idea is truly dynamic. Reading Murray's analysis of a person's life is like watching a movie, as opposed to looking at a series of snapshots. Because Murray sees personality as a story, he describes it with concepts that reflect the change and flow of events. Thema is one of these dynamic concepts.

Pro #3: The concept of thema as a need-press combination produces a theory that is interactional, a theory in which behavior is equally influenced by internal dispositions and external, situational factors. This kind of theory is more balanced than Freud's. The recent revival of interest in Murray's theory may also be due to the fact that interactionism has just been "discovered" by a younger generation of psychologists.

Pro #4: As long as personologists stick to describing events, they do not need to make philosophical assumptions. Personologists may exhibit bias in deciding which themes in a life story are the dominant ones, but that is not the same thing as making assumptions. Bias can be counteracted—Murray attempted to do this by using a team of observers; but assumptions are inevitable if one goes beyond description to causal explanation. To the extent that Murray sticks to description (which he does not do consistently), he avoids making unprovable assumptions.

Con #1: But by sticking to description in order to avoid making assumptions, Murray fails to provide us with causal explanations for behavior. Any theory that does not explain causes of behavior has little practical use, because it cannot tell us which factors to manipulate in order to change behavior. Murray's concept of need is, in fact, a causal explanation. Need, after all, is a hypothetical construct. Yet it often seems that Murray can't decide whether personology should be more like literary criticism, psycho-analysis, or mental measurement.

Con #2: This key idea does leave room for bias. When Murray himself picks out dominant themes in a life history, they are overwhelmingly psychoanalytic: urethral eroticism, castration complex, oral fixation, oral deprivation, cannibalism. Murray himself acknowledges that many readers will find these ideas farfetched. This con has less to do with Murray's key idea than with the way in which he applied it.

Con #3: Murray makes heavy use of jargon. This jargon lends an air of scientism to his theory; but if all the jargon were removed, Murray might be no more than a top-notch news reporter giving an "up-close" biographical segment.

REFERENCES

Allport, G. W., & Allport, F. H. (1928). The A-S reaction study. *Journal of Abnormal and Social Psychology, 23,* 118–136.

Allport, G. W., & Vernon, P. E. (1931). *A study of values.* Boston: Houghton-Mifflin.

Allport, G. W., & Vernon, P. E. (1933). *Studies in expressive movement.* New York: Macmillan.

Epstein, S. (1979). Explorations in personality today and tomorrow: A tribute to Henry A. Murray. *American Psychologist, 34,* 649–653.

Maddi, S. R., & Costa, P. T. (1972). *Humanism in personology: Allport, Maslow, and Murray.* Chicago: Aldine • Atherton.

Murray, H. A. (1938). *Explorations in personality: A clinical and experimental study of fifty men of college age.* New York: Oxford University Press.

Murray, H. A. (1940). What should psychologists do about psychoanalysis. *Journal of Abnormal and Social Psychology, 35,* 150–175.

Murray, H. A. (1981). In nomine diaboli. In E. S. Shneidman (Ed.), *Endeavors in psychology: Selections from the personology of Henry A. Murray* (82–94). New York: Harper & Row. (Original work published 1951)

Murray, H. A. (1981). American Icarus. In E. S. Shneidman (Ed.), *Endeavors in psychology; Selections from the personology of Henry A. Murray* (535–556). New York: Harper & Row. (Original work published 1955)

Murray, H. A. (1981a). The case of Murr. In E. S. Shneidman (Ed.), *Endeavors in psychology; Selections from the personology of Henry A. Murray* (52–78). New York: Harper & Row. (Original work published 1967)

Murray, H. A. (1981b). Dead to the world: The passions of Herman Melville. In E. S. Shneidman (Ed.), *Endeavors in psychology: Selections from the personology of Henry A. Murray* (498–517). New York: Harper & Row. (Original work published 1967)

Murray, H. A., & Kluckholn, C. (1981). Outline of a conception of personality. In E. S. Shneidman (Ed.), *Endeavors in psychology: Selections from the personology of Henry A. Murray* (204–234). New York: Harper & Row. (Original work published 1953)

Murray, H. A., & the Staff of the Harvard Psychological Clinic. (1943). Thematic apperception test manual. Cambridge, MA: Harvard University Press.

Shneidman, E. S. (Ed.). (1981). *Endeavors in psychology: Selections from the personology of Henry A. Murray.* New York: Harper & Row.

White, R. W. (1952). *Lives in progress.* New York: Holt, Rinehard and Winston.

White, R. W. (1975). *Lives in progress* (3rd ed.). New York: Holt, Rinehart and Winston.

PART TWO

Trait Theories

Trait theories of personality all share the commonsense notion that personality is composed of an individual's characteristics. The consistent, enduring, distinctive aspects of a person are that person's strongest traits. Put them all together and you have the personality. To be a bit more precise, personality is the pattern formed by various traits of various intensity. What makes you *you* may be not only the specific traits you have, but how these traits fit together.

Trait theorists typically regard traits as existing along a continuum from weak to strong. Individuals are different because certain traits are stronger in some than in others. Many trait theorists have developed elaborate psychological tests to measure the exact strengths of a person's traits. Trait theorists use psychological tests more often than any other psychologists.

Traits are seen as things that somehow belong to, and exist within a person—in the mind or elsewhere. The consistency that we observe in people's appearance, and which they themselves observe, certainly is a property belonging to those individuals. But trait theories go beyond that to say that the consistency that we observe in people's behavior, and which they themselves observe, is evidence of a disposition or tendency within each person to act in a certain way under certain circumstances. Traits, in other words, are tendencies to act in predictable ways. More precisely, traits are not the tendencies themselves, but whatever lies behind the tendencies. Some theorists consider it very important to specify what lies behind

each tendency, while others simply identify the tendencies and measure their strengths. All trait theorists believe, however, that there is something enduring and unchanging within each person.

Typologies, or theories of personality types, can also be included under the heading of trait theories. After all, type theories classify human beings according to their traits. To say that someone belongs to a certain personality type is simply to say that this person has a specific combination of traits. Jung's theory of psychological types, outlined in the box in Chapter 4 (Psychological Types), is an excellent example of a typology. Jung defines each personality type with a specific set of traits. Trait theories and typologies are very similar; the main distinction is that types are categories that flatly include or flatly exclude individuals; traits, on the other hand, are seen as characteristics almost everyone shares to some degree.

In the last analysis, both trait theories and typologies are ways of classifying personalities. Classification is the first step in any science. The classification of genuses and species in biology, and the classification of elements in the chemist's periodic table, are models followed by scientists in every discipline. Such systems of classification not only provide a convenient shorthand notation for scientific communication; they also allow scientists to convert huge blocks of disorganized information into coherent, bite-size chunks. Trait theorists strive to bring all of these benefits to the study of human personality.

7/Gordon W. Allport

A Biographical Sketch

Gordon W. Allport was the youngest of four sons born to a country doctor and his school teacher wife in rural Indiana. The year was 1897. The family later moved to several small towns in Ohio before Gordon's father finally established a sound practice in Cleveland. The domestic atmosphere was one of piety and hard work. It seems to have been pleasant enough, and secure, but there was little time for idleness or frivolity. Gordon helped, as did his mother and the other children, with a variety of chores associated with his father's practice, from relaying messages to washing up medicine bottles. From this work, Gordon acquired both a sense of responsibility and humanitarian concern for people's woes. From his mother he acquired a love of learning and a lively interest in religious matters. His maternal grandmother had been a preacher of some sort in a Free Methodist church.

The Allports had moved to Cleveland by the time Gordon began elementary school, and there he graduated from high school second in his class. Yet despite this academic distinction, he thought of himself as a rather routine student and had little idea what to do with his life, or where to go to college. It was his brother Floyd, a graduate of Harvard College, who pursuaded Gordon at the very last minute to apply to his alma mater. Gordon barely passed the entrance exam, but was admitted to the college in 1915. His association with Harvard would continue almost without interruption for the next fifty years.

College was an eye-opener for Allport. First there was the challenge of more rigorous intellectual standards than he was used to, a challenge he met by buckling down and studying harder. Second, there was the captivating array of opportunities. There were so many fascinating topics to study, so many compelling activities competing for his attention, it seemed as though there would never be enough time to explore them all. The young man who had come to college not knowing what he wanted to do, finished college wanting to do more things than he could possibly do.

What captured Gordon Allport's interest more than anything else in college was the discipline of social ethics—both as a topic of academic study and as a practical humanitarian endeavor. Social ethics at Harvard in those days seems to have been a combination of social work and moral philosophy. One of his social ethics professors arranged for Allport to supervise a boy's club in Boston's West End, a position he held throughout his undergraduate years. He was a volunteer home visitor for the Family Society. He was a volunteer probation officer. He worked with foreign students and displaced factory workers, helping to locate housing for these people. One summer he worked in Cleveland for the Humane Society. And he worked at the Phillips Brooks House at Harvard, a center for social service programs.

While Gordon was an undergraduate at Harvard, his brother Floyd was also there, finishing his doctorate in psychology. Floyd urged Gordon to take courses in psychology. Gordon did, and apparently he liked these courses, although he was a bit turned off by the mechanistic and **empiricist** emphasis he encountered in at least some of the faculty. Though they were all top-notch scholars, none of his undergraduate psychology professors would become Allport's mentor.

When he finished college in 1919, with a major in economics and philosophy, he could not decide whether to enter the social service or teaching profession. An opportunity materialized to try his hand at teaching while seeing another part of the world. For the year following graduation, Allport taught sociology and English at Robert College in Istanbul, Turkey. While he was there, he was offered a fellowship for graduate study in psychology at Harvard. From the moment he accepted this offer, he had no further doubts about his career choice.

Allport received his Ph.D. in 1922, writing one of the first, if not the first, doctoral dissertations on personality traits. Though he acknowledged his debt to the psychology professors he had had in graduate school— William McDougall, the father of social psychology; and Herbert Langfeld, who encouraged Allport to choose his own dissertation topic—they did not inspire him in the same way as the European psychologists he was to meet immediately afterwards.

A Sheldon travelling fellowship supported Allport during two years of postdoctoral study in England and Germany. The influence of the psychologists he met there can be seen throughout his later work. The innatist, structuralist orientation of the **Gestalt** psychologists provided him with an alternative to the empiricist-associationist approach in which he had been schooled. His fondness for the holistic approach also came from this source. Allport picked up his fascination with personality types from his association with Spranger. For years to come, Allport would be one of the leading interpreters of European psychology in the United States, and when the Nazis came to power he was instrumental in bringing European psychologists to this country.

Returning to Harvard in 1924 as an instructor in social ethics, Allport taught what he claims was the first course on the psychology of personality ever offered at an American college. In 1928, he became assistant professor of psychology at Dartmouth College. Two years later Allport was back at Harvard, this time to stay, and this time, finally, in the psychology department.

Richard Cabot, a cardiologist, moral philosopher, and Boston Brahmin philanthropist, played an influential role in Allport's career, serving as something like a wealthy patron. Cabot had been chairman of the social ethics department that granted Allport his first teaching position at Harvard in 1924. In 1935, Cabot directed the Cambridge-Somerville youth study, a longitudinal study of 300 delinquent boys. After serving on the staff, Allport became director of the study when Cabot died. Perhaps more important for the field of personality psy-

chology, in 1935 Cabot financed a semester's leave that allowed Allport to complete work on his personality textbook. In 1937, *Personality: A Psychological Interpretation* was published, sharing, with Ross Stagner's work of the same year, the honor of being the first textbook on personality psychology. Allport's book established him as the premier academic personality psychologist.

He never fell from that pinnacle, continuing for thirty more years to contribute to both personality and social psychology. His 1955 book, *Becoming,* is one of the most lucid explications of the phenomenon of the self in the whole literature of psychology. *The Individual and His Religion* (1950) may be the first study on that topic by a prominent academic psychologist since William James' classic work almost a half century earlier. In 1961, Allport published an extensive revision of his personality text under a new title, *Pattern and Growth in Personality.* Just a month short of his seventieth birthday, Gordon Allport died in 1967.

ALLPORT AS A TRAIT THEORIST

Gordon Allport deserves to be presented as the first example of a trait theorist in personality psychology, even though he is not the purest example—that honor belongs to Cattell. Allport certainly wrote a lot about traits—he said that traits are the foundation of personality—but he wrote a lot about other aspects of personality as well, whereas Cattell has focused his attention exclusively on traits.

Allport also deserves to come first because he is probably the greatest personality theorist outside the psychoanalytic tradition. If there were a hall of fame for academic personality psychologists, Allport would be the first to be voted in. This is a value judgment, of course, and the matter is very debatable. But without a doubt, Allport is one of the superstars of personality psychology.

Still another reason for introducing Allport first is his close connection to Murray. There is a continuity between the two, even though one is classified as a psychodynamic theorist and the other as a trait theorist. They were longtime colleagues in the Harvard Social Relations Department.

They undoubtedly influenced each other, and were both influenced in turn by other colleagues they had in common. Much of the same flavor pervades the works of both men.

Allport is a trait theorist because he says that personality is comprised of *traits*. When pressed for a definition, he says that traits are "the dynamic organization within the individual of those psychophysical systems that determine his characteristic behavior and thought" (Allport, 1961, p. 28). As you can see, traits have both a structural and a dynamic function in Allport's system—traits are what the personality is made of, and traits are what make people do what they do. But the hallmark of Allport's theory is his down-to-earth, commonsense approach. His view of traits is not much different from the view of the average layperson: Traits are simply a person's characteristics. When asked to write a letter of recommendation for someone, for example, most people would mention somewhere between three and ten prominent traits: aggressiveness, extroversion, athleticism, insensitivity, self-confidence, and so on. Allport calls these prominent attributes **central traits**. In addition to the central traits, each person has a number of **secondary traits**. These are more limited and do not extend throughout the entire personality. They are special talents or little quirks that surface only under rare, specific circumstances. Occasionally, a single trait will stand out so prominently, and so dominate the individual's personality, as to push all other traits into the background. Allport refers to these attributes as **cardinal traits.** But most of us have no cardinal traits, just a few central traits plus, at most, a dozen secondary traits. That is the gist of Allport's theory. There is not much more to say about it.

Although Allport's trait theory is not particularly distinctive as a whole, it contains a key idea—his own cardinal trait, if you will. That is where we will turn our attention now.

 **THE KEY IDEA**
INDIVIDUALITY

Allport's key idea is individuality. He says that every person is an unique individual, one of a kind. Just as each person is unique, so are each person's traits. Though we all share certain traits with the rest of the human race, each of us has certain traits that are ours and ours alone: individual traits.

Psychologists often express their view of human nature in the term they select to refer to human beings. Freud and Jung often use the term *psyche*, as though the mind were the only thing that mattered about a human being. Theorists in the Gestalt and holistic traditions refer to us as *the organism*, because they are so impressed by the organizing properties of perception. Rogers' object of study is always *the person*, because he wants to emphasize that people should not be treated as though they were inanimate objects or things. Allport always refers to the human being as *the individual*. That is

░ TRAITS DEFINED

Allport defined trait as a "neuropsychic structure having the capacity to render many stimuli functionallly equivalent, and to initiate and guide equivalent (meaningfully consistent) forms of adaptive and expressive behavior" (1961, p. 347). Several aspects of this definition are worth noting. First of all, by using the term "neuropsychic structure" Allport emphasizes that traits actually exist in some physical sense (perhaps represented by changes in the nervous system) within a person.

As a result, the nervous system is programmed "to render many stimuli functionally equivalent." This means that a person will react the same way to a whole class of stimuli. (Two stimuli are functionally equivalent if you react to them both the same way.) A red traffic light and a police officer with hand upraised, palm toward you, are functionally equivalent. You react to both by stopping your car. Sometime during your life, learning brought about a change in your nervous system, giving you the habit of stopping in response to these and similar signals. Although the class of stimuli that evoke this response constitutes a fairly general category (e.g., you also stop for a highway construction worker waving a red flag), it is not general enough to be called a trait. It is simply regarded as a habit. A trait renders *many, many* stimuli functionally equivalent. Consider the trait of orderliness. Orderly individuals react to a wide range of stimuli by trying to put things in order: their messy desks; a misunderstanding between two of their coworkers at the office; the club's business meetings that never start on time and rarely follow the agenda; flaunting of the law by everyone from tax evaders to plea bargainers; any confusion in their own minds about correct grammatical construction (Is it he and I, or him and me?). A trait triggers the same reaction to a wide range of stimuli.

Traits also *initiate* and *guide* behavior; they motivate. People do what they do because of their traits. Sometimes traits merely guide people's reactions to situational stimuli. The Interval Revenue Service stimulates everyone to file an income tax return, but orderly people far exceed the basic requirements for punctuality, neatness, and detailed declarations of assets in filing their returns. On other occasions, people's traits actually initiate their behavior, without the need for any external, triggering event—people are *proactive* as well as *reactive*. An orderly person, for example, might suddenly propose his trademark. For Allport, the single most important characteristic of personality is its individuality.

According to Allport, the business of personality psychology is to study what is unique about individuals. Furthermore, the object of personality psychology is to predict individual behavior. The predictions most psychologists make are **actuarial**—the kind insurance companies base their premiums on. An insurance company might predict, for example, that 583 persons will be killed in automobile accidents over the Memorial Day weekend. That figure may turn out to be exactly correct. What they do not predict, and what you really want to know, is whether a certain individual—you or one of your loved ones—will be killed. Predicting for individuals is, of course, much harder. But Allport stuck to his guns. He felt that any personality psychology that could not predict, or would not try to predict, individual behavior was not worthy of being called a personality that her or his club ought to have a constitution and bylaws. Allport's theory of motivation is interactional: Behavior is not caused by traits acting alone, but by traits interacting with situational factors.

Behavior, finally, may be *adaptive* or *expressive*. Adaptive behavior is "instrumental", or "coping," behavior; it is aimed at solving some problem. Orderly people carefully organize their lives into consistent patterns of routine and subroutine, so that they can efficiently accomplish each day's tasks and avoid the unexpected. This is their way of coping with the exigencies of daily living. The intended purpose of the routine is adaptation, adjustment. Allport's theoretical work is suffused with this strong functionalist tendency, deriving no doubt from the influence of William James, the originator of functionalism in American psychology. Functionalism explains behavior on the basis of its adaptive purpose.

But some behavior has no adaptive purpose; it is merely "expressive." A person performs it not to cope with any problem, but simply to express what kind of person she or he is. The stylistic component of behavior is an excellent example. People write in order to communicate.

Writing is therefore instrumental. But the style of a person's handwriting is expressive. The style has no coping function: An orderly person's handwriting is neat and clean simply because the orderly person is neat and clean. The style expresses the nature of its originator—a person with a strong trait of orderliness. Allport had a strong interest in expressive behavior as an approach to studying personality, particularly handwriting analysis. One of his early books was devoted to the study of expressive movement: gait, gesture, posture, and handwriting (Allport and Vernon, 1933).

To summarize, then, traits exist inside a person. They cause a person to respond in the same way to a great many different stimuli. (It is from such observations, in fact, that we infer the trait's existence.) Traits can merely guide behavior triggered by external stimuli, or initiate behavior without any external stimuli. The resulting behavior may be designed to cope with some problem or it may be expressive, like the whoop of delight that accompanies the thrill of victory.

---

psychology. True, it is sometimes worthwhile to predict how people in general will behave. Insurance companies obviously find such information useful. Marketing psychologists, too, want to know what proportion of the buying public will switch to their soap powder if they change the color of the box, though the behavior of individual customers does not interest them at all. I suppose that is right and proper, since they are not personality psychologists. But the psychologist who watches a depressed client slump out of his office after a harrowing therapy session is not helped by knowing that umpteen percent of persons in that state of mind commit suicide. The psychologist needs to know whether or not this individual patient will commit suicide. It is the job of personality psychology to make that kind of prediction. Personality is individual, according to Allport. Hence the object of personality psychology should be to predict individual behavior.

Baseball and apple pie, band concerts in the park on the fourth of

July—Gordon Allport was American through and through. The pioneer spirit, the frontier sense of independence, the ideal of rugged individualism permeated not only Allport's personality theory but his own character. With a puckish twinkle in his eye, he took delight in announcing that he was a maverick among psychologists. Not that he was looking to pick a fight; he simply rejoiced in the freedom every individual has in this country to express his or her own unique point of view. That attitude derived no doubt from his nineteenth-century, Protestant, midwestern background. He had been taught piety, honesty, and the value of good, hard work. And he had been taught a respect for people that bordered on reverence. If Will Rogers had not done so first, Allport might have coined the phrase: "I never met a man I didn't like." Allport was an individual who championed individualism. It is appropriate that he came not from Vienna, but from Ohio.

PERSONAL DOCUMENTS

The methods Allport advocated for studying personality were entirely consistent with his individualistic credo. *The Use of Personal Documents in Psychological Science*, published in 1942, outlines his approach: "The personal document may be defined as *any self-revealing record that intentionally or unintentionally yields information regarding the structure, dynamics, and functioning of the author's mental life*" (Allport, 1942, p. xii). Examples of such personal documents include: autobiographies, diaries, memoires, letters, interviews, and even literary productions. After collecting enough documentary material about an individual, psychologists can examine it with a variety of methods and theoretical perspectives. They can interpret it, for example, in light of Freud's psychoanalytic theory, producing something similar to what Erikson taught us to call psychohistory. Allport himself, of course, was not in favor of psychoanalytic interpretation. He was far from an admirer of Freud. Yet he acknowledged that psychoanalytic interpretation of personal documents was a useful way to study personality.

Another method Allport suggested was content analysis. In essence, content analysis is nothing more than counting how many times an item appears in a writing sample. Suppose, for example, you hypothesize that the individual whose personal documents you are studying is more an unhappy, than a happy, person. In that case, you might read the person's diaries. Every time you find an emotion recorded, you tally it up in either the happy or the unhappy column. When you get through, you add up the two columns. You might also want to use the diaries to examine specific periods in the person's life, in which case you might find that she or he was happier during some periods than during others. This method can be applied in any number of ways. For example, you can count how frequently various traits appear. The trick here is to define each trait well enough that anyone reading the document with your definitions in hand will come up with the same tally as you. This is a difficult process requiring considerable experience, but it can be done. In fact, Murray's method for scoring the TAT is a kind of content analysis of the subject's stories, in which the categories of need and press are tallied. McClelland (1961) used the same technique to assess the magnitude of needs expressed not only in stories triggered by ambiguous pictures, but in folk tales, nursery rhymes, and even pictures on Greek vases. Anything can be counted: the use of first-person singular pronouns; complaints about bodily aches and pains; optimistic and pessimistic statements; emotional experiences; likes and dislikes. Astute personality psychologists count only things that reveal something significant about the individual, things that allow them to compare various periods in the person's life, or to compare the person with another individual (or with the average individual). The advantage of content analysis is that it produces more objective data by quantifying observations. Computer technology has led to an increased use of content analysis, in recent decades, by allowing the vast quantities of data generated by this method to be handled easily.

We have already mentioned Allport's role in the Harvard Social Relations Department. White's *Lives in Progress* (1975) is very much in the Allportian tradition. More recently, Stanley King (1973) produced a work in the same genre, *Five Lives at Harvard*. The autobiographical statements of King's five subjects formed an important part of his data base. King's approach was longitudinal, more descriptive than analytical. Allport would surely have applauded it.

LETTERS FROM JENNY

A few years before his death, Allport (1965) published a book in which he followed his own advice regarding the use of personal documents: *Letters from Jenny*. He had collected the documents for this study two decades earlier, about the time when he wrote *Personal Documents*. During the 1940s, Allport was given a total of 301 letters, written between 1926 and 1937 by Jenny Gove Masterson and addressed to a certain Glenn and Isabel. These were friends of Jenny's only child, Ross, whom she disowned when he married a woman she disapproved of. Ross was born after his father died; and Jenny, all alone in the world, devoted her whole existence to raising her son. She endured great privation and much personal sacrifice on his behalf. When he was seventeen, Ross was sent off to college. Jenny was proud of what she had accomplished for her son, but also a little bit resentful that he might not be sufficiently grateful. World War I interrupted Ross's sophomore year at Princeton. He enlisted in the ambulance corps and served in France. Ross never went back to living with his mother in Chicago. He remained in the East, where he finished his college degree and worked without conspicuous success at a number of jobs. He got married without bothering to inform his mother. When she learned of the marriage, Jenny resolved never to see Ross again. But she continued writing letters to two of Ross's college friends, Glenn and Isabel, whom she had met just before Ross went off to France. Ross died in 1929, several months after surgery for a tumor of the inner ear. Jenny survived him by eight years, during which time she continued to correspond with Glenn and Isabel.

Allport is right when he says that Jenny's letters give an astonishingly vivid impression of her. One has no difficulty seeing her as a real, living person. Her image seems to coalesce and come into sharp focus right before your eyes. She is right there. Reading her letters, you feel no need for additional information, no desperate wish that you could call her back for one more question. You know all you need to know.

The picture that emerges is of a lonely woman, now past middle age, who bitterly relishes the role of martyr she adopted after her ingrate son, Ross, spurned her in favor of another woman. Jenny was fiercely possessive, jealously guarding everything that was hers—her son, her money, her few treasured books, pictures and momentos. With miserly zeal she hid her money away in mattresses, coat linings, her corset, and secret bank accounts. She meticulously destroyed her treasures one by one as she sensed that her life was drawing to a close, so that the vipers who ran the nursing home where she spent her last years could not get their hands on them.

Jenny was not a very trusting person. As time went on, she became increasingly suspicious that her mail was being tampered with. She thought that outgoing mail was being intercepted and delayed, read by prying eyes, and sometimes even destroyed. Incoming letters were also being censored, she said, occasionally arriving late or not at all. The culprits, depending on where she posted and received her mail during various periods of her life, included Ross, her employers, hotel keepers and landlords, even the staff of the home for aged women where she spent her last years. To guard against this invasion of her privacy, Jenny made every effort to deposit her outgoing mail directly into U.S. postboxes or post offices. She often instructed her correspondents to address her incoming letters "% General Delivery," so that she could pick them up in person at the post office. As an alternative strategy, she often suggested that the writer apply an additional seal over the flap of the envelope, or insert the envelope into a second envelope, so that she could detect whether the letter had been surrepititiously opened before she received it.

Jenny was obsessed with money. Hardly a letter goes by without some mention of it. Outright theft was only one of several threats she had to guard against. There were also shopkeepers who tried to cheat her by overcharging, shortchanging, or passing off shoddy merchandise. Rent-gouging landlords and greedy hotel keepers were a perennial problem, contributing no doubt to her frequent changes of residence. The prices she was charged for things rarely seemed fair to her. Even Ross, her own son, cheated her by borrowing money, squandering it on a succession of ladies of questionable virtue, then claiming that he could not repay it, even when she had certain evidence that he could.

Ross's lady friends were all of dubious moral character, from Jenny's perspective. "Prostitutes," she called them. Either they sold themselves to him, or as in the case of the one he married, bought him with their money. In any case, sex and money were tied together in Jenny's mind.

Even some of Jenny's own female friends, it seems, offered sex in exchange for money. The moment Jenny learned of this, she disowned them. There was the friend in New York, for instance, whom Jenny had known for several years and respected as a "high principled" woman. Jenny entrusted this woman with making her burial arrangements should she die, then was devastated to find her keeping a man in her apartment. And the man was not even intelligent! This "prostitute" had so little self-respect that she tried to justify her behavior by confessing that the man was not intelligent, but was kind and did have money.

Soon after this incident Jenny returned to Chicago, where she was met at the station by a woman she had known before moving East. Jenny had written her, and the woman had insisted Jenny stay with her for a few days until she found a place of her own. On the way to the apartment, the woman casually dropped a bombshell: She had a "boyfriend" living with her. Jenny was told not to worry. She would be no trouble at all and could stay with them as long as she liked. Needless to say, Jenny wrote this woman off as one more tramp and found herself other accommodations as quickly as possible. It was all a trap, Jenny realized later. By getting Jenny to live there, the woman hoped to legitimize her sordid arrangement, or at least to have some of Jenny's respectability rub off on her. The woman, you see, was still employed by the "strictly high class" company where she and Jenny had worked together years ago. She wanted to associate with Jenny in order to confirm her respectability.

Jenny was obsessively moralistic. Always at great pains to certify her own respectability, she often signed her letters "Lady M." Her dignified demeanor forbade that profanity should ever cross her lips, although occasionally, in the heat of anger, she allowed her pen to inscribe the abbreviation "d-f" (damned fool) in reference to some particularly abominable character. She regarded herself as a person of cultivated tastes. And indeed, to a certain extent she was. She frequented art museums and libraries and showed some familiarity with their contents. She made certain that Ross's upbringing included liberal exposure to such cultural benefits. When it came to schooling, Ross had to have the very best. Though Jenny herself was not well-educated, she valued education highly. Jenny was intelligent, even intellectual: She had an intellectual turn of mind and she valued intellectual pursuits. Circumstances forced her to work at rather menial jobs—telegrapher, adjustment department clerk, foundling home nursemaid—but she maintained her dignity and respectability by cultivating her intellectual interests. Inevitably, there were times when this intellectuality bordered on pretentiousness or snobbery, as when she was forced to work as a clerk in the art department of a department store, under the supervision of an ignoramus who did not know one artist from another.

Jenny seems to have been a very industrious, hard-working person, although during the period of her life covered by the letters she rarely held a job for very long. Some controversy always developed between her and her superiors, and she would either be dismissed or quit. This was all very depressing, of course, especially since she had barely enough money to live on. Time and again in her letters she talks of suicide—jumping off a bridge or building, or throwing herself into the sea. Over and over again she complains about ill health, aches and pains, her weak heart, her insomnia, exhaustion and fatigue. In almost every instance, this litany of complaints is linked to the ingratitude of her son Ross, for whose sake she has sacrificed her health. Jenny felt very, very sorry for heself; she was a morose, whining, pessimistic individual. Yet after cataloguing her tribulations in her letters, she coyly insists that the reader not feel sorry for her.

After Ross "left" her, Jenny was depressed and plagued by feelings of persecution. It is hard to tell whether she felt this way earlier in her life, because her letters were all written after Ross' departure. Obviously, she had devoted herself totally to him. He was her whole life, and after she lost him she had nothing to live for.

Jenny's letters offer a striking portrait of a unique individual. They support Allport's claim that personal documents provide a very illuminating basis for studying individual lives. Allport suggests three different approaches to interpreting the data from personal documents. He presents the first two—the existential and the depth approach—as primarily teaching devices and as a foil for the third, the structural-dynamic approach, which is clearly the one he prefers.

The structural-dynamic approach seeks to identify the traits that provide the key to Jenny's unique nature. These traits, according to Allport, are nothing other than the sum of Jenny's habits. "A *trait* is a family of habits or a widely generalized habit-system, illustrated by Jenny's solitariness, aestheticism, love of nature" (1965, p.193).

ANALYZING JENNY'S LETTERS

To discover these traits, Allport and his assistants used several of the methods we have already mentioned. Three dozen assistants read the letters and jotted down salient traits as they found evidence of them. When they had finished, they pooled their trait lists, combined synonymous traits under single headings, threw out items they could not agree on, and came up with 198 traits in nine separate categories. These nine categories constitute Jenny's central traits: (1) quarrelsome-suspicious; (2) self-centered; (3) independent-autonomous; (4) dramatic-intense; (5) aesthetic-artistic; (6) aggressive; (7) cynical-morbid; (8) sentimental; (9) unclassified. Allport did not claim that Jenny's personality was merely the sum total of these traits, since some of them, such as "aesthetic" and "sentimental," seem to overlap. The personality is, thus, as much a matter of how the traits fit together, their dynamic structure, as it is the traits themselves.

Allport's team attempted to get at these deeper structures by coding much of the material in the letters and subjecting it to various content analyses, some of them using sophisticated computer programs. Allport's faith in common sense appeared to be vindicated when even the most elaborate computer analysis spewed out a list of traits that was not very different from the one he had started with. In fact, the computer found only one previously unidentified trait ("sexuality," which referred primarily to the barely disguised incestuous nature of Jenny's relationship with Ross); and it failed to identify two from the existing list: "cynical-morbid" and "dramatic-intense." Allport plausibly attributed these two omissions to the ability of intuitive human readers to respond to stylistic nuances that eluded the computer's more concrete, literal approach.

Nevertheless, a computer program was designed to handle stylistic subtleties. Each word in Jenny's letters was coded with a category heading, or "tag word." For example, the tag word OVERSTATE was the code heading for words such as *always, never,* or *impossible.* By contrast, words expressing caution, reserve, or qualification (e.g., *perhaps, sometimes, probably*) would be tagged UNDERSTATE. Once the letters were coded and fed into the computer, a simple program query revealed that Jenny's letters contained far more instances of OVERSTATE than of UNDER-STATE. This confirmed the "dramtic-intense" category of the original trait list. If Jenny's letters gave the impression that she was given to over-statement, automated content analysis now demonstrated this objectively. This, Allport felt, is the value of the computer technique. It prevents the personologist from drifting too far away from the empirical data and getting lost in a fantasyland of abstract, theoretical constructs.

The tag-words technique also verified that Jenny was a loner. Her attitude toward women was negative; they are associated far more frequently with DISTRESS and BAD than with PLEASURE or GOOD. Men frequently appear under the heading AVOID. On the other hand, PLEA-SURE or AFFECTION is expressed in relation to art, nature, or books in 114 sentences.

Content analysis deals, of course, only with conscious content. When asked to find evidence for the psychoanalytic assertion that Jenny was motivated by guilt stemming from her unconscious homosexual and inces-tuous urges, the computer turned up almost no self-depreciatory state-ments by searching the tag words SELF, BAD, DEVIATION, and GUILT.

WHAT IS JENNY?

"Jenny," Allport concludes, "is pretty much what she seems to be" (1965, p. 207). An individual develops a set of habits in order to survive and deal with the world. Once established, those habits become a style of life, a style the individual is motivated to maintain consistently. People are likely to use the same approaches in the future as they used in the past, because people learn from experience that these approaches seem to work. Traits are learned habits that an individual acquires in the process of *actual* adaptation to the environment. Habits are learned when they *seem* adaptive to the individual who acquires them. Whether they are adaptive from somebody else's perspective is beside the point. Jenny's distrust of people, for example, might strike us as a fatal flaw in her character, the prime cause of all her misery. Yet to Jenny this habit made perfect sense, because she had been "burned" whenever she put her trust in someone else. Once her distrustful, suspicious attitude became an ingrained habit, it functioned as a self-fulfilling prophecy, poisoning her relationships almost before they began.

Allport conceded that he never managed to identify Jenny's "root habits and traits." But this failure to find the deep structure of her personality, he added, does not negate the validity of the structural-dynamic theory: "If we knew how Jenny was organized, we should then know why she behaves as she does" (Allport, 1965, p. 208). Readers of Allport's *Letters from Jenny* are likely to be disappointed. At the end of the book, they discover that even the expert does not have any magic keys to unlock the mystery of human personality. They might consider the author a fraud, a charlatan for breaking his promise to reveal the inner recesses of the personality.

Gordon Allport would smile wryly. He prized his integrity more than fame or charisma. If he did not know something, he was not ashamed to say so. If something was commonsense and simple, he would not try to show off his learning by giving a convoluted account of it. He was not pretentious. He was what he was. And he did not put on a different mask when he wrote about personality theory. Allport would simply answer that he had delivered *exactly* what he had promised. He had promised to show us, in fascinating and intimate detail, the life of a real, concrete, specific individual. Second, he had promised to "explain" her, not on the basis of "abstractions about personality-in-general," but as an individual who lived a particular, concrete life (Allport, 1965, p. x). To attempt even this, he said, was audacious. Yet he succeeded admirably. True, the reader will find little mention of the hidden parts of the personality (except, of course, in the chapter on psychoanalytic theories). Yet after reading Jenny's letters and Allport's analysis of them, the reader knows and understands Jenny very well. She comes alive for you. She is a three-dimensional character, not one of those cardboard cutouts that populate television soap operas and sitcoms. If there is anything more to explain about her, it is hard to imagine what that might be. In fact, we understand Jenny's personality so well that her behavior becomes almost totally predictable. When she tells how delighted she is to be admitted to such a fine retirement home, we know that in a matter of weeks she will be cursing it. When she patches things up with Ross, we know that it will never last. And we are not even surprised when she fires off a salvo at Isabel for sending her a package of food she cannot eat. Why? Because "that's Jenny." That's her style; that's what she's like. We know that she is like that because we have watched her for a long time, and she has always been like that.

Allport is telling us that if we want to predict an individual's future behavior, we need to take a long look at that individual's previous behavior. There is no better index of an individual's future behavior than her past performance. Above all else, personality structure is *individual*; and individuals will always strive to maintain their individuality.

PROS and CONS

Pro #1: This key idea appeals to common sense. Allport's key idea is a commonsense idea. If you want to know what a person will do in the future, look and see what she or he has done in the past. The idea is familiar enough. When gamblers set the odds on a boxing match, they consider the past performance of each fighter. When employers hire a new worker, they try to find out as much as they can about the person's previous record. College admissions officials have learned that the best predictor of a student's success in college is the student's grades in high school. We expect people to do in the future pretty much what they have done in the past. Sometimes we are wrong, but most of the time we are right. To ignore past performance would simple be contrary to common sense.

Similarly, the list of traits Allport derived from Jenny's letters appeals to our common sense. Even my brief account of her life should have allowed you to deduce many of those traits. People are individuals. They have individual traits (or at least unique combinations of universal traits). Everyone's *life story* is also unique; it has elements that stand out like the exaggerated features in a caricature. Even a layperson can identify these unique elements.

Because of its commonsense nature, Allport's theory makes use of very few **hypothetical constructs**—alleged psychic entities or forces, things that cannot be seen but are only inferred. The few constructs Allport uses, such as traits, are simple and easy to understand. In fact, his theory is hardly a theory at all; it is more like a careful, detailed description. Because Allport sticks close to observable facts, rarely venturing into the realm of theoretical speculation, he is less prone to commit errors. His theory is empirical in the most fundamental sense: It uses observable facts and resists the personality theorist's temptation to create psychic fictions.

The fact that people can understand what Allport is talking about is certainly a pro. More than any other personality theorist, Allport scrupulously avoided mystification. An individual's personality, he believed, is pretty much what common sense says it is.

Pro #2: This key idea affirms human dignity. Allport's key idea of individually certainly affirms the essential dignity of human personality. He is humanistic in the deepest sense of the word. Allport believes that every individual is valuable and has something unique to offer. For Allport, this was a deep religious conviction. It was also a value judgment, an assumption he made long before he began his psychological research. Obviously, there is no way to prove, or disprove, that assumption. But it is not easy to find fault with it either. In short, it is not a bad idea to live by.

Pro #3: This key idea has depth and breadth. The personal-documents approach is the logical consequence of Allport's key idea of individuality. This approach, which Murray also used, provides a thorough, intimate, long-term look at an individual personality. Psychoanalysts are forever claiming that their approach plumbs the depths of the personality, because it probes alleged unconscious mental activity. But the personal-documents approach of Allport provides both depth and breadth. A person's diary, for example may permit access to the most private and secret depths of the psyche every bit as well as hypnosis, free association, or dream analysis; and if the diary extends over many years of the person's life, it adds a longitudinal dimension as well—breadth as well as depth. If the job of personality psychologists is to examine the personality as thoroughly as possible, then they will have to look at an individual over as many years of his or her life as possible, and they will have to contrive to penetrate the innermost private recesses of that individual's mind throughout those years. Allport's personal-documents approach allows them to do exactly that.

Pro #4: This key idea remains relevant. Though Allport considered individual lives fascinating in their own right, he was ultimately interested, of course, in what individual lives tell us about human life in general. Jenny's letters are interesting because they teach us lessons we can apply to ourselves and to the people we know. Though we may be quite different from Jenny or Ross, all of us, as Allport observes, have been sons, or mothers, or potential mothers. At the very least, we have all had mothers. The problems Jenny faced are not so different from the problems we all face, and that is why the record of her individual life holds our interest. The only way to arrive at generaliztions about human personality is to start with the study of specific individuals.

In his presidental address to Division 8, the Division of Personality and Social Psychology of the American Psychological Association, Lawrence Wrightsman (1981) called for a return to the use of personal documents in the study of adult personality development. He regretted that little progress had been made in this area since Allport's pioneering work. The time had come to remedy that situation. While Wrightsman does not advocate using personal documents as the only source of data for the study of adult development, he maintains that they offer unique advantages. Certain personal documents, for instance, are particularly suited to specific theoretical traditions. Autobiographies, written by people who are looking back over their lives should be especially useful for testing the psychoanalytic claim that events in early life create a "lifescript" that the individual is destined to act out. Analysis of a random sample of autobiographies could check to see whether autobiographers actually visualize their lives in this fashion.

Diaries should be especially relevant for Eriksonian stage theories of development, since diaries contain day-to-day entries made over a long period of time. Stage theories could be tested by content-analyzing diaries to see whether the diary-writers are preoccupied with the specific crises the theory postulates, and at the specific times of life when these crises are alleged to occur.

Letters should be uniquely useful for testing **dialectical** theories of development, because letters constitute one half of a dialogue. Wrightsman regrets that the dialectical approach was not sufficiently "visible," when Allport wrote *Letters from Jenny,* to have been included in his analysis. Consequently, he feels

> that what is missing from the latter is a focus on the dynamic, changing relationship with Jenny's son, Ross, who is clearly the most important person or object in her world view. Jenny's feelings shift from trust and love to distrust and revulsion and back again. Early in the correspondence with Glenn and Isabel, she expresses feelings that Ross is lying to her, that he has abandoned her. On March 17, 1926, she writes "how impossible it would be for me to ever again believe one word that left his lips" (Allport, 1965, p. 14). There is, at this point, also envy over Ross's women friends, whom she calls "prostitutes." Later there is a reconciliation, Ross comes back, responds to her, and a mother-son romance of sorts ensues. Ross becomes an object of love. Subsequently Ross comes to "betray" her again; she describes him as a "contemptable cur." Yet, after Ross's death, there is a shift back to veneration and acceptance. We could employ various ways of labeling the dialectic that is operating within Jenny: a tug between trust and distrust of Ross; pulls between insistence upon her finanical independence and her reliance and dependence upon Ross and others; vacillations between helpless despair and realistic planning (Wrightsman, 1981, 377–378).

Jenny's letters certainly illustrate, even if they do not prove, the dialectical theory's principle that development is a process of perpetual change, characterized most conspicuously by conflicts between contradictory forces. These conflicts, once resolved, inevitably spawn new conflicts. If we had more collections of letters such as those of Jenny Gove Masterson, we could analyze them to see whether they, too, had this strong dialectical flavor.

More than a decade after Allport's death, fifteen years after he published *Letters from Jenny,* and almost forty years after his initial appeal for *The Use of Personal Documents* (1942), we find an eminent psychologist— Lawrence Wrightsman—using an auspicious occasion to lead his colleagues back to studying individual lives through personal documents. Wrightman's speech can only be interpreted as a very strong vote of approval for Gordon Allport's key idea of individuality. Perhaps the field of personology needs a bit longer to catch up to Allport.

Con #1: This key idea is not scientific.   The main points of our criticisms of Allport's key idea are borrowed from Robert Holt's 1962 article in the *Journal of Personality*. Holt contends, first of all, that Allport's theory of personality is more artistic than scientific, and that this is especially true of Allport's key idea, individuality. Science does not concern itself with individuals; it derives general laws—universal laws that permit actuarial predictions. That is what science is about. An in-depth portrait of a specific individual, which at best provides a "thrill of recognition," is an example of art, not science. There is nothing wrong with such portraiture, as long as you do not try to pass it off as science. And it cannot be science, because there is no such thing as an individual law. Laws are, by definition, generalizations. And science is concerned with finding laws. Allport's key idea of individuality may produce excellent portraits, but those portraits are works of art, not science.

Con #2: This key idea is not really individualistic.   Furthermore, it is impossible to conceptualize a truly unique event. Here Holt traps Allport in his own web. Allport says that each individual possesses certain traits that are unique to that person. But if that is true, then what words can be used to describe those traits? The words in the dictionary are all general concepts, terms that apply to a whole class of people. If my traits are really different from those of anyone else in the world, then a brand new word will have to be made up to refer to each one of them. But in that case the words denoting my traits are no longer concepts; they are more like proper nouns, containing no more descriptive information than my name or social security number. Telling you that I am John Doe, #021-76-8932, does not give you a very clear picture of my personality. Nor does it help you to know that my strongest cardinal traits are *glismality* and *dolitishness*. Of course, Allport did not invent words like that to refer to the individual, unique traits he discovered. As we saw in the case of Jenny, he used the same words we all use, words that are general concepts. Jenny was "aggressive," "independent," "artistic," "possessive," and "a martyr." We can certainly understand these familiar words, but Holt argues that they fail to capture Jenny's uniqueness. Are traits really unique or not? If they are, then they cannot be described with words that refer to general concepts. Unique traits can only be named, they cannot be turned into concepts.

Con #3: This key idea is impossible to implement.   But Allport's project is doomed to fail even as art, Holt says, because the rich reality of another person cannot be captured scientifically or artistically. It can only be experienced directly. Every description is an abstraction from reality, including the verbal description in a case study. Even if you made a movie of a person's entire life, with pictures and sound, you would still have an abstraction, something less than the actual person. The only way to know the personality of another individual is to know that individual. But as soon as you try to communicate that knowledge to some third person, you are dealing in abstractions. Hence Allport's project of capturing the unique features of individual personality is an impossible task—a nice idea, but one that cannot work.

In fairness to Allport we should point out that Holt's argument borders on the position that philosophers call **solipsism**: the idea that only the self can be known. Holt also fails to emphasize that the laws of science are themselves abstractions, meaning that every personality theory is abstract. It seems a little unfair to saddle Allport with a criticism that applies equally well to every other personality theorist. In the end, Holt seems to be saying that some abstractions are more acceptable than others.

CHAPTER SUMMARY

1. Allport, though not a typical trait theorist, did conceive of personality as comprised of traits: *central traits*, the three to ten prominent characteristics you would mention in a letter of recommendation; and at most a dozen *secondary traits* that are more limited and do not extend throughout the entire personality (special talents or little quirks that surface only in certain situations). But Allport's key idea is not his trait theory.

2. The idea that is distinctively Gordon Allport's is individuality. Every person is a unique individual with certain unique traits. Rather than studying human nature in general, personality psychologists should focus on what is unique about individuals. Furthermore, they should concentrate on predicting individual behavior rather than making actuarial predictions.

3. Consistent with his individualistic credo, Allport advocated using personal documents—autobiographies, diaries, memoires, letters, interviews, and literary works—to study personality. These documents can be analyzed from various theoretical perspectives and with various technical devices, such as content analysis. Content analysis logs the frequency of selected categories of statements in a sample of writing. McClelland's technique of tallying references to achievement themes is a famous example of content analysis. Manifestations of any trait or need can be totalled up; and if writings are available from several periods in a person's life, personality change and development may be reflected in changing totals.

4. *Letters from Jenny*, which Allport published in 1965, demonstrates how the personal-documents approach works. The book presents 301 letters, written between 1926 and 1937 by Jenny Gove Masterson and addressed to Glenn and Isabel, friends of Jenny's only child, Ross. Allport is right when he says that reading Jenny's letters gives us an astonishingly vivid impression of her as a real, living person.

5. To discover the traits that provide the key to Jenny's unique nature, Allport had three dozen assistants read her letters and jot down salient traits as they found evidence for them. They pooled their trait lists when they had finished, combined synonyms, threw out items they could not agree on, and came up with 198 traits in nine separate categories. This "manual" approach was followed by an elaborate computer-assisted content analysis. To Allport's credit, the traits discovered by the computer were very similar to those found in the initial analysis. In fact, the three dozen human readers intuitively picked up stylistic nuances that the computer was not programmed to recognize. Later Allport used a computer program designed to detect stylistic subtleties. This program could identify all instances of overstatement, for example, by counting the frequency of words such as *always, never,* and *impossible.* By comparing the OVERSTATE score with the UNDERSTATE score, Allport was able to confirm that Jenny was indeed given to overstatement, a habit that was congruent with her trait of dramatic intensity.

6.   For Allport, personality is pretty much what it appears to be, and Jenny is no different. Over the course of her life, she acquired a set of habits that seemed to work for her. Those habits may not actually have been adaptive, but because Jenny thought they worked she incorporated them into her style of life, which she was motivated to maintain consistently thereafter. In other words, Jenny's whole style—her set of learned habits, or traits—was summarized under nine headings. Although that hardly seems like a personality theory, after reading *Letters from Jenny* one does know Jenny very well. Her behavior becomes quite predictable, because we have come to understand Jenny's style. The impression we have of understanding Jenny's personality is not the product of any abstruse theorizing on Allport's part. He merely shows us, in fascinating and intimate detail, the life of a real, concrete, specific individual.

7. Pro #1:   Allport's key idea appeals to common sense. The notion that the best clue to future performance is past performance seems sensible. So does the list of Jenny's traits. A common sense theory uses few hypothetical constructs and is therefore very empirical. An added bonus is that ordinary people can understand it.

Pro #2:   Allport's key idea of individuality affirms the essential dignity of human personality and is therefore humanistic in the deepest possible sense.

Pro #3:   The personal-documents approach of Allport offers both depth and breadth in the study of personality. Diaries, for example, may permit access to the most private and secret depths of a person's psyche every bit as well as hypnosis, free association, or dream analysis. And if the diary extends over many years of the person's life, it adds the longitudinal dimension to the study as well.

Pro #4:   In his 1981 presidential address to the Division of Personality and Social Psychology, Lawrence Wrightsman called for a return to the use of personal documents in the study of adult personality development. In other words, Allport's key idea is still relevant. Wrightsman regretted that the dialectical approach, a particularly appropriate conceptual framework for analyzing letters, was not sufficiently "visible," when Allport wrote *Letters from Jenny,* to have been included in his analysis.

Con #1: Holt (1962) accused Allport's theory of being unscientific. Science seeks to discover universal laws, because there is no such thing as an individual law. The in-depth portrait of a particular individual is an example of art, not science.

Con #2: Allport does not give us unique, individual traits. If he did, he would have to name them with proper nouns. But he does not do this, he uses words that denote general, universal concepts. Where is the individual uniqueness in trait designations such as *aggressive, independent, artistic*? Truly unique traits can only be named, they cannot be conceptualized.

Con #3: Even as art, Allport's project was doomed to fail. The rich reality of another human being cannot be captured artistically or scientifically. The results of such efforts are mere abstractions. They inevitably leave something out. But what criteria does one use to decide what can be left out without distorting the picture? In the last analysis, nothing accurately represents a person except that person.

REFERENCES

Allport, G. W. (1937). *Personality: A psychological interpretation.* New York: Holt, Rinehart & Winston.

Allport, G. W. (1942). *The use of personal documents in psychological science* (Bulletin 49). New York: Social Science Research Council.

Allport, G. W. (1950). *The individual and his religion.* New York; Macmillan.

Allport, G. W. (1955). *Becoming: Basic considerations for a psychology of personality.* New Haven: Yale University Press.

Allport, G. W. (1961). *Pattern and growth in personality.* New York: Holt, Rinehart & Winston.

Allport, G. W. (1965). *Letters from Jenny.* New York: Harcourt, Brace & World.

Allport, G. W. & Vernon, P. E. (1933). *Studies in expressive movement.* New York: Macmillan.

Holt, R. R. (1962). Individuality and generalization in the psychology of personality: An evaluation. *Journal of Personality, 30,* 377–402.

King, S. H. (1973). *Five lives at Harvard: Personality change during college.* Cambridge, MA: Harvard University Press.

McClelland, D. (1961). *The achieving society.* Princeton: Van Nostrand.

White, R. W. (1975). *Lives in progress* (3rd ed.). New York: Holt, Rinehart & Winston.

Wrightsman, L. S. (1981). Personal documents as data in conceptualizing adult personality development. *Personality and Social Psychology Bulletin, 7,* 367–385.

8/Raymond B. Cattell

A Biographical Sketch

Raymond Cattell takes pride in the fact that despite his more than 35 years in the United States, he is still rarely taken for anything other than an Englishman. So fondly did he love his native Devonshire that he wrote what he calls a "travelogue" about it, entitled *Under Sail Through Red Devon* (1937). More to the point, his brand of psychology is English through and through.

Born in 1905 in the Midlands, Cattell did not move to Devon until he was six years old. His parents bought a house on the south coast, and Raymond spent some of the most wonderful days of his childhood sailing and climbing on the cliffs. His father and mother were both professional people, engineer designers who apparently operated their own consulting firm. They were bright—his mother had an IQ of 150, his father 120—and they were intellectual (his father loved history and literature as much as he did science). They were also politically liberal. Their child-rearing methods were permissive in allowing Raymond to do what he wanted with his time, but exacting in setting high standards for him. He was the second of three sons. His older brother seems to have become involved in a classic Oedipal struggle with his father, while Raymond kept a low profile and enjoyed a warm, sustaining relationship with his mother. There was sibling rivalry, it seems. Raymond was always competing, trying to catch up to his older brother. Intellectually he was able to overtake him, but physically he never could.

The Cattells were in Devon only three years when World War I broke out. The grim realities of war were brought home to young Raymond as the ships disgorged wave after wave of casualties, their bandages still oozing blood. A nearby mansion had been converted into a military hospital, and young Raymond helped care for the wounded there. This experience turned him into a very serious young man. He was profoundly impressed with the brevity and tenuousness of life, and he resolved never again to waste a moment of his time. At least this is the explanation Cattell offers for his habit, later in life, of regularly working in his laboratory until ten or eleven o'clock at night and rarely taking a holiday or vacation.

Apparently Cattell's interest in physics and chemistry goes back to his childhood. Among the mischievous pastimes he and his playmates enjoyed, he mentions making gunpowder in his "chemistry shed" in the apple orchard. Such pursuits held far greater fascination, it seems, than a game of football. At the age of 15, Cattell passed the Cambridge University entrance exam with first-class honors. But he declined to attend Cambridge, because London University seemed more appropriate for someone with such strong interests in science. His parents thought that he was too young to head off to the big city, however, and convinced him to wait a year. Still, it took Cattell only three years to graduate from the university with highest honors in physics and chemistry. He was then nineteen.

Before he graduated, however, Cattell had already given up all plans to become a chemist and had settled on a career in psychology. This decision came too late in his undergraduate days for him to change his major, so he simply finished his degree in the physical sciences. Nevertheless, for much of his senior year he was much more excited about psychology. He never actually took a psychology course, however. What apparently changed Cattell's mind, nudging him in the direction of psychology, was a combination of intellectual stimulation and pangs of social conscience. He attended lectures, for example, by Bertrand Russell, H.G. Wells, Huxley, and Shaw. That surely gave him plenty to think about. And the extremes of wealth and poverty he saw in London, the sheer dreariness of its slums, were themselves enough to shock this sensitive young man who had been reared in comfort among the orchards and clean sea air of the Devon coast. He wanted to do something more direct to help solve the world's problems than he felt could be done in a chemistry laboratory. As with so many of our theorists, when the time was ripe a fortuitous event occurred: He happened to attend a lecture by Sir Cyril Burt on the work of Sir Francis Galton. Galton had been an inventor of psychological tests, the discoverer of the technique of correlation, the founder of the laboratory and psychology department of London University, and, for all practical purposes, the first British experimental psychologist. Burt was Galton's pupil and one of his successors. The lecture by Burt provided Cattell with a concrete way to do something he felt was socially useful, yet also scientifically and intellectually respectable.

In 1924, Cattell therefore began graduate work in psychology at the University of London. The strength of his commitment to his new vocation can be gauged from the fact that, though he knew there were only six academic positions in psychology in all of England, he refused to be swayed by friends who reminded him of his bleak employment propects. Cattell did his doctoral work under the direction of Charles Spearman, who seems to have come as close as anyone to being Cattell's mentor. Most students today, if they know Spearman at all, recognize him as the author of the theory of the "g" factor (general factor) in intelligence. But Spearman was also the inventor of **factor analysis**, the statistical tool which is the heart and soul of Cattell's personality theory. In addition, Spearman was also a master test-builder who gave Cattell a firm grounding in the principles of psychological measurement. Though Spearman's interest was in the measurement and structure of abilities, rather than traits or motives, Cattell found he could apply almost everything he learned from Spearman to the study of personality. Of course, Cattell himself has maintained a lively interest in intelligence testing throughout his life and has insisted that ability traits be considered a part of personality. Cattell is very much in the mold of Spearman, who in turn was in the mold of Galton. The tradition is markedly British, with an emphasis on objective scientific methodology, mental tests, statistical analyses derived from correlation, and an interest in hereditary mechanisms in intelligence.

When Cattell received his Ph.D. in 1929, he was not besieged by job recruiters. In fact, he had to take a teaching position in the education department at Exeter University. He was back in the part of England he loved; but alas, he could do little in the way of research. As he began to conceive his grand strategy for investigating the structure of personality, he thought that he might profit from some clinical experience. To that end, and because of the lack of suitable university positions, in 1932 Cattell took a job as director of a school psychological service and clinic in Leicester. During the five years he was there, he gained an appreciation of clinical concerns and was influenced by psychoanalytic theories. He constructed a projective personality test, several **culture-fair** intelligence tests, and published the results of his research in at least six articles and four books. This single-minded dedication to work affected both his health and his marriage. His wife left him, and he developed a "functional stomach disorder." The year 1937 was the low point in Cattell's life.

An invitation from E.L. Thorndike to come to Columbia University as a research associate was Cattell's salvation. Though it grieved him mightily to leave his native land, Cattell was never to live in England again. After a year with Thorndike, he accepted a faculty post at Clark University. That, too, lasted only briefly. Next he moved to Harvard. During World War II, Cattell built and tested personnel selection tests for the Adjutant General's Office. But in the last analysis, life began for him at 40, when he was given an opportunity to set up his own personality research laboratory at the University of Illinois. There he labored from 1944 until 1973. Currently Cattell is Visiting Professor at the University of Hawaii. Over 300 articles and 30 books stand as a monument to the prodigious productivity of Raymond Cattell.

THE MODEL OF A TRAIT THEORIST

Raymond Cattell is the perfect example of a trait personality theorist. He believes that the personality is made up of traits—universal traits, not individual traits. Unlike Allport, Cattell does not insist on individual uniqueness. For him, traits are universal, like the elements he studied in chemistry. And just as every chemical substance consists of certain elements in certain proportions, so every personality consists of specific quantities of certain universal traits. The job of the chemist is to discover all of the elements in all of the substances in the world; the job of the personality psychologist, according to Cattell, is to discover all of the universal traits in all of the personalities in the world.

Cattell does deal with individuals, but in the same way that chemists deal with individual compounds. There is a game chemists play called quantitative analysis. (You probably did not get that far if you took only freshman chemistry.) Anyway,what they do is to give you some unknown compound—usually some powder or juice—and your job is to find out how much of which elements are in it. The professor knows, of course, because he or she just mixed the stuff up. To identify the elements you conduct a number of tests, beginning with simple things: If it is a powder, seeing if it will dissolve in water. When Raymond Cattell studies an individual's personality, he does exactly the same thing. He administers a number of personality tests—standardized paper-and-pencil personality tests—to find out which trait elements are present in the subject's personality, and how much of each trait the subject has. Traits exist in individual personalities in varying amounts; and those amounts can be accurately measured by properly constructed personality tests.

It should not surprise you now to learn that Cattell earned his bachelor's degree in chemistry. Nor should it surprise you to learn that Raymond Cattell is a master test-builder. As I mentioned, he did his Ph.D. at the University of London under Charles Spearman, who, in turn, had been a student of Sir Francis Galton—the originator of the idea of psychological tests. The mental testing tradition was very strong at the University of London. And when Cattell left his native land in 1937 to come to the United States, he came to another university where the mental testing tradition was very, very strong. He became E. L. Thorndike's assistant at Columbia University. Throughout Cattell's career, he has continued to construct more and more psychological tests. He is best known for his culture-fair intelligence tests and for his 16PF (Sixteen Personality Factor Questionnaire), a personality test that yields scores on sixteen different traits. He was instrumental in founding IPAT, the Institute for Personality and Ability Testing, whose catalogue offers about two dozen different tests for sale. Cattell is one of the foremost authorities in the field of psychological testing.

◤ THE KEY IDEA
DISCOVERING TRAITS
BY FACTOR ANALYSIS

Cattell is also one of the foremost authorities on the statistical technique known as factor analysis. Only L. L. Thurstone and J. P. Guilford are in his league. Cattell's *Factor Analysis* (1952) is now a classic. His key idea is that the basic trait elements in all individual personalities can be discovered by using factor analysis. You have no doubt seen the chemist's periodic table of 103 elements. Cattell theorizes that there must be some such list of elemental personality traits. And with factor analysis, he intends to discover what they are.

CATTELL'S RESEARCH STRATEGY

Factor analysis, Cattell says (1950, 1979), can be applied to three kinds of data. First, there are the L-data. "L-data" is short for life record data. What Cattell has in mind here are ratings made by one person of another person in an everyday life situation. For example, bosses might be asked to rate their employees on industriousness, perseverance, punctuality, cooperativeness, or intelligence. For each trait, they might rate each employee on a scale from 1 (extremely weak trait) to 7 (extremely strong trait). In other words, the data are converted into numerical form for statistical treatment. The second kind of data are called Q-data. Q-data stands for questionnaire data. The very same kind of rating scales may be used, except that here the individuals rate themselves rather than being rated by someone else. They rate themselves as they are in general, rather than as they perform in some specific situation; although this, too, would be possible. The third kind of data are T-data. T-data means test data. The tests consist of tasks on which an individual's performance can be objectively scored (a manual dexterity test, for example), or of paper-and-pencil tasks (you might be asked, for example, to identify which codes have been used to rewrite a series of messages). The preference is for tests that rate performance objectively and make responses hard to fake.

Cattell used L-data in the following example. The procedure would have been almost the same, however, had he used Q-data, or T-data. First, to make certain that his trait-rating scales included all possible traits, Cattell acquired a list of traits Allport had compiled in 1936, by combing the dictionary for every possible word that could be used to describe a human being. Allport left no stone unturned; his list ran to some 18,000 words. Nearly every trait in the English language appears somewhere on that list. But 18,000 was far too unwieldy a number. To pare it down to manageable size, Cattell combined words that were approximately synonymous with each other and threw out words that do not serve to distinguish one personality from another (e.g., "running"). The result of this distillation process was a list of 171 *trait-elements*, as Cattell called them.

His next step was to have people rate other people on each of these 171 traits. A supervisor, for example, would be given a sheet for each of his employees. Each sheet listed the 171 trait-elements, along with a scale from one to seven for each element. The supervisor then rated each employee on all 171 of the trait-elements. Cattell therefore received 171 numerical ratings for each employee (or other person who had been rated): 171 for Tom, 171 for Dick, 171 for Harry, and so on. And he may have used several hundred Toms, Dicks, and Harrys, so he had a lot of numbers to work with.

To reduce his list of trait-elements down to 171, Cattell had already combined all the synonyms. But he had a hunch that within that universe of 171 elements, there were a lot of traits that tended to go together. For example, an employee who is industrious is probably also punctual. Industriousness and punctuality are not synonymous, but a person who has one trait usually has the other. That person may tend to have some third trait, or fourth trait, or even a fifth trait as well. If Cattell could find out what trait-elements tend to go together, he might be able to condense his list of 171 even more.

There is a statistical process that does exactly that. It is called correlation, and it was invented by Galton and perfected by his student, Pearson. Every beginning psychology student has heard of the Pearson Product Moment Coefficient of Correlation. Spearman even developed a method for computing **coefficients of correlation** from rank-ordered data. Cattell was thoroughly schooled in the methods of correlation. He knew that the coefficient of correlation tells you the extent to which two or more things tend to go together. Take our example of industriousness and punctuality. Not everyone who is highly industrious is highly punctual; and not everyone who is punctual is industrious. Maybe the boss gave Tom a seven on industriousness and a seven on punctuality. And Dick rated a six on punctuality, but only a two on industriousness. Dick comes to work on time, but he goofs off a lot. If most of the employees earned similar ratings for industriousness and punctuality, however, you could conclude that industriousness and punctuality tend to go together in people. By taking the numbers that the boss gave all the Toms, Dicks, and Harrys on industriousness and punctuality and plugging these numbers into Pearson's mathematical formula, you come out with a single number called the coefficient of correlation.

A perfect correlation, indicated by a coefficient of 1.00, would occur if every employee who got a seven on industriousness also got a seven on punctuality, everyone who got a six on industriousness got a six on punctuality, and so on. That does not happen, of course, unless someone "fudges" the data. The correlation coefficient is normally some decimal smaller than 1.00—.83, or .26, or .07, for example. The size of that number indicates the extent to which the two traits tend to go together in people. A coefficient of .83 indicates a very strong tendency for those traits to go together; .26 indicates only a very slight relationship; and .07 indicates practically no correlation at all. Individual psychologists usually decide how large a coefficient of correlation must be in order to justify the conclusion that two or more traits go together. If they decide that the correlation must be 1.00, they will not find any traits that go together; if they decide that any traits showing a correlation of .70 or more go together, they may find some; if they make their cut-off point .40, they will find even more.

Cattell's cut-off point allowed him to reduce his list of 171 trait-elements to 40 clusters. These clusters were pairs or groups of trait-elements that correlated with each other at or above his cut-off point, but did not correlate well with any trait-elements outside the cluster. Cattell established his cut-off point by computing the coefficients of correlation for all combinations of the 171 trait-element ratings of all the Toms, Dicks, and Harrys who had been rated. The clerical task alone must have been prodigious. The number of coefficients of correlation he computed was 14,535! But from the universe of 171 trait-elements, Cattell had distilled 40 clusters, which he now referred to as **surface traits.** The process was almost like going from molecules to atoms; he was getting closer and closer to the most fundamental particles of personality.

Yet he had still not smashed the atom. It must be possible, he thought, to take these forty surface traits and break them down into some smaller number of still more basic building blocks. Indeed it was—and the way to do it was with factor analysis. He would compute the intercorrelations among all of the forty surface traits, then subject that **correlation matrix** to factor analysis. He would then discover what he would call **source traits,** the most basic particles of personality and the building blocks of all surface traits.

FACTOR ANALYSIS:
AN ILLUSTRATION FROM SPORTS

Factor analysis is simply an elaboration of correlational techniques. You can easily grasp the basic concept if you just think of some special ability, such as athletic ability. Take tennis-playing ability and ping-pong-playing ability, for example. These abilities are highly correlated—a person who is good at tennis is usually good at ping pong, and vice versa. If you measure a number of players' abilities at both games, by having them play each other and ranking them on the basis of the results, you can actually compute the coefficient of correlation between tennis-playing ability and ping-pong-playing ability. The correlation will probably be quite high. If you now have your tennis players play badminton, you will find another high correlation, though perhaps not as high as with ping-pong. Abilities in racquetball, squash, and handball will no doubt correlate highly with tennis ability too.

But if you take your tennis players and measure their baseball-batting ability you will find a considerably lower coefficient of correlation between baseball batting averages and tennis rankings. It will still be a positive correlation, but it will not be as high as the ones between tennis and other racquet sports. If you go still further afield, computing the coefficient of correlation between golf scores and tennis rankings, you will get an even smaller number.

These abilities (tennis-playing, ping-pong playing, etc.) are analogous to Cattell's surface traits. If we actually computed the intercorrelations among all pairs of these athletic abilites, we would come up with a table of twenty-eight coefficients of correlation: tennis with ping-pong; tennis with badminton; and so on; *but also* ping-pong with badminton; ping-pong with racquetball; etc. We would then subject that table (matrix) of twenty-eight coefficients of correlation to the mathematical operations that constitute factor analysis (this is typically done by computer nowadays). These mathematical computations would produce (1) some number of *factors;* and (2) the *loadings* on each surface trait of each factor. (See Table 8–1 for a whimsical example.) The computer would not name the factors; it would simply label them: FACTOR A, FACTOR B, and so on. But the factor loadings, expressed in decimals between 0.00 and 1.00, might indicate, for example, that FACTOR A was a very strong component in all of the surface-trait sports. "FACTOR A loads heavily on all of the sports" is the way a factor analyst would put it. We would then be faced with a job of interpretation. We would have to examine all of the sports closely, to see if there were one special skill they all had in common. In this case the answer is rather obvious: They all involve hitting a ball. Since there is no other skill they all have in common, we would be justified in concluding that FACTOR A must represent ball-hitting ability. Ball-hitting ability is a *factor* in all of these sports. The strength of this factor is indicated by the magnitude of the FACTOR A loadings for each sport.

TABLE 8-1

Hypothetical Factor Loadings for Various Sports

	Factor		
Sport	*A*	*B*	*C*
Tennis	.50	.41	.34
Ping Pong	.53	.22	.02
Badminton	.48	.44	.02
Racquetball	.44	.31	.10
Squash	.50	.35	.09
Handball	.45	.42	.06
Baseball batting average	.71	.19	.28
Golf	.37	.14	.19
100-yard dash	.08	.51	.41
Mile run	.11	.68	.36

FACTOR B might be found to load very heavily on tennis, badminton, racquetball, squash, and handball, but much less heavily on ping-pong, baseball and especially golf. This might lead us to conclude that FACTOR B represents a source ability such as footwork coordination or running endurance. If we wanted to check our hypothesis, we could perform the whole experiment again, this time including a hundred-yard dash and a mile run. If our hypothesis is correct, FACTOR B will show extremely high loadings on these two events. The new events will hardly load at all on FACTOR A, however, because being able to run and being able to hit a ball do not necessarily go together. In any case, our factor analysis would reveal a number of the most basic source skills shared by these surface abilities in athletics. There might be as many as half a dozen of these factors, including such additional things as physical strength, reaction time, and concentration. We would discover that the ability to excel in a given sport coincides with a specific combination of basic factors. Some basic factors would be found in all the sports, others in only a few.

SOURCE TRAITS DISCOVERED

Whether you are working with athletic abilities or personality traits, if you can measure them, you can factor-analyze them. Cattell did exactly the same thing with his surface traits that we have just done hypothetically with athletic abilities. He factor-analyzed his forty surface traits and identified fifteen factors, which he called *source traits*. These fifteen source traits, he concluded, are the most basic ingredients in all human personalities. They are also universal because they were distilled from a list of all the traits that exist—18,000 of them. It is as if Cattell has examined every athletic event in the world. According to Cattell, in any case, every human personality is made up of some combination of these fifteen source traits.

Cattell is not dogmatic about the exact number of source traits. He derived his fifteen traits from a factor analysis of L-data. From factor analyses using Q-data, he has come up with about twenty source traits. T-data have produced eighteen source traits and about fifteen ability traits. Many of the same traits are found, of course, in all of the analyses. (See Table 8–2 for a list of the source traits measure by the 16PF.) Cattell does not claim to have the final answer yet, but he does claim to have the right method.

PREDICTING PERFORMANCE

Once you have compiled at least a tentative list of the ultimate ingredients in personality—the source traits—it is a short step to developing a personality test that will measure the strength of each trait in an individual personality. Cattell accomplished this with his 16PF (The Sixteen Personality Factor Questionnaire). The 16PF allowed him to attain what he considers the ultimate goal of all personality psychologists—prediction. "Personality," he says, "is that which permits a *prediction* of what a person will do in a given situation" (Cattell, 1950, p. 2, italics added). This simple

TABLE 8-2

List of Primary Source Traits

Code Letter	Technical Name	Popular Label
A	Sizia–Affectia	Cool, reserved–Warm, easygoing
B	Low intelligence–High intelligence	Dull–Bright
C	Low ego strength–High ego strength	Easily upset–Calm, stable
E	Submissiveness–Dominance	Submissive–Assertive
F	Desurgency–Surgency	Serious, sober–Enthusiastic, happy-go-lucky
G	Low superego strength–High superego strength	Expedient–Consciencious
H	Threctia–Parmia	Shy, timid–Venturesome
I	Harria–Premsia	Tough-minded–Tender-minded
L	Alaxia–Protension	Trusting–Suspicious
M	Praxernia–Autia	Practical–Imaginative
N	Naivete–Shrewdness	Forthright, unpretentious–Astute, worldly
O	Untroubled adequacy–Guilt proneness	Self-assured–Apprehensive, guilt-prone
Q_1	Conservatism–Radicalism	Disinclined to change–Experimenting
Q_2	Group dependency–Self-sufficiency	Group dependent, a "joiner"—Self-sufficient
Q_3	Low self-sentiment–High Self-sentiment	Uncontrolled, follows own urges–Controlled, disciplined
Q_4	Low ergic tension–High ergic tension	Relaxed–Tense, driven

From Raymond B. Cattell, *Personality and Learning Theory, Volume 1: The Structure of Personality in Its Environments*, pp. 61-72. Copyright © 1979 by Springer Publishing Company, Inc., New York. Used by permission.

definiton is the rationale for the complicated, laborious process of factor-analyzing 18,000 traits to produce fifteen or twenty source traits, then developing a test to measure the source traits so that you can predict what a certain person will do when placed in a certain situation.

A person's behavior in any given situation, says Cattell, is a function of the sum of all the source traits that are relevant to that situation. Since some traits are more relevant than others to a particular situation, the strength of each relevant trait has to be weighted in proportion to its degree of relevance. Let us return to our tennis-playing example. The problem is to predict how well Martina will play tennis. We know that the traits of ball-hitting ability, footwork and running, and physical strength are all relevant to the tennis-playing situation. Our factor analysis of various sports told us this. For purposes of illustration, let us say that our factor loadings also tell us that tennis is 45% ball-hitting ability, 35% footwork and running endurance, and 20% physical strength. We can give Martina a test for ball-hitting ability, one for footwork and running, and another for strength. The tests give us a numerical score for each trait. Next we multiply her ball-hitting score by .45, her footwork-and-running score by .35, and her strength score by .20. Adding the three results together, we come up with a "tennis-playing ability" score for Martina. If we were to compute a tennis-

⫸ A TAXONOMY OF TRAITS

To avoid underestimating the thoroughness of Cattell's researches, you should know that the traits contained in Table 8–2 are by no means the sole determinants of behavior in Cattell's theory. Traits may, in fact, belong to any one of three categories: *ability traits, temperament traits* and *dynamic traits*. The traits in Table 8–2 are all temperament traits, except for B (high intelligence–low intelligence), which is an ability trait. Ability traits are those that determine how effective people are in achieving their goals. General intelligence and specific talents are obvious examples. Temperament traits involve characteristic energy levels, emotional tone, reactivity, and so forth. Dynamic traits are what set behavior in motion. They play the same role in Cattell's theory that the instincts play in Freud's theory, or the needs in Murray's.

Any of these three sorts of traits may either by learned or inherited. Cattell calls traits that are learned **environmental-mold traits**; he calls traits derived from heredity **constitutional traits.**

Cattell investigated dynamic traits with the same general strategy he had used to discover the source traits of temperament. Within the realm of dynamic traits, the surface level is occupied by *attitudes*. Cattell's concept of *attitude* corresponds fairly closely to the way the term is used by other psychologists, and even to its everyday usage. An attitude is a disposition to act in a certain way toward a specific object, or class of objects. A tendency to vote for conservation candidates is an attitude. So is a preference for Mexican food. Cattell used a variety of techniques to measure attitudes, then employed factor analysis to reveal dynamic source traits.

Cattell divides dynamic source traits into

playing ability score for Chris in the same way, we could predict whether or not Martina will beat Chris in their upcoming match. Cattell's specification equation describes the entire process very succinctly: Response = S_1T_1 + S_2T_2 + ... S_nT_n. *Response* refers to what the person will do in the situation; T stands for a trait that is relevant to the situation. (The subscript n says that the equation can handle any number of relevant traits.) S is a measure of how relevant a trait is to a particular situation. S-values and T-values are both derived from factor analysis.

Although Cattell is not interested in predicting the outcomes of athletic events, in essence he is like the major league scout who rates young prospects on each of the factors that make up the game of baseball: hitting, running, strength, alertness, etc. For obvious reasons, Cattell's theory is also applicable to personnel selection in business and industry. Suppose a corporation wants to know which of its employees will make the best managers and profit most from a course in management training. Cattell's theory can be used to analyze the tasks involved in management. Next, the theory can identify the traits that are relevant to managerial ability (and the ideal proportion of these traits) and test each candidate to find out how consitutional dynamic source traits, which he calls **ergs,** and environmental-mold dynamic source traits, which he calls **sentiments.** Ergs correspond to what most psychologists regard as primary drives. Ergs are innate and physiological, most people would call them instincts. Among the ergs Cattell found again and again in his factor analyses are the following: hunger; sex; gregariousness; parental protectiveness; curiosity; escape (fear); pugnacity; acquisitiveness; self-assertion; and narcissistic sex.

Sentiments, which are learned rather than innate, correspond to secondary, or acquired, drives. Cultural conditioning plays a large role in establishing these traits. Sentiments are the basis for a wide array of attitudes associated with social institutions. Some examples of sentiments: the religious sentiment; career sentiments; sentiments about home and family; and political sentiments. Other sentiments also emerged from Cattell's factor analyses: sentiments involving hobbies, sports, and mechanical interests; sentiments surrounding parents, spouses, sweethearts, and children; and finally, the self-sentiment. Cattell found the self-sentiment in almost all of his analyses; he accorded it a major role in his theory of motivation.

Even this extensive **taxonomy** does not include all of the factors Cattell had to analyze in order to predict behavior, but enough are included here to give a vivid impression of the complexity of his motivational theory. The information that must be fed into the specification equation before a response can be predicted includes properly weighted measures not only of ability and temperament traits, but of dynamic traits as well.

much of each trait she or he has. Some of the relevant traits will undoubtedly be abilities (general intelligence; knowledge of economics and finance; and knowledge of industrial processes). Other traits will involve temperament (being explosive or even-tempered; high-strung or relaxed; or being prone to depression.) Still other traits will be motivational (perseverance; gregariousness; even particular attitudes and interests). See Box: A Taxonomy of Traits.) As long as well-designed tests can measure these traits and determine their relevance to the tasks of management, then management ability can be accurately predicted. The same kinds of predictions can also be made for a wide range of personnel-selection problems, from admitting students to colleges or technical schools, to hiring salespeople and secretaries, to promoting assembly-line workers to shop supervisors. The IPAT catalogue even offers a screening instrument for selecting personnel "who need authorized, unescorted access to vital, protected areas of a nuclear facility" (*1983–1984 Catalogue of Psychological Tests*, p. 15). Though Cattell's specification equation is stated in a general way, implying that is can be used in any situation, it has been used most often to predict performance in jobs or in job-training programs.

PROS and CONS

Pro #1: This key idea echoes common sense. Despite the complexity of the mathematical procedures employed by Cattell, his basic idea that traits exist to a greater or lesser extent in people has profound common-sense appeal. We ordinarily take it for granted that people, including ourselves, have traits, and that some of these traits are stronger in some people than in others. The oldest surviving pieces of literature suggest that human beings have always thought in those terms about personality. Far more recently, some psychologists were telling us that traits played almost no role in determining behavior, and that situational variables were so powerful that we might as well forget about traits (Mischel, 1968). But common sense has long held what is fast becoming the majority opinion in psychology: Individual behavior is a product of traits interacting with situational factors (which, after all, is what Cattell's specification equation says). Folk wisdom acknowledges the role of situational factors, as evidenced in the widely held belief that even an honest man has his price. Yet no one doubts that some people are more honest than others, and that the trait of honesty does in fact exist. People have such obvious differences—physical stature; bodily health; temperament; special talents; moral character; likes and dislikes—that common sense tells us such traits must exist. By using this simple observation as his starting point, Cattell places his theory on very firm footing.

Pro #2: This key idea aims, like science, to measure. If traits exist in greater or lesser amounts in people, then it ought to be possible to measure them. Whether you can measure them accurately or not is another question. And whether the amount of a given trait in a person remains the same over a period of time is still another question. But the task of measuring a trait—say, conscientiousness—ought to be fundamentally similar to the task of measuring freestyle figure-skating ability. As we all know from watching the Olympic Games, a panel of expert judges observes the performance of each skater, then rates it on a common scale to come up with a set of marks. These marks are fed into a formula to determine the overall score. Thus something as ephemeral as an athletic and artistic performance is converted into numerical form; it is measured. True, there are occasions when we feel that it is not measured very accurately. It is also true that the skater who earned a 5.8 today may fall down tomorrow and receive only a 5.1. But the essential point remains: It is possible to measure very intangible aspects of a person's behavior and compare one person's performance with another person's. This is what Cattell strives to do. The fact that he cannot do this perfectly at the moment hardly seems reason for him to stop trying; on the contrary, present shortcomings provide a rationale for working to improve the precision of the measuring tools.

Pro #3: This key idea is an extension of our innate tendency to classify. Classification seems to be an innate activity of the human mind.

Those who deny the existence of innate ideas would disagree, of course. But even very young children will group similar objects. Playing alone and without instructions, they will, for example, spontaneously arrange all of the square blocks into one pile and all of the triangular ones into another. The mind generalizes; it picks out some general characteristic that runs through a number of particular objects and forms a classification system. The classification systems may vary, depending upon which characteristic is focused on. If some of the square blocks are large and some of them are small, and if some of the triangular blocks are large and some of them are small, the child may instead put all of the large blocks into one pile and all of the small ones into the other. But the child is still classifying, putting together all of the things that "go together," according to some criterion.

As we saw just a short while ago, the mathematical operation of correlation is nothing more or less than putting together things that go together. In other words, correlation is the mathematical formulation of a natural way of thinking. The mind is built to observe correlations. The mathematical formula simply expresses this innate propensity in numerical symbols. And since factor analysis is simply a logical extension of correlational methods, it too is a mathematical representation of a way of thinking that occurs quite naturally to the human mind. Correlation is not only natural, but ordinary—factor analysis represents an ordinary way of thinking. The example of the baseball scout sizing up a prospect is a case in point. The scout, quite naturally and without any knowledge of psychological statistics, evaluates the prospect in terms of each component or factor involved in playing baseball, and in light of the relevance of each of those components to overall baseball-playing ability. It does not occur to him that he is doing anything out of the ordinary. And, of course, he is not. He is only doing what comes naturally. Cattell, as a factor analyst, is doing exactly the same thing, except that he is doing it with more precision. We have to consider this one of the strengths of his theory. Cattell's approach has an inherent logic that is very hard to argue with.

Pro #4: This key idea is scientific.   The apparent precision and scientism of Cattell's system is alluring. Anyone who has been exposed to today's advertising knows that certain phrases—"doctor tested," "computer designed," "scientific tests prove"—sell products, because people in our society have put their faith in science and technology. Cattell is certainly the most scientific-looking of all the personality theorists we have considered. He uses computers; the mathematical operations involved in his factor analysis would surely impress most people; and he uses tests. All of that must be more scientific than just interviewing people.

I am not trying to suggest that there is anything fraudulent about Cattell's appearance of being scientific. It is quite genuine. Cattell *is* scientific, and he intends to be scientific. My point is simply that, given the extent to which this culture values things scientific, the more scientific a personality theory looks and is, the more likely it is to gain acceptance. And since this veneration of science pervades our entire culture, professional psychologists and laypersons alike will tend to be favorably impressed by Cattell's scientific sophistication.

Con #1: This key idea de-emphasizes situational variables.   Many personality psychologists today are emphasizing the importance of situational variables, as opposed to traits, in determining behavior. They say that if you are interested in predicting behavior, you would be much wiser to pay attention to situational or environmental variables, because compared to their influence, the influence of traits is practically nil. I will not reopen that argument here; there is much to be said for both sides. But there is no denying that at the moment, the situational-variables camp appears to be gaining momentum, while many champions of the trait approach seem to be in retreat—or at the very least, they are "stonewalling" it. While Cattell himself has managed to stay fairly aloof from the battle, as the arch trait theorist he is nevertheless regarded as outdated by the majority of young personality psychologists today. The current of the times is not flowing in his direction.

Con #2: Psychological testing has become unpopular.   The current of the times is antagonistic to another aspect of Cattell's project as well. Ever since the late 1960s, the entire psychological testing establishment has been under fire. Civil libertarians have criticized the intelligence tests used in schools for being culturally biased, prejudicial, and discriminatory. They have also held that the use of personality tests by government and industry constitutes an invasion of privacy. In more than a few instances the courts have agreed. Such tests have been outlawed in some school districts, and the personnel departments of many corporations have sharply curtailed their use. Even where they are still in use, freedom-of-information acts have been enacted to guarantee access to test results that were formerly kept secret. The whole psychological-testing industry is definitely on the defensive.

I shall not attempt to resolve this issue either. Suffice it to say that there have been abuses of psychological tests. Yet that hardly seems sufficient reason to throw away the baby with the bath water. Rather than discarding the tests, we ought to work doubly hard to construct better ones and to insure that they are used in a responsible manner. Cattell has been in the forefront of developing culture-fair tests of intelligence (tests that are not biased in favor of any particular cultural group). Nevertheless, to the extent that Cattell is associated with the psychological testing movement, and to the extent that tests are currently in disrepute, Cattell's key idea of discovering traits by the using personality tests is not likely to be very popular.

Con #3: Other factor analysts have found factors different from Cattell's.   Now that you are impressed by how scientific Cattell's factor analytic method is, you may be disenchanted to learn that other factor analysts have turned up factors different from the ones Cattel has identified. Precise and scientific though they may be, factor analysts in per-

sonality theory are no more in agreement than armchair philosophers. Hans Eysenck (1967), an eminent personality theorist in his own right, attempted to discover the basic elements of personality with factor analysis and came up not with fifteen, sixteen, eighteen, or twenty traits, but with three "dimensions" producing eight basic personality types. If one chemist told you there were 103 elements while another announced there were 204, you would not be inspired to have great confidence in the discipline of chemistry. Needless to say, the same applies to personality psychology. When the experts disagree among themselves, the public may be justified in taking their pronouncements with the proverbial grain of salt. While Cattell would claim that his factor-analytic approach to personality is superior because it is more scientific, the broader agreement one would expect to find among scientists has just not been evident. If agreement is the criterion of validity, then the superiority of the factor-analytic method has yet to be demonstrated.

One reason for the lack of consensus among factor analysts has to do with technical aspects of the mathematical operations involved. The number of factors extracted from any given correlation matrix depends on how the part of factor analysis called **rotation** is performed. Follow one convention for rotations and you might find four factors; follow another convention and you might find five. There are arguments, pro and con, for each method of doing rotations, but no consensus as to which is valid. Since the subtleties of the argument are beyond the scope of most people, we are left pretty much in the dark.

Another reason that two factor analysts may come up with different lists of traits is that the end product of the mathematical operations of factor analysis is, as we saw earlier, not a list of *traits* but a list of *factors*. The mathematical analysis does not name the factors, it only lists them and gives their loadings on each of the original tests or scales. The factor analyst who learns that Factor A loads heavily on tennis, racquetball, and baseball, but not at all on the hundred-yard dash and mile run, must still sit down in his or her armchair and reason out what the first group of sports has in common that is lacking in the other group. There is no mathematical formula for this; it is simply a matter of judgement. And though the decision is fairly cut-and-dried with a concrete problem like sports, it is far more complex and abstract when the target is something as intangible as personality traits. It is entirely possible that two factor analysts, given exactly the same table of factors, factor loadings, and other pertinent data, will come up with not only different names for the factors, but names that are not even close synonyms (cf., Anastasi 1983; Royce, 1982).

Despite all of this, the major reason why factor analysts come up with different lists of traits lies elsewhere.

Con #4: What comes out of a factor analysis is what went into it.   The main reason why factor analysts come up with different lists of traits is that factor analysis is applied not to the human personality itself, but to a personality test, a series of trait-rating scales, and ultimately, the

English language itself. In a sense, you only get out of a factor analysis what you put into it. Or to be more precise, you cannot get out of it anything that was not there to start with. A factor analysis of data from personality tests or trait-rating scales simply reduces the traits represented in those instruments to some more basic set of components or elements. Only components or elements of the traits represented in those instruments will be found, not any others. Clearly then, if you are looking for all of the elements of human personality, you must be absolutely certain that all possible human traits are represented in the tests or scales you start with. Some factor analysts are not as careful about this as others. Actually, it is not really a matter of carelessness; it is just that they do not always agree about what it means to be careful on this point. If factor analysts work with data from different personality tests and trait-rating scales, it is not surprising that they all find different trait factors making up personality.

Cattell has tried hard to be careful about this. That is why he started with all the words in the English dictionary that might possibly refer to traits. That approach seems to make sense. In fact, it might be the best solution available. Yet it has certain pitfalls. In the first place, if Cattell is looking for universal traits of human personality, he has limited himself by starting with the language of only part of the world's people. What, for example, if he had begun with the Japanese dictionary? Would he have ended up with the same fifteen source traits? Probably not, because each language considers a slightly different set of human characteristics significant enough to describe with words. There must be trait words in the Japanese dictionary that have no cognates in English and would therefore have been absent from Cattell's original pool. English-speaking people may have these Japanese traits, of course, but we do not have words for them. This example could be multiplied thousands of times: Not only are there many Japanese trait words without English cognates; the same is true for every other language in the world.

More is involved here than mere cultural bias. There is the larger question of verbal bias. If there are human traits for which there is no word in English, how do we know that there are not traits for which there is no word in any language? We have already seen that if traits are as individualistic as Allport says they are, there would be no word in the dictionary to refer to them. But even if they are more general, they might still be too complex or intangible to capture in a single word. That, after all, is why we have analogy, and metaphor, and even poetry. Some human characteristics will inevitably be lost if we limit ourselves to a simple WORD X = TRAIT Y formula. Yet Cattell assumed that personality traits were equivalent to the words people use to characterize each other. Consequently, his factor analysis is an analysis not of human personality, but of the words people use to describe personality. In the end, then, his analysis is no better than the words he started with. And there is nothing scientific about the way those words have come into use; they are simply the product of folk wisdom.

When chemists set out to analyze a chemical compound, they take the compound itself and break it down into its component elements. But when factor analysts set out to analyze human personality, they do not perform their operations on the personality itself, but on tests or ratings that already represent someone's *idea* of personality. There is a sleight-of-hand element here that most factor analysts would prefer us to ignore.

Con #5: Human nature is more than a series of holes in an IBM card. The portrait of human nature that emerges from Cattell's key idea (discovering traits through factor analysis) is rather barren and narrow. His goal is to reduce every individual to fifteen or twenty numbers—the individual's personality profile. First, factor analysis identifies the fifteen or twenty universal trait elements. Then some test, such as the 16PF, is built to measure the strength of each of these trait elements. Next, individuals are given the test. Their "personalities" are represented by fifteen or twenty numbers, the scores they got on each of the trait elements. The scores are arranged in a certain order on charts called personality profiles. Very seldom, of course, do two individuals end up with exactly the same profile, though that is possible. And the fact that it is possible suggests that there are aspects of personality that are not captured by this sketchy kind of portrait, because it is highly unlikely that a person observing these two hypothetical individuals with identical profiles would agree that their personalities were identical. One need not be as fanatical about individuality as Allport was to see that fifteen or twenty numbers cannot do justice to the richness of human personality.

But then, Cattell never aspired to be a portrait painter. His aim was to be a scientist. And true to that aim, his goal was to predict. The personality profiles that emerge from his tests do predict individual performance in a variety of settings. If that were not so, he would not have sold as many copies of them as he has. They are, in fact, among the best predictors available to business and industry for purposes of personnel selection and assessment. For cost effectiveness, a good testing program is undoubtedly the best way to screen candidates for new jobs, promotions, special training programs, etc. The tests accurately predict which individuals are most likely to succeed in such situations. Not perfectly, of course; but better than anything else we have, given the time and money available for these tasks. Predictions of this kind are Cattell's forte.

Cattell's approach is also useful for predicting academic performance in school settings. Here, however, the emphasis is more on ability factors than on what we would normally think of as personality traits. Nevertheless, Cattell maintains—and I think he has a strong argument here—that abilities are just as much personality traits as are characteristics such as introversion, aggressiveness, or suspiciousness. On the other hand, Cattell believes that academic success comes not only from abilities, but, more than is generally thought, from the influence of attitudes and sentiments.

In the clinical realm, Cattell's tests have been less widely used. This does not mean that personality tests are not used at all by clinical psychologists, because they are. Nor does it mean that his key idea of discovering traits through factor analysis is fundamentally antithetical to clinical psychological theories. The problem has to do with Cattell's own interests on the one hand, and the prejudices of clinical psychologists on the other. Despite five years of clinical experience at the beginning of his career, Cattell is less a practicing clinical psychologist than an academic researcher. He has maintained an interest in clinical psychology, and of late IPAT has published more and more tests designed to be used by clinical psychologists. Nevertheless, Cattell's theory is so complex, its mathematical foundations are so uncongenial to many psychotherapists, and his language is so unfamiliar, that the majority of clinicians are unwilling to expend the effort required to use either his materials or his theory. The traits that Cattell has discovered by factor analysis just do not fit the frame of reference of a good many psychotherapists. A test such as the MMPI (Minnesota Multiphasic Personality Inventory), for example, yields scores on traits that clinicians all understand and use all the time. Cattell's scheme of traits is not as familiar. Furthermore, many psychotherapists prefer a personality theory that places greater emphasis on the role of unconscious dynamics than Cattell does. These therapists, if they use tests at all, often prefer projective techniques—the Rorschach, for example. Apparently many clinicians feel that there is something missing from both Cattell's personality theory and his tests. Humanistically oriented therapists feel that he ignores the richness and uniqueness of personality, and psychodynamically oriented clinicians miss an emphasis on the unconscious.

Cattell has tried to reduce personality to a convenient number of test scores, in order to make predictions of performance in jobs and job-training programs, in academic studies, in rehabilitation programs, and in psychotherapy. The range of applications for his theory is fairly broad. The objective—to predict performance—is from certain perspectives narrow and limited. Predicting a person's performance may not be the same thing as understanding that individual's personality.

CHAPTER SUMMARY

Consistent with his background in chemistry, Cattell conceives of the personality as a compound made up of a limited number of universal elements. It is the job of the personality psychologist to discover those elements. To accomplish this feat Cattell employs personality and ability tests, coupled with a statistical technique known as factor analysis. Cattell's key idea is that factor analysis can identify the universal traits that make up all individual personalities.

1.   Cattell's strategy was to begin with a list of trait-words taken from the dictionary. By combining synonyms, he reduced the list to 171 *trait-elements*. He then had people rate other people on these. For example, bosses might rate their employees on a seven-point scale for such trait-elements as "punctuality" and "industriousness." Once he had collected a sufficient number of such ratings, Cattell computed the intercorrelations among all the pairs of trait-elements. Combinations that yielded a correlation coefficient above a certain criterion, e.g., .70, he considered trait clusters. These clusters, of which he found 40, he referred to as *surface traits*. Next he computed the intercorrelations among the 40 surface traits and factor-analyzed the resulting correlation matrix to discover *source traits*, the very basic particles of personality.

2.   The final factor analysis produced fifteen source traits. These traits are universal, because the entire universe—all of the traits in the English language—was included in the original pool. They are also the most elemental particles of personality, because there are no techniques for further analysis. Every human personality consists of a unique mixture of these source traits.

3.   The amount any given individual has of each source trait can be measured by tests constructed for that purpose. Cattell's 16PF is such a test. Once a psychologist knows how much of each source trait an individual possesses, the psychologist is in a good position to predict that individual's behavior. What a person will do in a given situation, according to Cattell, is a function of all of the person's traits that are relevant to that situation.

4.   "Personality," according to Cattell, "is that which permits a prediction of what a person will do in a given situation" (Cattell, 1950, p. 2). With his tests that measure the strength of source traits in individual personalities, Cattell is able to make predictions of the sort that are particularly useful in resolving personnel selection problems: admitting students to college or law school; placing recruits in various positions in the military service; hiring management trainees; or promoting assembly-line workers to shop supervisors.

5. Pro #1:   If you put aside the complex statistics, you can see that Cattell's key idea is very commonsensical. The idea that people have traits, and that these traits are stronger in some people and weaker in others, is as old as human history and taken for granted by almost everybody.

Pro #2:   Cattell actually measures personality; and that, after all, is the aim of science. If something so ephemeral as freestyle figure-skating ability can be measured, there is no intrinsic reason why personality traits cannot be measured.

Pro #3:   There is an inherent logic in Cattell's approach, that derived from the fact that correlation and even factor analysis are only formalized versions of our ordinary, natural modes of thinking. Quite naturally and spontaneously, we observe when things go together. Correlation merely mathematizes that process. Without thinking he is doing anything scholarly, a baseball scout (or even an ordinary fan) analyzes a baseball player's performance into hitting ability, fielding ability, baserunning ability, etc. Again, factor analysis merely mathematizes that process.

Pro #4: Cattell's key idea and resulting personality theory are scientific: He uses tests, computers, and formidable systems of mathematics. The theory also looks scientific, which is what Cattell intends it to be. In fact, Cattell is among the two or three most scientific theorists we will study.

Con #1: Unfortunately the other two most scientific theorists, Skinner and Bandura, maintain that Cattell's theory is almost totally useless, because it concentrates so much on traits while all but ignoring situational variables. If you want to predict behavior, they say, trait measurements are almost worthless; situational variables account for most of the differences in human responses. These critics say that traits, if they exist at all, are situation-specific.

Con #2: Psychological testing, one of the foundation stones of Cattell's theory, has been criticized for being culturally biased, prejudicial, discriminatory, and an invasion of privacy. Many courts, employers, and even college admissions officers agree with this criticism.

Con #3: Even psychologists who agree with Cattell that tests are good, and that hunting for traits with factor analysis is the best way to do personality psychology, sometimes discover source traits that are different from Cattell's. Factor analysts disagree among themselves. They disagree on what the proper mathematical procedures are. But there is also considerable opportunity for subjective interpretation at the point where the factors dervied from the mathematical analysis must be named and defined. This process is as much an art as a science.

Con #4: Yet the main reason why factor analysts come up with different lists of traits is that what comes out of a factor analysis is exactly what went into it. The thing that is factor-analyzed is not personality itself, but various alleged measures of personality: tests, rating scales, and perhaps even the English language itself. Obviously, if you were to begin with different tests or rating scales, or a different language, you might come up with different trait factors. Since the personality itself is not analyzed, the traits, whatever they may be, cannot be the elements of personality.

Con #5: The portrait of human nature that emerges from Cattell's key idea is barren and narrow. Fifteen or so numbers cannot do justice to the richness of human personality. They may provide enough data to make accurate predictions of performance in certain specific situations, but being able to predict performance may not be the same thing as understanding personality.

REFERENCES

Anastasi, A. (1983). Evolving trait concepts. *American Psychologist, 38,* 175-184.

Cattell, R. B. (1950). *Personality, a systematic theoretical and factual study.* New York: McGraw-Hill.

Cattell, R. B. (1952). *Factor analysis.* New York: Harper & Row.

Cattell, R. B. (1979). *Personality and learning theory: Vol. 1. The structure of personality and its environment.* New York: Springer.

Eysenck, H. J. (1970). *The structure of human personality.* London, Methuen.

Mischel, W. (1968). *Personality and assessment.* New York: Wiley.

Royce, J. R. (1982). Philosophical issues, Division 24, and the future. *American Psychologist, 37,* 258–266.

1983–1984 Catalogue of psychological tests, test services, and books. (1983). Champaign, IL: Institute for Personality and Ability Testing.

PART THREE

Behavioral Theories

Behavioral theories of personality have at least two distinguishing characteristics. In the first place, they hold that personality is exclusively the product of learning. Of course, no brand of personality theory denies that learning plays some part in the formation of personality; but the behaviorists claim that it plays the only role—the whole personality is learned. They contend that because you were born into this world with your mind a blank slate, there is no way that your personality could be anything other than what you have learned from experience since then. There is no room here for any instincts such as Freud postulated, or innate ideas such as the Jungean archetypes. Behaviorists even deny, or minimize, the role of hereditary individual differences in traits or abilities. They see mental retardation, for example, as the product of a developmental delay in learning (Bijou, 1968). Whether a person is a genius or a retardate, aggressive or a patsy, gay or straight, the personality pattern must have come about through learning, since personality has no other source.

The second distinguishing mark of behavioral theories of personality is allegiance to the principle that an individual's personality is the sum total of his or her observable behavior. People are what they *do*. In other words, behaviorists prefer to restrict their studies to what can be observed and measured.

The trouble with instincts and innate ideas is not only that they are alleged to be unlearned, they are also unobservable. Traits, too, are unobservable, though they are sometimes learned. Of course, the list of alleged psychic entities that are disqualified by behavioral personality theories extends far beyond these. It includes all concepts of self and ego identity; consciousness; the unconscious; dreams; fantasies; attitudes; wishes; values; and any sort of mental representation. In short, behavioral theories are "anti-mentalistic," against the idea that there is a mind that controls behavior.

There are, as we shall see, a wide range of positions on this issue within the behaviorist camp. At one extreme we find Skinner, whose theory has no room at all for internal mental processes. His hard-line, radical behaviorism equates personality exclusively with an individual's observable actions. At the other extreme is Bandura, who emphasizes the role of covert (hidden) cognitive processes in mediating behavior, but who nevertheless maintains that these processes only qualify for inclusion in his theory when they can be demonstrated to effect observable behavior.

Perhaps we should say, then, that the second earmark of a behavioral theory is that it seeks verification in observable behavior. Personality is defined as anything that affects behavior in an observable manner. If a person claims to have a certain attitude, but this attitude is not evident in his or her behavior, then behaviorists do not consider the attitude to be part of the individual's personality. The final test for the behaviorist is always *behavior*.

Thus behavioral theories, more than those of any other tradition, are typically founded upon experimental evidence. This is what they mean when they call their approach empirical. And since it is often more convenient to perform experiments using animals as subjects, many behavioral theories are based on evidence from animal experiments.

Coinciding with the behavioral theorists'

fondness for experimentation is their passion for prediction and control. They are ardent supporters of the following definition of psychology: *the science of the prediction and control of human and animal behavior*. That psychology, including the psychology of personality, ought to be a science, they have no doubt. That it is the business of science to predict and control, they accept as self-evident. It follows logically that the way to validate theories is to design experiments that will test predictions made on the basis of the theory.

This orientation also generates an interest, among many behavioral personality theorists, in behavior modification. Though all psychotherapists employ some theory of learning, it is the behavioral theorists who have systematically set out to apply principles of learning derived in the laboratory (usually from experiments with animal subjects) to the processes of psychotherapy and rehabilitation. They take the same methods they used for controlling the behavior of animals in the laboratory—the judicious application of contiguous stimuli or timely reinforcement—and apply them to the anxious behavior of neurotic patients, the antisocial behavior of criminals, the withdrawn behavior of **autistic** children, the untidy behavior of the severely retarded, the compulsive eating behavior of overweight persons, and to an endless variety of other human problems. Recently a whole new field has sprung up: behavioral medicine.

All of these behavioral technologies are based on the premise that behavior can be *controlled*. Again, there is some divergence of opinion among behavioral theorists concerning just what that means. Some hold that our behavior is controlled exclusively by external stimuli, while others allow room for a certain degree of internal self-control. But in either case, the emphasis is on control. *Control* is a word we hear being used by the behavioral theorists far more often than by any other personality theorists. This caused so much alarm among other psychologists that Albert Bandura felt compelled to use his presidential address to the American Psychological Association in 1974 to dispell fears that behavior modification might become the tool of a repressive, totalitarian political regime. Behavioral theorists' enthusiasm for control was apparently giving the whole movement a bad name.

In summary then, behavioral theories of personality hold that personality is the sum total of an individual's behavior, and that behavior is produced exclusively by learning. Behaviorists prefer to validate their theories with experimentation. They test predictions about what will happen when certain variables are manipulated. Their belief that behavior is controlled by these variables leads them to apply their theories to psychotherapy, education, and rehabilition.

REFERENCES

Bandura, A. (1974). Behavior theory and the models of man. *American Psychologist, 29,* 859–869.

Bijou, S. W. (1968). A behavioral theory of mental retardation. *Psychology Today, 2,* 47–51.

9/B. F. Skinner

A Biographical Sketch

Burrhus Frederic Skinner has left us a thoroughly charming account (1976) of an idyllic childhood spent in Susquehanna, Pennsylvania during the years before World War I. There he was born in 1904, the first of two sons, to William A. Skinner and Grace Burrhus Skinner. His father was a lawyer and sometime aspiring politician. His mother, whom Skinner says was the dominant parent, had achieved a modest local renown for her musical talents, both as a pianist and a vocalist. She was undoubtedly the source of Skinner's very strong interest in music, although his father had played the cornet at one time.

Young Fred Skinner spent the first twelve years of school in the same small brick schoolhouse. One of his earliest memories is of being taken by his third-grade teacher to his former second-grade classroom where he was exhibited as an inspiring model after turning in a perfect arithmetic paper. His parents did not lavish praise on him for his academic accomplishments, however; they simply took it for granted that he would excel. They had both graduated second in their respective high school classes. And Fred did excel. He seems to have been a rather bookish young man. At an early age he began to write stories. At ten, he published his first poem. But his lifelong fascination with gadgets is evident in the fact that he already had a typewriter and a printing press at that time. At thirteen, he began a novel, soon followed by a screenplay.

So fond was Skinner of school that during his high school years, he arranged for the custodian to let him into the building each morning before the first bell. Apparently he enjoyed physics almost as much as Latin. One of his teachers, Miss Graves, who was "promoted" through the grades at almost the same rate as Skinner, taught him drawing for twelve years and reading for six—not to mention Sunday School. Skinner credits Miss Graves with infecting him with his love of literature and art. She was clearly an important role model for him.

As a boy, Fred Skinner was forever concocting some kind of gadget or other. To put an end to his mother's pestering him to hang up his pajamas each morning, he devised a rope-and-pulley system by attaching the hanger in his closet to a sign over his doorway. When the pajamas were removed from the hanger, the sign descended to block the doorway; when the pajamas were hung up again, the sign disappeared. He also built a machine to smoke cigarettes, since he was forbidden to smoke them himself, but soon found that blowing smoke rings with an atomizer was not especially reinforcing.

Music is one of Skinner's great loves. After beginning at eight or nine with piano lessons, he graduated to saxophone. Before high school ended, he was playing in various bands, including weekend gigs with a jazz band. Nevertheless, it was opera and classical music that provided the greatest musical satisfaction for Skinner. And his interest in opera dovetailed with a love of theater, which was of course closely related to his interest in literature and writing.

Religion also played a major role in Skinner's upbringing. By the time he reached adolescence, he began to question the simplistic theology of his Sunday School teachers. Yet he had been indoctrinated so effectively that, for a long time, he was tormented by feelings of guilt over even minor misdemeanors. Characteristically he embarked upon a experimental test of the ability of faith to move mountains. He was about twelve years old when he stood on a scale and tried, in all good faith, to make himself lighter by virtue of sincere belief. Sometime later he announced to Miss Graves that he no longer believed in God.

Skinner went to college because it was always assumed that he would. On the advice of a family friend he chose Hamilton, a small college in upstate New York. Not surprisingly, composition was his favorite course during his freshman year. His commitment to a career as a writer continued to grow throughout his years at Hamilton, and he graduated with a major in English and a minor in Romance languages. He took no psychology, except for an incidental demonstration of the two-point threshold as part of a philosophy course. But a series of courses in biology, including advanced courses in embryology and anatomy, captured some of his interest. It was writing, though, that occupied the bulk of his time—writing for courses and for a variety of school publications. What finally made Skinner decide to become a writer was an experience during the summer following his junior year. He attended the

Middlebury School of English at Breadloaf, Vermont, and met Robert Frost. Frost consented to read some of Skinner's stories and returned them with an encouraging letter that was all the aspiring young writer needed.

Skinner tells us that he did not fit in very well with his classmates at college. He was not at all athletic, and he quickly acquired a reputation for being conceited. He chafed under some of the rigid requirements, such as complusory daily chapel. Looking back now, he feels he ought to have organized a student protest. Instead, he resorted to practical jokes. The most outrageous of these involved printing and putting up posters announcing a fictitious public lecture by Charlie Chaplin. The whole town fell for it; hundreds of people arrived to hear the famous movie comedian. Skinner also succeeded in sabotaging the graduation exercises and the contest for the oratory prize by delivering esoteric parodies at each. Apparently Skinner has long been something of an iconoclast.

Armed with his bachelor's degree, in 1926 Skinner set up a study in the attic of his rather disappointed parents' new home in Scranton, in order to begin his literary career. Nothing came of it. He could not write. Later he would conclude that he had simply had nothing to say. Hour after hour was frittered away. Before the year was out, he gave up the idea and took a hack job writing up the details of labor disputes for the Anthracite Board. When that job ended, Skinner entered a bohemian phase, spending six months living in Greenwich Village. After a tour of Europe in the summer of 1928, he entered Harvard to begin graduate work in psychology.

How did the budding young novelist settle on psychology? Apparently he had always pondered questions about human be-

havior. It was just that he made the mistake of expecting to find them answered in literature. In the midst of his despair over failing as a writer, Skinner remembered, with the force of a revelation, a quotation from Chesterton and a piece of advice from a friend. The crux of these recollections was that literary authors do not necessarily understand human behavior, and that science is the art of the twentieth century. He resolved, although not instantly, to pursue the scientific explanation of behavior.

As with so many of our theorists, a chance encounter with a book had decisive effect at this point (1927). In a journal he looked at regularly, Skinner came across an article by Bertrand Russell, in which Russell described the new behaviorism of John B. Watson. In quick succession Skinner read several of Watson's books, bought Pavlov's *Conditioned Reflexes* (1927), and wrote an article championing behaviorism, which he sent to the *Saturday Review of Literature*.

Skinner received his Ph.D. from Harvard in 1931. For five more years he stayed on there, supported by postdoctoral fellowships, conducting his classic experiments on the **operant conditioning** of rats (to which we will return shortly). In fact, most of Skinner's later professional accomplishments will be covered in the main body of this chapter. For now, it will suffice to sketch the broad outlines of his career. In 1936, he went to teach at the University of Minnesota. From there he moved in 1945 to the University of Indiana. Three years later he was invited back to Harvard, where he has remained ever since. At present, Skinner still spends a good portion of every day writing. Perhaps he forsook a career in literature, but he nevertheless has become one of the most prolific and persuasive American writers in any field.

SKINNER'S PRODIGIOUS ACHIEVEMENTS

If fame is the name of the game, B. F. Skinner is the hands-down winner among living psychologists. Of our entire cast of characters, in fact, none but Sigmund Freud can hold a candle to him in this regard. A recent survey showed Skinner to be the best-known scientist of any kind in the United States; and as early as 1970, he was included among the one hundred most important people in the world (Guttman, 1977). His picture has appeared on the cover of *Time* magazine. He is indisputably the most famous American psychologist of all time. Almost singlehandedly he has made *reinforcement* a household word, having taken over from J. B. Watson the role of standard-bearer for the behaviorist cause. None of the other psychologists included in this book, and very few (if any) in all the history of psychology, has ever written a best-seller to rival Skinner's *Beyond Freedom and Dignity* (1971) in sales and in popular acclaim. Neither are there many psychologists who are also popular novelists. Yet Skinner's *Walden Two*, published in 1948, is still in print. It has been read by hundreds of thousands of people who would never have read any of his more technical writings.

Skinner's fame is not the accidental, empty renown of the talk-show celebrity who is famous merely for being famous. Skinner's accomplishments are prodigious, and his influence has been profound. As a kind of Thomas Edison of psychological and educational technology, his influence derives as much from the usefulness of his gadgets as from the persuasiveness of his arguments. This is not to demean him by saying that he is nothing but a gadgeteer, but to support his view that influencing people involves changing the way they do things, rather than merely defeating them in an intellectual debate. In short, behavior is changed by changing behavior, not by changing minds. The full impact of Skinner's teaching machine and, more important, its software component—the learning program—has yet to be realized in the realm of human education. At some future date, however, Skinner's machine will probably be seen as one of those inventions that is dismissed as inconsequential at first, but has a tremendous impact when coupled with subsequent technology. Skinner's first teaching machines printed questions and answers on a paper tape that was stretched between two rollers. When the tape was advanced, the questions and answers were exposed through a slot in the face of the machine. Another popular way of presenting the learning program has been to include it in a programmed textbook, with the answer to each question printed either in a separate column that is covered with a piece of cardboard, or else at the back of the book. Needless to say, this is the kind of "horse-and-buggy" stuff that the computer made obsolete overnight. But if Skinner's hardware was made obsolete, it was only so that his software could undergo a quantum leap in its potential effectiveness.

Today you can buy programs for your home computer that will teach you everything from speaking French to managing your financial invest-ments. To some extent, they all use the principles developed by Skinner and his associates for constructing learning programs. Skinner's influence on formal education in schools and colleges has already been considerable, but it may become awesome now that education is moving, under the impact of computer technology, into homes, businesses and industries. For business and industry also impatient with the slowness of change in formal educational institutions, have been in the forefront of efforts to apply computer-assisted programmed learning to the training of employees. Skin-ner's influence on education outside the schools may well dwarf his already potent influence within the schools.

Skinner's influence in the field of mental health has been hardly less stunning. Here he has not done the job quite so singlehandedly; but by the same token, the changes are even more revolutionary. What were only recently regarded as mental illnesses are fast coming to be designated *behavior disorders*. Though the latest edition of the manual of the Am-erican Psychiatric Association is entitled *Diagnostic and Statistical Manual of Mental Disorders* (DSM-III, 1980), the symptoms listed in this work are no longer predominantly mentalistic. There is instead a strong emphasis on behavioral definitions of diagnostic criteria. At the same time, the people who foot the bill for psychiatric treatment are increasingly demanding that therapists be reimbursed for services only when they bring about demon-strable change in their patients' behavior. The growing use of biofeedback techniques and the establishment of departments of behavioral medicine point toward the acceptance of Skinner's ideas by the medical profession in general.

Behind all these developments lie a series of events that goes back at least to the time when Skinner and Lindsley invented the term *behavior therapy* (1954). Since then, behaviorism has come out of the animal labor-atory and into the clinic, where today behavior therapy is the only serious alternative to psychodynamic therapies. The application of behavior-modification techniques, based almost exclusively upon Skinnerian prin-ciples, to the rehabilitation of the mentally retarded has contributed might-ily to the deinstitutionalization of that population. Many of the same tech-niques have been widely applied to correctional institutions, ranging from maximum security prisons to group homes for juvenile offenders.

Though success in these settings has been somewhat less conspicuous, Skinnerian techniques have been used probably more than any other single brand during the past decade. It has even been possible to modify the psychotic behavior of mental-hospital patients with Skinner's *operant con-ditioning* procedures (Allyon & Azrin, 1965). Wards operated on the basis of behavior modification principles are commonplace in mental hospitals today. The result is not only that many patients recover more quickly, but that the hospital is a much cleaner, less violent, and less degrading envir-

◖ OPERANT AND CLASSICAL CONDITIONING

Skinner's theory and research concentrate on only one of the two kinds of conditioning known to psychologists. Skinner's is a theory of *operant* conditioning (also called *instrumental learning*). In operant conditioning the individual first behaves—does something; emits an operant, as Skinner puts it—and then suffers some consequence, which makes it either more or less likely that the behavior will be repeated. Reinforcement increases the probability of reenactment; absence of reinforcement decreases it. But the important point is that the learning process begins only when the individual spontaneously behaves.

In **classical conditioning**, the other major kind, the individual does not do anything. The learning process commences here when two stimuli impinge upon that person at the same time. If this process is repeated often enough, the second stimulus may come to evoke the same response as the first stimulus. Thus Ivan Pavlov repeatedly rang a bell at the moment he presented food to a dog. A dog's natural reflex reaction to food is to salivate. After the food and the bell were paired a sufficient number of times, the bell alone evoked salivation. Because the subject is a passive respondent in classical conditioning, it is also referred to as *respondent* conditioning.

Skinner does not deny the existence of classical conditioning; he simply thinks that operant principles have played a far greater role in the evolution of human personality and social institutions. He also thinks that operant principles are far more useful in practical applications such as behavior modification, programmed learning, and the design of a better world.

onment for those who must spend time there. Skinner's principles of operant conditioning are routinely applied today in treating a wide assortment of childhood behavioral problems, running the gamut from bed-wetting to hyperactivity. The extremely withdrawn, psychotic behavior of autistic children can also be treated as effectively with techniques based on Skinner's research as with any other method (Carr, Schreibman, & Lovaas, 1975).

Skinner's concerns have always been primarily practical and utilitarian, so it is appropriate that we should look first at his influence upon the practice of psychotherapy. Yet we cannot ignore the fact that more and more theories on the causes of abnormal behavior are based on the principles of operant conditioning. Skinnerian theories on the causes of depression, schizophrenia, infantile autism, and obsessive-compulsive disorders regularly turn up in the latest textbooks on abnormal psychology.

Even the bureaucracy of psychology has been influenced more powerfully by Skinner than by any other psychologist in recent history. Two widely distributed professional journals, the *Journal of the Experimental Analysis of Behavior* and the *Journal of Applied Behavior Analysis*, were created as the house organs for Skinnerian theory and research. And "Division 25 of the American Psychological Association (Division for the Experimental Analysis of Behavior) is exclusively a Skinnerian organization, the only section of APA identifiable with an individual psychologist" (Guttman, 1977, p. 324).

Skinner is famous and has been very influential. Perhaps this point has been made with overkill. Yet we have not even mentioned his invention of the Skinner box, the most popular piece of psychological laboratory apparatus in the world today, and probably the first association that most people have with the name *Skinner*. Given the scope of his influence, it is not possible to omit B. F. Skinner from our cast of personality theorists here, despite the ironic fact that Skinner has never considered himself a personality psychologist. Until recently, he has even denied that his work constitutes a theory (Skinner, 1969, p. vii–xii)!

THE KEY IDEA
CONTINGENCIES OF REINFORCEMENT

Skinner has had all this fame and influence in spite of the fact—or perhaps because of the fact—that his theory is more an elaboration of one simple idea than almost any of the others we consider in this book. Skinner is a cinch to analyze with the key idea technique. It is hard to think of another psychologist who has gotten so much mileage out of a single idea. For that to happen, of course, the idea (not to mention the theorist), must be extremely impressive. It also helps if the idea is already familiar. And it certainly helps if the idea is useful and practical. Skinner's key idea is all of these things.

Succinctly stated, Skinner's key idea is that *all behavior is determined by contingencies of reinforcement.* What this means is that our behavior in any situation depends on (is contingent upon) the kind or frequency of reinforcement in similar situations in our past. We are more apt to repeat behaviors that have been reinforced, less apt to repeat those that have not been reinforced or have been punished. In other words, the consequences of our past behavior determine our present behavior.

The parallel with Darwin's theory of natural selection is both strict and intentional. Skinner sees his idea of contingencies of reinforcement as a logical corollary to Darwin's theory. In evolution, environmental contingencies select who is to survive. **Mutations** occur, producing animals with new traits. Environmental circumstances either permit these animals to survive, or cause them to become extinct. Of course, the animals do not intentionally change in order to survive; the mutations are accidental. It is the environment that decides who will survive. This process extends over many generations, thousands of years, and involves the interaction of permanent changes in behavior with long-lasting features of the environment. But less stable features of the environment may exert the same kind of selective control over the more flexible behavior of individual organisms. The organism behaves—perhaps it is an infant who quite by accident vocalizes "mama"—and the environment reinforces, in this case by having an ecstatic mother run to pick up and hug her clever baby. The probability that this baby will again say "mama" is thereby increased. The environment has selected for that behavior. In each individual, contingencies of reinforcement select the behaviors that survive in the same way that environmental contingencies select the species that survive in nature. Behaviors that the environment does not favor are extinguished; those that it reinforces are reproduced. It is irrelevant whether or not the individual intends the behavior; in the end, environmental contingencies control the behavior's reproduction.

It follows quite logically from this that if you want to predict what a person will do in a given situation, all you need to know is what behaviors the environment typically reinforces in such a situation. Assuming that the person has been previously exposed to this or similar situations and that the environmental consequences are fairly consistent, it is a good bet that the person will do what is most reinforcing. The crucial point is that all of the information you need to predict behavior is in the environment, none of it is in the person's head. Skinner's theory is an example of extreme environmental determinism.

The other side of the coin is that Skinner is unremittingly anti-mentalistic. He does not need to know people's motives in order to predict their behavior. He does not need access to their feelings, intentions, dreams or aspirations. All he needs to know are the environmental contingencies. Skinner does not deny the existence of these internal contents-of-consciousness, or even of unconscious contents; he merely dismisses them as less useful for predicting behavior than a knowledge of the environmental contingencies. Surely the knowledge that dinosaurs were trying their damnedest to overcome the forces that led to their extinction would not lead one to predict that they would survive. Why then should the psychologist who is intersted in predicting what behaviors will survive in an individual **repertoire** be distracted by that individual's inner mental states?

The inner mental states come not before but after the behavior, both in the evolutionary history of the human race and in the personal developmental history of each individual. People were already behaving, long before the first cavepersons invented language and became consciously aware that they were consciously aware. Once that giant step was taken, it was a short step to observing the correlations between their own behavior and their mental states, and then inventing mentalistic explanations for their behavior. Because it feels painful when you stick your hand in the fire, people concluded that the reason we pull our hand out of the fire is because it hurts. But in fact whether it feels good or feels bad, whether it gives pleasure or causes pain, is beside the point. In the last analysis, the reason why we pull our hand out of the fire is that environmental contingencies during the course of evolution have selected mechanisms that result in that behavior. In short, cavedwellers who did not have the withdrawing-from-fire behavior or the mechanisms to learn it simply did not survive to reproduce. The pain of being burned is so intense, we simply conclude that the desire to avoid pain must be what causes us to keep away from fire. This rationale only adds a superfluous layer to the explanation, however, for we must still ask why we are constructed in such a way that fire causes pain. The answer, of course, might still be the argument from natural selection. But since that is the answer Skinner has arrived at already, what is gained by interjecting this intermediary step, which not only unnecessarily encumbers the explanation but also bogs it down in a notorious philosophical quagmire? I am referring, of course, to the mind-body problem.

How can something nonphysical, such as a desire to avoid pain, cause something physical, such as fire-avoiding behavior? How does the mind cause the body to move? That, in a nutshell, is the mind-body problem. And no one has ever come up with a satisfactory answer to it. Skinner's answer is that the mind does not move the body:

> The view that mental activity is essential to operant behavior is an example of the view that feelings or introspectively observed states are causally effective. When a person replies to the question "Will you go tomorrow?" by saying, "I don't know, I never know how I will feel," the assumption is that what is in doubt is the feeling rather than the behavior—that the person will go if he feels like going rather than that he will feel like going if he goes. (Skinner, 1974, p. 69.)

"He will feel like going if he goes" is just as plausible an assumption as the reverse. Feelings, desires, intentions, and other contents-of-consciousness may accompany that behavior, but there is no scientific evidence that they cause it. "There is no place in the scientific position for a self [for example] as a true originator or initiator of action" (Skinner, 1974, p. 225). The mind-body problem is a pseudoproblem, fabricated by the same kind of fuzzy thinking that invented the mind in the first place. If a mind or a self were required to initiate behavior, we would be at a loss to explain how prehistoric peoples, newborn infants, or even the family's pet dog is able to behave. If we were to hedge and say that only certain higher forms of behavior require a mind, we would be plunged into the morass of trying to specify the exact location of the dividing line between higher and lower behaviors. In fact, behavior is caused by contingencies of reinforcement. Feelings, thoughts, and even manifestations of what we are accustomed to calling "the self" are nothing other than various behaviors. They are not mind-stuff, they are behavior.

For behaviorism, the subject matter of psychology is behavior. There are "mental behaviors," but there is no mind apart from behavior. There are feeling behaviors, thinking behaviors, and behaviors such as self-description, self-prediction, and self-management. But where does the self go when it is no longer on stage behaving? The same place your shadow goes when the lights go out!

For Skinner, the subject matter of psychology is more specifically the prediction and control of behavior. Descriptions of inner states of consciousness may be interesting and an entirely worthy pursuit—Skinner himself has written poetry and aspired to become a novelist before he discovered psychology—but that is art and not science. As a science, psychology should be more practical, more useful. It should provide a technology for behavioral engineering. But in order to develop such a technology, it will need to discover the lawful relationships between contingencies of reinforcement and the behaviors that they cause. To discover these laws, Skinner has undertaken an experimental analysis of behavior.

THE EXPERIMENTAL ANALYSIS OF BEHAVIOR

Enter the notorious Skinner box. Not to be confused with the controversial baby tender in which one of Skinner's daughters spent most of her infancy, the Skinner box is a kind of vending machine for animals. Long before Coke and cigarette machines adorned every lobby, and Wurlitzer perfected the jukebox, Skinner built an automated food dispenser that delivered food pellets to laboratory rats when the rats pressed a lever.

He chose rats as subjects (a choice much criticized by his opponents) for several important reasons. A science must begin with less complicated cases, and the contingencies operating on human beings in the real world are far too complex. Behavioral analysis can begin to investigate them today, but it would have been foolhardy to begin there fifty years ago. Like many medical researchers, Skinner began with animals, not because he thought human beings were no different from rats, but because you can do things with rats that you cannot do with human beings. Control of extraneous variables is the most important consideration here. You can keep rats in captivity and control their entire life history, including such factors as their diet, feeding schedule, exposure to various stimuli, and even genetic endowment. Rats are cheap, easy to keep, and do not develop neuroses as readily as cats, dogs, or monkeys (Skinner, 1938, p. 48). But perhaps most important, the experimental apparatus for analyzing their behavior can easily be automated; after just six years of research, Skinner alone had studied two million responses (Skinner, 1938, p. 58).

The experimental box (Skinner himself does not call it a Skinner box) which made this prodigious feat possible was a compartment about one foot square, with a food tray, a water dispenser, a lever, and a light mounted on one wall. Connected to the food tray was a pellet dispenser, which could automatically be programmed to deliver a measured amount of food each time the rat responded by pressing the lever, or by exhibiting any other pattern of responses the experimenter chose to study. Connected to the lever was a cumulative recorder, a device which automatically traced a line on a moving roll of paper. The line jumped a fraction of an inch higher each time the rat depressed the lever. The result was a record of the animal's rate of responding: lever-pressings plotted against time (See Figure 9-1).

Skinner performed a radically empirical and functional analysis with the help of this ingenious contraption. He did not attribute any drives or instincts to the animals. He did not even report that a rat was hungry, only that it had not been fed for forty-eight hours. No interpretation; report only what you observe—that was the radically empirical part. In **functional analysis**, you change one thing at a time and see if it makes a difference in the subject's behavior. "Whenever I do this, he always does that" is the kind of knowledge that comes from a functional analysis. Its usefulness is obvious: If I want him to do that, then I have to do this.

The things Skinner changed to see if they made any difference in the subject's behavior were **discriminative stimuli** and **schedules of reinforcement.** We will examine both. Skinner analyzed the subject's behavior for changes in the rate of responding. Such change, of course, can be read directly from the cumulative record. A line rising ever more steeply indicates that the rat is pushing the lever more often, while a line beginning

FIGURE 9-1

A Typical Experimental Box

One side has been cut away to show the part occupied by the animal. The space behind the panel at the left contains the rest of the lever, the food magazine, and other pieces of apparatus.

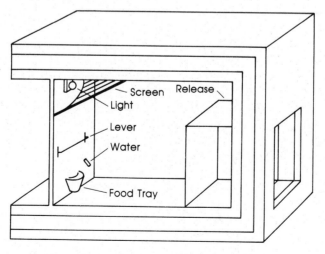

From Skinner, 1938, p. 49.

to level off shows that the subject is slowing down. A line that reaches a plateau and no longer climbs means that all lever-pressing has ceased.

A cumulative record can be obtained with the following procedure: (1) Dispense food to a hungry rat each time it pushes the lever. During this period the cumulative record line will rise more and more steeply. (2) Stop dispensing food at some point before the animal is satiated. Now the line on the cumulative record will start to flatten out. (3) If you wait long enough and still do not deliver any food, the animal will quit pushing the lever altogether and the line will be perfectly horizontal.

The rate of lever-pressing goes up when food follows each lever-pressing and goes down when it does not. Increasing the rate by giving food is what Skinner calls reinforcement. Reinforcement strengthens behavior—that, after all, is the **etymological** meaning of the word. Reinforcement is defined as *any stimulus which, when it follows a response, makes it more probable that that response will be emitted again.* Skinner's radical empiricism is evident here as well, in that he prefers to avoid using the word *reward* to refer to this phenomenon, even though it may look very much to you and me as if the rat is being rewarded for pushing the lever. Reward is a mentalistic concept that leads us to assume that the rat pushes the lever because it expects to get another bite to eat. That expectation is not only anthropomorphic, mentalistic, and liable to ensnare us in the mind-body problem, even more important, it is something we can infer, but never actually observe. All we can observe is that when food-delivery follows lever-pressing, the rat presses more and more, and when no food follows, it presses less and less—hence the definition of a reinforcer as a response-strengthener.

It follows that any continuing pattern of behavior must be caused by some kind of reinforcement. Amidst the complexity of daily life, it is often difficult to identify the reinforcers that cause certain behaviors to occur more frequently in ourselves, our friends, and even our pet cats. One reason for that, of course, is lack of control. We do not observe the cat's every move, or even our own for that matter. But another reason is that reinforcement does not need to follow each and every response to be effective. In fact, Skinner demonstrated very early on with his experimental box that intermittent reinforcement produces, astonishingly enough, an even higher rate of responding than does continuous reinforcement.

SCHEDULES OF REINFORCEMENT

Reinforcement that does not occur after every single response can occur after every fifth response, or it can occur every once in a while. This is a matter of programming, or scheduling, reinforcement. Reinforcement after every fifth response is an intermittent program of reinforcement that Skinner calls a *ratio schedule*. The ratio is this case is 1:5, but any ratio at all can be tried. If the ratio remains constant throughout the course of an experiment, or even a real-life situation, it is called a **fixed ratio schedule.** In fact, a real-life example of a fixed ratio schedule would be the migrant farm worker who is paid so much per basket for the grapes he or she picks. As Skinner demonstrated in the laboratory, this kind of schedule produces rates of responding high enough to endanger health, especially in the case of human beings. Labor unions have long regarded such pay schedules as exploitation and have bargained to have them eliminated.

Not all ratio schedules are fixed. The door-to-door salesperson, for example, works very often on what Skinner calls a **variable ratio schedule.** The reinforcement does not come after every fifth doorbell is rung, or indeed after any predictable number of sales attempts. Sometimes there will be long dry spells, yet on other occasions there may be two or more sales right in a row. The effect of this kind of schedule—this too has been demonstrated on laboratory animals—is to produce a high rate of responding that is particularly resistant to extinction. The organism continues to respond even during very long dry spells. Gambling is undoubtedly the most striking example of human behavior that is reinforced on a variable ratio schedule. People who have not won for many turns will go on putting coins into a "one-armed bandit," just as a rat will keep on pushing the lever long after the last food pellet drops into the tray, if lever-pressing has been reinforced on a variable ratio schedule.

In fact, many kinds of addictive behavior can be understood on the basis of variable ratio schedules. A drug or a drink does not produce the same buzz every time. In a case like this, the schedule "stretches" the ratios. Unless you increase your dosage, your increasing tolerance means that super highs will come less and less often. Getting hooked on watching a new television series works much the same way. For the first few shows, reinforcement may be quite frequent. Later, as the novelty wears off and the writers run out of ideas, the kicks are much less frequent. But many of us keep on watching long after all redeeming value has vanished. Even work can take on the character of an addiction, as indicated by the word "workaholic." A look behind the scenes usually reveals that the workaholic is responding to a ratio schedule. This is as true of the used-car salesperson working on commission as it is of the self-employed cabinetmaker who builds furniture to order. Even a salesclerk who does not get paid on commission may be operating on a variable ratio schedule, if the mere satisfaction of making a sale is at all reinforcing. In all these cases there is no need to look for an addictive personality. Nor is there some flaw in the character structure of the compulsive gambler, any more than there is a streak of virtue in the persevering self-employed artisan. Compulsive or persevering behavior may exist, but there is no need to postulate internal mental structures, *traits* of compulsiveness or perseverance, to account for it. The observation that behavior is maintained by a variable ratio schedule of reinforcement is the only explanation required.

Not everyone is a workaholic, of course. Why? Because not everybody is on a ratio schedule. Being paid a fixed wage or salary at regular intervals is an example of what Skinner calls an *interval schedule* of reinforcement.

An interval schedule can be programmed in the laboratory by rigging the food dispenser to deliver no more than one pellet every two minutes, or five minutes, or whatever interval the experimenter chooses, and then only if the animal has pressed the lever at least once during that interval. The important point here is that—unlike the ratio schedule, where the more you press the more you get—with an interval schedule, whether you press once or an hundred times during an interval, you only get one pellet at the end of the interval. Workaholics are not products of interval schedules.

Like ratio schedules, interval schedules may be fixed or variable. When the interval is fixed, the pattern of responses assumes a unique scalloped shape (see Figure 9–2). Early in an interval the rat presses the lever hardly at all, but as the end of an interval approaches the response rate increases sharply. Reinforcement is then delivered, and the lazy rat quits pushing again. This is reminiscent of college students who cram for exams, then ignore the material in the course until the next exam is scheduled. The students, of course, are no lazier by nature than the rats. It is the **fixed interval schedule** that causes lazy behavior to alternate with "cramming" behavior.

Professors who want their students to study the course material before every class, but who do not want to generate a lot of work for themselves by giving a quiz every day, can impose a variable interval schedule, in the form of occasional surprise quizzes. **Variable interval schedules** do not produce the scalloped effect of fixed interval schedules. The response rate on variable interval schedules, whether we are talking about rats or college students, is generally steady and can be kept quite high by shortening the

FIGURE 9-2

**Scalloped Pattern of Responses
Obtained with Fixed Interval Schedules**

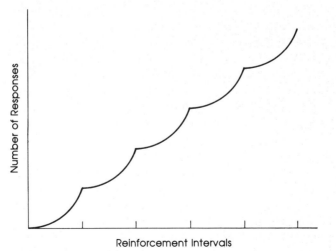

Reinforcement Intervals

intervals. The response rate varies with mean interval length—high for short intervals, low for longer ones.

Behavior maintained by variable interval schedules is also highly resist-ant to extinction. (Variable ratio schedules produce the same effect.) When you start work at a new job, the boss may look in every few minutes to see how you are doing. After you have been there a while, these checkups are much less frequent. But since you never know when they are coming, you try to look busy all the time. The variable interval schedule keeps you on your toes.

Different schedules of reinforcement therefore produce different pat-terns of behavior. Would that they were all as simple as the examples we have considered. But alas, life is much more complex than this, and any given human behavior is often controlled by more than one reinforcer and more than one schedule. Lately Skinner has been using computer programs to identify complex reinforcement schedules he cannot see by just looking at cumulative records. The results, though more complex, reaffirm the basic principle: Behavior is a function of environmental consequences. If those consequences strengthen a behavior, it will be repeated. How often, according to what pattern, and for how long depends upon how the conse-quences are scheduled.

DISCRIMINATIVE STIMULI

Skinner's simple little slot machine for animals, the Skinner box, demon-strated the powerful influence of another environmental factor in con-trolling behavior. Skinner found that if he reinforced the rat with food for pressing the lever when the light in the box was turned on, but withheld reinforcement when the light was off, the rat would soon press the lever only when the light was on and never when it was off. In fact, as soon as the light goes on in a dark box, a rat trained in this way will immediately begin to press the lever. This is an example of what Skinner calls the *stimulus control* of behavior. The stimulus, in this case the light, is called a *discrimi-native stimulus.* This kind of stimulus does not actually force the behavior to occur. All that we can say, from a strictly empirical standpoint is that the stimulus is present when the behavior is reinforced and will therefore be capable of increasing the rate of the response afterward (Skinner, 1969, p. 7).

It is extremely tempting to conclude that the rat learns to interpret the light as a cue, in effect realizing that there is a time and place for everything—a time to press, and time not to press. Examples of this abound in human life. The dinner bell rings and you come to the table. The bell does not force you to come to the table, and you would be quite capable of coming to the table without the bell. Yet the bell helps you to dis-criminate between the times when reinforcement is highly probable and the times when it is not. Actually, our pet cat shows a very similar pattern of behavior. Whenever he hears the electric can opener, he runs straight to the kitchen. Of course, all signals and signs are discriminative stimuli:

school bells, traffic lights, bus stop signs, restaurant signs, rest room signs: They all indicate the time and the place where a particular kind of behavior is most likely to be reinforced. There are many subtler social discriminative stimuli as well: the brief pause with which the other person indicates that it is your turn to pick up the conversation; the overly polite, patronizing chuckle after you have told your slightly off-color joke, letting you know that you have gone too far; the flirtatious look that suggests that your amorous advances will be welcome. Our environment is full of discriminative stimuli.

If you want to know why people do what they do, you must pay attention not only to schedules of reinforcement but to the presence of these discriminative stimuli. Skinner's key idea, you remember, is that our behavior in any situation depends on the kind and the frequency of reinforcement we have gotten in similar situations in our past. Discriminative stimuli permit us to identify the similarities between present and past situations. Any effort to predict and control behavior must therefore examine discriminative stimuli as well as schedules of reinforcement.

WHAT ABOUT PERSONALITY?

Personality is a term Skinner does not find particularly useful. If he uses it at all, he equates it with a person's behavior. People are what they do, or what they have done. Your personality is your life history, your biography, your cumulative record, so to speak. It is certainly not something inside of you. It is not even the sum total of all you have learned, as though you had memory banks filled with information inside. Personality is behavior; when you are not performing some act, your personality does not exist except as past history. Strictly speaking, personality is not something you have, it is something you do.

To do anything, of course, you need a physiological system: muscles, sense organs, brain, and nervous system. It is this system that is changed when the environmental contingencies of reinforcement cause a new behavior to be acquired. Although the changed system is something you have inside of you, it is not your personality; it is only that which mediates your personality. In any event, our knowledge of the system is too limited to be useful in predicting behavior. The body is also supposed to have an immune system, but immune responses do not exist, either, until the organism is invaded by environmental stimuli in the form of germs.

Nevertheless, Skinner finds it useful to speak of a repertoire of behavior. This, "like the repertoire of a musician or a company of players, is what a person or company is capable of doing, given the right circumstances" (Skinner, 1974, p. 138). Personality can therefore be defined as an individual's total repertoire of behavior.

Whether you look at it as what a person has done, what a person is doing at the moment, or what a person is capable of doing, personality is still almost exclusively the product of environmental contingencies of reinforcement. Skinner's one key idea, contingencies of reinforcement, is about all that is needed to answer the basic questions about personality—the questions of structure, dynamics, and development. If you ask the structural question, What does the personality consist of? the answer, as we have just seen, is behavior. If you ask the dynamic the question, What causes the personality to move? the answer is contingencies of reinforcement. And if you ask the developmental question, How did the personality get to be as it is today? the answer again is contingencies of reinforcement. What is more, if you also want to know how to change personality, your own or someone else's, the answer is that you must change the contingencies of reinforcement.

PROS and CONS

Pro #1:   This key idea is parsimonious.   A theory that can answer so many big questions with just one principle is certainly parsimonious. The job of science is to simplify, to account for the phenomena of nature with no more than a handful of fundmental principles. According to the "law of parsimony," also known as Morgan's Canon (after Lloyd Morgan, the father of animal psychology who developed it), whenever two or more plausible explanations exist for one phenomenon, the one that is simplest and requires fewest prior assumptions is most likely to be correct. Psychologists and other scientists accept Morgan's Canon as a rule of thumb.

As an abstract principle the law of parsimony is fine, but in practice it is often not so easy to apply. There may, for example, be no objective criteria for deciding which of two theories is simpler. More relevant to Skinner's case, it may be difficult to distinguish between the simple and the simplistic. Parsimony is fine, but oversimplification is not. Skinner has been accused of the latter and has constructed a bold defense.

Some people have trouble believing that all human behavior can be explained on the basis of contingencies of reinforcement. Skinner wonders why these people have so little trouble believing the germ theory of disease. You cannot even see germs, and yet people readily accept the simple explanation that germs account for all disease. Is it any more preposterous to say that contingencies of reinforcement account for all behavior? Darwin's theory of evolution is a model of parsimony, explaining the marvellous diversification of plant and animal life on the basis of one simple principle: natural selection. Skinner's theory, as a corollary of Darwin's, is equally parsimonious and no more simplistic. If Darwin is not simplistic, then Skinner is not simplistic. And if it is a pro for Darwin that his theory is parsimonious, then it is a pro for Skinner that his theory is parsimonious.

Pro #2: This key idea is dynamic.   The process of selection, in which the environment strengthens certain behaviors and weakens others, is just that—a process, something that goes on during every moment of life. Skinner's theory focuses on this process of behavioral evolution. A process is dynamic, always in motion. There is no such thing as stationary process. Personality psychologists are forever paying lip service to the idea of viewing personality as a process, yet none of them has done this as radically as Skinner. Perhaps that is because Skinner is the only radical behaviorist. He is the only one who resolutely excludes everything but behavior from his field of study, leaving nothing at all but process.

Behavior itself implies action. Yet Skinner is not interested so much in behavior itself as in how behavior is changed. The process of changing behavior: That is Skinner's topic, one that could hardly be more dynamic.

Skinner's decision to focus on the rate of responding, rather than on what he calls the topography of responding, also insures that he will deal with dynamic change, not static structure. The cumulative recorder, the hardware consequence of this decison, symbolizes Skinner's committment to dynamic analysis: The roll of graph paper on the machine is always in motion. Traditionally, psychologists have paid attention to what the organism does, the "topography" of behavior: a rat turns to the right or to the left in a T-maze; a person taking a Rorschach test reports seeing an elephant wearing a funny hat; of ten children who watch an aggressive model, nine subsequently behave aggressively. Skinner's objection to concentrating on the topography of behavior, while ignoring the rate of emission of behavior, is that topographical knowledge does not lead to a science of predicting and controlling behavior. The history of chemistry, he suggests, provides a parallel. For centuries chemists were fascinated by the colors and textures of elements and compounds, and by what happens when these substances are heated, dissolved, and combined. This was interesting and appropriate as the ground work for a science, but it was not a science in itself. It only became a science when someone noticed that the weights of the substances involved in reactions follow certain laws. Those laws were not apparent until someone decided to measure weight. By the same token, the laws of behavior could not come to light until someone realized that the key was in the rate of responding—not in what the organism does, but in how often it does it. Behavior is dynamic. It is action, movement, change. It stands to reason that the laws of behavior could be revealed by focusing on the process of change, as reflected in the changing rate of responding.

Skinner is not the only one of our theorists who is interested in the clinical applications of his work. All psychotherapists aimed to produce some kind of change in people. But behavior modification, which is largely the brainchild of Skinner, seems to be more obsessed with change than any of the other brands of therapy, perhaps because Skinner's method concentrates on bringing about explicit, observable changes. To the extent that behavior modification is single-mindedly devoted to producing change, it maintains Skinner's dynamic posture.

Most personality theories claim to be dynamic. Many even include the word *dynamic* in their brand name. Skinner's theory does neither, partly because the term *psychodynamic* has already been co-opted by the other side, where it means something quite different. Yet in the root—the *radical*—sense of the word, Skinners theory is dynamic in the extreme.

Pro #3: This key idea is applicable and testable. Skinner's key idea is both applicable and testable. The way in which environmental contingencies control behavior can be demonstrated in the laboratory, by placing animals in Skinner boxes. Principles discovered in the laboratory can be readily applied in the classroom or the clinic as well, to achieve educational and therapeutic objectives. The success of the principles in these settings constitutes another test of the theory's validity.

Consider a typical, though very simple, example taken from the first page of the first issue of the *Journal of Applied Behavior Analysis* (Hall et al., 1968). The setting is a third-grade classroom in an inner-city school, where most of the pupils are disadvantaged. The subject of the experiment is Robbie, a pupil who is especially inattentive and disruptive. In fact, careful observation showed that he was studying only about 25% of the time, and clowning around, distracting other pupils the rest of the time. These objective, unobtrusive observations of Robbie's usual behavior constitute what in the jargon of behavior modification is called a **baseline.** Obviously, the success of any program to change behavior can be gauged only by comparing behavior before the program is instituted with behavior after the program is functioning. In Robbie's case, the program simply aimed to reinforce his studying behavior. Whenever Robbie studied, the teacher now gave him a great deal of attention, encouragement and praise. When he did not study, she ignored him. This was something she had not done before, since his disruptive behavior was so exasperating. The effect was reminiscent of what happens when a rat in a Skinner box discovers that feeding is contingent upon lever-pressing. The frequency of Robbie's studying behavior shot up to about 75% (see Figure 9–3). That certainly made it look as though reinforcement, in the form of the teacher's attention, controlled his studying behavior. If you put a new bulb into a lamp and the lamp lights up, you can be fairly certain that a burnt-out bulb was the cause of the problem. But, there might have been a momentary power failure, so you reinstate the original bulb. If the lamp does not work with the old bulb but works when you reinsert the new one, you can be nearly absolutely certain that the bulb was the cause of the problem. The behavior modification experiment, also called the reversal design or ABAB design (it goes by all these names), follows the same logic. To test whether Robbie's increased studying is really due to the reinforcement the teacher is giving him, during the next phase of the experiment the teacher stops reinforcing his studying behavior and reverts to treating him as she did during the baseline period. The fact that his rate of studying declines during this phase, even though it does not fall all the way back to baseline, surely provides convincing evidence that the reinforcement provided by the teacher was the primary cause of his increased rate of studying in the previous phase. And when in phase four the teacher reinstates the program of reinforcement and Robbie's studying behavior again increases to approximately the rate seen in phase two, there can remain very little doubt that contingencies of reinforcement control behavior. The theory has not

FIGURE 9-3

Modification of Studying Behavior

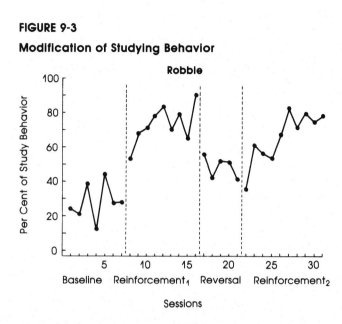

Robbie

Baseline Reinforcement₁ Reversal Reinforcement₂

Sessions

only been experimentally validated, but an educational and emotional problem has been resolved in a particularly humane manner.

Robbie was not threatened or punished. No force was used on him. He was given exactly what he wanted: attention. But getting that attention was made strictly contingent on his behaving appropriately in class. Now he feels good about what goes on in school and is obviously in a position to learn a great deal more than before. When his teachers tried to control his behavior with threats of punishment, he viewed going to school as a form of slavery. Now that his behavior is controlled by **positive reinforcement,** he feels that he is doing what he wants to do. Honey catches more flies than vinegar.

All of the applications of Skinner's theory use honey, not vinegar. Whether the task is reshaping an entire culture into a utopian community, or merely teaching a retarded person to eat with utensils rather than fingers, Skinner is adamant about using only positive reinforcement and avoiding all punishments and **aversive stimuli.**

Unwanted behavior should be analyzed, to reveal the contingencies that control it, and those contingencies should be changed so that the behavior is no longer elicited. In other words, the discriminative stimuli should be removed or the behavior no longer reinforced. Punishment should be avoided, if at all possible.

Skinner's utopia is a world without punishment. Perhaps his fondest idea is that people learn better when they are rewarded rather than punished. The best thing about the teaching machine, or any other programmed learning device, is that, like a personal tutor, it provides the student with immediate reinforcement following every response. Furthermore, students hardly ever experience the aversive consequences of failure; they answer almost every question correctly, because level of difficulty of the questions is increased very gradually and hints and prompts are systematically given. No dunce caps are awarded by Skinner's teaching machines. Even the slow learner is rewarded by being able to master a certain segment of the program. Like a stairway, the steps between each question and the next are small enough for anyone to climb. Some climb faster than others, of course, but a properly designed program permits everyone to progress. No student needs to get started on the dropout trail: "I can't do the work;" "I must be stupid;" "I'll just quit trying because I can't do it anyway."

In light of Skinner's very evident efforts to use his theory to help children learn, to alleviate the misery of the mentally ill, and to build an ideal society, it is hard to understand how some people regard him as an advocate of something approximating fascism. Part of the reason, I think, has to do with his fondness for hardware: the fully automated rat chamber; the air crib for his baby daughter; the teaching machine. Once the sinister, mad-scientist label was applied to him, his adversaries made it stick. They distrust his thoroughly rationalistic approach to everything. They say he is detached and analytical, just too calculating! It is true that his writings do not convey much warmth. They apparently have little room for emotion or intuition. Yet the main reason Skinner is maligned, especially by humanistic psychologists, is because of his position on the issue of determinism versus free will.

William James, whom most humanistic psychologists worship as a staunch advocate of free will, wrestled with this same issue. With perfect logical clarity, he pointed out that you cannot have a *science* that includes free will. If things are lawful in the scientific sense, they must be determined and cannot be subject to the whims and caprices of free will. Free will would make scientific prediction utterly impossible. How could Newton have discovered the law of gravity if apples, of their own free will, could decide to fall up on some occasions and down on others? No, if you are going to have a science of psychology, you cannot incorporate free will into it. Science, by its very nature, must be deterministic.

James acknowledged that he was perplexed by this dilemma. He knew his own will was free, yet he also believed strongly in the possibility and the value of a science of psychology. His "solution," if it can be called that, was to live with the contradiction. Since James was not directly involved in predicting behavior, he could afford to ignore the contradiction. But Skinner, precisely because he was so eager to apply his science to real human problems, had to accept determinism. If Skinner had been content to write descriptive accounts of psychological functioning, as James did, and never actually experiment with methods of changing behavior, he too could have ignored the contradiction. But Skinner is not just an armchair philosopher; he is a doer who believes that theories are pointless unless they are put to use.

Con #1: This key idea is deterministic. I am not really certain whether this discussion belongs under pros or cons, because Skinner himself is not perfectly clear about it. Or maybe he is perfectly clear, and I just do not want to believe that he means what he says. Recall the distinction we made between methodological assumptions and metaphysical assumptions. Methodological assumptions are things taken for granted about the best way to investigate a question. Metaphysical assumptions are things taken for granted about the nature of reality. If we think of science as something that is concerned with prediction and control, then determinism is a necessary methodological assumption. There can be no room for free will. In order to play the game of science, we must abide by the rules of determinism, just as in football we cannot run outside the sidelines to elude a tackle without being called down. Without such rules, we simply cannot have a game. Without sidelines we cannot play football; without determinism we cannot play science.

The problem arises at the point where Skinner confuses the game of science with reality. Science provides knowledge about functional relationships—if you do this, then that happens. Skinner seems to appreciate this when he says that his goal is a functional analysis of behavior. What science does not do is explain the nature of things. Science explains how things work, but not what they are. In order to explain how things work, science must make certain assumptions about what they are; but these assumptions are made precisely for the express purpose of speculating about how things work. The trick is not to be fooled, when your hypotheses about how things work are verified, into thinking that your assumptions about what they are have also been proven. Either Skinner has fallen into this trap, or he intentionally leads his readers into it.

Skinner acknowledges that people have a subjective experience of free will. But that is only a delusion, he says. Positive reinforcement of operant behavior is what produces the illusion of free will. Unlike reflex behavior, operant behavior is not caused or compelled by some obvious antecedent stimulus; and unlike **negatively reinforced behavior**, it is not an attempt to escape from pain or unpleasantness. Hence we feel that we perform operant behavior because we want to, "of our own free will," just as Robbie felt that he himself decided to study harder when the teacher began paying attention to him. Because this subjective feeling can perfectly well be ignored for purposes of prediction and control, Skinner writes it off as a delusion.

What is important, Skinner says, is that people controlled by positive reinforcement do not try to escape or counterattack. In short, they are happy with their lot and think that they are free. For many of Skinner's critics, statements such as this evoke images of the most insidious kind of totalitarian government—a society where people are led around like sheep and love it.

But then Skinner goes on to talk about countercontrol. Apparently the controlled also control the controllers. The government controls us, but we also control the government through the ballot box, letters to our legislators, media coverage, etc. Big business controls us, but we also control it through labor unions, consumer groups, and government regulatory agencies. For responding to all the individuals and agencies that seek to control us, we have at our disposal a potent arsenal of countercontrol measures, from turning off the television or hanging up the phone, to organizing a revolution and launching terrorist attacks. Strikes, work slowdowns, resigning your job, or leaving the country are all conspicuous examples of efforts at countercontrol. Truancy from school is a more prosaic one. There are thousands of much less momentous behaviors that qualify as efforts at countercontrol, behavior we all engage in every day.

If I can engage in countercontrol, then for all intents and purposes I am free—at least as far as I understand the meaning of the term *free*. We wonder, then, why Skinner sets up people who believe in free will as so many straw men to be knocked down. It is as if Skinner thinks that these are the same people who still believe the earth is flat!

At some level, Skinner must believe in free will. Otherwise what sense would it make for him to exhort us to join with him in building utopian societies? If people did not possess some degree of freedom, what sense would it make for Skinner to advocate using the principles of behavior modification on oneself to achieve self-control? And if people were merely rats in boxes, what sense would it make to speak of countercontrol?

Of course people are controlled, and of course people are free. The human condition is one of finite freedom, freedom within limits. Those limits are set by genetic endowment, culture, historical era, developmental experiences, and so forth. No one escapes the influence of these limiting factors; hence no one is absolutely free. Every human act is free and determined at the same time. None of our actions is completely free or completely determined (although some are freer than others); everything we do exists somewhere between the poles of freedom and necessity. Skinner is perhaps less opposed to the idea that people are free than to the idea that they are not determined. He can relax, however: The simplistic view that people must be either free or determined may have been held by the Sunday-school teachers Skinner rebelled against during his adolescence, but it is not defended by any serious theorist today.

Con #2: This key idea is much ado about nothing.   *Control* is a strong word, implying as it does absolute and even mechanistic determinism. What Skinner is really talking about is influence. His choice of the word "control" is provocative and misleading. A steering wheel controls the direction in which a car travels. An engineer controls a robot. But one human being *influences* another, unless we are talking about one of those five kinds of relationships in which there exists no effective countercontrol: "the care of the very young, of the aged, of prisoners, of psychotics, and of the retarded" (Skinner, 1974, p. 191). For those situations, the proper word is control. But for ordinary relationships between people who are more or less equal, a less misleading word would be *influence*.

The difference between a relationship between equals and a relationship between a jailor and a prisoner, for example, is a difference in power. When there is a difference in power, one person has something that the other person wants but does not have. The person who possesses the scarce resources is able to force the other person to perform certain actions in return for a share of the coveted resources. What is so amazing about that? Isn't it just a much simpler way of saying that behavior is controlled by environmental contingencies of reinforcement? What is there to explain? If you have something that people want, you can get them to stand on their heads to get it. If a corrupt jailor extracts sexual favors from a prisoner in return for leaving the cell unlocked, we do not need a theory to explain that behavior.

Our second con is that Skinner's key idea is much ado about nothing. Of course people are controlled. As long as there are people in the world who are more powerful than you, they will have some say in your behavior. As long as there are people who have something you want, your freedom will be limited. And if they have something you want very badly, such as the release of one of your children whom they are holding hostage, they will be able to control your behavior with a high degree of predictability. The more power they have—the more you want what they offer in return for your compliance—the more predictable your behavior will be. People will do what they have to do to get what they want!

Con #3: This key idea is based on circular reasoning. Another objection to Skinner's definition of reinforcement is that it is circular. Skinner never identifies the reinforcer ahead of time. His theory simply assumes that if the rate of a response increases, the stimulus that followed that response *must* have functioned as a reinforcer; it must have caused the increased rate of response. In other words, if you want to know what causes a behavior-changing response to be acquired, the answer is reinforcement. But if you want to know what reinforcement is, Skinner only tells you that it is whatever causes a response to be acquired. Round and round we go. Each word is defined in terms of the other, and we achieve no more insight into behavior change that we would get from being told that behavior changers are what cause behavior to change. Reinforcers (response strengtheners) are what reinforce (strengthen) responses. Skinner himself condemns this very kind of thinking when he says, "it is nevertheless a mistake to say that a fluid flows slowly because it is viscous or possesses a high viscosity. A state or quality inferred from the behavior of a fluid begins to be taken as a cause" (Skinner, 1974, p. 161).

Con #4: This key idea does not yield superior predictions of behavior. Skinner responds to this kind of criticism by pointing to behavior therapists' very real successes in modifying intractable and even life-threatening patterns of behavior. More than a few times when all other methods failed, behavioral techniques have achieved dramatic cures. Petulantly, like the little boy who threatens to take his bat and ball and go home if the game is not played his way, Skinner challenges people who are unpersuaded by his theoretical arguments to modify behavior as effectively as he can. If he is so adept at modifying behavior, we sometimes wonder why he does not modify the behavior of his adversaries directly, causing them to agree with him. The answer, of course, is that he does not have an absolute power advantage over them.

In an institutional setting such as a prison or a mental hospital, where the population is under constant surveillance and access to everything from food to physical safety is controlled by the staff, Skinnerian techniques predict and control behavior very effectively. As we saw under Con #2, the real reasons for that success may be less elaborate than Skinner's theory suggests. Be that as it may, our point here (Con #4) is that Skinner's ability to predict and control behavior is directly related to the captive state of his target population. The salient feature of the Skinner box as a piece of apparatus is not the lever, or its connection with the food-delivery system, but the simple fact that the rat is in a *cage*. Skinner's rats behaved predictably because they were in cages.

Human beings also behave much more predictably when they are in cages, whether the cages are real or imaginary, entered voluntarily or involuntarily. The astonishing success of behavior modifiers in work with the retarded has less to do with the fact that this population is not bright enough to beat the game than with the fact that they are captive. Again and again, the effects of behavior modification programs implemented in prisons have failed to extend beyond the prison walls when inmates are released into the community. Even patients who have never been locked up in institutions, patients who simply consult behavior therapists to help control their overeating or irrational fears, have voluntarily placed themselves under the authority of the doctor. For a certain number of hours each week, they have agreed to be held captive in the therapist's office. Little Robbie was right if he regarded his schoolroom as something akin to a prison, for he was indeed a captive there under the authority of his teacher. True, the mere fact of his captivity cannot account for the changes in Robbie's behavior. Those were indeed due to changes in the contingencies of reinforcement. Yet neither should the fact of captivity be regarded as just a methodological convention for controlling extraneous variables, as though those *extraneous* variables amounted to nothing more than a minor nuisance. From the point of view of controllers, it is always a nuisance when their subjects refuse to remain captive; but from the point of view of the subject, eluding captivity is a matter of freedom.

What Skinner offers is an improved technology for predicting and controlling the behavior of *captives*. Positive reinforcement works better than punishment, Skinner says, because it does not breed efforts at countercontrol. But that simply says that reinforcement does not breed efforts to escape captivity and find reinforcement elsewhere, or to rebell against the controller's authority and take by force what was previously offered only in return for behavior specified by the controller.

Skinner does not offer a superior (or even an effective) method of predicting and controlling the behavior of people who are not our captives, but who are related to us on a more nearly equal footing. My opponent on the tennis court—if only I could predict a split second earlier whether he will go down the line or crosscourt! The dealer at the flea market with whom I haggle over the price of a windsor chair—if only I could predict whether he will come down again if I threaten to walk away! My prospective employer at the job interview—if only I could predict whether she will be annoyed, or think that I stand up for myself, if I disagree with something she says! These are the kinds of things we would like to be able to predict. But at this point Skinner is no help. These things are all theoretically predictable, he would tell us, because these behaviors are all determined. But the contingencies are just too complex for us to make any such predictions at this point in history. Some day in the future perhaps, but not now!

Such behaviors are theoretically predictable for Skinner only because he assumes a priori that all behavior is determined. When his theory is attacked, Skinner often falls back upon his ability to predict behavior in an effort to bolster his argument. When it is brought to light that a good deal of ordinary human behavior is beyond his powers of prediction, he tells us this does not matter, since such behavior is theoretically predictable. If you begin to feel dizzy, it is because we are going around in circles again. If behavior is predictable, it must be determined. If it is determined, then it is theoretically predictable. In the very last analysis, Skinner can only tell us what he assumed without any proof long before the first pellet rolled down the chute of the first Skinner box: namely, that B. F. Skinner believes in the possiblity of a science for predicting and controlling human behavior.

CHAPTER SUMMARY

B. F. Skinner is the most famous American psychologist of all time, and his fame is deserved. He is a novelist and a writer of best-sellers. As the inventor of the teaching machine and of programmed learning technology, he is a sort of Thomas Edison of education. Skinner invented the term *behavior therapy* and is one of the moving forces behind the behavioral revolution in the mental health field. A division of the American Psychological Association, and several psychological journals, have even been established exculsively to disseminate research stemming from Skinner's theories.

1. All behavior is determined by contingencies of reinforcement—that is Skinner's key idea. It is a model of parsimony. We are more apt to repeat behaviors that have been reinforced, and less apt to repeat those that have not been reinforced or have been punished. The consequences of our past behavior determine our present behavior. Just as Darwin thought that environmental circumstances determine which species will survive and which become extinct, Skinner thinks that environmental circumstances cause every behavior to have a certain consequence that determines whether the behavior will survive in an individual's repertoire (i.e., be learned), or be extinguished.

2.   Because environmental contingencies select behavior, if you want to predict and control a certain behavior, you must observe and control the environmental consequences of that behavior. It is also useful to know whether the individual in question has performed these behaviors in the past, and if so, what the consequences have been. That is a matter of objective historical record; none of the information you need is hidden inside the person's mind.

3.   Skinner's radical behaviorism is anti-mentalistic. Knowing what is in peoples' minds does not help you to predict their behavior, because the contents-of-consciousness play no causal role in behavior. Hence they are totally superfluous in any explanation of behavior.

4.   Skinner's experimental analysis of behavior began with his studies of rats in what has come to be called the Skinner box. The Skinner box is a kind of vending machine for animals. In the cage, a lever is connected to a food dispenser and also to a cumulative recorder. A variety of signalling devices may also be included. The machine can be programmed to dispense food, contingent upon any pattern of lever-pressing the experimenter desires to reinforce. The cumulative recorder traces a line on a moving roll of paper, indicating the rate of the animal's responding. Changes in the rate of responding were what Skinner looked for as he methodically varied either the schedules of reinforcement or the discriminative stimuli.

5.   Reinforcement is any stimulus that follows a response and makes it more probable that that response will be emitted again. In the Skinner box, of course, reinforcement is the food that is dispensed following the response (the pressing of the lever). But reinforcement does not have to follow every single response. It certainly does not in real life.

6.   Knowing this, Skinner decided to study the effects of reinforcement delivered according to various schedules. When reinforcement is delivered after every nth response, we have a *ratio schedule*. If that ratio remains constant throughout an experiment—say the rat gets one food pellet after every five lever-pressings—it is called a *fixed ratio schedule*. Such a schedule results in extremely high rates of responding. A *variable ratio schedule* exists when reinforcement occurs after a variable number of responses—something like playing a Las Vegas one-armed bandit. Appropriately enough, such a schedule not only produces high rates of responding as well, but behavior that is particularly resistant to extinction. Addictive behavior is a case in point. *Interval schedules* dispense reinforcement not on the basis of the number of responses, but on the basis of the passage of an interval of time, during which the animal needs to respond only once to receive reinforcement. Additional responses during that interval do not affect reinforcement. Intervals, like ratios, may be either fixed or variable. *Fixed interval schedules* produce a pattern of responses that trace a scalloped line on a cumulative record, because the animal responds at a low or moderate rate early in each interval, but responds much more frequently as the end of each interval approaches. *Variable interval schedules*, in contrast, generate a steady rate of responding. Like variable ratio schedules, they produce behavior that is highly resistant to extinction. In short, each schedule produces a characteristic pattern of behavior.

7. Any stimulus that is present when a behavior is reinforced will be capable afterwards of increasing the rate of the relevant response. Skinner calls such stimuli *discriminative*. If a rat is reinforced for lever-pressing only when the light in the Skinner box is turned on and not when it is off, the rat will soon press only when the light goes on. Many signs and signals play the same role in human affairs: school bells, bus stop signs, flirtatious looks, etc. Discriminitive stimuli and schedules of reinforcement both control behavior.

8. Personality is behavior; it is not something inside a person. When a person is not behaving the personality does not exist, except as past history. Your personality is your life history, your cumulative record. Just as musicians have a repertoire of pieces they can play, so you have a repertoire of behaviors that you are capable of producing. Your total behavioral repertoire constitutes your personality. And that repertoire is the result of the contingencies of reinforcement to which you have been exposed.

9. Pro #1: Skinner's key idea makes for a beautifully parsimonious theory. To those who accuse him of oversimplification, Skinner points to Darwin's theory of evolution and the germ theory of disease as two examples of equally parsimonious theories that are accepted without such criticism.

Pro #2: Skinner's key idea is dynamic. What could be more dynamic than behavior! Perhaps only the process of changing behavior. And that is precisely what Skinner focuses on. In his experimental work he has chosen to focus on *changes* in the rate of responding, and in his applied work he has created behavior modification techniques to *change* behavior.

Pro #3: This key idea is eminently applicable and testable. A typical behavior-modification experiment attempted to increase the studying behavior of a third-grade pupil who was inattentive and disruptive in class. After observers had established Robbie's baseline rate of studying, the teacher introduced the treatment—she ignored him when he did not study and praised him lavishly when he did. His rate of studying increased dramatically. To confirm that this effect was indeed due to the teacher's making reinforcement contingent upon studying, she now reverted to her pre-treatment role. Robbie's rate of studying declined almost to the baseline level. When treatment was reinstituted, Robbie's rate of studying again increased. This ABAB design conclusively proved the efficacy of the program of contingency management, thereby testing Skinner's theory and doing Robbie and his classmates a lot of good. No punishment was involved. Robbie studies more now because he wants to. Skinner uses only positive reinforcement in every application of his theory. Skinner's utopia is a world without punishment.

Con #1: This key idea is deterministic. You cannot have a science that is not deterministic. If behavior is lawful and predictable, it cannot be subject to the caprices of free will. Determinism is a necessary methodological assumption if you want to do science. But it is a *methodological*, not a *metaphysical* assumption. Skinner confuses the two. Because it is necessary to assume determinism in order to conduct a functional analysis of behavior, he jumps to the conclusion that all human behavior is determined. Yet Skinner seems to believe in free will when he talks about countercontrol. And what sense does it make for him to exhort us to improve society, if all our behavior is determined?

Con #2: This key idea is much ado about nothing. You do not need a theory to explain that when one person has something another person wants, the first person is able to get the second to do his or her bidding. Obviously someone who has power over you can influence your behavior. And if that person has a great deal of power over you, she or he will be able to control your behavior with a high degree of predictability. No theory is required to explain that.

Con #3: Skinner's definition of reinforcement is circular. He says that reinforcement causes responses to be acquired, then defines reinforcement as that which causes responses to be acquired.

Con #4: Worse still, Skinner's theory does not yield the superior predictions of behavior he claims. When the behavioral engineer is in a position of power over clients, as typically occurs in institutions, schools, doctors' offices, or with animals in cages, Skinnerians can predict behavior rather well. But then so can anyone else (Con #2). Skinner does not give us a way to predict the behavior of people over whom we do not already have a power advantage, people who are our equals or superiors. Yet these are the very people whose next move we would most like to be able to anticipate. All that Skinner can tell us about them is that *in theory* their behavior is also predictable.

REFERENCES

Allyon, T., & Azrin, N. H. (1965). The measurement and reinforcement of behavior of psychotics. *Journal of the Experimental Anaylsis of Behavior, 8,* 357–383.

American Psychiatric Association, (1980). *Diagnostic and statistical manual of mental disorders* (3rd ed.). Washington, DC: Author.

Carr, E. G., Schreibman, L., & Lovass, O. I. (1975). Control of echolalic speech in psychotic children. *Journal of Abnormal Child Psychology, 3,* 311–351.

Guttman, N. (1977). On Skinner and Hull: A reminiscence and a projection. *American Psychologist, 32,* 321–328.

Hall, R. V., Lund, D., & Jackson, D. (1968). Effects of teacher attention in study behavior. *Journal of Applied Behavior Analysis, 1,* 1–12.

Skinner, B. F. (1938). *The behavior of organisms: An experimental analysis.* New York: Appleton-Century-Crofts.

Skinner, B. F. (1948). *Walden two.* New York: Macmillan.

Skinner, B. F. (1969). *Contingencies of reinforcement: A theoretical analysis.* New York: Appleton-Century-Crofts.

Skinner, B. F. (1971). *Beyond freedom and dignity.* New York, Knopf.

Skinner, B. F. (1974). *About behaviorism.* New York: Knopf.

Skinner, B. F. (1976). *Particulars of my life.* New York: McGraw-Hill.

Skinner, B. F., & Lindsley, O. R. (1954). *Studies in behavior therapy. Status reports II and III* (Contract NS–ORI–7662). Arlington, VA: Office of Naval Research.

10/Albert Bandura

A Biographical Sketch

Albert Bandura is the youngest of our theorists by several decades, and as such has not yet reached an age at which he deems it appropriate to sit back and survey all that he has accomplished. We do not have even a brief autobiographical statement from his own pen, nor has any other biographer contributed much information about Bandura's life. We do know that he was born in 1925, in a remote village of 600 inhabitants in northern Alberta, Canada. His parents were wheat farmers of Polish ancestry. (Bandura's first book was translated into Polish and published in Warsaw.) The town had only one school. Bandura's high-school graduating class consisted of only twenty pupils, and they had been taught throughout their high school years by only two teachers. A less auspicious academic beginning is hard to imagine. Yet Bandura reports that almost all of those twenty graduates went on to college, and eventually to successful professional careers. This was apparently due in large part to the resourcefulness of these youngsters in educating themselves. One can only surmise that the culture must have instilled a rather powerful achievement motive.

After he graduated from high school, Bandura got a summer job on a highway crew, patching holes in the Alaska highway. There he encountered a bizarre assortment of fugitives from civilization—people hiding from bill collectors and probation officers. His fascination with deviant behavior may well date from this unexpected exposure to mundane maladjustment. Whether there were other influences pushing him in the direction of psychology, we do not know. Apparently he settled on a career in psychology in his early days at the University of British Columbia in Vancouver; when he graduated three years later (1949), he won the Bolocan Award in psychology. This suggests that he was already doing outstanding work in psychology as an undergraduate. On the basis of the available information, in fact, it appears that Bandura followed a more direct path to his ultimate vocational goal than any of our other theorists.

For graduate study Bandura picked the University of Iowa, largely because of the presence there of Kenneth Spence, the prime exponent of Hullian stimulus-response behaviorism. At Iowa, learning theory was taught and tested with great zeal and scholarly rigor. Bandura's subsequent penchant for experimental methods and his emphasis on observational learning most certainly were acquired at Iowa, where the classic work of Neal Miller on imitation was held up to students as a model of excellence. In 1952 Bandura received his Ph.D. He spent the following year doing a postdoctoral clinical internship at the Wichita Guidance Center.

After the year in Wichita, Bandura secured an appointment as instructor in psychology at Stanford University. Still there today, he is now the David Starr Jordan Professor of Social Science in Psychology. At Stanford, Bandura was influenced by Robert Sears, a senior faculty member who was then doing research on the role of identification in learning and performing aggressive behavior. (Spence, Miller, and Sears had all studied at Yale with Clark Hull.) Bandura began a program of laboratory and field research on the social learning of aggressive behavior. That research culminated, in the 1970s, with his very persuasive demonstrations of the effects of television violence on young children. At the same time he was applying his research to these practical concerns, he was experimentally verifying the major constructs of his social learning theory. In the clinical realm, Bandura was also developing and testing his unique brand of behavior modification, based on the use of modeling techniques. More recently he has turned his attention to studying the effects of perceived self-efficacy on fear arousal and on the ability to confront threatening situations. Throughout these years of research and theory-building, Bandura has increasingly emphasized the role of cognitive factors in regulating behavior. As a consequence, his brand of behaviorism has become more and more mentalistic in comparison to Skinner's. In fact, the American Psychological Association's Distinguished Scientific Contribution Award for 1980 credits Bandura with having "sparked renewed interest in covert events," which is to say that he is largely responsible for the cognitive revolution in psychology. Thus Bandura's niche in the personality psychologists' hall of fame is secure, even though the full scope of his contribution to the discipline remains to be revealed by his astonishing creativity.

SOCIAL LEARNING THEORY

Albert Bandura's brand of cognitive behaviorism, which he calls *social learning theory,* is one of the most popular new theories in psychology. It has caught on with the force of an idea whose time has come. It *is* timely, representing as it does the confluence of classical behaviorism with a renewed enthusiasm for cognitive psychology—an enthusiasm signalled, on the one hand, by the rush to hop onto the Piaget bandwagon, and on the other, by an infatuation with the computer models of cognition that produced information theory and systems theory. Like a canny surfer, Bandura has picked out the very biggest wave and its now standing on its crest.

Bandura is a leader, as well as one of the originators, of the behavior-modification movement. Here too a new wave was rising. As the limitations of traditional psychotherapies became more and more evident in the 1950s and '60s, behavior therapies moved in to expand the frontiers. Demands for accountability by insurance providers and government agencies during the 1970s favored clinicians who could demonstrate tangible changes in their clients' behavior. The impact of behavioral techniques upon the practice of psychotherapy has been nothing less than revolutionary. And Albert Bandura is one of the leaders of that revolution.

For over two decades, Bandura has been concerned about violent and aggressive behavior. In the late 1960s and early 1970s, when the topic captured popular attention, Bandura was right there with his ingeniously designed experiments, demonstrating conclusively that violent shows on television contribute to violent behavior among viewers. Time and again Bandura and his associates experimentally verified that children imitate the violent behavior they see on TV. This conclusion is, of course, in perfect accord with common sense. It is a testimony to the power of the television networks that the issue was not definitively laid to rest until 1981, with the publication of a large-scale survey of the television-viewing habits of school children in California. Indeed, Bandura had been right all along. One of the pioneer researchers on the effects of television violence on viewers, and one of the acknowledged experts in that field, he has seen the the protest against TV violence grow from a mild swell into a mountainous wave. And once again, he stands atop the wave.

Whether Bandura's penchant for prediction allows him to pick out the best waves while they are still far from shore, or whether he somehow stirs up these waves himself, is the kind of question that has puzzled historians for a long time. Perhaps the waves Bandura is riding will continue to roll on. Perhaps they will fade away. Only time will tell. But if I were a betting man, I would wager that Bandura's waves will continue to swell and gain momentum, at least into the twenty-first century.

THE KEY IDEA
LEARNING BY OBSERVATION

True to his behaviorist heritage, Bandura maintains that personality is the product of learning. Everything that is personality was learned at one time. But how was it learned? In answering that question, Bandura departs from the traditional behaviorist party line. Mainstream behaviorism has long held that learning is the exclusive result of two factors, *contiguity* and *reinforcement.* Pavlov's dogs drooled when they heard the bell, because repeatedly the bell had been rung and the food presented at the same time—contiguously. Millions of rats have learned to press bars in Skinner boxes because pressing the bar is immediately followed by the delivery of a food pellet—reinforcement. In both cases there is a conditioned response, drooling or bar-pressing; and that response is conditional upon the reinforcement: food. No reinforcement, no response. Without a response, there is no learning; and without reinforcement, there is no response.

Now we can see just how radical Bandura's heresy is. Bandura proposes that learning can take place not only without previous reinforcement, but without any response. How is this possible? Through the perfectly commonplace phenomenon that you and I call *imitation!* "Monkey see, monkey do," "like father, like son," and an host of other hackneyed expressions all refer to the familiar observation that we can learn something by watching someone else. A slightly more technical term for this process is **observational learning.** Bandura usually prefers to call it **modeling**. It is a testimony to the popularity of this, his key idea, that *modeling* has caught on with a vengeance as a buzzword in psychology today.

Modeling, imitation, observational learning. Call it what you will, it is Bandura's key idea. It is also by far his most distinctive idea. Like most of the other key ideas we have encountered, this one was not invented by the theorist who made it famous. Bandura owes a great debt to John Dollard and Neal Miller (1941) for their pioneering work on the concept of imitation. Bandura acknowledges that their groundbreaking studies stimulated his interest in the topic. His particular slant on the subject has much to do with the influence of the **purposive behaviorism** of Edwin Tolman (1932), who pioneered the experimental study of observational learning. Yet Bandura has made this idea his trademark, and he has marketed it with a degree of success that eluded his predecessors.

Bandura has written a great deal about observational learning. Whether he is writing about aggression, or behavior modification, or self-competency—a topic that has captured his attention in recent years—observational learning is always a prominent theme in Bandura's works, giving them the characteristic flavor of social learning theory. (Incidentally, *social learning theory* is the brandname Bandura has given to his personality theory.) Imitation qualifies as Bandura's key idea, on the grounds that he has written more about it than any other idea.

Observational learning is a key idea in Bandura's social learning theory. Why this is so, of course, will not be completely apparent until we have examined the idea in more detail. Suffice it to say at this point that the much-celebrated cognitive emphasis in Bandura's theory is a consequence of the attention he pays to observational learning. Learning by watching somebody else is a kind of learning that takes place inside your head. It is cognitive and mentalistic. You do not have to do anything, nor does there need to be an observable behavior or response. If you accept the premise that we learn not only through conditioning, but through observation, then your theory will inevitably take a cognitive turn. In short, the key to Bandura's cognitive emphasis is his key idea—learning through imitation.

PROCESSES GOVERNING OBSERVATIONAL LEARNING

Bandura attempts to explain observational learning by identifying the variables that affect it. He wants to know under what circumstances it will, and will not take place. That is the sort of question social learning theory deals with. Note the very practical, utilitarian nature of the question: If you can find out what circumstances contribute to observational learning, you can encourage observational learning by arranging to have those circumstances present.

According to Bandura, four types of processes determine how much observational learning will take place: *attentional processes; retention processes; motor reproduction processes,* and *reinforcement and motivational processes.*

ATTENTIONAL PROCESSES

If you are going to learn by watching, you have to pay attention to what you are watching. That much almost goes without saying. In essence, that is all Bandura means when he says that observational learning depends on attentional processes. The ramifications of this commonsense principle are a little more complex. It follows, for example, that the more successful models are in capturing people's attention, the more likely people will be to imitate them.

Before models can capture your attention, you must be exposed to them. This is the principle parents follow when they try to find a good neighborhood in which to raise their children, and to prevent them from getting in with the wrong crowd. If children are not exposed to undesirable behavior, so the assumption goes, then they will not model it. The very same supposition underlies all forms of censorship, ranging from parental supervision of children's television viewing to Anita Bryant's anti-homosexual crusade. By controlling exposure, you can control attentional processes and thereby control what is learned by observation.

Nevertheless, mere exposure does not guarantee that attention will be paid or that imitation will take place. Some models attract attention much more effectively than others. Advertisers are particularly alert to this fact, and therefore populate their commercials with beautiful people. We are more apt to attend to people who are physically attractive, who have high social status, and who appear to be competent. This holds true whether we are exposed to them through the mass media or meet them face-to-face in our everyday lives. Children, for example, typically model their parents' behavior as well as the behavior of the leaders of their peer group.

Bandura demonstrated this process rather convincingly in an early experiment (1963), in which children were encouraged to imitate an adult who beat up an innocent rubber doll. This technique became the trademark of Bandura's experiments with observationally learned aggression and, appropriately enough, was imitated by many other researchers. Since Bandura's experiment, hundreds of Bobo dolls and other inflatable plastic mannequins have been assaulted and mercilessly pummelled as psychologists gleefully watched through one-way mirrors.

In another of Bandura's experiments, the crucial question was whether children would imitate the aggressive behavior of the adult model who controlled and dispensed desirable resources, or imitate the one who received those resources.

In the first part of the experiment, half of the children were assigned to groups in which an adult resource-controller gave toys, dolls and drinks to another adult while ignoring the third party, the child. The purpose was to see whether the child would identify with (and later imitate) the behavior of the adult who controlled the gifts, or the one who was rewarded by receiving them. The other half of the children were assigned to groups in which one adult gave the very same gifts to the child while ignoring the other adult. In both conditions, the sex of the adults was systematically varied so that the controller of resources would not always be a man. The groups, however, always included the child plus one male and one female adult.

In the second part of the experiment, a game was introduced. The children watched as the adults marched up to a pair of boxes, one of which contained a hidden prize, then smashed the rubber doll sitting atop one box and retrieved the prize. Each of the two adults carried out this sequence of actions in a distinctively different style, however. They selected different hats from a rack, marched with different gaits, and throughout the game said things that were not only different from each other, but unlike anything the child was apt to say without prompting. The aim of all this, of course, was to make it easy for the psychologist to identify which of the two adults the child was imitating.

Finally, the children got their chance to play the game. The adult who controlled the resources was the clear winner. Most of the children imitated that adult's behaviors more often, whether the controller was a man or a woman, and whether the child was a boy or a girl. Bandura concluded that children identify with powerful persons. They choose as models not people who get things, but people who have things. They do not think that to get things, you must be like the person who gets things. No, they are much more impressed by the person who has things, even if the person gives those things away. Power, defined as control over desirable resources, attracts attention and elicits imitation.

Paying attention to a model is the first step in learning by imitation. Without that attention, no learning will take place. The people who attract our attention are people who are powerful, in the sense that they have things we would like to have. Hence we are most likely to imitate them.

RETENTION PROCESSES

If you are going to learn by watching, then in addition to paying attention to what you watch you must manage to remember what you saw. It does no good to watch people do something if you cannot remember how they did it later on. Learning obviously implies that something is remembered. Consequently, in Bandura's theory the second process that determines how much observational learning will occur is the process of retention. The more you retain, the more you will be capable of imitating.

But what determines how much you retain? One factor is whether you are able to **encode** what you observe for storage in **long-term memory**. Putting what we watch into words and describing it to ourselves is a method we all use to help ourselves remember the actions of a model. Blocking that process should interfere with observational learning. Bandura has experimental evidence that it does.

The subjects for this experiment were again children who watched a model engage in physically aggressive behavior (Bandura, Grusec, & Menlove, 1966). The model was presented on a TV screen. The children were assigned to one of three experimental conditions. Children in group #1 described every aggressive action of the model to themselves as they watched. Group #2 simply watched passively and said nothing. Group #3 were kept mentally preoccupied by being required to talk about something entirely different while watching the film. After the presentation, the children were asked to act out all of the aggressive behaviors they could recall. Group #3 children scored much lower than the rest. Group #1 children, who had verbally encoded the model's actions, were able to to imitate far more behaviors than children from either of the other two groups, although the group #2 children, who had watched passively, did slightly better than the distracted group #3 children. Subjects who encoded aggressive responses in words remembered and, were able to imitate, 62% of those actions. Without verbal encoding, subjects remembered only 26% of the behaviors. The conclusion is obvious: Verbal encoding enhances retention and thus increases observational learning. To imitate a behavior, you must be able to remember what you saw the model do; and verbal encoding aids memory.

Words, of course, are not the only device that we use to encode information. We also use pictures, diagrams, and all sorts of mental images. As a Boy Scout, I was taught to tie a square knot by using the verbal memory device "left over right, right over left;" but I can also remember the procedure by picturing a properly tied knot in my mind. "Mental maps" are another kind of pictorial code we all use to help us remember how to get from one place to another. Athletes often concentrate by engraving the mental image of a successful performance into their minds. Afterwards, they try to imitate that image. The children in Bandura's experiment who did not use verbal encoding may have retained as much as they did with similar mental imagery.

Anyone who has ever prepared for an exam knows that even if information is adequately encoded, it is easier to retain if it has been rehearsed. If you keep saying something over and over again to yourself, or if you keep picturing the images in your mind, you remember better. Anything that interferes with such rehearsal interferes with memory. Rehearsal is therefore another process that affects retention and the permanence of observational learning.

In sum, learning by imitation is most effective when the information provided by the model is optimally encoded and frequently rehearsed.

MOTOR REPRODUCTION PROCESSES

Motor reproduction processes are the third factor affecting observational learning. These processes depend on the rather self-evident principle that watching can only teach you to do things you are capable of doing. Bandura cites the example of the young child who learns the sequence of actions necessary for driving the family car by watching his parents, but still cannot drive because his legs are not long enough to reach the pedals. Later, of course, when he is big enough to drive, that symbolically encoded sequence of responses may be enacted. This also holds true for most of the learning by imitation that occurs in childhood. Children observe and learn things that they cannot, or may not, imitate immediately. Perhaps they are not big enough, or strong enough, or smart enough; or perhaps they are not allowed to imitate the behavior (e.g., drinking Daddy's beer or smoking Mommy's cigarettes). In this case, the memory is stored away for future reference, perhaps to be transformed into overt behavior years later.

This principle is not confined to children. I can watch Scott Hamilton demonstrate how to do a triple-axle jump on ice skates, encode that information verbally and pictorially, and retain it with perfect clarity; but I will still never perform a plausible imitation of Scott Hamilton doing a triple axle. You can learn to do a lot of things by observation, but you cannot learn to do things beyond your capacity.

On the other hand, very often you can learn to do things beyond your present ability by practicing the subskills that are the basis of the observed behavior. Someone who had the coordination and the physique to do a triple axle might watch Scott Hamilton's demonstration. But if the observer did not know how to ice skate, he or she would still not be able to imitate Hamilton's jump. Yet if this person practiced and acquired the necessary subskills—skating, gymnastics, ballet, and so forth—she or he could transform into overt behavior the mental representations of a demonstration that may have been observed some time ago.

Learning the necessary subskills and successfully executing the composite behavior depends, in turn, upon the process of self-observation and the availability of feedback information. That is why ballet dancers practice in front of mirrors. To imitate successfully, you need to be able to see how well your movements conform to the picture you have stored in your mind. Lacking a mirror, you can have someone else watch you and comment on your performance. This, of course, is the role of a teacher or coach. You can also try to be especially attentive to your own bodily sensations. But in the end, in order for learning by imitation to take place the learner must have a way to observe his or her own performance and receive some feedback.

Motor reproduction processes play a role in observatonal learning. If some handicap prevents a person from performing an observed behavior, obviously that person will not be able to imitate the behavior. Limitations in ability affect what can be learned through observation. If people do not possess the necessary subskills to perform a complex behavior, they will not be able to imitate that behavior until the necessary repertoire of subskills has been acquired. Furthermore, unless people are able to monitor their own behavior or receive feedback from some source, they will not be able to imitate what they have observed. The better the feedback, the better the imitation.

REINFORCEMENT AND MOTIVATIONAL PROCESSES

A behavior may be learned by observation, effectively encoded, remembered well and frequently rehearsed in imagination, yet never translated into action. Why? Because the behavior is socially or morally unacceptable. We all learn by observation hundreds of behaviors that we will never perform. By reading a spy thriller, I may learn how to assassinate the president. Yet, it is unlikely that I will act out that behavior, since it is contrary to my moral code and would also bring severe punishment. Whether a behavior learned by observation is actually imitated in overt actions or not depends on its expected consequences. If performing the behavior at a particular time and place is likely to bring pain, punishment, social disapproval, feelings of guilt, or any other kind of negative consequences, then I will probably not imitate the behavior. On the other hand, if the behavior is likely to bring pleasure, comfort, praise, or feelings of self-esteem—in short, if it promises positive reinforcement—I will probably put it into action. Reinforcement encourages imitative performance.

For Bandura, unlike many other behavioral theorists, the learner does not actually have to receive the reinforcement in order for it to have an effect on his or her actions; the learner simply has to expect the reinforcement. The mere anticipation of reinforcement is sufficient to influence what a person does. Because Bandura's theory refers to such mentalistic factors as expectations and anticipations, he is called a cognitive behaviorist.

If the expectation of reinforcement serves as an incentive to perform a behavior that has already been learned, there is no reason why that same kind of expectation should not motivate the learning process itself. The processes of attention, retention, and motor reproduction are all enhanced by the expectation of positive reinforcement. You do not pay much attention to the airline stewardesses who model the lifejackets before each flight; but your attention would be galvanized if they offered the same demonstration moments after the captain announced that you were about to crash-land in the sea. You may have difficulty remembering people's names, but if you are introduced to someone you find especially attractive, or someone who offers you a high-paying job, you will probably make a special effort to find some memory aid that will help you retain that person's name. You will probably say the name over and over again to yourself and preview mental filmclips of imaginary interactions with the person. People learn what they think will be useful to them. The more observational learning promises to pay off, the better people will learn; they will attend more carefully, encode for memory more effectively, and rehearse more frequently.

Granted that how much we learn from observation and later perform, depends on how much reinforcement we expect, we still need to ask where these expectations come from. How are people able to anticipate the consequences of their actions? According to Bandura, they do it on the basis of past experience. The child who is slapped down by his father for imitating an obscene gesture he learned on the street will become wary about doing it again, at least in front of his father. If, on the other hand, it brings cheers from his friends when he does it behind the teacher's back, he may be encouraged to repeat the performance in that setting. Discriminative learning has taken place; the child has acquired the expectation that this bit of imitative behavior can have negative or positive consequences, depending on the nature of the audience.

Bandura calls this kind of reinforcement *external*. It is administered by persons or forces outside of the learner. The reinforcing agent does not have to be a person. The child who imitates daddy's shaving behavior and cuts himself with the razor learns to beware of razors on his own, without having his father punish him. The essential feature of external reinforcement is that learners themselves perform the imitated behavior and also suffer the consequences (social or physical) at the hands of the environment.

Fortunately, as Bandura points out, we do not have to learn everything from the consequences of our own actions. We are able to profit from the experience of others. The human race, he reminds us, would never have survived unless we were able to learn from the mistakes and the successes of others. Learning by external reinforcement can be extremely expensive. What if each of our prehistoric ancestors had had to learn from direct experience which animals in the forest were dangerous, rather than being told or seeing someone else mauled? What if all of us had to learn what plants were edible by trying them out ourselves? We simply would not be around today. The great evolutionary advantage that human beings have is their ability to learn from the experience of others, and to pass that knowledge on to succeeding generations.

This ability to learn from the experience of others depends upon what Bandura calls **vicarious reinforcement.** (The word *vicarious* simply means "in place of another person.") You can watch the reinforcement consequences of someone else's actions and use that information as a guide for your own behavior. The primary function of reinforcement, according to Bandura, is to provide information—information about the anticipated consequences of a particular behavior. That is the role of both external reinforcement and vicarious reinforcement. Reinforcement does not make a person do something; it does not cause behavior. It simply provides information that a person can use in deciding how to behave. Vicarious reinforcement is just as useful in that respect as external reinforcement, and it is much less costly.

Bandura demonstrated that vicarious reinforcement actually affects imitative performance. He did this with yet another of his Bobo-doll assault experiments (1965). In a film shown to nursery-school children, an adult model badly abused a large Bobo doll, simply because the doll refused to get out of his way. He sat on the Bobo doll, punched it in the nose, hit it over the head with a mallet, and as if that were not enough, peppered it with rubber balls. Each aggressive action was accompanied by distinctive verbalization—for example, "sockeroo" with each blow of the mallet. The children were divided into three groups. All three groups saw the very same film, but each was shown a different ending. One group of children saw the model being rewarded for beating up Bobo; another group saw the model being punished for his attack; the third group saw no ending at all and was therefore given no clue about the consequences of the model's aggressive behavior. After the film session, each child was taken to a playroom that contained, among other toys, a Bobo doll. Psychologists watched through one-way glass while the child played unsupervised for ten minutes. Children who had seen the model punished imitated significantly fewer of his aggressive actions than those who had seen him either being rewarded or getting away with no consequences. The children did not have to be punished themselves to learn to inhibit their aggressive behavior. Vicarious punishment provided sufficient information for them to curb that impulse.

A second source of expectations about the consequences of our imitative behavior is therefore vicarious reinforcement. We note what happens to other people when they do certain things, and we infer that the same rewards or punishments may be forthcoming for us if we engage in such activity. Thus we are more likely to imitate behavior we see rewarded, and less likely to imitate what we see punished.

Bandura names a third source of expectations about the consequences of our behavior. This source, which he calls **self-reinforcement**, indicates just how far he has departed from the traditional behaviorist party line. Bandura's concept of self-reinforcement comes very close to Freud's notion of *superego*. Self-reinforcement refers to the fact that we all develop an internal set of standards for evaluating our behavior. In everyday language, you or I would call this our *conscience*. When we do something that violates those internal standards, we punish ourselves by feeling guilty; if we do something that lives up to or exceeds those standards, we congratulate ourselves. But of course, this does not happen only after the fact. Again, you do not have to wait until you have done something "naughty" to know that it will make you feel bad. Your conscience functions as an early-warning system, letting you know ahead of time what to expect as a consequence of certain actions. Thus people are less likely to imitate actions they expect to feel ashamed of, and more likely to imitate those of which they expect to feel proud.

Parents and other socializing agents instill these self-reinforcing systems in us when we are children. Like every other aspect of the personality, the criteria for self-reinforcement are learned. They are learned in all of the same ways that anything else is learned. Parents use external reinforcement, for example, to shape children's behavior, consistently praising them for playing cooperatively with their friends, and consistently punishing them when they fight with other children. Eventually, children will internalize these standards and conform to the parental commandments, because the children want to be able to approve of their own behavior and to avoid self-criticism. The standards the parents set for the child gradually become the child's own standards. But the standards the parents set for themselves are often also adopted, by the process of imitation, by the child. This may be why the boy whose father consistently beats the living daylights out of him for fighting with other children is surprised to find his son getting into more and more fights. The power of example may be greater here than the power of external reinforcement. The boy identifies with his father. The beatings inform the boy that his father approves of physical violence as a way of getting others to do what you want them to do. Imitating that behavior, the boy treats his playmates the very same way his father treats him. The expectation of a beating does not stop the boy's fighting, which is reinforced by his growing sense of self-approval. The threatened punishment only teaches him to avoid getting caught, or if caught to have a ready alibi.

The mention of alibis brings to mind a further comment Bandura makes about self-reinforcement. He remarks that when people are impelled by social pressures to act contrary to their internal standards, they are able to avoid self-condemnation by engaging in self-deceptive machinations (Bandura, 1973). *Advantageous comparison* is one such technique. "You think I'm bad, look at him," is the essence of this maneuver. Thus the American government sought to justify its aggression in Vietnam by magnifying the cruelty of the Viet Cong. Reprehensible aggression can also be justified by *appealing to higher principles.* Throughout history, self-righteous crusaders and witch-hunters have employed this tactic to assuage their consciences. *Displacing responsibility* is another way of escaping self-condemnation. "I was only following orders," was the excuse not only of Nazi death-camp executioners, but of the American lieutenant in charge of the My Lai massacre. *Dehumanization of victims* is another handy way of sanctioning otherwise unacceptable aggression. The aggressor who is able to make the enemy into "gooks," "pigs," or "degenerates" is able to "waste" them with minimal pangs of conscience. *Blaming the victim* can also salve the conscience. If they had it coming to them because of their own stupidity or provocation or villainous character, then clearly I am justified in letting them have it. All of these self-deceptive machinations may therefore serve to modify, or even subvert, the effects of self-reinforcement, according to Bandura.

To get back, then, to the question of how we know in advance whether imitating someone's actions is going to bring us pleasure or pain: the answer is that we learn from past experience to anticipate future consequences. If our past experience has nurtured a set of standards that the behavior to be imitated will violate, we know before performing it that it will bring us pain. Our self-reinforcing systems enable us to anticipate such consequences. If we see someone else rewarded for performing a certain action, we learn to expect that by performing the same action, we will reap the same reward. This vicarious reinforcement tells us what consequences to expect from our behavior. Finally, "learning the hard way"—recollecting the consequences of our own past actions—also provides a basis for expectations. External reinforcement has taught us to expect success from things that have worked before, and to anticipate failure if we keep doing things that never worked in the past.

Our expectations about the consequences of our behavior derive from all three of the kinds of reinforcement. In turn, these expectations function as incentives or motivators in our observational learning. In general, we are more likely to learn and imitate behaviors we expect to be reinforced, and less likely to learn and imitate those we expect to bring punishment.

In sum, there are four kinds of cognitive processes that affect observational learning and imitation: attentional processes; retention processes; motor reproduction processes; and reinforcement and motivational processes. Bandura's theory has clear practical implications for changing personality through observational learning. If as a therapist you want to optimize your clients' observational learning, you must first capture their attention with attractive, powerful models who control resources the clients desire. You must also instruct clients to pay special attention to certain aspects of the model's performance. Next, you must teach clients the most effective methods for coding observed behavior, so that they can retain a mental representation of it for future reference. Then you must encourage clients to rehearse the observed behavior mentally and to practice it overtly. Better still, have them practice it in front of you or some other coach who will give them accurate and immediate feedback concerning their performance. At the same time, you might also try to improve their powers of self-observation by sensitizing them to important aspects of their performance. The next step is to expose clients to models who are rewarded for performing the desired activity, so that the clients can profit from vicarious reinforcement. You must also arrange for clients to be reinforced when they perform the action themselves. In this regard, it is especially important to keep them from trying out the behavior in a real-life situation until they have perfected it enough to be fairly sure of success. On top of all this, you should try to engender a set of internal standards that will allow clients to feel pride and self-satisfaction when they perform the target behavior. This self-reinforcement guarantees that clients will continue to perform the behavior even if it occasionally fails to bring the desired results.

This program of therapy, according to Bandura, is an extremely powerful agent in changing personality. Personality is behavior, and by systematically applying social learning principles in order to modify specific behavior patterns, personality can be changed.

VICARIOUS CONDITIONING

We should also mention another type of observational learning to which Bandura has devoted considerable attention. Ever since Pavlov taught his dogs to drool at the sound of a bell, psychologists have known that animals can be classically conditioned. When J.B. Watson conditioned little Albert by clanging an iron rod whenever Albert reached for a harmless white rat, he demonstrated that humans can acquire simple phobias through the same classical conditioning process. Now Bandura has shown that similar fears can be instilled in someone who merely observes someone else being conditioned. You do not have to be bitten yourself by a dog to develop a fear of dogs; witnessing someone else screaming and bleeding as a growling dog tears at his or her flesh may be more than adequate. After that, when you see a similar dog, your heart may beat a little faster. Of course, you do not have to witness the event firsthand for the conditioning to occur. Seeing it on TV or in the movies, or even reading about it in the newspaper, can have some effect. Bandura points out that we acquire all manner of emotional responses, not just fears, through the process of **vicarious conditioning**. Emotional attitudes toward minority groups, for example, may be passed along in this fashion. In fact, all of our likes and dislikes, tastes and preferences, are capable of being established by vicarious conditioning.

Bandura has also applied the notion of vicarious conditioning to psychotherapy. He knew that Joseph Wolpe had already demonstrated that many fear responses can be extinguished—that is to say, *unconditioned*—by having the person confront the feared object while feeling relaxed, safe, and secure. In this way, the feared object becomes associated with positive feelings, rather than negative, anxious ones. Bandura reasoned that if you can acquire a fear by watching someone else being conditioned, you should be able to lose a fear by watching someone else's fear being extinguished or counterconditioned.

Bandura's (1969) dramatic snake-handling experiment seemed to show that he was right. Adult subjects with strong snake phobias were randomly assigned to one of four experimental groups. Subjects in the control group received no treatment at all. A second group received Wolpe's *systematic desensitization* therapy. After being taught techniques of deep muscle relaxation, under the therapist's guidance, these subjects imagined progressively more threatening encounters with snakes. Their treatment involved no contact with real or even toy snakes. They only imagined encountering snakes. Nevertheless, Wolpe and his followers had already shown that this treatment is quite effective in removing a wide range of phobias. The third group of subjects received a **symbolic modeling** treatment. This is a form of vicarious conditioning. The subjects watched a film showing fearless models handling plastic toy snakes, then progressing gradually to more and more contact with live king snakes. These subjects were also instructed in deep muscle relaxation before viewing the film. Furthermore, the presentation of the film was under the subjects' control. They could stop the film or reverse it whenever they found the scenes too anxiety-producing. The fourth group of subjects was given a **live modeling** treatment. This too was a vicarious conditioning experience. These subjects watched firsthand as fearless models handled live king snakes, first behind glass, then right in front of them. When they became comfortable with watching the models, the subjects donned gloves and graduated to touching the snakes themselves. In the end, they were able to hold the snakes in their bare hands.

Subjects from all four groups were then given a posttest. They were asked to approach a live king snake, pick it up, and hold it near their faces. The control-group subjects, of course, were no more able to do this than they had been before. (The same test had been given at the outset to establish a baseline.) Subjects treated with systematic desensitization, however, showed considerable improvement. Many of them were now able to handle live snakes. The subjects from group four, those who had had the live-modeling treatment, were of course still able to handle the live snakes. In fact, this treatment was far and away the most successful in alleviating the fear of snakes. However, the most striking result was achieved by the symbolic-modeling group, the group that had seen snakes only on film and who consequently had had no actual practice in handling live snakes. These subjects did better on the posttest than the systematically desensitized subjects. Though they were not as fearless as the group exposed to live modeling, their superiority over the systematically desensitized group demonstrates the effectiveness of vicarious conditioning as a method of eradicating phobias. Both of the methods that used vicarious conditioning were more effective than the systematic desensitization.

This experiment not only provided evidence in support of Bandura's theory, it had a marked influence on the practice of psychotherapy. Psychotherapy, as advocated by Bandura, is much more an educational process than a healing process. The social learning therapist is a teacher whose approach, insofar as modeling techniques are used, says: "Here, let me show you how to do that." Coaching people on how to deal with life's problems is the stock and trade of this approach. If the therapist models effective behavior and models it well, clients should get better. Apparently they do: More and more psychologists today are using live-modeling techniques to help clients overcome various fears and compulsions.

DISTINCTIVE FEATURES

Bandura's key idea—the important role of observational learning in the formation of personality, and the nature of that process—gives his social learning theory a distinctive flavor. The theory is cognitive and purposive. In contrast to instrumental learning, where the learner performs trial-and-error behavior and is selectively rewarded and punished for it, observational learning does not require any behavior to be performed (and consequently reinforced) in order for learning to take place. Observational learning is learning that takes place without previous reinforcement. Reinforcement, or at least the anticipation of reinforcement, may be required for the actual performance of the behavior, but learning and performance are two different things. Learning is a *cognitive* process; performance is behavior itself. People do not express everything they learn in their actions, according to Bandura. His emphasis on observational learning forces Bandura's theory away from traditional behaviorism and toward a more cognitive orientation.

Even when he talks about the *performance* of modeled behavior, Bandura recognizes this obvious fact: Behavior is performed without any past reinforcement. But Bandura does not want to give up completely the behaviorist principle of reinforcement. He therefore contends that imitational performances are motivated by the *expectation* of reinforcement. In other words, he says that these behaviors are probably learned in the first place because they promise reinforcement. The expectation of future reinforcement, which is of course a cognitive phenomenon, somehow feeds back into the present to motivate the person to learn and perform the behavior. Thus Bandura's theory takes on a *purposive*, or future-oriented, flavor. Bandura sees personality not only as the product of forces from the past that drive a person, but as something that involves planning, anticipating, and striving to achieve future goals.

Again, Bandura's says that expectations of future reinforcement feed back into the present to affect observational learning, which in turn feeds back to affect future performance. The way in which all of this happens gives Bandura's theory its third distinctive quality. The theory is **cybernetic.** This simply means that it focuses on the manner in which feedback systems control and regulate behavior. The ordinary household thermostat provides a familiar example. The thermostat includes a monitoring device, the thermometer, that measures the temperatures in the house. It also contains a control device, a switch, that turns the furnace on or off. When the temperature drops below the selected point, the thermometer informs the switch, which then sends a message to the furnace to send up more heat. When the temperature has risen a few degrees, the thermometer tells the switch to turn off the furnace. This process of feedback control is no different from the one a child uses in learning to ride a bicycle. In this case the semicircular canals of the ear monitor balance, the nervous system contains the switches, and the muscles put out the energy. All imitative learning, according to Bandura, works the same way. The task for the psychologist, then, is to identify the monitoring devices, the control devices, and the resulting behavior, and then to explain how information flows within this system. Because Bandura chose to concentrate on observational rather than instrumental learning, his attention was drawn to the information-conveying properties of models and the feedback-loop structure of the pupil-coach relationship. In observational learning, the two-way relationship between a model and an imitator gives meaning to the word *social* in Bandura's brandname—social learning theory.

Because observational learning plays such a major role in Bandura's theory, the theory is inevitably cognitive, purposive, and cybernetic. But social learning theory has two distinctive features that are not logically required in a theory based on imitation. As I have tried to illustrate, Bandura's theory is distinctly *experimental* and distinctly *applicable*. The tenets of social learning theory cannot be accepted until they have been experimentally verified. Bandura stands firmly in the behaviorist tradition in regarding the experiment as the final arbiter of truth. What is a little less stereotypically behaviorist is his humanistic interest in the clinical applications of his theory. Bandura is no ivory-tower, laboratory scientist. His extensive research on the effects of television violence on children and his development of effective behavior modification techniques reveal a deep concern for the betterment of human society and the alleviation of human suffering.

PROS and CONS

Pro #1: This key idea is a classic.   Imitation, Bandura's key idea, has an illustrious heritage in the history of ideas. It is a time-honored idea that has been accorded a central role in personality-formation by some of psychology's most eminent thinkers. Freud, who is seldom given the credit he deserves for appreciating the powerful role of learning in the development of personality, referred to observational learning under the rubric *identification*. *Identification* is Freud's word for imitation. The role of identification in shaping personality, according to Freud's theory, is pervasive. Identification plays an important part in the formation of the superego. Sex roles are learned when the child works through the Oedipus complex and identifies with its mother or father. Identification with a powerful person or organization may function as a defense mechanism.

It is interesting to note that when Bandura began his teaching career, he worked at Stanford University with Robert Sears, who conducted a series of experiments to test the Freudian concepts referred to in chapter three of this book. Shortly before he went to Stanford, Sears was the senior author of a book reporting research on child-rearing patterns. The research had as its "central theoretical innovation... 'identification,' viewed as a secondary motivational system" (Woodward, 1982, p. 404). The history of this key idea can therefore be traced from Freud to Sears to Bandura.

Piaget also accorded a central role to observational learning in his theory. His basic concepts of **assimilation** and **accommodation** refer to the ways in which we use feedback from observing our own performances, and those of others, to construct mental representations of reality. As early as 1945, he published a book on the role of imitation in the cognitive development of children (Piaget, 1951). Though there is little evidence that Bandura was directly influenced by Piaget, Bandura's cognitive and cybernetic emphasis is very much in the Piagetian tradition.

The purposive slant in Bandura's theory is in the tradition of another great psychologist, William James (Woodward, 1982). Here, too, the influence is not direct, although the genealogy of the idea can be traced from Bandura back to James. James was against a merely mechanical theory of learning. What he said, essentially, was that people learn habits because habits work. If habits do not work, if they are not effective, they are not learned. For James, learning is functional; it serves a purpose. Bandura's contention that reinforcement does not automatically and mechanically cause learning, but instead provides information about future consequences, is in very much this same tradition.

By selecting observational learning—with its cognitive and purposive implications—as his key idea, Bandura is following in the footsteps of the giants in psychology. For all but the most ardent iconoclasts, that is a pro. The fact that Bandura has so much in common with theorists representing such different traditions shows that he is eclectic and nonsectarian as well.

Pro #2: This key idea appeals to common sense.

The idea that we learn by watching others is such a commonsense idea that we wonder how behaviorists could have ignored it for so long. It is normal and natural to ask someone to show you how to do something. The most common method of teaching is teaching by example. Children are little monkeys, copycats whose penchant for mimicry, though it may sometimes catch us off guard, is nevertheless a quality even the most untutored parent takes for granted. Again, Bandura's key idea is a commonsense idea.

Everyday experiences also make it clear that you can learn without reinforcement. How many silly slogans from radio and television commercials stick in your mind, and later invade your consciousness, even though you make no effort to remember them and there is no conceivable payoff for doing so!

Learning something and performing it are two entirely different things. Psychologists overlooked this commonplace fact for decades, until Bandura insisted they pay attention to it.

It is a definite advantage that Bandura's key idea and its many ramifications coincide so well with common sense, though Bandura himself would not advocate common sense as a criterion for testing the validity of a theory. For Bandura, a theory is true only if it can be verified by experiment. Perhaps he would concede, nevertheless, that it could not hurt that it corresponds to common sense.

Pro #3: This key idea is applicable.   Bandura's key idea is highly applicable. It is not just a fascinating "ivory tower" speculation; on the contrary, it is easy to put in to practice. Bandura has answered the demand that psychology be relevant to human problems. His step-by-step analysis of modeling processes is easy to translate into a series of behavior-modification techniques that teachers, rehabilitation counselors, and therapists can use. The amount of training required to learn these techniques is considerably less than that needed, for example, to become a psychoanalyst. What is more, these techniques work. In fact, Bandura contends that they work faster than other methods for changing behavior. The enthusiasm with which practicing psychologists have rushed to adopt Bandura's modeling techniques in recent years suggests that he may be right.

Practical applicability alone does not justify a theory, nor does the success of a therapy based on it, yet both of these things add to its value. Bandura's key idea is valuable because of its many practical applications—pro #3.

Pro #4: This key idea has democratic implications.   Bandura is optimistic about the possibilities for changing behavior with modeling and other behavior-modification techniques. Our behavior, and thus our personalities, are not cast in stone. We are not condemned by fate to carry every emotional handicap, every annoying habit, and every crippling intellectual deficit around with us for the rest of our lives. A theory such as Bandura's, which views personality almost exclusively as a product of learning and places extreme emphasis on environmentalism, is naturally optimistic about the possibility of changing personality. If a pattern of personality was learned, then it can be unlearned and a new one relearned in its place. There are no massive internal structures, such as traits, to be dismantled; nor any hidden instincts to be unearthed and defused. The personality is far more flexible in Bandura's view. As he sees it, the personality "travels light"; it carries little or no baggage, in the form of hereditary traits or instincts. It rolls with the punches, changing and adapting itself to meet the requirements of new situations. If the situation changes the personality will also change.

This means that, given the proper observational learning experiences, any cockney Liza Doolittle can be made into my fair lady. Differences among personalities are not due to innate endowments, but to chance environmental circumstances. As long as these circumstances can be reversed, undesirable aspects of the personality can be corrected. In other words, everyone is potentially equal: Bandura's theory is democratic and egalitarian. It is completely in accord with our ideals of equal access for all citizens to free public education. After all, the theory implies that all social inequities can be remedied with techniques that are basically educational.

Bandura's key idea has implications that are profoundly democratic; it shows faith in the improvability of human nature; and it is optimistic about the value of education. Those features constitute a pro, because the implicit values correspond so closely to the principles upon which our nation was founded.

Pro #5: This key idea is supported by experimental evidence. We have already discussed the final pro at some length: Bandura's key idea is supported by experimental evidence. Bandura is scrupulous in not admitting anything into his theory unless it can be experimentally verified. His concepts are **operationally defined** and his hypotheses are stated in testable form. The catalogue of experiments he and his followers have conducted is formidable. Many of these experiments are elegantly designed and ingeniously conceived. They all have that same practical bent that permeates Bandura's work. Bandura uses people, not animals, as his experimental subjects. He places these people into very lifelike situations, not artificial and contrived laboratory situations. When the children in the Bobo-doll experiments played games with their teachers, for example, they used familiar toys in almost the same way they would on an ordinary school day. Needless to say, experimental results garnered from real-life situations can be more confidently generalized to other real-life situations. Bandura's experiments usually have this kind of manifest practical relevance.

I should emphasize that the word *experiment* is being used here in the narrow, technical sense, to refer to research designs in which variables are manipulated in order to disclose causal relationships. Occasionally Bandura collects survey data or uses correlational methods, but by and large, his research is experimental. This means that he divides his subjects into different groups and exposes each group to a different treatment—for example, rewarding aggression in one group and not rewarding it in the other. This is what psychologists call "manipulating a variable." The variable in question here is the payoff for aggression. The payoff is manipulated, in the sense that it is given in different amounts to each group. The results, of course, are analyzed to see if these different treatments make a significant difference in the subsequent behavior of one group of subjects, as compared to the other group. If they do, then the experimenter may infer that the difference in treatments *caused* the difference in subsequent behavior, since in all other respects the two groups were treated identically. The experimental method's ability to discover causes makes it very attractive to Bandura and accounts for its favored status among psychologists in general.

Since the majority of psychologists agree that the most compelling evidence for a theory is experimental evidence, the fact that Bandura's key idea is supported by massive amounts of experimental evidence is certainly one of its strong points.

Con #1: This key idea does not really explain. What is a theory for? What constitutes an explanation? These are questions that have divided personality psychologists for decades and are likely to do so for years to come. For Bandura, the purpose of a theoretical explanation is to predict and control behavior. On this point he is adamant. But we must ask whether being able to predict an event necessarily means that you understand it. Does Bandura's key idea explain, in the sense of conferring true understanding, or does it merely serve the utilitarian end of forecasting? Admittedly, it is useful to be able to make accurate forecasts; but if you know how to forecast, do you know everything you always wanted to know about personality?

Concepts such as *modeling* and *vicarious conditioning* do not really explain, they merely name. They provide us with a label to stick on behaviors that are already familiar to us. In the absence of reinforcement or some other motive, these concepts do not indicate *why* some behaviors are learned while others are not, although experiments such as the one showing that children model the controller of resources are a step in that direction.

It all boils down to the questions personality theorists choose to ask themselves. Bandura poses the question: Under what circumstances will imitation take place? He does not deal with the question of why we imitate. What causes imitation, according to Bandura, are situational circumstances. But the thing that causes imitation in the first place—the ultimate reason why we imitate—does not interest him. If that is your question, Bandura's key idea does not have your answer.

Con #2: This key idea is not comprehensive.   Bandura's key idea is not part of a comprehensive theory of personality. As we have just seen, his theory does not include a concept of motive. He tells us that people find certain events reinforcing, but he does not tell us why. He does not relate human satisfaction to any internal system of wants or desires. Even where prediction itself is concerned, Bandura's theory is not very helpful, since it provides no basis for knowing ahead of time what a person will find reinforcing. Unless you know what a person wants, it is impossible to say what she or he will find reinforcing.

Bandura does have a pretty good idea of what people want, of course; and unlike most other behaviorists, he does say that people have motives and intentions. But true to his behaviorist heritage, he maintains that such motives are almost always products of social learning. Consistent with his extreme situationalist position, he also contends that such motives are predominantly produced by momentary circumstances, rather than permanent traits or dispositions. As a result Bandura's theory—in marked contrast to psychodynamic theories—contains no well-defined, systematic theory of motivation.

Nor does Bandura have a theory of development about observational learning. Though he is plainly interested in the process of imitation in children, his research casts no light on the manner in which that process changes as the child grows older. We are left with the impression, after reading Bandura, that observational learning in children is no different from observational learning in adults. Bandura's theory may be cognitive, but it is not cognitive developmental. According to cognitive developmentalists such as Piaget, the processes of acquiring knowledge change in important ways as a person grows from infancy to adulthood. Bandura largely ignores this developmental aspect of cognition.

Although *self-reinforcing systems* is a thinly disguised structural concept, Bandura does not have a theory of personality structure. He disdains the trait approach, because assessed traits do not predict behavior as effectively as situational factors. Psychodynamic theories, he says, postulate causes that cannot be empirically demonstrated and are deficient in predictive power. By and large, Bandura seems to feel that ideas about the structure of personality are superfluous. They are largely irrelevant to his concern with predicting and changing behavior.

We are left with the question: Where is the person in Bandura's personality theory? Granted, there is a little bit of structure. Admittedly, there is a motivational concept of sorts. But there is no attention to development. The sum total of Bandura's ideas cannot add up to a whole person. Bandura's key idea is not the basis for a comprehensive personality theory. At best it is the major concept in a fragmented personality theory.

In short, Bandura's theory is not a grand theory in the tradition of Freud; it is a mini-theory. It does not answer all the questions we can ask about personality. That failure is a con, especially for those of us who want answers to all of those questions. If Bandura claims to answer all those questions, he is misrepresenting his product.

Con #3: This key idea has antidemocratic implications. With the publication of *Beyond Freedom and Dignity* in 1971, B. F. Skinner incurred the wrath of many liberal thinkers by insisting that human behavior is totally controlled by environmental contingencies of reinforcement. Free will, he said, is an illusion. Behavior-modification techniques thus came to be viewed by many as dangerous tools that could be used by a totalitarian state to enslave a defenseless populace. When Bandura became president of the American Psychological Association in 1974, he wisely used the occasion of his presidential address to the annual convention to disassociate himself from this extreme position. In an attempt to stake out a position that was more moderate, more representative of the majority of American psychologists, Bandura (1974) bent over backward. He insisted that reinforcement does not control human behavior automatically and mechanistically, that human beings have a certain amount of freedom in making choices, and that even the most effective behavior modifiers are not able to manipulate other people at will.

The basis of Bandura's disagreement with Skinner is Bandura's concept of *reciprocal control*. This has to do with his previously mentioned cybernetic orientation. Although the environment does exert control over human behavior, human behavior also affects the environment, he says. The control process is a two-way street. While "it is true that behavior is regulated by its contingencies, . . . the contingencies are partly of a person's making" (Bandura, 1974, p. 866). Bandura's (1974) position is still deterministic, but it is reciprocally deterministic, in the sense that it "does not imply the fatalistic view that man is but a pawn of external influences" (p. 867).

Does this mean, then, that Bandura is an exponent of free will in personality theory? The answer depends on what you mean by free will. What Bandura (1974) means is clear from the following statement: "Within the social learning framework, freedom is defined in terms of the number of options available to people and the right to exercise them" (p. 865). The question is wrongly phrased, according to Bandura, as freedom-versus-determinism. In reality, human beings are free to choose from a number of determined alternatives. Note that Bandura prefers the term *freedom* to *free will*. This is appropriate, since the thing he is talking about is not really free will; it is only a somewhat more complex form of determinism. This determinism may not be the antithesis of freedom as Bandura defines the term, but it is most certainly the opposite of free will.

The reinforcement, or expected reinforcement, that controls behavior in Bandura's theory need not come directly from the environment. This is where his *options* come in. The environment may promise you the reinforcement of a day's pay if you get up and go to work today, but that reinforcement does not move you automatically, like a puppeteer's string. You have the option of rejecting that incentive and staying in bed instead. Indeed, this does look like free will. But here is how Bandura would explain it. Your decision to stay in bed, while not dictated by the environmental contingencies of the present day, is the product of your past history of reinforcement, whether external or vicarious. Over the years you have learned, either by trying it yourself or by observing others, that staying in bed instead of going to work has certain positive benefits of its own. The expectation of these benefits is controlling your behavior in this instance. In any case, you are not controlling your behavior yourself. Parents, teachers, and other models from your past are ultimately controlling your behavior, since if you had been reared to believe there was absolutely nothing to be gained from staying in bed, you would hop up and go to work. In either case, your past social learning history determines which options you have and which ones you are most likely to choose. If Bandura did not believe this were so, how could he possibly hope to predict behavior.

Any theorist whose aim is to predict and control must of necessity be a determinist. This may be a science-fiction scenario, but I am sure Bandura would agree that if you knew the entire social learning history of an individual, right up to the present moment, you could predict that person's next act with absolute certainty. Why? Because when what has gone before in your life interacts with the environmental conditions impinging upon you at this moment (including what you can foresee), *there is only one* specific act possible for you in the next moment. This is what determinism means in personality psychology. To call this situation freedom, and to settle for that, is a con in my book. Unlike the democratic implications we saw in Bandura's theory earlier, this feature compromises human freedom and is potentially anti-democratic.

CHAPTER SUMMARY

Bandura's social learning theory is currently enjoying great popularity, partly because its cognitive emphasis is so timely. But its popularity is due also to its applicability to behavioral therapies, the most rapidly growing brand of psychotherapy. Bandura's research on the effects of television violence on children was also timely.

1. Bandura's key idea is, quite simply, that a great deal of learning takes place through imitation, something he prefers to call *observational learning* or *modeling*. Unlike conditioning, observational learning can occur in the absence of any reinforcement or response. It is therefore learning that takes place in your head. This attribute makes Bandura's theory cognitive, and perhaps mentalistic.

2. Bandura set out to identify the variables that affect the amount of observational learning that will occur. The first of these variables is *attentional processes*. To learn by watching, you must pay attention to what you watch. Hence anything that captures attention will maximize observational learning. One of Bandura's more famous experiments demonstrated that children imitate models who control desirable resources.

3. The second variable affecting observational learning is *retention processes*. To learn, you must remember what you saw. Anything that aids retention, aids learning. Another experiment demonstrated that verbally encoding a model's actions optimized observational learning. Rehearsal is also an effective technique to aid retention.

4. *Motor reproduction processes* are the third variable affecting observational learning. Observation can only teach you to do things you are (or can become) capable of doing. Children often learn behaviors they will not be capable of reproducing until they grow bigger or stronger. Aspiring athletes and dancers may learn complex performances by observation, performances which they are able to reproduce only after mastering the requisite subskills. Feedback—in the form of careful self-observation, pointers from coaches, videotapes, or even mirrors—is extremely helpful in perfecting motor reproduction. Nevertheless, if a handicap or physical limitation places the behavior to be learned beyond the capability of a person, that person will never be able to imitate the observed behavior.

5. Bandura calls the fourth and final variable that affects observational learning *reinforcement and motivational processes*. We learn by observation only behaviors that we expect to be reinforcing. If we did not expect them to be reinforcing, we would not bother to learn them. But where does this expectation of reinforcement come from? Bandura points to three sources. The learner may have performed similar behaviors in the past and suffered the consequences (*external reinforcement*). Or the learner may watch, or simply hear about, someone else performing the behavior and suffering certain happy, or unhappy, consequences (*vicarious reinforcement*). By now it is clear that the primary function of reinforcement is to provide information about the consequences we can expect from various behaviors. In addition, learners may consult their own consciences, asking themselves whether they can expect to feel proud or guilty if they imitate a behavior they have observed (*self-reinforcement*). In general, we are more likely to learn and imitate behaviors for which we expect reinforcement, and less likely to learn and imitate behaviors for which we expect to be punished.

6.   *Vicarious conditioning* is a specific type of observational learning that Bandura has devoted considerable attention to. In vicarious conditioning, an observer is conditioned by watching someone else being conditioned. The classic case is acquiring a fear of dogs by seeing someone else being bitten. Bandura's snake-handling experiment demonstrated how this process could be reversed and used to remove fears. Subjects who watched models handle snakes were able to overcome their snake phobias through this process of vicarious conditioning.

7.   Bandura's emphasis on the role of observational learning gives his social learning theory a distinctive flavor. As we have seen, his theory is *cognitive* and *purposive*. Because we learn behavior in the expectation that we will receive reinforcement at some future time, the image of human nature Bandura gives us is of beings who are planning, anticipating, and striving to achieve future goals. Bandura's theory also has a cybernetic flavor. It focuses on how feedback systems control and regulate behavior. It is important to note that Bandura's work is resolutely *experimental* and always *applicable*.

8. Pro #1:   Bandura's key idea of learning by observation is part of a classic tradition. Freud advanced the same notion under the rubric of identification. Piaget's ideas about observational learning have the same cybernetic flavor as Bandura's, and William James' view of learning may have influenced Bandura to be purposive. Freud, Piaget, and James are good company for any psychologist.

Pro #2:   What could be more commonsense than the idea that you can learn by watching somebody else? Aren't children born imitators? Furthermore, if we have ever had a silly commerical stick in our minds, we know that we can learn without reinforcement.

Pro #3:   Bandura's notions about observational learning are very useful in psychotherapy, rehabilitation counseling, and in many teaching situations. Applicability may not prove the truth of a theory, but it certainly establishes its value.

Pro #4:   Bandura's key idea has democratic implications. With its extreme emphasis on environment (as opposed to heredity), it is very optimistic about the possibility of restoring the health of every distressed personality. It is an egalitarian philosophy with a strong faith in the virtue of education.

Pro #5:   Bandura is scrupulous about not admitting to his theory anything that has not been experimentally verified. His experiments are models of design. What is more, he uses people, not animals as subjects and places them into lifelike situations, not artificial laboratory settings.

Con #1:   Despite all this, Bandura's key idea does not really explain. Concepts such as *modeling* and *vicarious conditioning* merely label phenomena, they do not explain them. Nor does being able to predict something prove that you understand it. Bandura may be able to tell us under what conditions imitation is likely to occur, but he never tells us why we imitate—what causes imitation in the first place.

Con #2: Bandura's key idea is not the basis for a comprehensive theory of personality. At best it is the major concept in a fragment of a personality theory. Bandura has no concept of motive—he does not explain why people find certain events reinforcing. Nor does he have a theory of development to show us how observational learning grows and matures. Of course, he has no concept of personality structure either, because traits do not predict behavior nearly as well as situational variables. We wonder where the person is in Bandura's personality theory.

Con #3: Despite Bandura's efforts to reassure us that behavior modifiers do not control people like puppets on a string, Bandura's theory is deterministic. A theory that aims to predict and control behavior can make no provision for free will. According to Bandura, if it were possible to know the entire social learning history of an individual, up to the present moment, you could predict the person's next act with absolute certainty. Free will does not enter into this at all. There is one, and only one, "next act" possible for a person with a specific history of social learning.

REFERENCES

Awards for distinguished scientific contributions: 1980: Albert Bandura. (1981). *American Psychologist, 36,* 27–34.

Bandura, A. (1965). Influence of model's reinforcement contingencies on the acquisition of imitative responses. *Journal of Personality and Social Psychology, 1,* 589–595.

Bandura, A. (1973). *Aggression: A social learning analysis.* Englewood Cliffs, NJ: Prentice-Hall.

Bandura, A. (1974). Behavior theory and the models of man. *American Psychologist, 29,* 859–869.

Bandura, A., Blanchard, E.B., & Ritter, B. (1969). The relative efficacy of desensitization and modeling approaches for inducing behavioral, affective, and attitudinal changes. *Journal of Personality and Social Psychology, 13,* 173–199.

Bandura, A., Grusec, J.E., & Menlove, F.L. (1966). Observational learning as a function of symbolization and incentive set. *Child Development, 37,* 499–506.

Bandura, A., Ross, D., & Ross, S.A. (1963). A comparative test of the status envy, social power, and secondary reinforcement theories of identificatory learning. *Journal of Abnormal and Social Psychology, 67,* 527–534.

Miller, N. & Dollard, J. (1941). *Social learning and imitation.* New Haven: Yale University Press.

Piaget, J. (1951). *Play, dreams, and imitation in childhood* (C. Cattegro & F.M. Hodgson, Trans.). New York: W.W. Norton. (Original work published 1945)

Tolman, E. (1932). *Purposive behavior in animals and men.* New York: Appleton-Century.

Woodward, W.R. (1982). The "discovery" of social behaviorism and social learning theory, 1870–1980. *American Psychologist, 37,* 396–410.

PART FOUR

Humanistic Theories

Humanistic theories of personality are identified by the following characteristics: (1) they use a **phenomenological** approach to the study of personality; (2) they insist that personality be viewed holistically; and (3) they hold that human beings have free will. In marked contrast to the psychoanalytic or the behaviorist position, these assumptions affirm the intrinsic value of human experience and the dignity of human nature. This more affirmative posture is the essence of what is meant by *humanistic.*

Humanistic theorists take the phenomena of subjective experience seriously. Behaviorists prefer to ignore the private mental world; humanistic theorists take that inner stream of consciousness as their starting point. They do not ignore behavior, but their orientation is more mentalistic than behavioristic. On this score they are closer to the psychoanalysts. But unlike the psychoanalysts, who claim to know better than you why a specific thought came into your head at some particular moment, the phenomenological approach, employed by humanistic theorists, simply accepts your conscious experience at face value, without reducing it to some allegedly more basic drives or instincts. Experience is taken as a given, and phenomenology does not try to go behind experience. It does not even assume, as psychoanalysis does, that anything exists behind experience. Experience, as it presents itself to us, is where phenomenologists begin. They start out by describing experience—inner, private experience—as accurately, and in as much detail, as they possibly can. This is the approach used in all observational sciences. Astronomers look through telescopes and record their observations, often with the aid of precise measuring instruments. Biologists describe and classify what they see under their microscopes. Phenomenologists do the same thing, except that instead of looking outward, they look inward.

One of the first things you discover, when you begin looking inward and taking subjective experience seriously, is that our experience is integrated, organized and centered. It coalesces around some core. Your stream of consciousness has one continuous, central filament running through it. That core filament, of course, is what in ordinary parlance we refer to as our "self." You should not be surprised, then, to learn that the concept of *self* plays a prominent role in humanistic theories of personality.

Because they believe that our experience is centered and integrated, humanistic theorists insist on a holistic view of personality. As the Gestalt psychologists demonstrated so many years ago, our conscious minds are specifically designed to organize the chaotic input from the world into meaningful wholes. When we look at the picture on the front page of the morning paper, we do not see hundreds of separate black and grey dots, but a picture of the latest terrorist bombing, or of the president addressing the National Press Club. When we look at a movie, we do not see a series of still pictures flashed on the screen in rapid succession, but one continuous flow of action. The normal function of consciousness is to make sense by making things whole. True, we can employ our consciousness to dissect and analyze experience, but the result is something artificial and irrelevant. After all, a handful of musical notes, played without regard to time or order, is not a melody. The melody is a patterned, organized whole, which is not changed even when all the original notes are transposed into another key. For humanistic theorists, then, to dissect personality by reducing it to basic instincts or energy sources, or to a list of universal traits, or to a collection of stimulus-response connections, is to lose sight of personality itself. A boxful of parts is not the same as the finished product. The whole is more than the sum of its parts.

Consistent with their holistic emphasis, most humanistic theorists denounce the tendency of many other theorists to separate the mind from the body. The person is one psychosomatic unity, they hold. There are no disembodied minds floating about, nor are there any human bodies without some kind of mind. Personality does not reside only in the mind, and it certainly does not exclude the body. In fact, the humanists say we should stop speaking of mind and body as though they were separable, because they are not. We are whole persons; and if we happen to get sick, we are not sick in our minds or sick in our bodies (mentally ill or physically ill), but sick in our persons (personally ill).

Also consistent with their holistic emphasis, most humanistic theorists refuse to split personality into conscious and unconscious portions. If personality is whole, half of it cannot be under separate management. While most humanistic theorists acknowledge that a certain amount of mental activity may go on outside the realm of sharply focused awareness, they find some way other than the Freudian unconscious to conceptualize this process.

Not only does a phenomenological approach reveal a self that is whole, it reveals a self that is free to decide and to choose. Thus every humanistic theorist holds that human beings have free will. This is not to say that human behavior is not partly determined by inner biological factors and external environmental stimuli. Manifestly it is. Nor is this to discredit the contribution to our understanding of human personality of those psychologists who concentrate their research efforts on examining the influence of those factors. It is simply to say that those factors alone do not constitute the whole story. By concentrating exclusively on those factors, the humanists say, psychology has come up with a one-sided picture of human nature. They also say that the subjective experience of constantly having to choose among alternatives in order to make decisions is so close to the essence of human personality that any psychology of personality that dismisses

this topic as uninteresting, or secondary, can only be regarded as fatuous. No one denies that human beings experience themselves as being free to make decisions, but the psychoanalysts and the behaviorists regard that experience as an illusion. True to their phenomenological creed, humanistic theorists do not decide in advance that this experience is either illusory or secondary. Instead, they study it, because they believe it is no less important than the people who have it say that it is!

The decisions and choices that phenomenological description says the self freely makes all refer to the future. While walking along the road of life, in other words, we choose among the paths that lie ahead, not behind. (We have already made our decisions about those that lie behind.) The point, according to humanistic personality theorists, is that human personality is future-oriented. It is purposeful and goal-directed. We are not pushed blindly from behind by libidinous forces or past conditioning; we plan and aspire, and we direct our efforts toward the achievement of those plans and aspirations. Many humanistic theorists even go so far as to postulate an innate tendency toward self-actualization. According to this notion, it is the overarching goal of every individual to find personal fulfillment by becoming everything that she or he potentially is. The personality is built to grow toward mature perfection. In this sense as well, human nature strives toward the future.

In sum, humanistic theories of personality, relying on the methods of phenomenology, prominently feature the concept of the self. Because they take the experience of selfhood seriously, their perspective is strongly antireductionistic and holistic. Because it affirms free will, their perspective is also antideterministic.

11/Carl Rogers

A Biographical Sketch

Carl Rogers' life story reiterates many of the themes we have seen in the lives of our other theorists: a love of books; a deeply engrained devotion to hard work; rebellion against a conservative religious training which nevertheless left its mark; and a significant change or two in career goals. The story begins in 1902 in a suburb of Chicago, where Carl was born into an upper-middle-class family, the fourth of six children. His father was an engineer who had formed his own contracting business. His mother, who had also attended college, was a deeply religious person in the fundamentalist tradition. Rogers grew up with family prayers, much Bible reading, and no smoking, drinking, or card-playing.

Apparently Carl was precocious. He learned to read long before he went to school, and when he did begin school he was put directly into the second grade. Though he always did excellent school work, Rogers says that he was a dreamy youngster, absentminded and lost in a fantasy world. His schoolmates derisively called him "Professor Moony."

As Carl entered adolescence, his father took up agriculture and moved the family thirty miles out of Chicago to a farm he had bought. This brought numerous changes in Carl's life. For one thing, he was now required to perform a daily round of chores that were physically exhausting, but taught him responsibility and self-reliance. The move also meant that Rogers would commute long distances to three different high schools, which he would have to leave every day immediately after classes. Thus he never could participate in extracurricular activities or form close friendships with classmates. This, in turn, meant that his only social group was his own family. But the move also brought him close to nature, which he loved so deeply that he became an amateur naturalist. He not only learned everything he could about giant night-flying moths, for example, but collected and raised their caterpillars through the entire twelve-month cycle, until they emerged as moths. Finally, because his father insisted upon operating the farm according to the latest scientific principles, Rogers acquired an early appreciation and understanding of the experimental method. True, he was only comparing the effectiveness of different fertilizers and animal feeds, yet he learned how to design experiments and conduct statistical tests of hypotheses.

When it came time to go to college, Rogers naturally chose to major in scientific agriculture. The year was 1919, and the college was the University of Wisconsin, where his mother, father, two older brothers, and sister had all gone. At Wisconsin, Rogers became an active member of a Sunday-morning religious group sponsored by the YMCA. The sense of closeness and intimacy he experienced within that group, Rogers says, is something he had not previously known outside the context of his family. The group seems to have been conducted in a fashion that today we might call non-directive or even Rogerian. Clearly, this was a formative experience for Rogers.

It was during his sophomore year that Rogers "heard the call." During Christmas vacation he attended a fundamentalist, evangelistic student conference where the speakers whipped the audience to a peak of religious fervor. Rogers came away committed to a career in the Christian ministry. Since agriculture did not seem an appropriate preparation for the ministry, Rogers changed his major to history.

During his junior year, Rogers was selected as one of ten American students to attend the World Student Christian Federation Conference in Peking, China. This experience had a thoroughly liberalizing effect on him. Before it was all over, our young evangelical zealot concluded that perhaps Jesus was not divine after all. This profound change came about after six months of travel, not only to Peking, but throughout China and the Philippines. Rogers met people from markedly different cultural and religious heritages. Meeting students from other countries at the conference also had a leavening effect. Even some of the American religious leaders who sailed with the student group had a liberalizing influence.

Liberalized but not yet secularized, Rogers had not changed his mind about his vocation: He would still go into the ministry. In 1924 he graduated from college. He had lost a year because of his extensive travels, and because of a bout with a duodenal ulcer after his return from the Orient. In fact, while recuperating from this illness he took a correspondence course in psychology, his only undergraduate course in that subject.

Rogers' liberal theological views were not well received by his family. And when he chose to attend Union Theological Seminary in New York because it was the most liberal, his father tried to bribe him with an offer to pay all expenses if he would go instead to Princeton, the stronghold of fundamentalism. But Rogers declared his independence from his family. In August of 1924, just before they set off together for New York

City, Carl Rogers and Helen Elliott were married despite the protests of both sets of parents.

At Union Theological Seminary, Rogers encountered not only the usual courses in theology and scripture, but a course in "Working with Individuals," in which the professor brought in psychologists and psychiatrists as guest speakers. Rogers realized for the first time that this manner of helping people was a possible career choice. He also had the opportunity at "Union" to participate in another unstructured, intensive group experience: a seminar in which there was no teacher and the students chose the curriculum. As students wrestled with their own questions in that seminar, Rogers says, most of them decided to quit religious work. He himself was one of these. The transition, however, was relatively smooth and painless. He had already taken some courses across the street at Columbia University Teachers College. Now he took all his courses there, in the doctoral program in clinical and educational psychology.

A fellowship at the newly founded Institute of Child Guidance provided financial security for the growing family—their first child was born in 1926—and introduced Rogers to an eclectic Freudian perspective that contrasted, in an intellectually stimulating way, with the statistical mental-measurement approach he was getting at Columbia.

For his dissertation, Rogers constructed a personality adjustment test for children, based upon insights gleaned from his work at the clinic. He also began at this time to develop some confidence in his skills as a therapist.

In 1928, partly due to the financial pressure created by the imminent arrival of a second child, Rogers accepted a position in Rochester, New York, with the Society for the Prevention of Cruelty to Children. He was to spend the next twelve years there, laboring in relative obscurity. He did teach summer courses at Columbia, and part-time at the University of Rochester. But ultimately it was his first book, *Clinical Treatment of the Problem Child* (1939), that brought him to the attention of the search committee at Ohio State University. He was appointed full professor there in 1940. In 1945, Rogers moved to the University of Chicago, where he had been invited to establish a counseling center. The twelve years he spent there were perhaps his most productive. He was lured away in 1957 by an offer from the University of Wisconsin, promising him just about carte blanche to do whatever he liked. Things, unfortunately, did not work out as well as expected, and in 1964 Rogers moved to California, where he has been ever since—first at the Western Behavioral Sciences Institute, and since 1968 at the Center for Studies of the Person.

CLIENT-CENTERED THERAPY

If people know anything about Carl Rogers, it is that he has something to do with non-directive counseling. Actually, Rogers called it *client-centered therapy*. It is so uniquely his product that the name *Rogerian therapy* may well be its most common label. It is entirely appropriate that people should associate Carl Rogers' name primarily with a brand of psychotherapy, because Rogers spent almost every day of his professional life in the practice of psychotherapy.

Carl Rogers' personality theory derives almost exclusively from his experiences as a therapist. When asked what were the most important influences on his theoretical thinking, Rogers always said it was his clients. The people who came to him for counseling taught him far more, he said, than any other source. He admitted he had also learned something from reading books and working with students and younger colleagues; but he had no mentor, no master teacher whose work, like a good disciple, he carried on. Quite the contrary, he found his way alone, for many years in the face of obstinate resistance from psychology and psychiatry alike.

Rogers spent the first ten years of his professional career unlearning what he had been taught in graduate school about how to do therapy, and trying out and revising the methods prescribed in the professional literature of the time. In those days, psychotherapy was the exclusive province of the medical profession. A psychologist doing psychotherapy was viewed by psychiatrists as an illegitimate practitioner of medicine—an opinion that was shared, if they bothered to consider the issue, by most psychologists. This state of affairs seems incomprehensible today, largely because of changes brought about by the pioneering efforts of Carl Rogers.

Because psychotherapy was exclusively a medical specialty when Rogers broke into it, it was modeled along the lines of "doctor knows best." The client, or patient, was viewed as sick and helpless, and the therapist as the all-knowing expert who would prescribe appropriate remedies to cure the patient's problems. But the more Rogers listened to his clients in Rochester, the more he became convinced that clients, not the doctor, know best how to cure themselves. Over the years, Rogers gradually abandoned the kind of questioning that resembles a clever lawyer's cross-examination. More and more, he allowed his clients take the lead in choosing topics for discussion. Lo and behold, he found that clients knew what their problem was! Even more important, they knew *when* they were ready to face up to it. But most surprising of all was the discovery that clients had the resources for dealing with their problems. Rogers found that as a therapist, all he had to do was provide a safe, non-threatening, warm, accepting, non-judgmental atmosphere, and clients would eventually find a solution to their own problems. Thus, client-centered therapy was born.

Rogers was not satisfied, however, with merely discovering a method of therapy that worked. He was more than a psychological repairman. He wanted to extract the meaning from what he was learning from his clients. What was the significance of these revelations for a philosophy of human nature? Such questions had perplexed him at least since his days as a student at Union Theological Seminary. And from still earlier in his life, he recalled a method for investigating such questions. By the age of fourteen, as a result of the family's moving to the farm, Rogers had mastered the experimental method. He knew how to apply it to evaluating the effects of various fertilizers on crop growth, or of various feeds on milk production. Another hobby during those teenage years also helped him to develop the investigative skills he would later apply in his clinical work: Young Carl Rogers was a collector of moths. He was fascinated by the great night-flying moths that lived in the woods near the farm—so fascinated that he bred them in captivity, raised the caterpillars, kept cocoons over the winter, and assiduously observed and recorded the entire process. Years later in Rochester, Rogers became the first to record a therapy session on motion-picture film. Since that time, he has filmed and recorded thousands of interviews.

Today, when students regularly bring tape recorders to class to record a professor's lecture, it may be difficult to appreciate the significance of Rogers' innovative application of the then-new technology in 1938. Before that time, students of psychotherapy had no objective way of knowing what a therapist did or said during the process of psychotherapy. The only records that existed were the recollections and notes of the therapists themselves. The opportunities for selective forgetting and perceptual distortion, whether intentional or unintentional, were obvious and numerous. The odds that therapists would find confirmation for their own pet theories in their experiences with patients were enhanced by bias, despite well-intentioned precautions against this. By exposing the process of psychotherapy to public scrutiny, recordings and films made it possible, for the first time, to do bona fide scientific research on personality. That is exactly what Carl Rogers did.

Freed from the need to consider research hypotheses during the therapeutic session, he could now devote his energies single-mindedly to helping his clients. Afterward, he could play back his tapes for himself and other researchers, observing the process with the same discerning eyes that had once watched caterpillars transformed into moths. Just as he had once tested the effects of various fertilizers on crop growth, he could now test the effects of various therapeutic methods on personal growth. Carl Rogers was one of the greatest pioneers in developing methods for research into the process of psychotherapy, a fact that was recognized by the American Psychological Association as early as 1956. In that year, the first in which such awards were given, the association presented him with the Distinguished Scientific Contribution Award. This, he maintains, is still his most cherished honor (Rogers, 1974, p. 117).

Rogers' research demonstrated that psychotherapy did more than help people solve specific problems in their lives; it stimulated profound changes in their personalities. As Rogers and his associates studied their ever expanding-library of taped interviews, and as Rogers reflected upon his own experience as a therapist, it became clear to him that therapy is a process that nurtures personal growth. Like fertilizer, it may even accelerate growth—growth toward maturity and personal fulfillment, growth toward realizing full human potential. The more Rogers watched his clients grow and mature in his therapeutic greenhouse, the more firmly convinced he became that their growth held the answers to the most important questions in personality theory. Not only did his clients carry within themselves the solutions to their own problems, they also had the answer to the question of what it means to be fully human!

Rogers' experience as a therapist confronted him with two basic questions: (1) What is the nature of the state of being that is produced by psychotherapy? (2) What are the factors that produce that state? The answers to these two questions, answers Rogers insists can be found by observing his clients in therapy, constitute Rogers' key idea.

◤ THE KEY IDEA
PERSONHOOD CREATED
BY BEING VALUED

Through psychotherapy, clients become **fully functioning persons.** Rogers' concept of *the person*, or to be more precise *the fully functioning person*, is the first half of his key idea. Psychotherapy is not the only process that enables you to become a person; but it provided Rogers with a convenient laboratory situation where he could study that larger process.

Clients become fully functioning persons, Rogers concluded, by being unconditionally valued. Rogers' concepts of **conditions of worth** and **unconditional positive regard** are the second half of his key idea. Wherever these conditions obtain, whether in psychotherapy or in everyday life, they help to actualize the innate potential everyone has to become a fully functioning person.

When you understand Rogers' concept of the fully functioning person, and the quality of interpersonal relationships that fosters that state of being, you have the key to all of Carl Rogers' personality theory.

THE FULLY FUNCTIONING PERSON

"To be that self which one truly is"—a phrase Rogers borrowed from the Danish philosopher-theologian, Søren Kierkegaard—defines that goal of becoming a person, which Rogers regards as the number one project in everyone's life. All people have this need to find out who they really are, to look behind the masks and the many roles we all play and discover the real self, the person beneath the outward appearances. We become so easily entangled in the habitual modes of impressing others, lying to ourselves, and distorting our perceptions that we lose contact with our true selves, with the person behind the *persona*.

Rogers claims that his experiences with his clients have taught him that there is such a person, that someone actually lives behind the facade. This is "what human beings appear to be striving for," he says, "when they are free to choose" (Rogers, 1961, p. 164). Given an atmosphere of safety, warmth, and empathic understanding in client-centered therapy, people strive to become persons.

MOVING AWAY FROM THE SELF ONE IS NOT

Down with facades.   Initially this striving to become a person takes the form of moving away from the false self, from the self that one is not. One thing that occurs is a gradual dismantling of facades. Tentatively at first, and then more boldly, the masks are laid aside. Strategies of self-concealment are relinquished. Disgust and dissatisfaction with accumulated hypocrisies surfaces, often accompanied by a torrent of rage and remorse, which, once expressed, leaves the client feeling washed clean.

There is a sense of release at being done with phoniness, and an evident desire for authenticity and integrity. People want to be real. They do not want to be fakes or counterfeits. People—all people—Rogers says, want to be genuine. They want to become real persons.

Banishing "oughts."   A second aspect of this emancipation occurs as clients move away from "oughts." They begin to stop doing things, and being certain kinds of people, just because they think they *ought* to act or be like that. They stop living someone else's design for their life and begin designing it themselves. The person stops fulfilling someone else's prescription. Maybe it was his father who just always assumed that he would grow up to take over the family business, or his mother who would have been so proud to have a professional man in the family. Maybe it was the kids on the playground who branded him a clumsy klutz so often that eventually he got into the habit of tripping over curbstones just to get a laugh. Maybe it was his grade-school teachers hounding him to stop being such a dreamer that persuaded him he ought never consider himself a very practical person. Whatever the source of these prescriptions, the amazing thing is how uncritically most of us adopt them as specifications for the kind of person we ought to be.

The desire to earn a parent's love, the need for acceptance by one's peer group, the effort to get attention from the teacher: Any of these motives can lock people into a pattern of behavior that they mistakenly come to accept as the manifestation of their own true selves. As client-centered therapy proceeds, they gradually realize that these are artificial selves—not the selves they want to be, merely the selves others think they ought to be. In therapy, clients begin to give up acting the way they *ought* to act to meet someone else's specifications for their selves, and start to act the way they *want* to act in order to be true to their own real selves.

Anti-conformity.   Rogers found that clients in therapy began their journey toward personhood by moving away from cultural expectations. In a word, they became increasingly *nonconformist*. Not only do individual parents, teachers, and friends put pressure on us to be the selves we ought to be; the larger culture defines for us what a beautiful person, a normal person, and even a worthwhile person is. Fully functioning persons are individuals with minds of their own, who resent and resist the attempts of business organizations, educational institutions, and other manifestations of the mass culture, to mold or shape them.

Please yourself.   In the process of becoming a person, the client moves away from pleasing others. Many clients, Rogers found, have formed themselves by trying to please others. Probably it starts out when the individual, as a child, becomes obsessed with pleasing his or her parents; but for some people it becomes a characteristic way of relating to nearly everybody. Thay want people to like them; and they think people will not like them unless they please. The resulting paradox is that the harder they try to please others—and they do try harder and harder—the less satisfaction and personal fulfillment they feel. This, of course, is a great source of consternation, since they have no idea why this should be so—no idea, that is, until client-centered therapy emancipates them by radically eliminating the need to please. Confronted by a counselor who accepts them warmly, whether they try to please or not, clients gradually give up trying to please the counselor and glimpse, perhaps for the first time in a long time, the possibility of pleasing themselves. The realization filters into consciousness that these selves fashioned to please others were not their real selves, and that to find their real selves they must give up always trying to please others.

This does not imply that fully functioning persons are selfish, or that they never do things to please other people or to meet their obligations. It is not so much a matter of what they *do* as of what they *are*. They may do things to please others or because they are expected to do them, but they will not be persons whose selves, whose identities, whose very essences, are designed and defined by someone else. They must be their own persons. They must be the architects of their souls. They must live by Shakespeare's famous dictum: "To thine own self be true."

MOVING TOWARD ONE'S OWN TRUE SELF

As the caterpillar emerges from the cocoon, it sloughs off its old self and moves toward a new self. By moving away from one mode of being, one inevitably moves toward another. Growth toward becoming a fully functioning person is a process in which the moving away and the moving toward are in one sense always simultaneous, even though at certain times the moving away may appear predominant while at other times the moving toward is more salient. Fully functioning persons are defined by what they are and by what they are not. We have seen what they are not. Let us turn our attention now to the more positive characteristics that mark what they are.

Opening up.   As clients move away from facades and come out from behind their masks, they necessarily move toward being more open. The trouble with masks—or any kind of armor, for that matter—is that while they offer some degree of protection, they also serve to close you in. A mask may keep others from seeing you, but it also may make it harder for you to see out. A bulletproof vest may make you invulnerable to a forty-five caliber slug, but it can also diminish the pleasure of a tender caress. Persons who are on their way to becoming fully functioning start to open themselves up. They begin dropping their defenses. They get rid of their masks and strip away their armor. They do it cautiously at first, fearing that their nakedness may be mocked. But client-centered therapists do not mock. They do not attack at all. And so, the client opens up a little further. Before long the clients begin to realize that their real selves are coming out into the open. The authentic persons that lay hidden for so many years behind the facades are being uncovered, so that even the clients can see them. Another problem with masks, you see, is that if you wear one all the time, whenever you look into a mirror all you see is the mask. After a while, you begin to take the mask for your real self. Our defenses not only hide us from others, they hide us from ourselves. The opening up that occurs in client-centered therapy reintroduces clients to their long-lost selves.

Openness, Rogers says, is the antithesis of defensiveness. The fully functioning person is receptive to experience. The attitude Rogers alludes to seems to me remarkably similar to what many describe as the aesthetic attitude. Imagine sitting down to listen to your favorite piece of music. You don your stereo headset, sink back in your easy chair, and just bathe yourself in the music. All critical faculties are put aside. You just let the music do its thing on you. If it moves you to tears, all right! If it makes you get up and dance, OK! You do not fight it, you go with it, and it gets into you. And because you have opened yourself to the music, you are open to your own feelings. You may even discover a depth of feeling you never knew you had.

Fully functioning persons are open to their feelings in the same way. But they are open to their feelings in all kinds of situations. They adopt this same aesthetic attitude toward all of their experiences, not just listening to music. They allow things to move them emotionally, and they do not block or hide the resultant feelings from themselves. In short, they are in touch with their feelings. And since for Rogers the feelings are close to the core of the real self, they are also in touch with their real selves. The more aspects of your experience you can open yourself up to fully, the more you will be able to get in touch with your feelings; and the more you are able to get in touch with your feelings, the more your real self will come into focus.

Being open to experience also means that you perceive reality more accurately. Listening to music with a receptive, aesthetic attitude enables you to hear what the music really has to say. Defensiveness, on the other hand, distorts perception—there is a large body of psychological research to support that claim. Openness clarifies perception. Rogers agrees with Maslow here and cites Maslow in support of his contention. In fact, Rogers' fully functioning person has many of the same characteristics as Maslow's **self-actualizing person**. Both have more accurate perception of reality because they are not crippled by defensiveness.

Accurate perception of reality is, of course, a criterion of positive mental health that is almost universally accepted by psychologists and psychiatrists. People who distort reality—either external reality or their own internal reality—are *ipso facto* mentally ill. It follows, then, that the more accurate a person's perception of reality, the healthier that person is. Fully functioning persons, because they are open to experience and thus perceive reality more accurately, are mentally healthy human beings.

Trusting the organism.   The openness of fully functioning persons is closely related to a second characteristic: their increasing trust in their organism. Clients who are progressing toward becoming fully functioning become increasingly able to trust their impulses and intuitions. The hackneyed phrase, "If it feels right, do it," becomes their guideline. Most people are too inhibited to act on impulse. They hunt around for rationalizations to disguise the fact that they make important decisions on the basis of nothing more than whims. They fear that slick salespersons will take advantage of them by playing on their emotions. Their ideal is to be deliberate and rational, to think things through. Not so with fully functioning persons. They are comfortable with their impulses. They have no need to summon up their intellectual faculties continually in order to keep their impulses in check. If it feels right, they do it. And ninety-nine percent of the time, "it" turns out to have been the right thing to do.

The reason why fully functioning persons do the right thing can be traced back to their characteristic openness. A person faced with making a decision will make the best decision when she or he has all of the relevant data to work with. Rogers' fully functioning persons have all the data. Their openness permits them to perceive reality accurately, preventing the data from being distorted. Unlike less adequately functioning individuals, they are not handicapped by defenses that block out important bits of information. The result, Rogers says, is that fully functioning persons, like automatic computing machines, intuitively make wise decisions, decisions based simply on their feelings about a situation. Of course, they occasionally make errors, but most of the time they are right. And the more their decisions turn out to be good decisions, the more they learn to trust their impulses.

A side effect of this is that fully functioning persons find it relatively easy to make decisions. We all face agonizing decisions from time to time; becoming fully functioning will not deliver you from that fate. But have you ever noticed how many people are in an almost permanent state of paralysis, unable to make even the simplest decisions without lengthy rumination? And the more choices they have, the harder it is for them to decide. It may not be far from the truth to say that most people who seek psychotherapy urgently need someone to help them make up their minds about something they cannnot decide on their own. Choices are hard to make if you cannot trust your impulses. But fully functioning persons, because they trust their impulses, do not procrastinate over decisions or suffer undue anguish in making them.

Trusting one's organism involves more than just trusting one's emotional reactions, however; it includes feeling confident about one's judgment and having a strong sense of the rightness of one's internal standards of value. Rogers cites the examples of several creative artists and scientists whose work was rejected at first, but who nevertheless persisted because they firmly believed in their own ability to judge what was good. El Greco, he points out, must have realized early in his career that good painters did not paint the kind of pictures he did, yet he continued to trust his own inner vision of what was good art. Einstein must have known that his thinking represented a serious departure from traditional theory in physics, yet he trusted his own judgment more than that of the scientific establishment.

This phenomenon is not unique to artists or genuises, Rogers says; it is typical of all fully funcrioning persons. Fully functioning persons trust their own judgment and internal standards of excellence more than those of external authorities. And because fully functioning persons are open to experience and thus more accurate in their perceptions of reality, the trust they place in their judgment is vindicated more often than not.

Willing to be a process. A third characteristic of person who are in the *process* of becoming fully functioning is just that—they are in *process*. In fact, they *are* processes. A person is not a thing, an entity; a person is a process. And even when persons become fully functioning, they do not arrive at some motionless state of rest; they continue to function, and to function fully as processes. But then, all people's lives are processes. Whether they function fully or only partially, all people are processes.

The difference between the fully functioning person and the rest of us is that the fully functioning person accepts the fact that his or her life is in a perennial condition of flux, while the rest of us cherish childish fantasies that some day, when we have gotten it all together, we will be able to lean back and relax. The notion that we can reach some permanent beatific state of being, where the endless struggle with unpleasant decisions will cease, is an extraordinarily popular fantasy. It is also a defense, of course. Fully functioning persons, since they relinquish all defenses, do not need that fantasy. They accept the fact that they will never have it "made in the shade." They abandon the goal of having all of their problems solved some day. They concentrate on being processes, rather than regretting that they are not yet finished products. In fact, they welcome the chance to be processes, to be undisturbed by the prospect of continual change. Fully functioning persons relish the sense of adventure that comes with accepting oneself as a process.

This zest for life is similar to what Rogers elsewhere refers to as *increasingly* **existential** *living* (1961, pp. 188–189). (The characteristics of the fully functioning person are a composite sketch from a number of articles written by Rogers over a span of many years.) Because fully functioning persons accept themselves as processes and abandon all hope of arriving at some quiescent terminal state, they are able to live fully in each present moment. They relish each moment because they are open to experience. Their receptive attitude and lack of rigidity permit them to "go with the flow." They do not try to mold events to fit their preconceptions, and they are not annoyed by the fluid qualities of existence. They participate in, rather than criticize, the ever-changing flow of phenomena. This is what Rogers means by *increasingly existential living*, the condition he sees his clients approaching as they progress in client-centered therapy.

These three characterisitcs—openness to experiences, trust in one's organism, and willingness to be a process—define the essence of the fully functioning person. Rogers does, however, mention several other characteristics that we can safely regard as secondary. Either they are partially derived from the three primary characteristics, or they are to some extent redundant. I will mention them briefly just to round out the picture.

Self-direction. Fully functioning persons are self-directed; they have a strong sense of autonomy. As clients progress in therapy, Rogers finds that they become more and more willing to take responsibility for their own choices. They choose their goals themselves and make decisions on their own; they also accept responsibility for the consequences. They do not invariably make good decisions; but if things go wrong they do not blame others or try to excuse themselves on the basis of unforeseen circumstances. They are free agents who are in the process of gaining the courage to resist the universal temptation to escape from freedom by having someone else make their decisions for them.

Being complexity. Closely related to the willingness of fully functioning persons to be a process is their moving toward *being complexity*. They face and accept the contradictions in themselves, in their feelings, and in their relationships. Their ambivalent feelings, for example, do not threaten them, and are therefore not denied. They sometimes cordially hate the persons they love most, but they do not see anything wrong with that. They also allow themselves to feel hate just as enthusiastically as they feel love. Contradictions do not make rational sense, and most people conceal part of themselves behind a facade in order to project an image of rationality. Not so with fully functioning persons, according to Rogers. They must be true to themselves. They must go with their feelings. And since they are human, their feelings are complex and contradictory.

Acceptance of others. A by-product of the openness to experience in fully functioning persons is this last characteristic: acceptance of others. They approach other people with the same receptive, aesthetic attitude that they direct toward all their experience. According to Rogers, they value others and appreciate them for what they are. They do not criticize them for not being what they "ought" to be. Borrowing a quotation from Maslow, Rogers points out that just as we do not fault the water for being wet, so fully functioning persons do not judge others for being what they are. They simply accept those others uncritically, and without judgment.

Carl Rogers was interested in human potential. He wanted to know what human personality would look like if it were allowed to grow under optimum conditions. To explore that question he built his own little greenhouse, called client-centered therapy, then put people in there and watched them grow. He found that in that secure and protected environment, they voluntarily shed their defenses and became more open to their experience. They dared to make contact with their feelings and grew to trust their impulses, even when the impulses were complex and contradictory. The prospect of perpetual change was transformed for them from a grim necessity, to be denied if possible, into an exhilarating, welcome adventure. What made this transformation possible was the clients' growing conviction that they were more and more in control of the direction these changes would take. They gave up following the demands of others, trying to meet the expectations of society, and attempting to live their lives to please others. In return, they became more autonomous and self-directed. They continued to change, of course, but for them change was no longer shaped by external forces; it was a flowering of all the potential contained in the seeds of their true selves. As a flower exists potentially in a seed, Rogers argued, the fully functioning person exists potentially in every individual. The distinguishing characteristics of human personality are revealed not by taking the seed apart, but by nuturing it to grow to its fullest, then examining the mature, blossoming organism.

WHAT CONDITIONS PRODUCE THE FULLY FUNCTIONING PERSON?

How do you get the organsim to flower? Rogers recalls that as a therapist he tried a hundred and one different things to cure his clients before realizing that, in order to cure them, he had to stop doing anything *to* them. They did not seem to improve, he found, when he explained the causes of their problems and prescribed steps they ought to take to solve them. Rogers discovered, ironically, that if he wanted to help clients he had to give up trying to help them directly. He had to learn instead simply to accept and appreciate them as valuable human beings. When he did this, the clients seemed to find ways to help themselves. Being valued as an intrinsically worthwhile individual was the key ingredient in Rogers' greenhouse, the formula that helped his clients to flower. Not content with mere speculation, Rogers and his colleagues conducted numerous researches to test the validity of this hypothesis. Not surprisingly, these researches demonstrated that clients made most progress toward becoming fully functioning persons when they felt that their therapist accepted and valued them unconditionally.

But how do therapists let clients know that they value them unconditionally? Do they annouce it as a matter of company policy immediately following the introductory handshake? Do they have signs all over the office saying: "We value every person unconditionally"? Obviously they do not. And if they did, the client's private response would undoubtedly be a cynical "I'll bet you do." The unconditional acceptance of the client, if it is to be effective and credible, must be communicated by the quality of the ongoing therapeutic relationship. Rogers identified three crucial attributes in this regard: (1) the therapist is congruent; (2) the therapist expresses unconditional positive regard for the client; and (3) the therapist understands the client empathically.

CONGRUENCE

Congruent therapists are sincere persons, persons who are not phony or artificial. They do not hide behind a facade of professionalism. They are in contact with their own feelings in the relationship, and they reveal these feelings to the client. They do not smile benignly if the client says something that arouses their hostility, nor do they seek to disguise their affection if they feel attracted to the client. They make themselves fully present to the client, as real persons. They are not defensive or evasive, and they do not have some secret strategy. They do not play games with the client. They are what they seem to be. In short, what you see is congruent with what you get. Rogers chose the word **congruence** for this quality because he wanted to emphasize the perfect match between therapists' inner feelings and desires and their observable outward actions.

It is this congruence that makes therapists, and everything they say, credible. When Joe Namath proclaims the virtues of the "great smell of Brut" aftershave and cologne on TV, more than a few viewers may doubt his sincerity, because his message contains a number of incongruities: rude, macho Joe Namath, fearful that his aroma may offend; egocentric Joe Namath, taking a personal interest in me by letting me in on one of the secrets of his legendary success with women. It just does not fit together—it is incongruous. That is why so many TV announcers, used-car salesmen, and politicians strike us as untrustworthy. There is a lack of congruity, a mismatch, between what they say and what they are. Not so with client-centered therapists, Rogers says. They are congruent; and because they are congruent, clients trust them and believe what they say. Without this congruence in the therapist, all the "unconditional positive regard" and all the "empathic understanding" in the world would still strike the client as no more credible than a television commercial. The therapist's congruence is the basic guarantee for everything else that happens in the relationship.

The therapist's congruence is enough to show clients that they are valued. Unlike psychoanalysts, who sit where the patient cannot see them and assume the role of the great stone face, client-centered therapists assume some risk on behalf of their clients. They let themselves be seen, not just physically but psychologically as well. By disclosing themselves and their feelings to clients, they encourage much more mutuality in the relationship; but they also make themselves much more vulnerable to clients. By letting down their defenses, therapists open themselves to attack. This vulnerability tells the clients that the therapist trusts them, and more important, that the therapist cares about them. We do not remove our masks for people we do not care about. Because client-centered therapists remove their masks and are congruent, clients sense that these therapists value them.

UNCONDITIONAL POSITIVE REGARD

A congruent therapist who expresses *unconditional positive regard* toward clients communicates to those clients that they are persons of intrinsic worth, regardless of what the clients (or anyone else) may think of their own feelings, desires, and behavior. *Unconditional positive regard* refers to the client-centered therapist's attitude of total acceptance of the client and the client's feelings. The therapist is non-judgmental, consistently refusing to make any evaluation, positive or negative, of anything the client presents. Praise, of course, can be as tyrannical as criticism, since it implies that the opposite behavior is bad, establishing a standard which, if not achieved in the future, instills a sense of failure. Unconditional positive regard, like the aesthetic attitude, is not critically evaluative; it is an attitude of receptive appreciation. According to Rogers, client-centered therapists appreciate their clients; they "dig" people.

There are no conditions of worth that clients must meet to *qualify* for the therapist's acceptance. They do not need to *earn* approval here; it is freely given. The therapist cares about them, likes them, prizes them (Rogers uses all these terms), on the basis of no apparent ulterior motive. Incredulous clients, like little children, often react to this at first by trying to be bad in order to test the therapist's limits. They miss appointments, or talk crazy, or tell the therapist off, just to test whether this acceptance really does not have any strings attached. If the therapist manages to weather this storm and congruently maintain a warm, positive regard for the client, the client gradually begins to believe that someone really and truly does care about him or her. The next step is to draw the conclusion: Since someone who knows all my faults cares about me despite those faults, I must be worth something as a person.

Unconditional positive regard is the most direct way that therapists communicate to clients that they are valued. It manifests itself partly, as we have seen, in what therapists do not do. They do not cross-examine clients in order to affix a diagnostic label; they do not even give any advice, or offer expert opinions, about what the client ought to do; they do not prescribe any agenda of topics to be discussed. For the most part, they just listen attentively. They seem to be genuinely interested in hearing what the client has to say. They seem to be earnestly trying to understand. Willing to follow where the client leads, they do not prod, pry, or probe. When they do respond—and they are responsive, demonstrating a genuine willingness to work just as hard as the client in a mutual search for solutions—their response is often something like this: "Let me see if I understand what you just said," whereupon they restate what the client has just said. They do not give an exact quotation but paraphrase, endeavoring to amplify or clarify the feeling-content of what the client has just said. There is no evaluation of the client's statement, only a reflection; but it is a reflection that highlights certain points, in order to show the client the deeper meaning of the feelings he or she has just expressed, feelings the client may have perceived only dimly until they were mirrored in the therapist's restatement.

EMPATHIC UNDERSTANDING

If therapists listen carefully enough, if they are sensitive to the client's condition and do not amplify too much, the client will feel understood—in fact, understood in a deeper, more sympathetic, and more supportive way than ever before. Rogers' word for this kind of understanding is **empathy:** This is the third crucial ingredient in client-centered therapy.

With empathy, therapists put themselves in the client's place and see the world as the client sees it. They adopt the client's internal frame of reference and hence understand what things mean to the client, and what feelings things stir up inside the client. By adopting some sort of imaginative, "as if " attitude, therapists appropriate the perspective of the client, looking at the world through the client's eyes, yet somehow never losing their own objectivity.

Therapists communicate this empathic understanding by accurately reflecting the client's statements back to the client. They convey understanding not only with what they say, but with the tones of their voices, their facial expression, and all of their other bodily expressions of emotion. Clients know when a therapist understands their lack of self-confidence, for example, because the therapist adopts a hesitant, timid, diffident demeanor in order to echo the client's feelings. Just as one plucked string sets up sympathetic vibrations in a nearby string, a client-centered therapist tunes in to clients and reproduces their emotional tones—client and therapist are on the same wavelength. And the whole person is involved, not just the intellect. Empathy, Rogers claims is much more than just an intellectual game in which the therapist subtly persuades clients to accept certain of the therapist's ideas as insights.

When they feel understood, clients also feel accepted and valued. After all, it takes a real effort to achieve this kind of understanding. Rogers says therapy is the hardest work he has ever done. Clearly, therapists would not work so hard if they did not value their clients. The therapist's empathy communicates to clients that they are worth understanding, that their inner meanings and private hopes and fears have value. Why else, Rogers asks, would their therapist be willing to risk getting so emotionally involved with them? The risk of involvement empathic therapists assume for the sake of their clients further convinces the clients that their therapists genuinely care about and value them.

When individuals become convinced that another person cares about and values them, Rogers says, they begin to value themselves. This gives them the freedom to start becoming fully functioning. The core of this therapeutic relationship, the basic conditions that tell clients they are valued, are the congruence of therapists, their unconditional positive regard, and their empathic understanding. Each of these conditions tells clients not only that they are valued, but valued unconditionally. Clients do not have to prove their value; they do not have to earn this acceptance, because it is freely given. In fact, try as they may, they cannot disqualify themselves. They are accepted and valued with no strings attached. Being valued unconditionally is the essence of the experience clients have in Rogerian therapy; it is the key, Rogers claims, to unlocking the potential that every individual has to become a fully functioning person. This, then, is the other half of Rogers' key idea.

THE KEY IDEA IN A NUTSHELL

Rogers says that people become fully functioning persons when they are unconditionally valued. By experimenting with different approaches to psychotherapy, Rogers believes that he has demonstrated this. He has used the therapist's office as a kind of laboratory. And what he has discovered there, he contends, applies to people from all walks of life. If parents are congruent with their children, show them unconditional positive regard, and understand them empathically, the children will grow into fully functioning persons. If teachers value their pupils unconditionally, the pupils will start to become fully functioning. If businesses and other organizations conduct their affairs in accord with these principles, their employees and members will become more creative and productive. Wherever people are involved in interpersonal relationships, Rogers argues, applying these principles will foster growth toward full human personhood.

What does it mean to be an authentic, human person? That is the question, Rogers seems to be saying, a personality theory should answer. What is personality? What is the nature, the essence, of being a person? Rogers says that the answer to that question becomes evident when growing conditions are optimal, when human beings are encouraged to blossom and flower, to realize every last ounce of their innate potential. The fully functioning person is Rogers' picture of human personality in bloom.

PROS and CONS

Pro #1: This key idea is humanistic.   It is refreshing to find a key idea in personality psychology that does not demean human nature. The idea that everyone of us has the potential to become a fully functioning person is very flattering. Most of us would prefer this idea to either the Freudian image of us as savages with thin veneers of civilization, or the behaviorist model of us as trained animals jumping through hoops. Reading Carl Rogers makes us feel good about the human race. His outlook is decidedly mellow. No personality theorist is more optimistic about the perfectibility of human nature than Carl Rogers; and no psychotherapist has so integrated his conviction of the essential goodness of human nature into his manner of conducting psychotherapy. Rogers lives his optimism about human nature; he practices what he preaches. He is congruence itself.

The term *humanistic*, applied to Carl Rogers, refers to this attitude of reverence for human personality and celebration of human potential. Rather than viewing human nature as something that carries the seeds of its own destruction within itself, Rogers sees it as the bud of its own glorious flower. Rogers trusts the organism; he has faith in humanity. In the deepest sense, this is what it means to be humanistic.

Rogers' emphasis on positive mental health is, of course, entirely consistent with his humanistic perspective. Some psychologists argue that by studying the mentally ill, they can get an accurate picture of normal personality, because among the mentally ill, normal personality processes are magnified and therefore easier to identify. No so, according to Rogers! Disease is not a magnification of the normal, it is deformity. To avoid a distorted image of human nature, personality psychologists must study health, not illness. Human nature reveals its essence when it is in full flower. Much more can be learned by studying what causes personality to grow and flourish than by concentrating on what cripples and warps it. It is remarkable that Rogers, a clinician faced with a cavalcade of psychological misfits in his daily practice, came to such optimistic conclusions about human nature.

Consistent with his humanistic orientation, Rogers is adamantly in favor of free will, as opposed to determinism. His debate with B.F. Skinner on this issue is one of his most frequently reprinted papers (Rogers & Skinner, 1956). The conviction that human beings are free, rather than determined, is absolutely essential as a foundation for Rogers' key idea. His whole program was to find out what human beings will strive for when they are *free* to choose. That is why Rogers' approach to psychotherapy—very unlike that of the behavior modifiers—carefully avoids making clients' choices for them. In fact, Rogers makes every effort to remove all extraneous constraints, so that clients can make their own decisions with absolute freedom of will. According to Rogers, people choose to become fully functioning persons when they are permitted optimum exercise of their free will. It is perfectly clear, then, that if there were no such thing as free will for human beings, Rogers' portrait of the fully functioning person would not be an accurate picture of human personality. Rogers' key idea of the fully functioning person, and of the conditions that lead to that state, absolutely requires allegiance to the concept of free will. In fact, any humanistic theory of personality cannot help coming down on the side of free will.

Unlike the trait theorists, who dissect personalities into a dozen or so distinct traits; unlike the psychoanalysts, who picture the psyche as an house divided against itself; and unlike the behaviorists, who view us as an aggregation of millions of separate stimulus-response connections, Rogers sees the person as a *whole*. He does not attempt to dismantle the personality into its alleged constituent parts. His key idea deals only with the whole person. When you begin to take persons apart, he says, they cease to be persons; they are no longer human. Rogers' holistic emphasis is therefore entirely consistent with—and in fact is required by—his humanistic position.

Another typically humanistic feature of Rogers' theory is his respect for people's subjective experience, particularly their feelings about themselves. Rogers' insistence that an individual can only be understood through an empathic process, in which we imaginatively put ourselves inside that other person, also pays tribute to human nature by implying that our inner experience is important and valuable. Traditionally, behaviorist theories have had no use for subjective experience; and though psychoanalysts have been willing to listen to it, they have insisted that they know better than the patient does how to interpret the patient's experience. Neither approach values this unique human attribute; one ignores it, the other merely uses it. Neither approach recognizes something that every human being believes with absolute certainty: The stream of conscious thoughts and feelings that passes continually before my mind's eye is my most important possesion; without it, I would be neither human nor myself. Carl Rogers, on the other hand, showed his profound appreciation of this fact, basing his personality theory on a phenomenological approach that tries to apprehend a person's internal frame of reference, and by concentrating especially on the person's self-concept.

Pro #1 is that Rogers' key idea is humanistic, for a variety of reasons. It stresses that human nature is innately good; it focuses on positive mental health; it affirms that human beings have free will; it is holistic; and it takes subjective experience seriously, including the experience of being a self. For the most part, these assertions resemble philosophical assumptions: They can be debated, but they cannot be proved. Yet if we do not have some faith in human nature, life hardly seems worth living. Rogers' key idea dignifies human nature, rather than demeaning it. I take that to be a pro.

Pro #2: This key idea is interpersonal.

Pro #2 is that Rogers' key idea takes the *interpersonal* processes involved in personality development seriously. Although all individuals have the potential to become fully functioning persons, Rogers says that they will never achieve that goal unless they encounter a certain quality of interpersonal relationship. They must be accepted and valued by another person, or persons, if they are to actualize their innate potential. In other words, building fully functioning persons is not a do-it-yourself project. Personality, fully functioning or otherwise, exists within a context of interpersonal relationships. To ignore that context, as so many other theories do, is to arrive at a truncated model of personality. Personality is not just a set of traits to be tallied up on a profile sheet, like so many credits and debits on the statement of your personal bank account; it depends on the quality of a whole social network of interpersonal relations. Quality, then, is just as important as quantity; and for Rogers, this quality resides not so much in individuals themselves as in their relationships. Personality psychology must focus not only on what is *in* persons, but on what is *between* persons. In the last analysis, according to Rogers, real persons do not exist except in relationships. There is no personality, in the sense of personhood, except in relationships. To be human, one must be related.

Rogers' strong emphasis on interpersonal relationships seems appropriate in light of the social nature of human development. Perhaps all psychology is social psychology; at the very least, all personality psychology ought to be social psychology. Contemporary theorists appear to be increasingly aware of this requirement. Remember, for example, that Albert Bandura incorporated a systems-theory slant into his social learning theory. Here was a theorist from a rival school who wound up placing the same emphasis on interpersonal relationships as Rogers. Rogers' interpersonal emphasis is a pro because it makes sense, and because contemporary theorists are beginning to catch on to that fact.

Pro #3: This key idea is supported by empirical research.

The American Psychological Association gave one of its first Distinguished Scientific Contribution Awards to Carl Rogers, honoring him for his empirical research. Not surprisingly, pro #3 is the fact that Rogers' key idea is supported by an impressive amount of empirical research. Rogers knew that philosophical arguments and anecdotal stories about successful counseling sessions would not persuade his colleagues in the APA. If he was going to convince them that his theory was valid, he would need experimental evidence. And so, with the help of a small army of graduate students and younger colleagues, he set about collecting it. The Q-technique developed by Stephenson in the early 1950s provided Rogers with an empirical measure of the changes clients underwent in therapy.

The Q-technique presents a client with a deck of cards, each containing a self-descriptive statement such as: "I am a submissive person"; "I don't trust my emotions"; "I feel relaxed and nothing bothers me"; "I am afraid of sex"; "I usually like people." Clients are asked to sort the cards into nine piles, ranging from statements that are most characteristic of them to those that are least characteristic. The number of cards that must be placed in each of the nine piles is specified, producing a pattern similar to a **normal distribution curve**—that is, more cards are put in the middle piles and fewer in the extreme categories. The purpose of this exercise is to make possible a certain kind of statistical analysis. Once clients have sorted the cards, describing how they perceive themselves at the present moment, they are asked to sort the cards again, this time to describe the ideal selves they would like to be. The difference between clients' descriptions of themselves as they are, and as they ideally would like to be—expressed as the coefficient of correlation between their two Q-sorts—produces a measure of congruence, of the extent to which they are being their real selves. To evaluate progress in psychotherapy, these measures can be taken at a number of points in time: before therapy begins; during the course of therapy; after therapy is completed; and even months, or years, later. Using this Q-technique, Rogers (1961) and his colleagues have verified that individuals in client-centered therapy do become more congruent persons than subjects in control groups who received no treatment.

Once he had a way of measuring the progress clients made in therapy, Rogers could begin to identify the features of therapy that contributed most significantly to that progress. A doctoral dissertation by one of Rogers' students, G. T. Barrett-Lennard, illustrates how this can be done. Barrett-Lennard developed a Relationship Inventory that allowed him to measure several aspects of the therapeutic relationship that, according to Rogers' theory, promote personal growth. The inventory contained a number of statements aimed at finding out the extent to which clients felt they were being *empathically understood* by the therapist. Examples: "He appreciates what my experience feels like to *me*"; "He tries to see things thru my eyes"; or "He understands my words but not the way I feel." Clients were asked to respond to each item on a six-point scale from strongly true to strongly not true. The Relationship Inventory also contained items designed to measure how much *positive regard* the client felt from the therapist. Statements such as "He cares about me," and "He is curious about 'what makes me tick,' but not really interested in me as a person," were included to assess the level of regard perceived by the client. The *uncon-ditionality* of the therapist's regard for the client was measured by still other items, such as: "Whether I am expressing 'good' feelings or 'bad' ones seems to make no difference to the way he feels toward me"; or "His interest in me depends on what I am talking to him about." The therapist's *congruence*, as seen by the client, was also assessed with items such as: "He behaves just the way that he *is*, in our relationship"; or "There are times when his outward response is quite different from his inner reaction to me." There were, of course, many more items than the examples given here. They were all mixed in together to make up the Relationship Inventory.

The important point is that this inventory was a reliable way to quantify clients' subjective experience of their therapists' empathic understanding, level of regard, unconditionality of regard, and congruence. With the inventory, plus the Q-technique for measuring progress toward becoming fully functioning, Rogers' key idea could now be tested empirically. The procedure was simply to ascertain whether the clients whose Relationship Inventory scores credited therapists with a high level of congruence, unconditional positive regard, and empathy, were the clients who had made most progress toward becoming real persons, as indicated by their Q-sort scores.

They were. Barrett-Lennard's data showed a statistically significant, positive correlation between the therapist's perceived congruence, level of regard, unconditionality, and empathy, on the one hand, and the degree of personality change achieved during therapy, on the other. Of the four factors, empathy was most highly correlated with positive personality change; but the contribution of the other three factors was also significant.

> Thus we can say, with some assurance, that a relationship characterized by a high degree of congruence or genuineness in the therapist; by a sensitive and accurate empathy on the part of the therapist; by a high degree of regard, respect, liking for the client by the therapist; and by an absence of condition-ality in this regard, will have a high probability of being an effective therapeutic relationship. These qualities appear to be primary change-producing influences on personality and behavior (Rogers, 1961, p. 265.).

The Barrett-Lennard research does provide empirical support for Rogers' key idea, but I have not included it here in order to prove Rogers' theory conclusively. I simply wanted to give you some of the flavor of Rogers' research, and to show how it is possible to measure and statistically analyze some of the subtle, subjective aspects of the therapeutic relationship. Rogers himself refers to these researches as "pioneering." As such, they lack the methodological sophistication of more recent work. But Stephenson's Q-technique, and studies in the Barrett-Lennard tradition, are the foundation on which hundreds of subsequent research studies have been built. The resulting body of research, taken as a whole, argues persuasively for the validity of Rogers' key idea. In short (Pro #3), Rogers' key idea is supported by empirical research modelled on the pioneering studies described above.

Pro #4: This key idea is widely applicable.   Carl Rogers has always been first and foremost an applied psychologist. He has a philosophical bent for theorizing; and as we have just seen, he has a strong commitment to empirical research. Far more crucial than either of those concerns, however, is his dedication as a therapist to helping his clients. His main reason for concocting this key idea was to help his clients. Not surprisingly, the idea also turned out to be applicable in a wide range of other contexts (Pro #4). Reviewing the areas to which Rogers' theories have been applied, Farson (1975) says: "Professionals from education, religion, nursing, medicine, psychiatry, law, business, government, public health, law enforcement, race relations, social work—the list goes on and on—all came to feel that here, finally, was an approach which enabled them to succeed on the previously neglected human dimensions of their jobs, to reach the people for whom they felt responsible but were often unable to help" (p. xxx).

Of all these many fields, education provides perhaps the best example of how the same key idea that guided Rogers in his counseling practice can become the chief ingredient of a theory in another field. If psychotherapy ought to be client-centered, then perhaps education ought to be student-centered. Rogers cautioned teachers never to forget that they teach students, not subject matter. They do not teach math, or English, or history; they teach *persons*. They may teach these persons *about* math or English or history, but they must never allow the student to become secondary to the subject matter. "Student-centered," in other words, is the opposite of "subject-centered."

Just as client-centered therapy assumes that clients have the potential for curing themselves, Rogers' student-centered theory of education assumes that students already know how to learn. One person cannot really teach anything to another person; all that teachers can do is to facilitate learning in their students. Again, the analogy of farmers and their crops is brought to mind. The plants have an inner potential for growth; all that farmers can do is to make sure the plants get plenty of warm sunshine, water, and perhaps a little fertilizer. Teachers, like therapists, can do no better than to follow this recipe. This means that teachers must also be *congruent;* they must also show their students *unconditional positive regard;* and they must also communicate *empathic understanding* to them. The same conditions that foster personal growth in psychotherapy will promote learning in the classroom, Rogers maintains.

The practical consequences of this approach, when it was first spelled out by Rogers, struck many professional educators as nothing short of radical. Congruent teachers, for example, are real persons to their students, not aloof repositories of expert knowledge who hide behind a facade of intellectual superiority. Consequently, instead of lecturing at students, the congruent teacher joins them in their search to find answers to their questions, simply helping them to discover their own answers. Since their regard for students is positive and unconditional student-centered teachers do not evaluate the answers their students discover; they merely support them in their search. They do not make public comparisons among students, telling one student that his answers are dumb and another that hers are correct. In fact, if they are to be entirely consistent in providing unconditional positive regard, student-centered teachers must refuse to assign grades to their students. Rogers sometimes permitted students in his courses to grade themselves. Examinations evaluated by anyone other than students themselves are also taboo. The primary task of student-centered teachers is to understand their students' questions empathically; and, by reflecting those questions back to the students, to aid them in clarifying their questions and tentative answers as they struggle to discover new knowledge for themselves. The rationale for this approach is Rogers' conviction that only the knowledge that one discovers for oneself is truly learned.

This is not the place to go into a discussion of the ferment these ideas created in educational circles. The ideas are presented here only to illustrate how Rogers' key idea can be (and was) transferred lock, stock, and barrel to another discipline. People have also attempted to transfer Rogers' idea to many of the other fields listed in the quotation from Farson. If it is a virtue for a key idea to be widely useful, in the sense that it can easily be applied to a vast number of other disciplines, then Rogers' key idea certainly deserves a pro for its applicability.

Con #1: This key idea is based on self-deception.   Though Carl Rogers' key idea rests on a broad foundation of empirical research, it is still not immune to criticism. Like most research results, his data are subject to more than one interpretation. Rogers' own interpretation may very well be colored by wishful thinking.

You will recall that Rogers' initial strategy was to provide clients with a safe, accepting environment where they were free to choose, and then to observe what kind of person they chose to become. This was how Rogers "discovered" the characteristics of the fully functioning person. He took great pains not to influence his clients, to be *non-directive*. He refused to interpret or evaluate; he simply reflected, like a mirror. His was a hands-off kind of approach: Don't do anything *to* clients; just let them grow in the direction they choose. Only, of course, if he succeeded in *not* influencing his clients, would it be fair for him to conclude that the way they turned out was due to some universal, innate growth process in them, and not his influence. His whole notion of the fully functioning person is based on the assumption that the characteristics of the fully functioning person represent the flowering of innate human potential and are not the result of the therapist's influence.

But how can therapists not influence their clients? And is it not curious how closely the beliefs and values of clients who have successfully completed client-centered therapy resemble those of Carl Rogers himself ? In fact, the portrait of the fully functioning person looks suspiciously like Carl Rogers' philosophy of life.

Albert Bandura (1961) has an explanation, from a different perspective of course, of why this should be so. What it boils down to is that therapists—whether they are Rogerian, Freudian, Jungian, or something else—*do* influence their clients; and they influence them according to certain well-known principles of learning. For example, the fact that client-centered therapists do not explicitly approve or disapprove of clients' behavior does not mean that they do not influence the clients' behavior. Though the therapists do not respond with approval or disapproval, they do in fact respond to some—*but not all*—of the things the client says and does. Those responses, those displays of interest, by the therapist are sufficient to reinforce certain kinds of behavior. When the therapist gives a little smile, leans forward a bit to listen more carefully, or simply emits a reassuring "uh-huh," clients receive a clue that they are on the track the therapist wants them to follow. If these reinforcements do not continue, the client will eventually abandon that track. Because neither Rogers, nor any other therapist, responds, or responds in the same way, to every statement a client makes, then obviously the therapist is covertly, or perhaps unwittingly, shaping a client's behavior in accordance with the laws of operant conditioning. Bandura (1961) concludes that "consistent with the results from verbal conditioning experiments, content analyses of psychotherapeutic interviews suggest that many of the changes observed in psychotherapy, at least insofar as the patients' verbal behavior is concerned, can be accounted for in terms of the therapists' direct, although usually unwitting, reward and punishment of the patients' expressions" (p. 150).

In addition to being covertly conditioned, there is good reason to believe that Rogers' clients were also influenced by the process that Bandura calls *modeling. Modeling* refers to learning by imitation. Bandura (1961) presents experimental evidence to support his contention that "affectional nurturance is . . . an important precondition for imitative learning to occur, in that affectional rewards increase the secondary reinforcing properties of the model, and thus predispose the imitator to pattern his behavior after the rewarding person" (p. 152). Needless to say, Rogers' client-centered technique, with its emphasis on unconditional positive regard, provides clients with an abundance of "affectional nurturance." Consequently, it is not surprising that "client-centered patients, . . . tend to produce the client-centered terminology, theory, and goals, and their interview content shows little or no overlap with that of patients seen in psychoanalysis who, in turn, tend to speak the language of psychoanalytic theory" (Bandura, 1961, p. 154).

In a nutshell, Con #1 says that, by unwittingly using subtle rewards and punishments and the modeling process in his client-centered therapy, Rogers turns his clients into little Carl Rogerses! If this is so, then the fully functioning person Rogers claims to have discovered is nothing other than the mirror image of Carl Rogers himself. In that case, what Rogers has discovered in his clients is not some innate human potential, but his own philosophy and values.

Part of the problem comes from Rogers' farmer-and-fertilizer analogy. Despite all the claims about the virtues of talking lovingly to your houseplants to make them grow, it is extremely unlikely that plants are influenced by the same learning processes that affect human beings. Plants do not learn from human beings; but human beings learn from other human beings. A flowering plant may be the product *only* of its innate potential, nurtured by a supportive environment; but to ignore the influence of learning, to assume that mature human beings are likewise *only* products of their innate potentials, is to assume too much. Rogers' key idea may have a lot to do with the brand of fertilizer he uses.

Con #2: This key idea is too optimistic.

Rogers' critics have accused him of being anti-intellectual, romantic, and utopian. The anti-intellectual criticism comes from either rationalistic academics or from cognitive psychologists, who decry what they regard as his one-sided emphasis on feelings, as opposed to rational thinking. "If it feels right, do it," strikes them as a simplistic, and even dangerous, maxim. Rogers' technique is easily lampooned, as when Bob Newhart, playing a somewhat ineffectual but well-meaning psychologist on his TV show, counsels a particularly distraught patient to "Go with that feeling." Or consider the cartoon that depicts an irate patient climbing over the desk to strangle his therapist, who calmly observes: "Mr. Jones, you seem to have strong feelings about this."

Romantic has several connotations. On the one hand, it refers again to Rogers' emphasis on feelings. The romantic movement, which sprang up in the nineteenth century and influenced art, music, philosophy, and science, was characterized by a fascination with nature and an exaltation of feeling and emotion. Darwin's theory of evolution is romantic; it represents a natural process as a passionate, and even bloody, struggle for survival. Beethoven's music is romantic because it appeals to the emotions and often takes its themes from nature. Freud's theory is romantic, with its emphasis on clashes between unconscious, irrational emotions. Even the existential philosophy of Søren Kierkegaard, which Rogers credits as the source of his key idea, is typically romantic; it stresses the anguish of making personal choices. When applied in this sense to Rogers, the term *romantic* is not necessarily derogatory; it simply classifies his theory within a particular tradition. Whether you like that tradition or not is pretty much a matter of taste. On the other hand, *romantic* can also be used in a derogatory sense to mean *sentimental*, *fanciful*, or *unrealistic*. In this case, the implication is that Rogers' theory is little more than a pipe dream.

Utopian means much the same thing. Rogers' concept of the fully functioning person represents an ideal state of human existence. While this state may be much admired and much desired, it will never become a reality. It would be more accurate to describe what Rogers calls a *real person* as an *ideal person*. Real people are not like that; no one is as good as Rogers would have us believe.

At the root of most of these criticisms, it seems to me, is the belief that Rogers' view of human nature is overly optimistic. Rogers is as extreme in his optimism about the perfectibility of human nature as Freud is in his pessimism. Logic demands that both men cannot be right, and it suggests that the truth may lie midway between the two extremes. From a logical standpoint, human nature, even when its potential is fully actualized, is neither as magnificent as Rogers contends nor as depraved as Freud would have us believe. In fact, this is the conclusion favored by most personality theorists.

Yet there is another possible conclusion—namely, that both Rogers and Freud are correct, and that human nature is a paradox, a logical contradiction. According to this dialectical view, neither extreme should be watered down to produce some muddy middle ground; the two contradictory extremes should be allowed to exist in full force, at one and the same time. This, of course, is contrary to logic. But that is precisely the point the dialectical view is trying to make: Human nature does not follow the rules of logic. The essence of human nature is a paradox. Human nature is both heroic and tragic; human beings are totally free and totally determined, not a little bit of one and a little bit of the other. We are a bundle of contradictions. It is curious that Rogers overlooked this viewpoint when he was reading existential philosophy, since it is at the very heart of Kierkegaard's system. Actually, Freud's concept of the struggle between life instincts and death instincts is much closer to the dialectical view than Rogers ideas are. By ignoring one half of the fundamental dialectic of human existence, Rogers not only overlooks half of human nature, but misses its very essence. Pascal alluded to that essence long ago, when he wrote: "Know then, proud man, what a paradox you are to yourself."

CHAPTER SUMMARY

Rogers was first and foremost a therapist. He invented client-centered therapy. He was also a researcher—the first to make an audio recording of a therapy session. Rogers pioneered empirical research on psychotherapy.

1. Successful therapy, Rogers claimed, enabled clients to achieve a state that he called *full functioning*. Rogers thought that this state of fully functioning personhood represented the essence of human personality, because fully functioning persons are in the process of actualizing their potential and becoming everything that a human being can be. Watching clients advance during therapy toward becoming fully functioning persons, Rogers concluded that they were moving toward becoming their true selves and moving away from being inauthentic selves.

2. Clients moved away from their inauthentic selves by gradually relinquishing their facades and discarding hypocrisies. They began to stop acting in the way they had been told they "ought" to act, and started acting in a manner more expressive of their true selves. This included rejecting certain cultural expectations. In effect, people in the process of becoming fully functioning tended to be non-conformist. A final characteristic: They gave up trying always to please other people and began to concentrate more on pleasing themselves.

3. Clients moved toward their true selves, first of all, by opening up. They dropped their defenses and became more receptive to experience. Consequently, they perceived reality more accurately. Second, they were able, more and more, to trust their impulses and intuitions—something Rogers called *trusting the organism*. As a result, they made decisions more readily and their decisions usually turned out for the best. Third, people in the process of becoming fully functioning were willing, Rogers found, to be in process. Rather than wishing that things would settle down and stop changing, they welcomed, even relished the prospect of change. They were also self-directed, making decisions on their own and accepting responsibility for the consequences. They were also open to (and accepting of) the contradictions in themselves, in their feelings, and in their relationships—something Rogers called *being complexity*. Finally, they were very accepting of other people. These, then, are the characteristics of human personality when it is fully functioning, when it is operating at its optimum level.

4. What conditions promote this full functioning? Rogers discovered that clients made most progress toward becoming fully functioning when they were in therapy with a therapist whom they perceived to accept and value them unconditionally.

5. What characteristics of therapists lead clients to perceive that they are accepted and valued unconditionally? Rogers found, first of all, that the therapist had to be congruent. Congruent therapists are genuine, not phony. They are in touch with their own feelings and they are involved in the therapeutic relationship. They do not hide themselves from the client, but willingly risk emotional involvement. By voluntarily making themselves vulnerable in this way, they communicate to clients that their therapist trusts and values them.

6. The second characteristic Rogers discovered in therapists who were perceived as valuing their clients unconditionally was that they expressed unconditional positive regard. Their attitude toward their clients was one of total acceptance. They were non-judgmental and consistently refused to make any evaluation, positive or negative, of anything their clients presented.

7. The third characteristic of therapists who were perceived as valuing their clients unconditionally was empathic understanding. Empathic therapists are able to put themselves in their client's place and see the world as the client sees it. This kind of understanding is communicated when a therapist accurately reflects a client's statement so that the client responds: Yes, that is exactly how I feel. When clients feel understood, they feel accepted and valued.

8. These observations extend far beyond psychotherapy. If people are treated with congruence, unconditional positive regard, and empathic understanding in any kind of relationship—parent-child, teacher-student, employer-employee—the result will be growth toward full human personhood.

9. Pro #1: This key idea is humanistic. It reverences human personality; emphasizes positive mental health, rather than disease; insists on free will; is holistic; and takes subjective experience seriously.

Pro #2: This key idea emphasizes the interpersonal nature of personality development; it focuses attention on the quality of interpersonal relationships.

Pro #3: This key idea is supported by empirical research. Beginning with the invention of Q-technique in the 1950s, Rogers and his associates have demonstrated how the intangible qualities of relationships can be measured, and how they can be shown to affect something as abstract as development toward fully functioning personhood. Rogers was the catalyst for thousands of subsequent research studies.

Pro #4: This key idea is practical; it has endless applications. Rogers himself developed a program for what he called student-centered education.

Con #1: This key idea is based on self-deception. Rogers assumed that because he was non-directive, he did not influence his clients. Bandura has argued persuasively that therapists inevitably influence their clients by operantly conditioning them, and by modeling various behaviors. If this is true, then Rogers has simply been making his clients into little Carl Rogerses, and the picture of the fully functioning person he claims to have discovered is nothing more than the mirror image of his own values and philosophy.

Con #2: This key idea is anti-intellectual, romantic, and utopian. It is altogether too optimistic. Its one-sided emphasis on feelings is sentimental, fanciful, and unrealistic. Rogers' *real persons* are in fact *ideal persons*, living in a state of being that can be imagined, perhaps even strived for, but which can never be attained in this real world. Far more realistic is the dialectical view that recognizes the paradoxes inherent in human existence.

REFERENCES

Bandura, A. (1961). Psychotherapy as a learning process. *Psychological Bulletin, 58*, 143–159.

Evans, R. I. (1975). *Carl Rogers: The man and his ideas.* New York: E. P. Dutton.

Farson, R. (1975).Carl Rogers, quiet revolutionary. In R. I. Evans, *Carl Rogers: The man and his ideas.* New York: E. P. Dutton.

Rogers, C. R. (1939). *Clinical treatment of the problem child.* Boston: Houghton Mifflin.

Rogers, C. R. (1961). *On becoming a person.* Boston: Houghton Mifflin.

Rogers, C. R. (1974). In retrospect: Forty-six years. *American Psychologist, 29*, 115–123.

Rogers, C. R., & Skinner, B. F. (1956). Some issues concerning the control of human behavior. *Science, 124*, 1057–1066.

12/Abraham Maslow

A Biographical Sketch

Abraham Maslow seems never to have been seriously committed to a career goal other than psychology. Even so, he did not arrive at his adult identity without going through his share of turmoil. Born in 1908 to uneducated Russian Jewish immigrants in New York City, he was a victim of the combined effects of prejudice, discrimination, and financial insecurity. Since the Maslows were the only Jews in their neighborhood, Abraham grew up a lonely child, shunned by his peers at school and on the street. Books and libraries became his haven. He grew up in libraries and he had no friends. Later in his life, Maslow marvelled that such an environment had not made him psychotic. We may marvel that it did not make him bitter, and that it produced a theorist who was so optimistic about human nature.

Maslow's parents left no doubt in his mind that he was to rise above the lowly station in life that they had bequeathed him, and that he was to accomplish this with good hard work. Maslow had no shortage of achievement motivation. He seems also to have displayed more than a modicum of filial piety, for he followed his father's dictates after he finished high school by enrolling in law school. It is not hard to understand the father's desire that his son enter a practical profession. Abraham endured two weeks of law school before a class session devoted to cases involving the building of spite fences turned him off completely. He went home that night and solemnly informed his father that he could never become a lawyer. The confused elder Maslow listened as Abraham described how he wanted to study everything that he could, in order to answer personal and theoretical questions for himself. Reluctantly the father acquiesced, and Abraham took up a liberal arts rather than a professional curriculum.

There was, however, an additional family controversy. At the tender age of 16, Maslow fell in love with the woman who would become his wife. Soon he and Bertha were talking of marriage. As you may well imagine, his father was strongly opposed. In part to escape this atmosphere of domestic tension, Maslow left home to take his sophomore year of college at Cornell. This seems to have been a compromise. Probably his parents supported the move, hoping it would get him away from Bertha. If they did, they were to be disappointed. For his junior year Maslow transferred to the University of Wisconsin; and before he graduated in 1930, he and Bertha were married. His father did finally give his blessing, and Maslow says that when he married Bertha and went to Wisconsin, his life really began.

A man of strong passions, Malow was not only head over heels in love with his young bride, but was utterly captivated by the new behaviorism of John B. Watson. He went to Wisconsin already sold on behaviorism as a program that could help him to change the world. Maslow stayed on at Wisconsin for his graduate work. Harry Harlow was just then establishing his primate research center at Wisconsin, and Maslow was the first to earn a Ph.D. under Harlow's direction. His research and his doctoral dissertation had to do with dominance hierarchies among monkeys, as related to their sexual behavior. The influence upon Maslow's later research of the training he got in Harlow's laboratory is a matter to which we will return later in this chapter. In 1934 Maslow received his Ph.D. He had already

been teaching as a graduate student, and now he stayed on for another year at Wisconsin under a postdoctoral fellowship.

Maslow retained his interest in sexology. In fact, he did significant work in the field long before the Kinsey Report appeared. But Maslow did not retain the behaviorist orientation he had so ecstatically embraced earlier, and which he went to Wisconsin to imbibe. He did not, of course, become the father of humanistic psychology overnight. It was a long process, extending over perhaps a decade.

Reading Freud and Gestalt psychology led Maslow to question behaviorism. Various other intellectual encounters also helped pave the way for his eventual disillusionment. But the experience Maslow says was most crucial in demonstrating to him the bankruptcy of behaviorism was a personal one—the birth of his first child. "Becoming a father changed my whole life, it taught me as if by revelation," he says (Maslow, 1968, p. 57). "Our first baby changed me as a psychologist. It made the behaviorism I had been so enthusiastic about look so foolish I could not stomach it anymore" (Malsow, 1968, p. 55).

In 1935, when Maslow returned to New York to spend two years as a Carnegie Fellow at Columbia University, he made contacts that would carry him still further from behaviorism. He met and worked with psychoanalysts such as Alfred Adler, Karen Horney, and Erich Fromm. Eventually he himself was psychoanalyzed. Max Wertheimer, the father of Gestalt psychology, and Ruth Benedict, the first great female anthropologist and Margaret Mead's teacher, both made a profound impression upon Maslow at this time. Later in his life he would realize that they were his first models of self-actualizing persons. He absolutely adored them. They were, of course, at the opposite pole from behaviorism. Maslow identified with them and incorporated much of their orientation into his own developing theoretical notions.

The eruption of World War II completed the process of change that transformed the ardent behaviorist into an outspoken humanist. By this time Maslow was teaching at Brooklyn College, where he was Associate Professor of Psychology from 1938 until 1951. One day in 1941, soon after the attack on Pearl Harbor, Maslow solemnly resolved henceforth to do everything in his power to promote the course of world peace, and to put an end to persecution and senseless killing. His strategy was to put aside anything that was not relevant to that goal and concentrate single-mindedly on developing the theory of human nature that you will read about in this chapter. His theory, as we shall see, is a utopian conception which, if it could be put into practice, would bring people together to live in peace and harmony. Maslow made this resolution suddenly, as he was driving home from work one night and had his way blocked by a patriotic parade. That moment, he says, changed his life. Perhaps it would not be too great a distortion of fact to say that at that moment in 1941, he discovered his true vocation.

Actually, Maslow's mature theory was also beginning to take form as early as 1941, when he coauthored an abnormal psychology textbook (Maslow and Mittelman, 1941) that contained an exposition of his hierarchy of needs. In 1951 Maslow was invited to become chairman of the psychology department at the newly founded Brandeis University. While there, he published the book that established him as a major personality theorist, *Motivation and Personality* (1954). During the 1960s Maslow became, along with Carl Rogers, one of the chief architects of what he liked to call the "third force" in psychology—the movement for a humanistic psychology. An opportunity to spend a year free of academic responsibilities came in 1969, when Maslow was appointed the first resident fellow at the Laughlin Foundation in Menlo Park, California. Tragically, Abraham Maslow died in the following year, 1970, at the age of 62, the victim of a second heart attack. Among the theorists we study in this book, only George Kelly was granted so brief a time in which to accomplish so much.

MASLOW THE HUMANIST

At his death in 1970, Abraham Maslow was riding the crest of a decade-long wave of popularity among college students. This popularity is not hard to account for. More than any other eminent psychologist of that time, Maslow embodied the values and aspirations of the flower children of the 1960s.

His was an anti-establishment stance. The establishment he challenged was the psychological establishment, not the military-industrial complex, but the revolutionary sentiment was the same. He publicly goaded his colleagues to make their research relevant to serious human problems. He took an interest in oriental philosophies, especially the mystical experiences produced by various meditational techniques. He said that human beings were basically good—no original sin, no tragic flaw, no animalistic id instincts. Society is what corrupts an otherwise innocent human nature. If human beings could just be raised in an environment where all their needs were gratified, they would blossom into perfect specimens of humanity. It was a kind of utopian blueprint. In an era when thousands of kids were running off to live in communes, Maslow addressed himself to the question that most students wanted psychology to answer: how should we live?

THE KEY IDEA
A SCIENTIFIC ETHICS

At heart, Abraham Maslow was more interested in ethics than he was in psychology. Psychology was only a means to an end for him. It is absolutely essential that we grasp this point, not only to understand why Maslow was so germane to the youth of the sixties, but to understand his personality theory itself. The clue to Maslow's personality theory—the concept that deserves to be called his *key idea*, is his conviction that a scientifically verifiable code of ethics could be derived from a psychological study of the essence of human nature. At first glance, you might think that Maslow's key idea was his notion of self-actualization, or his famous hierarchy of needs. But you would be overlooking the grand project that guided him for over half of his life—the search to discover a set of principles for living a life that could be described, with certainty, as morally good. In psychology Maslow believed he had found the tool that would make such a discovery possible. In other words, Maslow developed his personality theory as a tool for answering an ethical question.

Every month in *Yankee Magazine*, the Savogran Company runs an ad depicting a peculiar tool from colonial times that is now preserved in some New England museum. Above the picture, the words "what's it?" challenge the reader to identify the mysterious gadget. The question has stumped me every time I have looked at it. Yet when the next month's issue reveals that December's "what's it" was, for example, a roofer's tool, used for replacing shingles and removing nails, I understand completely. To understand a tool, you need to know what it was used for. The same thing is true of Abraham Maslow's personality theory.

BASIC NEEDS

In his search for the good, Maslow pursued at least three main lines of attack. His first strategy was to try to discover, once and for all, what the essence of human nature is. Deep down in their hearts, are human beings basically good, are they evil, or are they some combination of both? The question has to do with motives. Is it natural for human beings to *want* to do good, or to *want* to do evil? Clearly, Maslow would have to begin his quest by studying motivation.

THE FREE-CHOICE STRATEGY

Human beings want what they need; they are motivated to gratify their needs. But what are these needs? How can we find out which are true needs and which are only wants, since not everything people want is necessarily something they also need. Maslow lists a dozen or so strategies for answering that question, but picks out four as the most important. The first and simplest way to discover which needs are essential is to place human beings in a free-choice situation and observe which needs they elect to gratify. This reminds me of the classic cafeteria-feeding experiments with infants, in which twenty or thirty different foods were set down in front of babies at mealtimes. The babies were allowed to eat as much as they liked of whatever they liked. Nutritionists found that the babies chose a diverse well-balanced diet in the long run, although they might gorge themselves on only one food during certain meals. The important point is that they chose what they needed, what was good for them. Hence if you did not know whether human beings needed salt in their diets, for example, you could design an experiment that allowed infants to choose between salted and unsalted foods. If they regularly chose the salted foods, you could conclude that salt is a basic human need.

The very same technique was used by Harry Harlow, the psychologist under whose guidance Maslow earned his doctorate, to identify basic psychological needs. No introductory psychology textbook would be complete without a picture of one of Harlow's tragically orphaned baby monkeys confronting the choice between a wire surrogate mother and a cloth one. The wire manikin dispenses milk from a nipple protruding from one of the holes in the mesh that represents her epidermis. The cloth mother, standing in the opposite corner of the cage, has no food to offer. She is constructed of the same wire mesh, but her mesh is covered with soft terrycloth toweling, and a small light bulb is installed in her loins to generate warmth. We all know that baby monkeys need food. What we learned from Harlow's experiment is that they also need something he called *contact comfort*, since the babies spent all the time when they were not eating cuddling up to the non-nourishing, cloth mother. Apparently the cloth mother was providing something that monkey nature needs.

Not only will the organism choose what it needs when allowed to select freely from alternatives, but it will work to earn what it needs. Rats will push levers to get food. Monkeys isolated in solitary confinement will learn to solve puzzles just to open a window and look out of their cells. If you want to find out what an animal needs, find out what serves to reinforce that animal. The basic needs are primary reinforcers.

THE FRUSTRATION STRATEGY

A second strategy Maslow suggests for separating the basic needs from those that are nonessential is to observe the effects of frustration. If you frustrate a basic need, the organism will develop pathology. If you frustrate a need that is not basic, no such illness will result. Again Harlow's work provides an exquisite example. In a series of experiments, he raised monkeys in various degrees of social isolation. Those raised without any contact with other monkeys grew up to be severely autistic. Monkeys, it seems, have a basic need for some kind of social contact.

THE GRATIFICATION STRATEGY

Frustrating a basic need produces pathology. Gratifying a basic need, according to Maslow's third strategy, has the opposite effect. It positively promotes health, growth, and full functioning. Maslow (1970) maintains

> that there is nothing esoteric or nonscientific about this criterion. It can easily be put on an experimental basis, or even an engineering basis, if we remember only that the problem is not very different from choosing the right oil for a car. One oil is better than another if, with it, the car works better. It is the general clinical finding that the organism, when fed safety, love, and respect, works better, i.e., perceives more efficiently, uses intelligence more fully, thinks to correct conclusions more often, digests food more efficiently, is less subject to various diseases, etc. (p. 92).

If you want to find out whether a need is basic, just gratify it and see if the organism grows and flourishes.

THE HEALTHY SPECIMEN STRATEGY

Of course, instead of putting different kinds of oil in your car and then waiting around to see how it runs, you could just pick out a few excellent-running cars and see what kind of oil they use. You can discover basic needs, Maslow suggests, by this fourth strategy of observing directly what needs are expressed by people who are already healthy and fully functioning. If a person is healthy, that should indicate that his or her basic needs have been gratified. Consequently, the clue to which needs are really basic can be found by observing which needs are gratified in all healthy individuals.

THE HIERARCHY OF BASIC NEEDS

Employing these strategies, Maslow divined five categories of basic needs in the human personality: (1) physiological needs; (2) safety needs; (3) love and belongingness needs; (4) self-esteem needs; and (5) self-actualization needs. He also mentions that human beings seem to have some basic cognitive needs—a curiosity drive, mastery motive, or competency need—although he does not find a neat place to fit them into his fivefold hierarchy. For a more detailed discussion, see the Box: Maslow's Hierarchy of Basic Needs.

These basic needs define human nature; revealing the intrinsic design of the human personality and telling you what a person must have in order to become fully human. As such, they answer a question in personality

MASLOW'S HIERARCHY OF BASIC NEEDS

To appreciate the radical nature of Maslow's theory of motivation, you must recognize that almost all previous theories of motivation limited basic needs to those drives that are clearly biological, such as hunger, thirst, and sex. These were the classic Darwinian instincts, and they met the requirement that instincts should be universal in the species. Only motives necessary for the present and future survival of the species were considered *primary drives,* or *basic needs.* All others—needs for love, knowledge, beauty—were regarded as *secondary,* that is to say, learned through association with one or another of the primary drives. Thus the need for love might derive from the hunger drive, since infants are typically treated affectionately while they are suckled.

Maslow, however, argued that the reason these so-called secondary drives do not appear in all human beings, and are not apparent at birth, is not because they are not basic, but because they are not *prepotent.* Needs, Maslow observed, are organized in the order of their prepotency. You may, for example, be ravenously hungry, but if you suddenly begin to suffocate and start gasping for air, your need for food immediately vanishes and your need to breathe takes over and directs your behavior. This does not mean that your need for food does not exist, simply that it is masked by another need which has temporarily become prepotent. Even such higher needs as love, knowledge, and beauty may actually exist, but

merely be masked. People living on the edge of starvation do not have much time to indulge their aesthetic creativity, for example. But if the lower, more prepotent needs are gratified, then the higher needs are free to emerge. A need remains active in directing behavior only so long as it remains ungratified. Once a need is gratified, it ceases to motivate. As long as you are hungry, you are preoccupied with finding something to eat; but once your appetite is assuaged, you are free to attend to other needs.

Basic needs can be organized in a hierarchy of prepotency. Maslow's five categories of basic needs are sometimes visualized as steps in a pyramid:

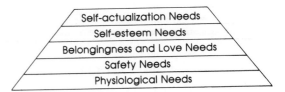

Actually, he proposed that they were arranged more like a nest of boxes, where each succeeding box is slightly smaller than the preceding one and just fits inside it. Thus you cannot see the smaller box until the bigger one is removed. Need gratification is what removes each larger box. Yet even that is not a perfect analogy, since need gratification is not necessarily an all-or-nothing proposition. Lower needs may be partially gratified, permitting higher

psychology, but they also answer the ethical question of how we should live. How should we live?—in accordance with our nature! We should live in a way that allows us to become all we were designed to be. What is good?—gratification of basic needs is good. What is evil?—frustration of basic needs is evil. Society, especially in the form of parents and teachers, should be permissive, it should not restrict and frustrate the basic needs of children.

Note Maslow's list of basic needs does not include any that are evil. There are no hostile or aggressive impulses. All of the basic needs are good, needs to emerge only partially. Perhaps we should visualize several of the boxes only partially removed from each other.

The five categories of basic needs that Maslow hypothesized, beginning with the most prepotent, are: (1) physiological needs; (2) safety needs; (3) belongingness and love needs; (4) self-esteem needs; and (5) self-actualization needs. The physiological needs include all of the body's requirements; food, water, air, sex, sleep, warmth, exercise, rest, and so forth. Maslow resists making a list, because the nature of such a list depends entirely upon the degree of specificity desired. The need for food, for example, can be specified more precisely in terms of the need for salt, sugar, protein, fat, various minerals, etc. The principle of prepotency applies, however, in any case. If you lost a lot of salt through vigorous exercise, for example, you may experience a craving for salty food until that deficit is made up. For the vast majority of middle-class American adults, physiological needs are well gratified and hence play only a minor role in motivating behavior.

When physiological needs are gratified, safety needs emerge. Safety needs include the need to avoid physical harm and threats of violence, as well as the need for order and predictability. The behavior of most middle-class Americans is not heavily motivated by these needs, partly because these needs are largely gratified, and partly because this group is taught to hide its safety needs. In any case, safety needs are most evident during wars and natural disasters, and in children. Safety needs quickly come to the fore when a young child is cornered by a snarling dog or convulsed by a sudden colic.

When people's belongingness and love needs emerge, people hunger for relationships with other people. This need seems identical to Murray's need for affiliation. Loneliness is an especially painful affliction for people experiencing these needs. Maslow thinks that thwarting these needs is the most common cause of psychopathology in our society.

Esteem needs emerge next. They have two aspects. On the one hand, we have a need for achievement, mastery, competence, and confidence; on the other, we need prestige, status, attention, and the respect of others.

Finally, if all the lower needs are gratified, the need for self-actualization emerges. This refers to a person's need to become all that he or she potentially is. (A more detailed discussion follows later in this chapter.).

We can sum up the concept of the *hierarchy* of basic needs as follows: (1) When lower needs are gratified, higher needs emerge; and (2) when lower, more prepotent needs are frustrated in a person who is operating at a higher-need level, that person will regress to the level of those lower needs, at least until they are again gratified.

---

or at the very least morally neutral. "It can certainly be granted by now that our knowledge is sufficient to reject any claim that human nature is in its essence, *primarily, biologically, fundamentally* evil, sinful, malicious, ferocious, cruel, or murderous," Maslow concludes (1970, p. 118). Human nature is basically good. If human beings do evil things—and Maslow does not deny this—that is because their basic needs have not been gratified. Frustration of basic needs results in pathology; and aggressive, destructive behavior is precisely the form such pathology takes. Aggression is not a fundamental ingredient of human nature, as Freud believed; it is a secondary reaction to the frustration of nature's intrinsic plan for human growth and development. Maslow clearly believes that the consequences of this fact are primarily ethical (1970):

> The recognition that man's best impulses are appreciably intrinsic, rather than fortuitous and relative, must have tremendous implication for value theory. It means, for one thing, that it is no longer either necessary or desirable to deduce values by logic or try to read them off from authorities or revelations. All we need to do, apparently, is to observe and research. Human nature carries within itself the answer to the questions, how can I be good; how can I be happy; how can I be fruitful? The organism tells us what it needs (and therefore what it values) by sickening when deprived of these values and by growing when not deprived (p. 102).

Maslow's hierarchy of basic needs is manifestly a psychological theory of human personality dynamics. But to understand it more fully, we must see it as a tool designed explicitly to answer the ethical question, what constitutes the good life?

SELF-ACTUALIZING PERSONS

Along with his research on basic needs, Maslow used another approach to discover the essence of human nature and to answer the question of how we should live: studying superior specimens of humanity—psychological Olympians, so to speak. Freud, well versed in the medical tradition, had concentrated his attention on specimens of pathology. But pathology, by definition, is a distorting or deforming of humanity as nature designed it. Pathology is a deviation from the good. If you are looking for "the good," why not study the best? Not just people who show no signs of sickness— why not go all the way to the opposite extreme and look at those who illustrate human potential developed to its fullest? That is where you will get the most highly magnified view of what human nature is capable of becoming.

Self-actualizing is the term Maslow used to refer to these exemplars of positive mental health, because their most conspicuous characteristic was full use and exploitation of all their talents, capabilities, and potentialities. This total liberation of human potential is made possible, of course, by the gratification of basic needs. Self-actualizing people are people whose physiological, safety, love and belongingness, and self-esteem needs have been gratified. In that sense, they no longer "need" anything; they are no longer operating in the red. Since they no longer have to grub around for need-gratifiers, no longer have to compensate for shortages and deficiencies, they are set free to be just what they are. They no longer do what they do because they need to. Their behavior becomes an expression of what they are; they do what they do simply because it is their nature to do so. In the same way that all other living things grow and develop not to make up for any lack or deficiency, but simply because their natures are intrinsically designed for this purpose, the human personality also grows and develops naturally; in fact, it blossoms when it is no longer obstructed by having to gratify basic needs. It follows, then, that if you want to see human nature in its purest, most undistorted form, you must study self-actualizing people. The characteristics of self-actualizing people constitute the essence of human nature.

What characteristics did Maslow (1970) find typical of self-actualizers?

1. Their perceptions are more accurate than those of other people. They show exceptionally good judgment in a wide variety of situations because they do not stereotype, and because their own needs (already being gratified) do not distort their perception.

2. Self-actualizing people are very accepting of themselves, of others, and of nature in general. They are "good animals," with good animal appetites, who do not feel guilty about their natural impulses or ashamed of their natural bodily functions. And they accept others in the same non-judgmental, almost stoical fashion.

3. Spontaneity is conspicuous among self-actualizers. Rather than just reacting to other people or circumstances, they are self-propelled. One side effect of this is that they are likely to appear unconventional.

4. Most self-actualizers focus the major portion of their life's energy on some problem outside themselves. They have a sense of mission in life.

5. Many ordinary people are afraid to be alone for very long and waste such time when they have it. Not so with Maslow's self-actualizing people. They relish solitude, needing it more than most people do. And they use it very well.

6. They are autonomous and self-sufficient. They do not need the approval of society to find satisfaction in their accomplishments, nor are they intimidated by what the neighbors think.

7. There is a childlike naivete in their appreciation of things. They see something new at each encounter, even with the most mundane objects. Their ability to be fascinated every day makes life an adventure that they anticipate with zest.

8. In fact, self-actualizers venture beyond the boundaries of normal consciousness, into the realm Maslow calls **peak experiences**, far more often than the rest of us do. Many of them are mystics of one sort or another.

9. They feel very deeply, and very strongly, at one with the entire human race—not with any one ethnic or national group, but with humanity as a whole. They sincerely want to do the very most that they can to benefit humanity. They are explicitly anti-nationalistic.

10. Their interpersonal relationships are characterized by very deep ties of friendship with rather few people. They are not joiners of clubs.

11. Still, Maslow insists that they are democractic in the deepest possible sense. What this means is that they have a profound conviction that every human being has a fundamental and equal right to actualize his or her unique potential.

12. Self-actualizers are strongly ethical. They have a highly developed sense of right and wrong, and they may pursue ends they regard as right without regard to the means.

13. Though self-actualizing people may seem a rather serious and sober lot, they have a sense of humor that permits them to poke fun at their own foibles. But they never laugh at someone else's expense. Their sense of humor is never hostile and they do not mock others.

14. Self-actualizers are creative, though there are wide individual differences in the manner in which this creativity manifests itself. Some may be arty, others philosophical. Still others are creative in quite ordinary, mundane pursuits. Maslow's examples include shoemakers, carpenters, and clerks.

15. Whatever their vocations or avocations, self-actualizing people resist enculturation. They transcend their particular culture, considering themselves citizens of the world. As such, they appear detached from the particular culture in which they live.

16. What are conflicting dichotomies for most people are often resolved in self-actualizing people. For them there is no difference between work and play, for example. Neither is there a conflict between heart and head. What they feel they want, and what they know intellectually to be right and good, are one and the same.

17. Finally, when they love (and self-actualizing people are very loving persons), they are able to drop all their defenses and let the other person know them completely. They respect and accept the one they love, without trying to remake him or her into some fantasy they have of the perfect partner. And they are not possessive. They simply desire that the person they love actualize the potential that is uniquely his or hers. At the same time that they maximize their own individuality and thus maintain a kind of detachment, they are able to attain a more complete fusion with the person they love than can ever be found among less healthy individuals.

Like Maslow's research on basic needs, his research on self-actualization revealed that human nature is good. Self-actualizers are not hostile, aggressive, or destructive. In fact the majority of their characteristics are ethically admirable: They are democratic in the deepest sense; they focus their energies on some problem outside of themselves; they desire to help the entire human race; they are loving people; they are strongly ethical; etc. But this emphasis on ethical qualities is not surprising when you remember that, though he was seeking to answer the psychological question, what is human nature, Maslow wanted to use the answer to that question as a key to answering the ethical question, what is the right way to live. No clearer statement of that intention can be found than in the words he wrote shortly before his death. Referring to the study of self-actualizing people, he said:

> I believe also, on the positive side, that this great frontier of research is our most likely source of knowledge of the values intrinsic to human nature. Here lies the value system, the religion-surrogate, the idealism-satisfier, the normative philosophy of life that all human beings seem to need, to yearn for, and without which they become nasty and mean, vulgar and trivial (Maslow, 1970, p. xxii).

Maslow's personality theory always served as a preface to his ethical system. Only when you understand that can you appreciate why he chose to investigate the particular questions that he did.

PEAK EXPERIENCES

Maslow (and Maslow alone) did a great deal of research in another area in order to discover the essence of human nature and answer his ethical question. That is the area he called peak experiences.

Peak experiences are ecstatic mystical experiences. Though they are often produced in a religious context, they are just as common in connection with sexual orgasm, philosophical insight, athletic success, watching a dance performance, or bearing a child, according to Maslow. Certain drugs, he observes, may also provide access to these realms of expanded consciousness. These experiences, though infrequent, are not abnormal. They are healthy, not morbid, and have nothing whatsoever to do with hallucination or delusion. On the contrary, peak experiences are one of the signs of self-actualization, although non self-actualizers may have them too. These experiences are rare, even in individuals who try to cultivate them. And they are transient—no one has discovered how to make them last more than a few fleeting moments. During those moments, time may seem to stand still, or perhaps all of time may seem to be compressed into a single instant. But wherever "peakers" go on their trips, the visits always seem to have been all too brief afterwards. Hence peakers invariably yearn to go back again. The peak experience is a positive good, yearned for and desired as an end in itself. People describe such experience as the high point of their lives. They never felt better, they say. Some even say afterward that they would gladly die, suggesting that they feel they have tasted the ultimate reward.

If peak experiences truly represent humanity's best moments, then the rationale that led Maslow to study self-actualizing people applies here as well. There the question was why not study the best people, here it is why not study people's best experiences. If the peak experience constitutes an expedition into the higher reaches of human consciousness, if it truly represents an expanding of human consciousness beyond its usual boundaries, then it should yield further insight into human potential. It should show us just how far human nature is capable of growing and maturing.

The peak experience is, as we have seen, a rapturous emotional experience, but it is also an intellectual, cognitive experience. To be more exact, the dichotomy between emotional and intellectual is overcome in the peak experience, so that feeling and knowing are one and the same process. But the knowledge conferred by the peak experience is knowledge of a unique kind. Most of our knowledge is knowledge for use, problem-solving knowledge; the knowledge characteristic of peak experiences is knowledge for its own sake, knowledge for the sheer enjoyment of knowing. It is, like aesthetic appreciation, an end in itself. Most knowledge deals only with surface properties of objects. It classifies, and stereotypes, and attempts to predict reactions to various stimuli. But the knowledge from peak experiences knows the object in and of itself, in its essence and in its individual uniqueness.

Maslow calls these two ways of knowing **D-cognition** and **B-cognition.** D-cognition is the ordinary kind of knowing, which is based on deficiency needs. D-cognition of an apple, for example, would include knowing that it is a member of the class of objects we call food, and that it can therefore be used to alleviate the nutritional deficiency I experience as hunger. B-cognition of the same apple, on the other hand, would come to know it as an apple unlike any other apple in creation, an object that is intrinsically fascinating, quite apart from any use to which it might be put. B-cognition does not seek to get anything out of, or do anything to, the thing that it knows. This kind of knowing is self-forgetful and egoless. Yet there is intense concentration and total absorption in the object. B-cognition is a more passive, receptive, appreciative kind of knowing, not an active, prodding, interfering kind. The accompanying emotional tone is one of wonder, awe, and humility before the experience. B-cognition would not analyze the apple, but would see it whole, as a perfect unit from which nothing is missing and to which nothing needs to be added. In short, through B-cognition one would come to know this particular apple in its being. B-cognition is cognition of being.

The knowing that occurs in peak experiences is of course B-cognition. Both Maslow and all those who report such experiences insist that it really *is* knowledge. Not only is it valid knowledge, it is superior knowledge—superior because it is knowledge gained by human nature at its height. Peak experiences, with their attendant B-cognition, offer us a glimpse of the absolute pinnacle of human development. From the vantage point of this summit, truths that could only be guessed at from below are clearly discernible.

Maslow's studies of peak experiences and B-cognition explored a neglected aspect of human nature. Today's much publicized researches into right brain-versus-left brain function vindicate his once controversial interest in these topics. Brain researchers now tell us that each hemisphere of the brain has a different cognitive style. The right side is intuitive, holistic, and without language. The left hemisphere controls speech and analytical thinking. This sounds very much like Maslow's distinction between D-cognition and B-cognition.

But Maslow's interest in studying peak experiences and B-cognition was more than just an effort to explore a neglected aspect of human nature; it was an attempt to verify ethical principles. Peak experiences are always good; they are never evil or painful or undesirable. They can even be regarded, at least according to the reports of those who have them, as the highest good. As such, they create values—true values, because perception is not distorted by deficiency needs. Maslow calls these values *values of being* or *B-values.* B-values are absolutely true and eternal, because they are grounded in the essence of human nature. They include such qualities as honesty, beauty, wholeness, spontaneity, uniqueness, justice, order, and the transcendence of contradictions (Maslow, 1959, 1964, pp. 92-94).

The validity of these B-values is confirmed for Maslow by the observation that peak experiences promote healthy personality development. Psychotherapy, when it succeeds in overcoming pathology, does so by encouraging B-cognition. The insights that occur in psychotherapy are really B-cognitions, and patients regard these insights as peak experiences. A peak experience has the power to heal, to unify, and to make whole. The practical consequences of this observation include attempts by various therapists—from the use of psychedelic drugs to induce peak experiences in alcoholics to the practice of meditation, hypnosis, and relaxation techniques (sometimes biofeedback-assisted)—to produce similar states in a wide range of clients. The results have sometimes justified Maslow's optimism; in other instances they have been rather disappointing.

Maslow's three major contributions to personality psychology—his hierarchy of basic needs, his study of self-actualizing people, and his explorations into peak experiences—are best understood as efforts to establish a scienced of ethics. Along the way, he happened to construct a theory of personality. But the questions he chose to investigate in the field of personality were always determined by this one guiding ambition: to replace a system of ethics based on what considered ideological authoritarianism with a set of ethical principles firmly grounded in a science of human nature.

PROS and CONS

Pro #1: We sincerely hope that this key idea is true.   Who would not like to believe that Maslow's theory is valid? Only the most sadistic **psychopath** would be disappointed if it were proved that human nature is fundamentally good. How encouraging it would be to know for certain that war and crime and violence would vanish if only basic needs could be gratified. I would certainly perfer to believe that, rather than the dismal Freudian contention that human beings, despite a veneer of civilization, are naturally vicious. The Freudian portrait of human nature is disparaging and derogatory; Maslow gives us an image we can be proud of.

Of course it may simply be our nature to prefer a portrait that flatters us. The fact that we would like to believe Maslow's theory does not make the theory true. But it is only fair to say that our hopes do not make the theory false either. The theory is not suspect just because it flatters us, just because we want it to be true. Although our wants and desires sometimes distort our perceptions, they do not always blind us to reality. If we did not start with the unproven assumption that our natural instincts are selfish and acquisitive, perhaps we would not be so distrustful of our impulses, desires, and feelings. Perhaps we would come to agree with Maslow that what the heart longs for, and what the head knows to be true, are one and the same thing.

Maslow's key idea is utopian. He was convinced that by studying essential human nature, he could extract a set of ethical principles that would allow human beings to live together in peace and harmony, each fulfilling his or her unique potential. Our sincere hope that Maslow's idea is valid (Pro #1) should be taken seriously, not lightly dismissed as mere wishful thinking.

Pro #2: This key idea can humanize many endeavors. The ethical principles Maslow derived from his study of human nature were relevant to all areas of human endeavor. Education, however, seemed to be the application that interested him most. Though it has many other roots, the body of pedagological theory loosely known as humanistic education is very much in accord with Maslow's doctrine.

Perhaps the most basic aim of humanistic education was to avoid squelching a child's innate curiosity, a curiosity which, if it were nurtured rather than frustrated, would be more than powerful enough to motivate learning throughout the school years and for the rest of one's life. With such an intrinsic, growth-oriented motivator, teachers and parents would not need to use threats, punishments, or bribes (such as grades) to induce children to learn. Children would learn because it it in their nature to learn; they would learn for the sheer joy of learning. And they would learn without the dehumanizing, demeaning, and counteraggression-producing effects of the traditional repressive system.

Permissiveness is a cardinal virtue in the humanistic code of ethics. If we want to nurture the precious, fragile seedling of curiosisty, if we want to encourage it to grow, we must give it free rein. Children must not be made to feel ashamed or guilty when they inquire about natural bodily functions, nor should they be spanked if they take the vacuum cleaner apart. School curricula should be designed to allow each child to explore his or her own individual interests at his or her own pace. Educational materials should be designed in such a way that these explorations will lead the child to discover essential principles. All children should explore the territory their curiosity leads them to. They should not be forced, in lock-step fashion, to listen day after day to lectures on topics that have no immediate interest, for that will gradually destroy their curiosity—an effect which, once accomplished, is almost impossible to reverse.

The application of some of these very principles is being blamed today for the steady decline of SAT scores in the 1970s, and the inability of many high-school graduates to read and write as well as they ought to. "Back to basics" is the slogan today, and humanistic educators are now the ones who are on the defensive. Undoubtedly, some of the criticisms of humanistic education are justified. Yet its proponents can argue that it never was really tried, at least not on any large scale, and that many of the excesses perpetrated in the name of humanistic education had little or no relation to the principles of its best architects. No matter what becomes of humanistic education as a self-conscious movement, however, it has made an impact on education. Even as we go back to basics, we have been forewarned that we must never again lose sight of the fundamental principle that we do not teach arithmetic or spelling or music, we teach persons.

I consider it a pro that Maslow's key idea leads to such applications in humanistic education. I am one of those who believes that the basic principles of the idea are sound, although they were not always applied in a consistent, or wise, manner. And I also think that the principles of humanistic education continue to exert a beneficial influence today in the field of education. These are value judgments, of course, but as Maslow himself pointed out, psychologists and educators who try to avoid value judgments are deceiving themselves.

Pro #3: This key idea presented a third alternative for psychology.

Maslow's key idea produced a personality theory that was an alternative to behaviorism, on the one hand, and psychoanalysis on the other. For this reason, he often referred to his theory as "third-force" psychology. Unlike Maslow, most behaviorists and psychoanalysts did not proclaim that their objective was to discover a system of ethics. Most of them, in fact, have disclaimed any interest at all in values. Nevertheless, both behaviorism and psychoanalysis contain implicit values and have ethical applications and implications. Skinner (1948, 1971) surely demonstrated this in *Walden II* and in *Beyond Freedom and Dignity*. Within the psychoanalytic camp, Erich Fromm (1955) has always been an outspoken crusader for ethical causes. But the ethical principles that derive from Maslow's personality theory are markedly different from those that derive either from behaviorism or psychoanalysis, making Maslow's theory a distinct alternative.

The most basic disagreement between Maslow and the behaviorists is the issue of whether human nature is proactive or reactive. Behaviorists adhere to the blank-slate doctrine. According to this notion, the human organism has no inborn motives or instincts. Its behavior can be understood entirely as a series of responses to external stimuli. If there were no stimuli coming in from outside, the organism would not do anything at all. It is not self-starting, nor does it have an internal program or guidance system. It does not act except by reacting. And the nature of those reactions is determined not by anything within the organism, but by the nature of the stimulus.

Maslow's view presents strong contrast. For him, human nature is proactive and human beings are self-starters. Like seeds planted in the ground, they grow whether there is any external stimulus or not. They are also pre-programmed; they have a built-in agenda that provides direction and aims toward a specific goal. None of this denies that the human organism often behaves by reacting to external stimuli. Maslow does not disagree with the stimulus-response explanation of certain behaviors, but he does object strongly when it is advanced as an explanation of *all* human behavior. For Maslow, the potential for growth toward self-actualization is built into every human being and unfolds automatically, without any specific stimulus, as long as the individual's basic needs are gratified.

The greatest bone of contention between Maslow and the psychoanalysts is whether human nature is basically good or basically evil. The Freudian view of humanity is, of course, anything but flattering. According to the pleasure principle, human beings are selfishly out to get as much as they can for themselves. Later on, when Freud added the death instincts to his theory, he proposed that all human beings have a mean, destructive streak. Socialization fortunately subdues most of these uncivilized tendencies, so that they are not evident, at least on the surface, in most normal behavior. But beneath the surface, that is the nature of the beast.

Maslow did not agree that aggressive, destructive instincts were original equipment for human beings. Selfishness he saw as a result of a shortage of gratifiers. In a society where there was enough for everyone's basic needs to be gratified, there would be no selfishness, no conflict, and no competition. Human beings are not naturally selfish and competitive. It is the frustration of basic needs that deforms their essential nature and emerges in this pathology. But potentially, human nature is caring, sharing, and cooperative.

My point (Pro #3) is not that Maslow's position on the proactivity-versus-reactivity and good-versus-evil controversies is better, but simply that Maslow's position constitutes a clear and distinct alternative to the other positions. That is why I have highlighted the specific issues that make the contrast very clear. Maslow had many other disagreements, of course, with both behaviorism and psychoanalysis. Most scientists and philosophers agree that it is beneficial to have this kind of public debate about theoretical issues, no matter which side one favors. The fact that Maslow's key idea stimulated a lot of theoretical discussion in personality psychology, by providing a third alternative, is a significant pro.

Pro #4: This key idea made psychologists examine their values. Another advantage of Maslow's key idea is that it forced psychologists to recognize that a science, especially a science of human personality, cannot be value-neutral. To speak about motivation, whether in terms of instincts or needs or reinforcements, is to speak about what a person wants or desires—what the person values, in other words. What a person wants is also what a person values; and as soon as you begin talking about values, you enter the realm of ethics. You cannot develop a theory of motivation without at the same time promulgating a theory of ethics.

Until the mid-1960s, most psychologists preferred to deny or ignore this logic. Since that time, more and more articles in the psychological journals have examined the philosophical assumptions and value orientations implicit in psychological theories. Maslow is at least partially responsible for this trend, which is still growing and now seems firmly established. To say that it is a beneficial trend is of course a value judgment; but it is one with which I concur, and so I list it as a pro.

Con #1: This key idea begs the question. Attractive though Maslow's key idea may be, we must consider the criticism that, in the last analysis, he begs the question. His reasoning may be circular. The image of human nature he discovered may be nothing more than his own reflection in the glass. To find out what human nature is like at its best, he selected a group of what he called self-actualizing people and studied them. But if he did not already know what human nature looks like at its best, how did he know which people to select as self-actualizers? The implicit criteria Maslow used to select his self-actualizing people are the very same characteristics he later "found" in these people. What is more, they are the same characteristics he used as the basis for his scientific ethics! The criticism here is not that some other psychologist might have picked a different group of people as prototypes of self-actualization, nor even that someone from another culture might have made different choices. The criticism is simply that Maslow already knew what he was going to find before he set out to hunt for it. It is as if his thinking went something like this:

> What is the good? The good is what good people do. Who are good people? They are people who do good. Well then, if we can just find some people who are doing good, we will know that they are good people. We can see what kind of good it is that they are doing, and then we will have discovered what goodness really is.

Maslow's basic needs research is not quite as vulnerable to criticism as his self-actualization studies, but even there he may be begging the question. He defines basic needs as those that produce pathology when frustrated, and promote health when gratified. In other words, the cornerstone of Maslow's scientific system of ethics is the assumption that since health is good, gratification of basic needs must be good; and since pathology is bad, frustration of basic needs must be bad. The problem here is that health and pathology are not objectively defined conditions. Is homosexuality a sickness? Well, not if the person is happy and satisfied with that life-style, according to the latest pronouncements of the American Psychiatric Association. But what about moderately psychopathic commodity-options swindlers who are perfectly satisfied with their life-style? Are they healthy?

What is healthy and what is pathological is ultimately a question of values. There is widespread consensus on many of these values, as we see in diagnostic manuals such as the **DSM-III**, but they are still values. This means that Maslow's list of basic needs is a mirror reflection of his definition of psychological health, which in turn is an expression of his values. He starts out with an image of what he considers good, calls it health, observes what contributes to it, then completes the circle by concluding that he has scientifically established what is good.

The situation with regard to peak experiences is similar. There he begins with experiences that people describe as supremely good. Peak experiences are by definition always good; they are never bad. Then he examines reports of these experiences and deduces from this analysis the nature of the good. This kind of reasoning borders on **sophistry**. When Maslow calls this reasoning scientific, this man who wanted to separate ethical systems from all authoritarian dogma is simply appealing to another authority. Apparently he found some authorities more tolerable than others.

Con #2: This key idea has elitist implications. Maslow's key idea has unfortunate elitist implications. His search for self-actualizing people is a logical outgrowth of his effort to discover the essence of human nature, which he hoped would provide a foundation for a system of ethics. But his self-actualizing people constitute a kind of aristocracy. Certainly they are an exclusive group. Though he says everyone has the potential to become self-actualized, Maslow took great pains to tell us how rarely that potential is realized. He screened three thousand college students and found only one self-actualizer. In the end he was forced to work with a sample of only about two dozen, because that was as many as he could find. Maslow himself used an apt metaphor to explain this. There are not many Olympic gold medalists, he said, even though everyone has the potential to win a gold medal. But if it is true that everyone has the potential to win an Olympic gold medal, it is very obviously true that some people have more potential than others. The very same thing applies to self-actualization, although Maslow would not have liked to admit it.

It all comes down to privilege. Self-actualizing people are a privileged group of people, an elite. True, they are not a elite based on land or capital or even blue blood, but they are an elite nonetheless. And privileged people somehow have a way of demanding more and more privileges. Consider this extreme hypothetical question: Who should we allow to go into the bomb shelter when a nuclear attack is launched? Shouldn't the human race make every effort to preserve its best specimens? Do Maslow's self-actualizing persons, who are supposed to be democratic in the deepest sense, really think that you and I have as much right to that shelter as they do? Stoically reasoning that if they survived they could contribute more good to more people than you or I, they would shut the door with clear consciences and leave the rest of us to face the holocaust.

Privileged persons have a privileged view of things. The very first characteristic Maslow attributes to self-actualizing people is that they have a more efficient and more accurate view of reality than ordinary people. This follows logically from the observation that they have no ungratified lower needs to distort their perceptions. During peak experiences, glimpses of this same view may occasionally be snatched, in the form of B-cognition, by ordinary people, but once again, peak experiences are much more frequent among the self-actualizing. This discussion of the privileged view of reality leads us directly to Con #3.

Con #3: This key idea has totalitarian implications.   Maslow's key idea of discovering a scientifically verifiable system of ethics has dogmatic, and even totalitarian, implications. After enjoying the exclusive view from the summit, Maslow was undoubtedly convinced that he knew what was best for the human race. The question is, how far would he or any one of his disciples be willing to go to force his "normative philosophy" upon the rest of us. If his code of ethics were scientifically proven to engender psychological health, would anyone have the right not to follow it?

The tyranny of health is already evident in the medical field, where we are forbidden to use everything from saccharin to laetril because science has proved that these things are bad for our health. If psychological health is treated in the same way, is it not possible that we will move toward a society where certain behaviors are outlawed because they are bad for your *mental* health? If so, why fault the Russians for putting political dissidents in mental hospitals when they proclaim decadent bourgeois thoughts that are injurious to mental health? How is a psychiatric examination different from the Spanish inquisition, except that each appeals to a different authority? The inquisitors, the best of them at least, genuinely believed that they were working in the best interests of their clients, doing what was good for them. Whenever people try to pin down its nature with scientific proof, health—especially mental health—tends to become an authoritarian, dogmatic principle that leaves little room for free choice.

An outcome like that would certainly be diametrically opposed to what Maslow intended; his sentiments were manifestly humane, humanistic, and humanitarian. But whenever people become convinced that they know what is best for somebody else, there is a danger that they will try to impose their superior knowledge on the other person, limiting his or her freedom.

CHAPTER SUMMARY

1.   Maslow wanted to discover the nature of human personality, because he believed it would answer his questions about how to live the morally good life, and how to design a perfect society. The good life is a life lived in accordance with your nature. But how do you find out what constitutes your nature?

2.   One of Maslow's strategies for discovering the essence of human nature was to try to isolate the essential needs—*basic*, he called them—from the myriad wants, desires, likes, and preferences we all have. If a need is basic, it is an essential feature of human nature, something without which we would not be human.

3.   To separate basic needs from non-essential needs, Maslow suggested that researchers allow subjects to choose freely among gratifications of many different needs—in carefully designed experiments, of course. The needs subjects consistently choose to gratify, when given a free choice, must be the basic needs.

4.   A second strategy for determining whether a need is basic or non-essential is to observe the effect of frustrating that need. If frustrating a need causes the person to become ill or to malfunction in any way, then the need must be basic. If frustration does not result in pathology, the need is not essential.

5.   A third, related strategy involves gratifying the need in question to see whether it is basic. If it is basic, gratification should cause the organism to grow and flourish; it should promote positive mental health. If this does not occur, then the need must not have been basic.

6.   One other way of identifying which needs are basic, according to Maslow, is to observe people who are already healthy and fully functioning, in order to see which needs they all gratify. Those are the basic needs.

7.   Using these strategies, Maslow discovered the following hierarchy of basic needs: (1) physiological needs; (2) safety needs; (3) love and belong-ingness needs; (4) self-esteem needs; and (5) self-actualization needs. These basic needs define human nature. To live well, one should gratify these needs. An ideal society is one that allows its citizens to gratify these needs. Human nature itself is good; pathology, aggression, destructiveness result only from the frustration of basic needs.

8.   Maslow also tried to discover the essence of human nature by studying individuals with superior mental health. He called these people *self-actualizing persons*. They are model human beings who have gratified all their basic needs and are therefore free to realize their full potentials. Self-actualizing persons are examples of undistorted human nature, human nature at its best. Among the characteristics Maslow attributed to self-actualizing people are: accurate perceptions; self-acceptance; spontaneity; childlike naivete; taste for solitude and mystical experiences; autonomy; anti-nationalistic humanitarianism; non-hostile sense of humor; creativity; non-conformism; and lovingness.

9.   To gain further insight into the essence of human nature, Maslow studied the ecstatic mystical experiences he called *peak experiences*. These include not only experiences occurring in a religious context, but some that happen in connection with sexual orgasm, philosophical insight, athletic success, watching a dance performance, giving birth to a child, or even using certain drugs. Peak experiences are obviously emotional highs, but they are also cognitive experiences of a unique sort. The knowledge con-ferred by peak experiences is the result of what Maslow calls *B-cognition*, that is, cognition of being. Unlike the deficiency-motivated knowing of everyday experience, which Maslow calls *D-cognition*, B-cognition knows its object in and of itself, as an end in itself—not as a thing to be used, but as a thing that is intrinsically fascinating. Ordinary dichotomies, such as the distinction between emotion and intellect, or subject and object, are over-come in peak experiences. B-cognition, because it is not distorted by ungratified needs, yields superior knowledge. Like self-actualizing persons themselves, the momentary flashes of actualization that occur in peak expe-riences, give us glimpses of human nature in its essence. By studying peak experiences, Maslow found that certain qualities—honesty, beauty, whole-ness, spontaneity, uniqueness, justice, order, and the transcendence of contradictions—were absolutely true and eternal values grounded in the essence of human nature.

10. Pro #1:   We sincerely hope that Maslow is right about this key idea. If he is, then human nature is innately good, and human beings have the potential to live together in peace and harmony (if we can design a society wherein basic needs are gratified).

Pro #2:   The application of Maslow's key idea can humanize many endeavors. Humanistic education is a case in point. Though it may now be considered passé, Maslow's idea had a lasting and beneficial effect upon our educational institutions.

Pro #3: Maslow's key idea produced a psychological theory that represented a viable third alternative to behaviorism and psychoanalysis. Maslow's theory sparked a spirited debate that clarified issues and positions on all sides, and led to revisions and, ultimately, even to new theoretical formulations. Such ferment is healthy for any discipline.

Pro #4: Maslow forced psychologists to abandon the fiction that their discipline is value-neutral, and instead to examine the values implicit in their theories.

Con #1: Maslow's reasoning is circular; he begs the question. How, for example, could he pick out self-actualizing persons to study if he did not already have a pretty good idea what their characteristics were? When basic needs are frustrated, he tells us, they produce pathology; when they are gratified, they produce positive mental health. But Maslow's list of basic needs is only a mirror image of his criteria for positive mental health, criteria that he never proved and already had in mind before he "discovered" the basic needs. Peak experiences are by definition always good, he says; when Maslow deduces the nature of goodness from these experiences, he is therefore practicing sophistry.

Con #2: Maslow's key idea has elitist implications. His self-actualizing people are an elite, privileged group, a kind of aristocracy. They have, according to Maslow, a superior view of reality.

Con #3: Unfortunately, this elitism creates the potential for dogmatism, and perhaps even totalitarianism. A group of people who are absolutely convinced that they know, better than anyone else, what is good for the human race may find it difficult to avoid imposing their ideas (by force if need be) on the rest of us. Nothing would be farther from Maslow's intentions, but whenever people become convinced that they know what is best for someone else, the danger of coercion exists.

REFERENCES

Fromm, E. (1955). *The sane society.* New York: Rinehart.

Maslow, A. H. (1954). *Motivation and personality.* New York: Harper & Row.

Maslow, A. H. (1959). Cognition of being in the peak experiences. *Journal of Genetic Psychology, 94,* 43-66.

Maslow, A. H. (1964). *Religions, values, and peak-experiences.* Columbus: Ohio State University Press.

Maslow, A. H. (1968). A conversation with Abraham H. Maslow. *Psychology Today, 2*(2), 35-37; 54-57.

Maslow, A. H. (1970). *Motivation and personality* (2nd ed.). New York: Harper & Row.

Maslow, A. H., & Mittelman, B. (1941). *Principles of abnormal psychology.* New York: Harper & Row.

Skinner, B. F. (1948). *Walden two.* New York: Macmillan.

Skinner, B. F. (1971). *Beyond freedom and dignity.* New York: Knopf.

13/George Kelly

A Biographical Sketch

George Kelly may have decided to become a psychologist earlier in life than some of the theorists we have studied, but by that time he had undoubtedly tried more (and perhaps more diverse) occupations than any of the others. Kelly's background is in some ways reminiscent of Carl Rogers' and Gordon Allport's. All three came from religiously pious, conservative Protestant families in the rural Midwest.

George Kelly, an only child, was born in 1905 on a farm near Perth, Kansas. His father, who had been educated for the Presbyterian ministry at Princeton, abandoned that career shortly before George was born and became a farmer. In 1909, Kelly's father fitted out a covered wagon and moved the family to a homestead in Colorado. Lack of adequate water on the land forced the Kellys back to Kansas before long. Young George's schooling was sporadic, although his parents made up for much of the deficiency by tutoring him themselves at home. What he learned at home, in addition to his sums and his ABCs, was the virtue of prayer and good hard work, and the evils of drinking, dancing, and card playing.

From the time he was thirteen until he graduated, Kelly attended four different high schools. He lived away from home for most of this time, because the schools were too far away to make commuting practical.

Aiming to become a mechanical engineer, Kelly spent three years at Friends University and his senior year at Park College, where he earned a B.A. in physics and mathematics in 1926. Like Cattell, Kelly seems to have realized almost before he graduated that something else interested him more. He had been active in the debating club as an undergraduate, and apparently some of the social issues he had been forced to consider became matters of deep personal concern. It is perhaps worth noting that in debating, one role-plays the part of an advocate, or a critic, of a particular ideological position. Kelly may have discovered that when you argue a position, you make it your own in a way you never can by just reading or hearing about it.

In any case, in September of the same year (1926), he enrolled in a master's degree program in educational sociology at the University of Kansas. His thesis was on how workers in Kansas City spent their leisure time. (He had elected to minor in labor relations.)

After receiving his M.A. in 1927, Kelly did so many different things in the space of a few years that it is hard to keep track of them all. In Minneapolis he taught part-time in a labor college, offered classes in public speaking to the American Bankers Association, and taught citizenship classes for immigrants. Next he got a job at a new junior college in Sheldon, Iowa. One of his activities there was coaching students in drama. After a year and a half at Sheldon, he won an exchange fellowship to Edinburgh University; but before he went off to Scotland, he taught sociology in the summer session at the University of Minnesota and picked up a few dollars more working as an aeronautical engineer in Wichita.

At Edinburgh, Kelly earned his Bachelor of Education degree, which customarily took two years, in only nine months, thanks partly to credits he received for previous academic work. His thesis, on the prediction of teaching success, was done under the direction of the famous educator and statistician Sir Godfrey Thomson. It was during this time, apparently, that Kelly turned to psychology. Earlier, his first undergraduate course in psychology, taught from a stimulus-response perspective, had failed to capture his interest. While working for his master's degree at the University of Kansas, he had read Freud but had found him muddled and unscientific. Yet in 1930, Kelly enrolled in the State University of Iowa as a candidate for the Ph.D. in psychology. The following June he received his degree, doing his dissertation on common factors in speech and reading disabilities. He arrived at this point in his life only after studying mathematics, physics, education, sociology, labor relations, measurement and statistics, speech pathology, and cultural anthropology.

The nation was in the throes of its worst depression, and things were not to improve much for at least a decade. Kelly managed to get an appointment to the faculty of the State College at Fort Hays, Kansas, where he was to spend the next thirteen years. It was during this period that he laid the foundations for his psychology of **personal constructs.** First, however, he had to give up his interest in physiological psychology and come to terms with the obvious fact that Fort Hays really needed a clinical psychologist. Next he had to develop some techniques for helping people with their problems. Kelly developed a counseling service for both the college and the public schools in Fort Hays. He also established traveling clinics that went from school to school around the state. Turning back to psychoanalytic writings for help, Kelly found that he could make use of many Freudian concepts in his clinical work.

Nevertheless, Kelly's clientele in rural Kansas schools was not at all like Freud's Viennese neurotics. Perhaps Kelly's emphasis on rational decision-making reflects not just a personal preference, but also the kinds of cases he dealt with. At any rate, Kelly was soon experimenting with a variety of psychotherapeutic techniques. Toward the end of the 1930s, he became aware of Moreno's techniques of role-playing and psychodrama. Similar notions had long fascinated him and it was not long before he came up with his own technique of **fixed-role therapy** (to which we will return later in this chapter). The key concept in Kelly's mature theory—the concept of the personal construct—was also taking form during this time, partly due, no doubt, to his discovery of a book by Alfred Korzybski that emphasized how the language we use shapes the way we think.

World War II brought George Kelly out of rural Kansas and elevated him to national prominence. After a brief stint training civilian pilots in Kansas, Kelly was called to Washington, given a commission in the Navy, and assigned to the Aviation Psychology Branch of the Bureau of Medicine and Surgery.

When Kelly returned to academia in 1945, he went not to Fort Hays, but to the University of Maryland. He stayed there for only one year before moving (1946) to Ohio State University, to accept an appointment as professor and director of clinical psychology. Here he came into full flower, doing the research and theoretical formulation that established his reputation as a giant in the field of personality psychology. Kelly stayed at Ohio State nineteen years. During that time he built an excellent graduate program in clinical psychology. He also became a moving force in the national effort to enhance the status of clinical psychology as a profession. In 1955, the two-volume work which constitutes the essence of his theoretical system—*The Psychology of Personal Constructs*—was published. Kelly lectured at a number of other universities in this country and around the world, especially in the Caribbean and South America. In 1960/61 he went on a world tour sponsored by the Human Ecology Fund, lecturing in London, Moscow, Madrid, and Warsaw on the relevance of personal construct theory to the resolution of international problems.

In 1965 Kelly was appointed to the Riklis Chair of Behavioral Science at Brandeis University. This was a very prestigious position; even more important, it gave complete freedom to pursue his own scholarly interests. That made it all the more tragic when George Kelly died the following March (1966) at the age of 62. Writers who knew George Kelly consistently mention his warmth as a human being, his unselfish friendship, and his sincere modesty.

PIGEONHOLES IN THE MIND

The human mind does not simply record its experience; it organizes experience into various categories, the way a postal clerk sorts incoming mail. So much happens to us, we are bombarded with such a profusion of incoming stimuli, that we need some way of sorting it all out. We need some system of pigeonholes into which we can classify all this information if we are to make any sense out of it at all.

While eating my breakfast cereal, I catch sight of a black speck swimming in the milk along with my Rice Krispies. Is it animal, vegetable, or mineral? Which pigeonhole am I to sort it into? It will make quite a difference in my subsequent behavior. To eat a bug would be "gross"; if it is a pebble, I might break a filling; on the other hand, if it is merely a burned Rice Krispie, it will not hurt me to eat it. No matter which category I assign this alien speck to, I will act accordingly. In this case, the categories involved are fairly objective and the chances of error in classification are slight, but this may well be the simplest task of categorization that confronts me that day.

A few hours later, I answer the doorbell and discover a well-dressed young man carrying a brief-case. He announces that he wants to interview me as part of a public-opinion survey on hazardous waste disposal and associated environmental issues. As he stands there on the doorstep making his pitch, I try to size him up. I search for relevant categories. Animal, vegetable, mineral will be of little use here; I need to sort this character into categories like honest or dishonest, pushy or submissive, interesting or boring, fanatic crusader or open-minded researcher. The categories I call into play in this situation may say as much about me as they say about the person standing on my doorstep. Like my responses to a Rorschach inkblot, they reveal the issues that I am concerned about. My interest in whether the visitor is honest or dishonest may tell you that I am a little bit paranoid, that I am suspicious of people's motives, or that I am a fearful individual who thinks everybody is out to rob me or con me. When I place "pushy or submissive" high on my list of categories, that may imply that I am a person who sees interpersonal relationships as a matter of dominating or being dominated. My use of the "interesting–versus–boring" category might shed some light on my values. Perhaps it suggests a taste for stimulating, novel experiences, rather than the same old thing again and again. And the "fanatic crusader–versus–open-minded researcher" category clearly reveals a part of my value system: I am in favor of unbiased, calm, judicious intellectual inquiry, and I cannot tolerate uncompromising zealots.

I would probably use more than just these four categories to size up my visitor. I might not even be aware of some of these categories. After all, it happens so fast. But I would try to classify him into some set of pigeonholes I had already constructed in my mind. You would do the same if you found him standing on your doorstep, but the categories you would call into play, the pigeonholes you have in your mind, might be quite different. You might try to classify him as either intelligent or stupid, attractive or repulsive. No doubt you have already thought of other categories. But whatever they might be, the point is that they reflect your own values and concerns. In fact, if we could somehow see the whole set of pigeonholes you use to classify all the people you know, we would have a pretty good idea how your mind works. We would understand how you think.

THE KEY IDEA
YOUR MENTAL PIGEONHOLES
ARE YOUR PERSONALITY

The key idea in George Kelly's personality theory is as simple as that. If you understand how people think, then you understand their personalities. If you know the pigeonholes they use to categorize their experiences, then you know what kinds of people they are. The way they categorize other *people* is more important than the way they categorize *things*, because people are more important than things, and because there are greater individual differences in our categorizations of people than in our categorizations of things. The principle is the same in either case, however. Your personality consists of a specific combination of the pigeonholes you use to categorize your experiences. This is the key to Kelly's theory of personal constructs.

Kelly's theory is called a cognitive theory because it emphasizes the way in which people think. The word *cognitive* refers to thought processes. A person is as a person thinks, according to Kelly. This is in contrast to psychodynamic theories that emphasize how a person strives, what a person needs, or how a person is driven. It is also different from **affective** theories such as Rogers', which stress the importance of feelings. Kelly deals with feelings and, in a roundabout way, with motives, but his primary emphasis is on how people think.

The word cognitive also refers to the processes that enable us to understand and interpret our experience. Kelly employs one of his favorite terms in this context—the word *construe*. It means to interpret or to understand, though you may be more familiar with its negative form, *misconstrue*, which means to misunderstand. Anyway, Kelly says that the mind is perpetually engaged in a process of construing reality. Things happen to us, from the revelation of a speck in our breakfast cereal to the appearance of a caller at the door, and then we try to make some sense out of them. We subject them to some interpretation. We construe them.

PERSONAL CONSTRUCTS

But of course we do not have to start out from scratch in construing every event that happens to us; our past experience teaches us that many events are similar. The consequence is that when two similar events occur, the first one gives us a way to understand the second event. Such ready-made ways of construing are none other than the pigeonholes, or categories, we have been talking about—*personal constructs*, Kelly calls them. What Kelly means by *personal constructs* are pigeonholes such as honest-dishonest, or pushy-submissive. They are mental frameworks we build on the basis of our past experience, in order to help us interpret or construe what happens to us later on. We build them ourselves: Each one of us erects an edifice of pigeonholes in his or her mind. Kelly chose the term *personal construct* very carefully. We construct our pigeonhole edifices; we build them on the basis of experience. These "constructs" are also personal; each person's mental building is unique, different from anyone else's.

But Kelly's choice of the word *construct* also refers to his observation that each person's picture of reality is a *construction*. We are all constantly engaged in interpreting reality. I do not know for certain whether the self-proclaimed pollster on my doorstep is honest or dishonest, pushy or submissive, etc.; but I construct a personality sketch of him just the same. Whether my construction corresponds to reality, whether my picture of him is accurate, I cannot know at that moment. But that is fine, because it is a subjective construction; it is not objective reality. All construing is construction. The two words have the same root. That is why Kelly says that we *construe* the things that happen to us by using a system of personal *constructs*.

CONSTRUCTS AS TENTATIVE HYPOTHESES

The constructions we make out of reality are tentative, hypothetical. When I construe the pollster as honest and invite him into my living room, I am well aware that my construct may not correspond exactly to reality. I simply hypothesize that he is honest, then remain on the alert for any evidence that may either confirm or contradict that hypothesis. I may even attempt to test the hypothesis actively by demanding further identification, or by quizzing the man about environmental issues. In the light of what I discover as the interview proceeds, I may revise my hypothesis. In other words, construing is an ongoing activity, one we engage in every moment of our waking lives. Sometimes we make constructs with relative confidence—perhaps I am quite sure that he is honest. In that case the construing will not seem so hypothetical to me, and I will make no conscious efforts to test it. I would still be capable of revising it, however, if sufficient contradictory evidence came to my attention. In short, our personal constructs are guesses or hunches about the nature of reality, hypotheses that are confirmed or disconfirmed by future experience.

Because of their hypothetical nature, our personal constructs have a forward-looking posture. They are future-oriented and anticipatory, rather than just descriptive. True, their purpose is to enable us to understand what is happening at the moment; but the object of that understanding is not simply to satisfy our intellectual curiosity. Personal constructs help us to anticipate, to predict future events and plan our own strategies. I do not wonder whether the door-to-door pollster is honest or dishonest simply for the sake of knowledge. I want to put that knowledge to a specific use: namely, to predict whether my answers to the questionnaire will have an impact on public policy, or whether my house is going to be burglarized by this man a few nights from now. We construe reality in order to prepare ourselves to deal with it. Personal constructs are survival mechanisms.

CONSTRUCTS AS GUIDES FOR BEHAVIOR

We behave according to how we construe events. If by the time the pollster left my house I had revised my hypothesis and construed him as dishonest (on the basis of his claim to have lost his identification card and his almost total ignorance of environmental issues), I might take extra precautions against burglary for the next couple of weeks—leave the outside lights on all night; ask the neighbors to keep an eye out; maybe even buy an alarm. Construing an event is like turning the steering wheel of a car: It guides the vehicle in one direction or another as it moves into the future.

But one direction may not be as good as another. Steering in one direction may get you to your destination quickly, comfortably, and without burning much gas. Turning another way may lead you into all kinds of dead ends, forcing you to back up again and again. A third direction might involve you in a serious accident. Since the direction in which you steer your future behavior depends on how you construe the present situation, some constructs inevitably work better than others.

Kelly did not care whether an individual's constructs were accurate or true in any ultimate, philosophical sense. His only criterion was whether they work effectively and efficiently to steer that person's behavior toward his or her desired destinations. Each one of us has some constructs that work well and some that make us waste our energies, perhaps even getting us into trouble. Furthermore, no two people have exactly the same system of constructs. Some people have a system that works very effectively, while others have a construct system that leads continually to frustration, disappointment, and distress.

CONSTRUCT THERAPY

The implications of Kelly's idea for psychotherapy are obvious. People who seek psychotherapy are people whose personal constructs do not work very effectively. But events can be construed in a variety of different ways—a fact Kelly referred to with the term **constructive alternativism.** Not only different people construe events differently; each individual can choose to construe an event (or person) in any number of ways. Therapy therefore consists in teaching patients how to make alternative constructs to replace their ineffective constructs. This involves a kind of construct transplant, accomplished through the use of role-playing. Once the therapist has determined which of a patient's constructs need to be changed and in what direction they need to be changed, the therapist writes up a character sketch of a fictitious person whose thinking makes regular use of the new constructs to be implanted in the patient. The patient is presented with the sketch and asked to play-act the role of that character, first with the therapist in the office, and then outside the office in daily life for the next couple of days or even weeks. If the therapist has done a good job, the patient will begin to discover that the construct system of the character he is role-playing is far more effective than his own construct system. The patient gradually adopts the new constructs and is thereby cured. His or her personality is changed. After all, if your system of personal constructs equals your personality, then changing your constructs equals changing your personality. (Needless to say, the actual methods Kelly used in psychotherapy were not nearly as simple as this, nor were cures effected this quickly. Still, these are the core features of his *fixed-role therapy.*)

MEASURING YOUR CONSTRUCTS

Before we go on to the pros and cons of Kelly's key idea, perhaps you would enjoy having a look at your own personal construct system. Kelly has devised an ingeniously simple technique for identifying an individual's most basic personal constructs. He calls it the Rep Test, short for *Role Construct Repertory Test.* If you had gone to Kelly for therapy, he would have given you the Rep Test as one way of helping him understand how you construe your world.

Figure 13–1 on page 300 is a reproduction of what Kelly calls the grid form of the Rep Test. To begin work on the test, turn the grid so that the word *Figure* appears at the top. In the space next to the number 1 under the word *Figure,* write your own name. Next to number 2, write your mother's name. Follow this procedure. as outlined in Kelly's original instructions (reproduced below), all the way through number 22.

Instructions for Figure List (from Kelly, 1955, p. 270)

1. Write your own name in the first blank here.
2. Write your mother's first name here. If you grew up with a stepmother, write her name instead.
3. Write your father's first name here. If you grew up with a stepfather, write his name instead.
4. Write the name of your brother who is nearest your own age. If you had no brother, writer the name of a boy near your own age who was most like a brother to you during your early teens.
5. Write the name of your sister who is nearest your own age. If you had no sister, write the name of a girl near your own age who was most like a sister to you during your early teens.

FROM THIS POINT ON DO NOT REPEAT ANY NAMES. IF A PERSON HAS ALREADY BEEN LISTED, SIMPLY MAKE A SECOND CHOICE.

6. Your wife (or husband) or, if you are not married, your closest present girl (boy) friend.
7. Your closest girl (boy) friend immediately preceding the person mentioned above.
8. Your closest present friend of the same sex as yourself.
9. A person of the same sex as yourself whom you once thought was a close friend but in whom you were badly disappointed later.
10. The minister, priest, or rabbi with whom you would be most willing to talk over your personal feelings about religion.
11. Your physician.
12. The present neighbor whom you know best.

13. A person with whom you have been associated who, for some unexplained reason, appeared to dislike you.
14. A person whom you would most like to help or for whom you feel sorry.
15. A person with whom you usually feel most uncomfortable.
16. A person whom you have recently met whom you would like to know better.
17. The teacher whom you have recently met whom you would like to know better.
18. The teacher whose point of view you have found most objectionable.

FIGURE 13-1

The Rep Test: Grid Form

1	2	3	4	5	6	7	8	9	10	11	12	13	14	15	16	17	18	19	20	21	22	Sort No.	CONSTRUCT	CONTRAST
																			0	0	0	1		
																0	0	0				2		
												0	0		0							3		
					0	0	0															4		
	0	0	0																			5		
					0											0			0			6		
	0							0								0						7		
		0															0	0				8		
				0								0				0						9		
					0							0				0						10		
					0									0							0	11		
				0				0						0								12		
					0									0					0			13		
		0			0	0																14		
			0		0	0																15		
							0	0							0							16		
0			0	0																		17		
																0	0				0	18		
		0	0											0								19		
0													0	0								20		
						0						0	0									21		
0					0		0															22		

Reprinted from *The Psychology of Personal Constructs. Volume 1, A Theory of Personality,* by George A. Kelly. By permission of W. W. Norton & Company, Inc. Copyright 1955 by George A. Kelly. Copyright renewed 1983 by Gladys Kelly.

19. An employer, supervisor, or officer under whom you served during a period of great stress.
20. The most successful person whom you know personally.
21. The happiest person whom you know personally.
22. The person known to you personally who appears to meet the highest ethical standards.

When you have filled in the names of all 22 of your figures, turn the grid so that the words *Construct* and *Contrast* are at the top of the sheet. You will notice that just to the left of the number 1 in the column headed *Sort No.* there appear three small circles, one each under numbers 20, 21, and 22. "This means that you are first to consider the three people whose names appear" above these respective numbers in the *Figure* column—your most successful person, happiest person, and most ethical person (Kelly, 1955, p. 273).

Think about these three people. Are two of them *alike in some important way that distinguishes them from the third person?* Keep thinking about them until you remember the important way in which two of them are alike and which sets them off from the third person.

When you have decided which two it is, and the important way in which they are alike, put an "X" in the two circles corresponding to the two who are alike. Do not put any mark in the third circle.

Now write in the blank under "Construct" the word or short phrase that tells how these two are alike.

Next write in the blank under "Contrast" what you consider to be the opposite of this characteristic.

Now consider each of the other nineteen persons whose names appear at the heads of columns 1 to 19. In addition to the persons whom you have marked with an "X," which ones also have this important characteristic? Put a check Mark (✔)—not an "X"—under the name of each other person who has this important characteristic . . .

[Now proceed to Sort No. 2.] Think about persons number 17, 18, and 19—the three who have circles under their names. In what important way are two of these distinguished from the third? Put "X's" in the circles to show which two are alike. Write the "Construct" and the "Contrast" in the blanks at the right just as you did before. Then consider the other sixteen persons. Check (✔) the ones who also have the characteristic you have noted.

Complete the test in the way you have done the first two rows (Kelly, 1955, p. 273).

Now for the interpretation. What does it all mean then? The twenty-two words you have written under the heading *Construct* are, of course, your own personal constructs. Constructs, according to Kelly, are dichotomous or bipolar—like black and white, or good and evil. Thus, what you have written under the heading *Contrast* is simply the opposite pole of each of these twenty-two constructs. Sometimes Kelly referred to what you have written under *Construct* as the *emergent pole* of the construct, and what you have written under *Contrast* as the *implicit pole*. Whatever we call them, each of the twenty-two pairs of words represents one of your personal constructs. These are not all the constructs you have, of course. Obviously this test taps only the constructs you use in construing other persons, and even at that, only some of the many persons you interact with every day. Nevertheless, Kelly has selected these *figures* because they probably represent the most significant people in your life; hence, they should elicit the most important aspects of your system of personal constructs.

Many elaborate techniques have been devised for analyzing the Rep Test and the many variations on the grid technique that have been invented since Kelly first concocted it (Fransella & Bannister, 1977). Kelly himself described how the grid could be factor analyzed (1955). Most of these approaches will probably be beyond your range of convenience unless you have already joined the computer revolution by buying your own home computer. But there are a few things you can easily do beyond just seeing what your personal constructs are.

You can, for example, classify your constructs as either *situational* or *psychological*. Situational constructs (also called physical constructs) are those which simply describe some aspect of a person's outward appearance, such as "young" or "old," "both teachers" or "not a teacher," "overweight" or "not overweight"; or that refer to a situation in which you encounter these people, such as "neighbor" or "not a neighbor"; "plays tennis with me" or "does not play tennis with me"; "both drive a Chevrolet" or "does not drive a Chevrolet." Psychological constructs are those that describe traits of personality, attitudes, personal values, and social skills; for example: "understanding" or "not understanding"; "very religious" or "not very religious"; "tense" or "easygoing"; "shares my political ideas" or "does not share my political ideas." You can scan your list of personal constructs and see how many of them are situational and how many are psychological. Generally speaking, the more psychological constructs you have, the more sophisticated your personal construct system is. It may be, however, that some of your constructs that at first glance appear to be situational are actually used in a way that is more psychological. This may become apparent only after you have completed the next stage of analysis.

In this stage, you proceed to an examination of the grid itself. Take a sheet of paper and place it on the grid directly under the row of check marks and Xs you have made for construct sort number 1. Copy along the top edge of the paper all the check marks and Xs you have written on the grid for construct sort number 1. Now slide the paper down one row to construct sort number 2. See how many of the check marks and Xs in sort number 1 match those you made in sort number 2. If they all match exactly, give yourself a score of –3. If they all match except for one mark, give yourself a score of –2. And if they all match except for two marks, give yourself a score of –1. Now move the paper down to the row for construct sort number 3 and repeat the procedure. Go through the whole grid this way, all the way down to sort number 22, to see to what extent each sort matches sort number 1.

Now turn the piece of paper to expose a fresh edge and align it under the row for construct sort number 2. Copy the pattern of check marks and Xs you have written for sort number 2. Then slide the paper down to row number 3, inspect for matches, and score. Go on in the same manner to score rows 4 through 22. When you have done that, find a fresh edge on the paper and copy your marks for sort number 3, and slide the paper down row by row, scoring for matches in all the rows below. Go on to copy row number 4, scoring for matches in the rows below it, and so on until you have copied all of your responses down to the bottom of the grid, giving yourself a score of –3 each time there is a perfect match, –2 each time there is a match except for one mark, and –1 each time there is a match except for two marks. When you have finished, add up all of your scores. What you will have is a measure of cognitive complexity (Bieri, 1955).

Now, if two construct sorts result in the same, or even almost the same, pattern of check marks and Xs, that means that the constructs in question, even though you may have named them differently in each sort, are used in the same way and hence are functionally equivalent. If you have, for example, five such constructs, each of which is repeated only once, that means that your construct system does not contain 22 *different* constructs but only 17. And if one or more of those constructs is repeated more than once, then the total number of different constructs is still smaller. A construct system with only 17 constructs is not as complex as one with 22. Hence the lower your score (remember that the scores were negative numbers), the lower the complexity of your construct system. A score of zero represents the most complex construct system. Scores less than zero represent decreasing complexity.

Returning now to the matter of situational constructs–versus–psychological constructs, you can see that if a construct to which you have attached a situational name happens to have a pattern of markings that matches another construct to which you have given a psychological name, then the first construct may in fact be functioning in your system as a psychological construct, despite the name you have given to it. Check to see if there are any such instances in your grid, and revise your situational/psychological construct score accordingly.

Let me caution you that these complexity scores should not be taken too seriously. There has been considerable controversy about the validity of cognitive-consistency scores derived from grids of this kind, and the simple method of scoring presented here has been superseded by far more elaborate techniques during the three decades since it was first introduced (Fransella & Bannister, 1977). In fact, it is not at all impossible to find reputable psychologists who question the reliability of the Rep Test itself, as well as measures of cognitive complexity derived from it (Bavelas, 1978). In a word then, whatever your score, take it with a large grain of salt. Consider it rather as an exercise that demonstrates, in a very simplistic fashion, how numerical scores may be derived from Kelly's Rep Test by using the grid technique.

The Rep Test is an ingenious, concrete application of Kelly's key idea.

THE FUNDAMENTAL POSTULATE AND ELEVEN COROLLARIES

Kelly's personal construct theory can be summarized with one fundamental postulate and eleven corollaries.

THE FUNDAMENTAL POSTULATE

The fundamental postulate states: "A person's processes are psychologically channelized by the ways in which he anticipates events" (Kelly, 1955, p. 46). In everyday language, this means that how you behave depends on what you expect to happen. Kelly uses the word *processes* to refer to people's thinking and feeling, as well as their overt actions. He describes these processes as *channelized* rather than determined, meaning that they are influenced and encouraged, but not forced, to follow a certain direction. When Kelly says anticipation of events directs our behavior, he shows his allegiance to the humanistic notion that future goals, rather than past traumas, provide the best clues to future behavior.

People operate, Kelly says, in much the same fashion as a research scientist. They develop little theories about things—about why people act the way they do; the best way to study for a psychology exam; the comparative virtues of various health-food diets. They form hypotheses from these theories; test the hypotheses; and refine their theories in light of their experimental results. Most people do this, of course, without even being aware of it. But we all do it, Kelly says, so that we can predict or anticipate the future better. In effect, Kelly is saying that we strive for some degree of control over the future.

THE CONSTRUCTION COROLLARY

How do people know what to expect in a given situation? They expect what happened in similar situations in the past to happen again, that's how. The construction corollary says that we anticipate events first by noting their similarity to events we have already experienced, then by constructing (imagining) the same outcome.

THE INDIVIDUALITY COROLLARY

The individuality corollary says that each individual anticipates (constructs) in a different way.

THE ORGANIZATION COROLLARY

The systems of constructs people use to help them anticipate events are not just disjointed conglomerations of hypotheses; they are *organized*. Some constructs, for example, are more general than others. Several specific constructs may be filed under one of these general headings: e.g., *smart-dumb* and *fat-thin* might both be subsidiary to *good-bad*.

THE DICHOTOMY COROLLARY

They are structured according to an either-or, black-or-white format. They are polar opposites.

THE CHOICE COROLLARY

In a given situation, people will apply the pole (of a dichotomized construct) they think will help them most to improve and strengthen their

Assuming that an individual's personality equals his or her personal construct system, all you need to do to get a picture of that individual's personality is to discover the most important constructs she or he uses to construe his or her world. The Rep Test does exactly that. And it does it in a most straightforward manner. It does not use inkblots or ambiguous pictures. It does not attempt to measure the strength of traits imposed upon the subject by the test-builder. It simply asks subjects to tell how they overall construct system, ultimately improving their general predictive ability.

THE RANGE COROLLARY

Not every construct can be applied to everything. *Loud-soft,* for example, is applicable to sounds or even to colors, but not to apples or peanuts. Each construct is appropriate to those things within its *range of convenience.* The range of some constructs is broader than that of others.

THE EXPERIENCE COROLLARY

Learning occurs as people modify their construct systems in the light of experience. Constructs that predict well are retained and strengthened; those that function poorly are discarded or revised.

THE MODULATION COROLLARY

The modulation corollary refers to the rigidity or flexibility of people's construct systems. Kelly says that constructs can be more or less *permeable* or *impermeable.* Having impermeable constructs is like wearing blinders. The range of convenience of impermeable constructs is sharply defined and inflexible. Permeable constructs, on the other hand, are more open-ended and hence promote learning and personality change. Kelly chose the word *modulation* to refer to the fine-tuning of constructs that occurs when constructs are sufficiently permeable to be changed by new experience.

THE FRAGMENTATION COROLLARY

People are not consistent. They may apply logically incompatible constructs to successive events. Though Kelly portrays human nature as highly rational, he stops short of claiming that anyone's construct system is perfectly consistent. He does say, however, that people strive for consistency and that most behavior is at least consistent with people's dominant constructs.

THE COMMONALITY COROLLARY

If two people interpret events using the same system of constructs, they are likely to think and act very much alike. (This is, in effect, the converse of the individuality corollary.) Note that it is not necessary for these people to be exposed to the same events, only for them to employ the same system of constructs.

THE SOCIALITY COROLLARY

The final corollary states that if you can understand (construe) how another person views events—what system of constructs the other person uses to interpret reality—then you can play the role of the other person, which is the basis for social interaction with that person. What Kelly is referring to here seems very close to what Rogers called *empathy:* the ability to see the world as another person sees it. Both agree that it is the basis of social relationships.

construe important people in their lives. The basic assumptions are obviously that people themselves know better than anyone else how they view the world, and that if you ask them, they will tell you. These are of course assumptions and not established facts, and they, along with several other assumptions on which Kelly's key idea rests, are open to question. By considering the pros and cons of Kelly's key idea, we will bring some of these assumptions into sharper focus.

PROS and CONS

Pro #1: This key idea is cognitive.   Psychology's current infatuation is with anything cognitive. If you want to sell a book, a new personality test, or even a workshop on biofeedback to psychologists, just get the word *cognitive* into the title and the success of your venture is all but guaranteed. The history of psychology can be likened to the California gold rush, in that as soon as one "prospector" hollers that he or she has struck paydirt, everybody scrambles to dig in the same territory. After a while somebody makes a strike somewhere else, and everybody deserts the previous mine, which has proved to be pretty tough digging after all, and dashes over to this new site. Pursuing this analogy, we could say that cognitive psychology was not a newly discovered deposit but the reopening of an abandoned mine that had not been worked for fifty years. But no matter, the effect is the same—psychologists by the thousands are flocking to the neighborhood to dig into the lode of cognitive ore.

As the first and only thoroughly cognitive personality theory, George Kelly's psychology of personal constructs is perfectly in step with the times. You might even say that the rest of psychology has finally caught up with Kelly. Kelly's key idea—how you think is what you are—is an idea whose time has come. It is a definite pro for Kelly's key idea, and for the theory that derives from it, that it is relevant and timely.

For too long, too many psychologists were willing to reduce the higher mental processes to a mere hyphen between stimulus and response. They had abandoned studying thinking, hoping that thinking would not matter. But Kelly insisted that if did matter. And though he cannot be given sole credit for engineering the cognitive revolution in psychology, surely his influence had some impact, especially in the realm of clinical psychology. Jean Piaget surely was the prime mover in getting psychologists to attend once more to cognitive processes. And the electronic information-processing wizards who build computers that do everything from playing chess to landing a man on the moon threaten to steal the show if psychologists fail to get into the cognitive act. Many, many influences have precipitated the much needed cognitive revolution in psychology. Perhaps George Kelly's role might be described as best supporting actor. For that he deserves, if not an Oscar, at least a pro.

Pro #2: This key idea is simple and commonsense.   The idea that if you know how a person thinks you know a lot about his or her personality is so evident to common sense that it is difficult to understand how psychologists could have ignored it for so long. Kelly's key idea has the immediate appeal of a simple, self-evident truth: Anyone can see that it makes sense. We all take it for granted in our everyday interactions with other people. We are constantly engaged in analyzing the statements of others for some clue to what, and how, they are thinking. And we assume that people behave at least to some extent on the basis of how they think. Kelly took these mundane observations and made them the foundation of his theory.

And he kept it simple. Kelly's theory is parsimonious. It has few theoretical constructs—only one fundamental postulate and eleven corollaries. The eleven corollaries can almost all be guessed once you know the fundamental postulate, which states that "a person's processes are psychologically channelized by the ways in which he anticipates events" (Kelly, 1955, p. 46). This is Kelly's way of saying that if you know what mental pigeonholes a person uses, you understand that individual's personality. The eleven corollaries, which constitute the remainder of the theory in its entirety, follow logically and with transparent simplicity. For example: The *sociality corollary* says in effect that people who think alike will understand each other; the *individuality corollary* observes that different people think differently; the *range corollary* points out that certain mental pigeonholes are applicable to certain situations but not to others (animal, vegetable, mineral was useful for the speck-in-the-cereal situation, but not particularly helpful with the stranger at the door); and the *experience corollary* proposes that most people will modify their constructs if experience demonstrates that they do not work very well. Once you have Kelly's key idea, it is not hard to deduce the rest of the theory. The connection between Kelly's key idea and his handful of theoretical constructs is direct, clear, and inevitable. This, together with the manifest commonsensicality of the key idea itself, constitutes a strong pro for George Kelly.

Con #1: This key idea is too simple.   If you understand how a person thinks, you know a lot about his or her personality, but do you know everything about his or her personality? Kelly did not say explicitly that your system of personal constructs *equals* your personality, yet he did not seem to think it necessary to include anything else in his theory of personality, nor to try to change anything else in the patients who came to him for therapy. Con #1 has to do not so much with what Kelly said as what he did not say. We can only applaud the fact that his cognitive orientation provided a much needed corrective to a psychology that had for too long ignored the role of thinking in human personality. But if we apply this corrective too enthusiastically, we risk unbalancing our model of personality in the opposite direction. We must avoid the gold-rush mentality that makes prospectors desert perfectly good mines in order to dash off after the rumored mother lode. There is no mother lode in personality psychology; there is no one key idea that will encompass the rich complexity of human personality.

Of course, how a person thinks is important. But how a person feels is important too. And Kelly has reduced feelings to mere by-products that accompany the effective (or ineffective) functioning of our personal construct systems. If our constructs lead us to anticipate events correctly, we are happy; if we anticipate wrongly, we are anxious. How we think determines how we feel. There is little provision for the possibility that how we feel influences how we think—an equally plausible hypothesis, and one on which Freud built his not inconsiderable reputation.

How a person learns is also important. This is subsumed under Kelly's experience corollary, which says in effect that personal constructs that work well will be strengthened, and those that do not will be discarded. Behaviorists might not be prepared to concede that that tells the whole story, yet Kelly seemed to feel it required little further elaboration.

How a person's wants and urges arise is also important. But Kelly expressly denied the need for any concept of motivation in his theory of personality. For him, instincts, drives, and needs were all abstract theoretical constructs of psychologists, not real life personal constructs used by ordinary people. Furthermore, they were superfluous to him. People do not need drives and instincts to set them in motion and make them behave. People move and behave because they are alive. No other explanation is called for. To be alive is to be in motion. Kelly's effort to dismiss all of dynamic psychology in this cavalier manner strikes many people as akin to hunting elephants with a flyswatter.

Kelly's key idea, if it were to become one ingredient in an eclectic theory of personality that included the insights of dynamic psychology and learning theory, would provide a nice balance. But if Kelly's key idea is advanced imperialistically as the answer to all questions in personality theory, it can lead to a seriously unbalanced view of human nature. That imbalance is the essence of Con #2,

Con #2: This key idea depicts people as too rational. Philosophers have traditionally viewed the mind as comprised of three faculties: cognitive, **conative**, and affective. Affective refers to the emotions, conative to the will, and cognitive to the intellect. To say that a theory is cognitive, then, is another way of saying that it focuses on the intellectual processes. And the primary characteristic of the intellect is that it is rational. Con #2 is simply that Kelly's key idea is too rational. Human beings are not as rational as Kelly would have us believe.

People will adopt that system of personal constructs that works most effectively and efficiently for them, according to Kelly. In fact, Kelly's psychotherapy is based squarely on the belief that if you can demonstrate to a client that another construct works better than the one she or he is now using, she or he will readily adopt it. The implication is that individuals conduct a kind of cost-benefit analysis in evaluating their own thinking habits. And just as most businesses in recent years have switched, in their data-processing operations, from using more cumbersome computer languages to using the more streamlined COBOL language, because it is more cost-effective, so individuals will switch from one set of mental pigeonholes to another if their internal "auditors" can demonstrate that the move will increase their chances of gaining their objectives. It all sounds terribly cerebral and highly calculating. Maybe people do operate that way, and then again maybe they do not. Even if they do, Kelly has still dodged the fundamental question.

Kelly says, in effect, that people will adopt and strengthen the set of constructs that proves most effective in helping them get whatever it is that they want. What he does not tell us is how they decide what they want. He virtually admits that thinking only serves an instrumental function in the gratification of wants—it calculates the best strategy for people to get what they want—but he does not tell us where the wants come from. We become aware of our wants and construe them, organizing them thoughtfully. But our wants do not come from our thoughts; they are already there. Kelly recognized this when he said—and here I am paraphrasing again—that to be alive is to want. And what all human beings want, according to Kelly, is to be able to predict and control the future better and better. They want to know and to understand. They want to make rational sense of their experience. What they want is something rational, but the want itself is not rational. It does not derive from reason; it seeks reason. Wanting to know is not knowing, it is wanting. Wanting is wanting, and that is something quite different from knowing. Conation (wanting) and cognition (knowing) are separate and distinct processes. Each has its own unique character. Cognition is rational—or at least it can be rational. Conation is not rational; it is appetite. It is not irrational, but neither is it rational. The rationality–irrationality dichotomy does not apply here.

Kelly's concentration on the thought processes leaves us with the impression that human behavior is guided by rational calculation. Yet he knew that wants are simply appetites before they are reflected upon and construed as thoughts, and that as unconstrued wants they are neither rational nor irrational. And he knew that gratification of these non-rational wants was the unacknowledged (and largely unexamined) reinforcement principle, or motivational construct, in his personality theory.

The personality equals an individual's system of personal constructs—that is Kelly's key idea. But individuals have adopted those particular constructs because the constructs enable them to predict the future in such a way that they get what they want and get it cost effectively. Different people have different systems of personal constructs, according to Kelly. That is why their personalities are different. But is it not clear that they have different construct systems because they have different wants to start with? And does it not follow, then, that the more fundamental explanation of why people have different personalities is that they have different wants?

Yet this is the question that Kelly dismisses as uninteresting. Why one person wants one thing and another wants something else, is an issue he simply does not deal with. He just assumes that that is the way it is; he takes that as his starting point. That certainly is his prerogative. Plenty of worthwhile theorizing can be done while postponing that issue. But it should be made clear that it is only postponed, since ultimately it cannot be avoided if one is to build a comprehensive theory of human personality. Kelly was a bit slippery on this point. By not making it clear that he was just postponing answering the question, Kelly implied that the question was not important. And by ignoring that aspect of personality that is non-rational and concentrating on the rational aspect, he left us with a portrait of human nature that is one-sided, all head and no heart.

CHAPTER SUMMARY

1. People are continuously categorizing their experience, filing away every event like a postal clerk sorting incoming mail. They sort different events into different categories. But different people may sort the same event into different categories because, unlike the post office where the system of pigeonholes is the same for every clerk, people's mental pigeonholes are their own highly individual constructions. As such, they reveal as much about the individual as they do about the event he or she is categorizing.

2. Kelly's key idea is that the sum total of the mental pigeonholes used by a person to categorize his or her experiences constitutes that individual's personality. If you know how a person thinks, then you understand that person. Kelly's theory is called *cognitive*, because *cognitive* means *having to do with thinking*. People construe—interpret—their experience.

3. Kelly refers to our mental pigeonholes as *personal constructs*. We build them up by noticing that certain events are similar and others are different. These, of course, are subjective interpretations.

4. Kelly says that these constructs are hypotheses about the nature of reality, hypotheses we operate with—like a detective following a lead—until additional evidence confirms, or forces us to revise them. Hence, our constructs are not merely descriptive; they enable us to anticipate future events and thereby guide our actions.

5. Construing an event one way leads to a certain kind of behavior; construing it another way leads to quite different behavior. Yet some behaviors are more effective than others in getting people what they want. Hence some constructs work better than others.

6. For the person whose constructs lead to wasted energy, interpersonal conflict, and eventually distress and frustration, there is construct therapy. Since events may be construed in any number of alternative ways, an individual has the option of exchanging some of his or her constructs for new ones—trading them in on new models. Kelly calls this interchangeability of constructs *constructive alternativism*. His therapy consists of teaching patients alternative constructs that can replace ineffective ones. This is accomplished in part through role-playing.

7. Kelly developed the Rep Test (Role Construct Repertory Test) in order to reveal the principle features of an individual's personal-construct system. The test first asks you to list the names of twenty-two important people in your life. Next it asks you to look at these people in groups of three and to identify some characteristic that two of the people have in common, but not the third. It then asks you to come up with a verbal label for that similarity, and another one for the difference. The twenty-two pairs of similarities and differences you produce constitute the core of your personal construct system.

8. Pro #1.   Cognitive theories are currently enjoying great popularity in psychology, and Kelly's key idea is cognitive. His key idea may even be responsible for that popularity to some extent.

Pro #2. The idea that knowing how a person thinks leads to an understanding of that individual's personality makes such common sense that it is hard to see how psychologists could have ignored it for so long. And Kelly's theory is parsimonious.

Con #1: But understanding how a person thinks does not tell you everything about that individual's personality. Kelly largely ignores how the person feels, learns, and is motivated. Hence the theory is unbalanced.

Con #2. Kelly assumes that people are rational. He says that people adopt the construct system that is most effective in getting them what they want. What he does not explain is how they decide what it is that they want. Wants are by definition not rational; They are appetitites. And since wants exist prior to construing, we can only conclude that Kelly has failed to explain the non-rational source of personal constructs.

REFERENCES

Bavelas, J. B. (1978). *Personality: Current theory and research. Monterey, CA: Brooks/Cole.*

Bieri, J. (1955). Cognitive complexity-simplicity and predictive behavior. *Journal of Abnormal and Social Psychology, 51,* 263–268.

Fransella, F. & Bannister, D. (1977). *A manual for repertory grid technique.* London: Academic press.

Kelly, G.A. (1955). *The psychology of personal constructs; Vol. 1. A theory of personality.* New York: W. W. Norton.

14/Conclusion

Our shopping tour has come to an end. We have had a look at each of the major brands of personality theory. There is a dazzling assortment of models and special features. The key idea format was introduced to help keep the information glut under control. Let us begin this wrap-up by listing the theorists and their key ideas.

☐ Sigmund Freud: unconscious motivation; pansexualism; stages of development
   ☐ Carl Gustav Jung: the collective unconscious
   ☐ Erik Erikson: identity and ideology
   ☐ Henry Murray: personality as themes in your life story
   ☐ Gordon Allport: individual uniqueness
   ☐ Raymond Cattell: elements of personality
   ☐ B. F. Skinner: contingencies of reinforcement
   ☐ Albert Bandura: observational learning
   ☐ Carl Rogers: personhood—the result of being valued
   ☐ Abraham Maslow: a scientifically verified system of ethics
   ☐ George Kelly: personality as your system of mental pigeonholes.

We have also evaluated each of these key ideas in relation to its pros and cons, because we are not merely window shopping, we are looking to buy. Maybe you still have not decided which theory to buy. Sometimes the pros and cons may have yanked you around quite a bit. Perhaps you thought you were all ready to buy a theory after you read the pros, and then the cons pulled the rug right out from under you. Once or twice you may have wished that I would just come out and tell you which theory I thought you ought to buy. It may still be confusing, even with all the key ideas laid out in front of you. Maybe by grouping them in various categories I can further highlight the basic issues that should guide your choice.

SCIENCE OR HUMANITY

The most fundamental rift in personality psychology, it seems to me, is between theorists who view the discipline as a branch of the natural sciences and those who see it as something akin to the humanities. Of course, most psychologists pay lip service to the ideal that psychology is a science. Given our culture's reverence for science, and the need for psychologists to compete with biologists and electronic engineers for government and university funding for their research (and with medical doctors for third-party payments for their therapeutic services), it is unlikely that many psychologists will willingly cast off the mantle of scientific professional. None of the theorists we have considered admits to doing anything less than science. Nevertheless, it is quite clear that what some of them do is much closer to biography than it is to biology.

Erikson, Murray, and Allport have all produced works of biography, and their personality theories all advocate a biographical approach as the best way to discover what personality is and how it works. In fact, Erikson's name is uniquely associated with the discipline of psychohistory. Much of Jung's data comes from historical research, and his methods often smack more of **ethnography** than of psychology. Maslow's true vocational calling, as we saw, was ethics, that branch of philosophy which seeks to answer the question of how we should live. Biography, history, ethnography, and ethics are all humanities; they are not, in the usual sense of the word, sciences. Yet all of these personality theorists persist in referring to their work as science.

Skinner would, of course, ridicule such a claim. For him a science of psychology is that which makes possible accurate prediction and control of behavior. Both Bandura and Cattell would agree that personality psychology ought to be that kind of enterprise. Though Skinner and Bandura seek the causes of behavior primarily in the external environment while Cattell probes for them within the individual, all three are aiming at the kind of explanation that says: If cause X operates, then effect Y necessarily follows. What we usually accept as the scientific model are explanations that trace chains of cause and effect in this if-then fashion. Clearly this is not the only possible way of explaining things. What is not so clear is whether it is the only *scientific* way of explaining things.

Skinner would say that it is. Maslow, for one, would say that it is not. He would say that explanations based on the goals and purposes of behavior, on the structural and intentional properties of personality, are not only valid but equally scientific. He held, for example, that the basis of his ethical system was scientific. More is involved here than merely the desire to partake of the benefits accruing to scientists in our society.

Sigmund Koch, who should have a perspective on this issue, since he edited the classic six-volume *Psychology: A Study of a Science* (1959, 1962, 1963), concludes that "psychology cannot be a coherent science," and that at least part of psychology ought to be regarded as a branch of the humanities or the liberal arts (1981). No one denies that part of psychology is a science; Koch simply says that all of psychology cannot be one unified, coherent science. The distinction between arts and sciences cuts right through the middle of psychology.

Amadeo Giorgi looked at the same problem, the problem of two psychologies, and refused to concede that one was more worthy than the other to be called a science (1970). He proposed the term *human science* to refer to his brand of phenomenological theory, and the term *natural science* to refer to theories that are modeled after physics or biology. Both have their place in psychology, and both, he insists, are equally scientific. They simply represent different kinds of sciences.

Whether or not you choose to regard personality theories that resemble biography as scientific, it is difficult to deny that they are quite different from personality theories that emulate physics, chemistry, and biology. It is almost impossible to include components from both in one system. They are just not compatible, because they are based on radically different assumptions. Your choice will depend on which assumptions you can live with most comfortably.

Personality theories in the natural-scientific tradition are based on the assumptions of determinism, objectivity, and atomism. Because their goal is the prediction and control of behavior, these theories must assume that behavior is lawfully determined. If they allowed for the capricious operation of free will, these theorists would not be predicting but merely guessing. Natural-scientific theorists strive to find methods that are as objective as possible, in order to guard against the intrusion of personal bias and to insure that all observations will be capable of being replicated. Their goal is to detach themselves insofar as possible from their subject matter. To this end, they often quantify their observations and frequently record them automatically with machines. They prize the experimental method and make every attempt to minimize subjective interpretation. The natural-scientific approach is also characteristically atomistic. It assumes that understanding comes about by reducing the thing being studied to its most elemental particles. The success of physicists in delving ever deeper into the nature of matter—advancing from elements to atoms, from atoms to electrons and protons, and from there to positrons and quarks—is taken as evidence for the wisdom of this strategy. And though holistic field theories in physics have made significant contributions to our understanding of matter during the twentieth century, only Bandura has moderated his atomistic approach in that direction; Cattell and Skinner maintain a strongly atomistic stance. These assumptions, though plausible, are unproven and unprovable. Thus natural science's claims to truth rest upon a foundation that is less secure than most scientists are willing to admit.

Personality theories in the historical-biographical tradition, however, may not have any firmer foundation. As any historian with even a modicum of sophistication will confess, all history is **historiography.** This means that there can be no history without interpretation. The notion of history is merely an ideal; what exists in actuality are various interpretations of history. One of these may be the official interpretation, or even the interpretation agreed upon by the majority of scholars. It may even pass for history. But it is not history; it is the interpretation of history. Even if you had a camera crew on hand to film every event as it happens, that video record, which we so often accept uncritically as an objective account, would still not constitute history. Why not? Because the camera is selective. It does not photograph everything; it aims in one direction and not in others. The picture frame has borders. What is included within those borders and what is left out can make a tremendous difference, as cinematographers well know, in the impression that is created in the viewer. Again, history cannot be recorded, it can only be interpreted. Biography, the study of individual life history, is of course subject to the same limitations. Biographers can develop methods, such as Henry Murray's scrupulous ones, to guard against the introduction of systematic bias. Scholars may reach a consensus, or even unanimous agreement, regarding the interpretation of an individual life history. Yet the final product is always an interpretation, and interpretations inevitably rest upon certain assumptions.

Whether you choose a personality theory in the natural-scientific tradition, one in the tradition of the humanities, or one somewhere between the two, there is no way to avoid making a priori assumptions and thus no guarantee of absolute truth.

THE FOUR CATEGORIES OF PERSONALITY THEORIES

As a further aid in your choice of theoretical options, let us examine the assumptions underlying each of the four types of personality theories we have studied—psychodynamic theories, trait theories, behavioral theories, and humanistic theories.

If psychodynamic theories are equated with psychoanalytic theories (and all four of the psychodynamic theories we studied were psychoanalytic), and if humanistic theories all use a phenomenological approach (and certainly Rogers and Kelly do, with Maslow leaning in that direction), then we can safely say that these psychodynamic and humanistic theories represent the preference for an internal perspective on personality, as opposed to the external perspective preferred by the trait and behavioral theories. Phenomenology and psychoanalysis are similar, in that both concern themselves with the inner mental world of the person as that person sees it. Their viewpoint, insofar as this is possible, is from the inside looking out. Trait and behavioral theorists, on the other hand, prefer to take up their vantage point on the outside, then attempt to look in. Behaviorists are not at all concerned with the individual's inner mental world. Trait theorists are also uninterested in the person's inner world, in focusing on the person's subjective experience and how it is construed. They assume, rather, that the internal traits that they seek to discover are properties of the person, not significantly different in kind from blood pressure or reaction time; and that these traits can best be measured from the outside. Hence psychoanalysis and phenomenology are alike in that they both assume an internal perspective, and behaviorism and trait theories are alike in the they both assume an external perspective on personality.

But oddly enough, there is a way in which behaviorism and phenomenology are alike. Both claim to be empirical. What this means is that they deal only with what is given directly to experience. They try to stay away from interpretation, and to avoid accounting for what is observed by appealing to hypothetical forces or theoretical abstractions. The concrete givens of experience are their subject matter. Of course behaviorism views those concrete givens from an external perspective, while phenomenology looks at them from an internal perspective. Both, however, differ radically from psychoanalytic and trait theories, which infer the existence of forces and entities in the personality that cannot be observed directly. Instincts and traits are hypothetical constructs. Their presumed effects can be observed, but they themselves can only be inferred—they are abstractions. More assumptions, (though not necessarily less tenable ones) are involved in theories of this sort. Thus behavioral theories and phenomenological theories are alike, in that they both deal with empirical events; while psychoanalytic and trait theories are alike, in that they both infer hypothetical forces or entities in the personality. This information is summarized in Table 14–1.

There are some similarities between the diagonally opposite blocks in Table 14–1. Phenomenological and trait theories of personality, for example, are both alike in that they take a descriptive, structural approach to their subject matter. Phenomenological theories attempt to produce a descriptive analysis of the structure of subjective experience. In the same way that the first botanist who looked at a leaf under a microscope was able to describe a structure of which we were previously ignorant, the phenomenologist who examines conscious experience aims to achieve enough power of magnification to see previously undiscovered features. Trait theories also search for structural features, but see them as properties of the person, rather than simply of conscious experience. Their perspective is external. Nevertheless, trait theories, like phenomenological theories, are essentially descriptive. True, they frequently quantify their descriptions, and that does make them seem more scientific. But they are still descriptions and not explanations. Trait theories are concerned with discovering

TABLE 14-1

Two Dimensions of Personality Theories

	Empirical Events	*Hypothetical Forces or Entities*
Internal Perspective	Phenomenology	Psychoanalysis
External Perspective	Behaviorism	Trait

traits that comprise the structure of personality, and then measuring the quantity of each of those traits in various individuals. The project involves describing structural features.

The other two diagonal opposites in Table 14–1, psychoanalysis and behaviorism, are alike in that they are both engaged in producing functional explanations of what people do. They are more concerned with the question of how the personality works than with the question of what the personality is, although this is admittedly more true of behaviorism than psychoanalysis. Functional explanations attempt to trace chains of causes and effects. The causes are typically conceived as forces applying an impetus either from within the personality or from the environment. Since these forces are thought to determine action, the strategy of both psychoanalysis and behaviorism is to identify these important forces and the lawful principles according to which they operate. In this respect, even such traditional adversaries as psychoanalysis and behaviorism have much in common.

In fact, every possible pairing of the four types of personality theories reveals certain similarities. Though they all differ sharply from each other, each one has something important in common with at least one other type. As a result, the history of psychology has been a succession of shifting alliances, sometimes producing rather strange bedfellows.

For the consumer who is shopping for a personality theory, this means that the task of choosing a theory can be reduced to answering two or three dichotomous questions. Do you want a theory that takes an internal perspective, or one that assumes an external perspective? Secondly, do you prefer a theory that is based on empirically observable events, or are you willing to postulate the operation of hypothetical forces or the existence of hypothetical entities? Actually, if you answer just those two questions, you will have decided which of the four types of personality theory you want to buy. The third question serves as a kind of check on your selection: Would you like a theory that is structural and descriptive in its emphasis, or one that is functional and explanatory? If your choices are clearly and logically thought out, the answer to this question will lead you to the same one of the four types of personality theory that you have already chosen on the basis of your answer to the first two questions.

CHOOSING A SPECIFIC THEORY

BASING YOUR CHOICE ON ASSUMPTIONS

Even if you have narrowed your choice down to one of the four types of personality theories, you may still have some difficulty choosing among the specific theories within that category. Perhaps you can make that choice easier for yourself by considering, and personally evaluating, the basic assumptions upon which each theory rests. Some assumptions will undoubtedly be more palatable to you than others.

Many of the issues surrounding the most important assumptions made by each theory have been discussed under the pros and cons in each chapter. However, the stand of each theorist on every assumption has not necessarily been explicated. Table 14–2 indicates the position of each of our theorists on the six assumptions discussed in the introductory chapter. This list of assumptions is by no means exhaustive. Every theory makes many more assumptions than are listed here. I have selected these six, however, because they illuminate the most fundamental disagreements among the various theories. Not every theorist takes a strong stand on each of these six assumptions. Hence not every theorist's name is listed in Table 14–2 alongside each assumption. Only theorists whose position on a given assumption is extreme are included.

Let us review these six assumptions very quickly. Whether you assume freedom or determinism depends on whether you believe that the things you do are produced by your conscious choices and decisions, or caused and programmed by forces beyond your control (and quite possibly outside your knowledge). Do you run the show, or do you just sit there and watch it? That is about what this issue boils down to. Rogers is the most vociferous exponent of the free will position. Skinner has been his archrival, arguing effectively for the deterministic position.

Whether you assume rationalism or irrationalism depends on whether you think that human beings operate primarily on the basis of intellect, or on the basis of impulses and passions that make us do the things we do. It

TABLE 14-2

Positions of Theorists on Basic Assumptions

Freedom	Rogers, Maslow, Allport	Freud, Skinner, Cattell, Erikson, Murray	*Determinism*
Irrational	Freud, Jung	Skinner, Kelly, Allport, Bandura, Rogers, Maslow	*Rational*
Good	Rogers, Maslow, Allport	Freud	*Evil*
Environment	Skinner, Bandura, Erikson	Freud, Jung	*Heredity*
Subjective	Rogers, Kelly	Skinner, Cattell	*Objective*
Holistic	Jung Maslow, Rogers, Murray	Freud, Skinner, Cattell, Bandura	*Atomistic*

was Freud, of course, who built his career on unearthing secret passions and hidden impulses. He even suggested that rationality was nothing but an illusion. Freud's extreme position at the irrationality end of the continuum cannot be offset by any theorist at the rationality end, since no one takes as strong a stand in support of rationality as Freud does for irrationality.

The choice between goodness and evil obviously refers to the issue of whether human nature is intrinsically good or somehow tainted, and hence inherently evil. The so-called tragic view of human nature, dating at least from the days of classical Greece, holds that there is some basic flaw in human nature which limits human perfectibility. Theological doctrines of the fall of Adam and original sin are similar. Freud is unique among the personality theorists we have considered in making this tragic view a fundamental ingredient of his theory. Self-actualization theorists, such as Rogers and Maslow, strongly disagree and assume an extreme position in favor of the essential goodness and perfectibility of human personality.

Assumptions based on the heredity–versus–environment controversy are familiar enough to require little further comment. The issue is simply whether the personality is primarily a product of learning and life experiences, or mainly a product of nature, in the form of instincts, physiological structures, or developmental schedules. The tremendous amount of heat generated by arguments over this issue is due in large part to the implications for political and educational policy that derive from a commitment to one or the other of these assumptions. Skinner is undoubtedly our most outspoken champion of the environmental position, whereas Freud places the greatest emphasis upon the role of hereditary factors in the formation of personality.

The assumption of objectivity or subjectivity is a methodological matter. The question is whether the personality is best understood from the perspective of a detached, dispassionate observer regarding it from the outside, or by an engaged, involved observer looking at it from the inside. The distinction, unfortunately, is not quite so clear-cut as the simple objective-subjective dichotomy implies, since it may be possible, as phenomenologists claim, to study subjectivity objectively. Kelly, for one, would insist that that is his program. Similarly, Rogers resists the implication that he is purely subjective. Nevertheless, both are obviously much less objective, or objective in a different sense, than Skinner, who makes the most extreme argument in favor of objective methods for studying personality.

The assumption of either holism or atomism is also a methodological matter, although it also has metaphysical implications. The methodological question is whether the personality is best understood by regarding it as an indivisible unit, or by breaking it down into some number of constituent parts. The metaphysical question asks whether these alleged constituent parts really exist or are mere abstractions in the mind of the analyst. Maslow, who called his theory *holistic-dynamic,* argued most insistently for the holistic point of view. Skinner, who pictures the personality as the sum total of millions of conditioned responses, and Cattell, who sought to find elements analogous to those in chemistry, represent the most extreme atomistic position.

The more frequent appearance of the names of certain theorists in Table 14–2 indicates that some theorists are more prone than others to assume extreme positions on these issues. It also serves to highlight several very fundamental differences, as well as some unexpected similarities, among the theorists we have studied. For example, Freud and Skinner, whom you might not expect to agree on anything, appear together in their support of determinism and the atomistic approach. They clash violently, however, on the rationality–versus–irrationality and heredity–versus–environment issues. Freud and Rogers disagree on four of our six assumptions, and their names never appear in the same box in Table 14–2. Freud holds to determinism, irrationality, evil, and atomism; Rogers assumes freedom, rationality, good, and holism. Rogers and Skinner, arch-rivals in the debate over freedom–versus–determinism, agree on rationality; yet they disagree on freedom–versus–determinism and holism–versus–atomism.

BASING YOUR CHOICE ON QUESTIONS ADDRESSED

Still undecided? Another manifestation of a theorist's basic assumptions is the nature of the questions his theory is designed to answer. Perhaps it will help you decide which theory is right for you if we reiterate the key question that each of these theories aims to answer. The theory you prefer may be the theory that best answers your question, the question that is of most interest to you personally.

Just as Freud's theory could not be reduced to only one key idea, it also resists being boiled down to one question. Nevertheless, a single unifying theme runs through much of Freud's writing. It is the theme of control. *Freud* asks: *How can a person gain control over his or her life?* Freud's notions of the sexual instincts and unconscious motivation depict the individual as ruled by forces over which there is no rational control. The aim of Freud's psychoanalytic therapy was to decrease the proportion of a patient's behavior that was impulsive and uncontrolled, and to increase the proportion that was under voluntary control. He tried to achieve this aim by making the unconscious conscious. "Where id was, there let ego be," was his motto. The question his theory aims to answer, then, is how this state of affairs can be accomplished.

The question that perplexed *Jung* for all of his professional life, and which his theory consequently is designed to answer, is: *Why are the same themes and symbols produced by people in such widely separated times and places?* Do they represent some universal structures in the human mind? What are those structures, and how do they influence behavior?

Erikson, of course, was captivated by the question of identity. *How does a person answer the question: Who am I?* That is the issue his theory is designed to illuminate.

For *Murray* the question was always: *How shall we capture or characterize personality?* His goal was to devise some shorthand notation with which he could epitomize any individual personality. An x-ray of the mind, a set of psychological fingerprints—the fantasy of finding something of this sort was a lifelong preoccupation of Henry Murray.

Allport was fascinated by the variety of human individuality. His question was: *What makes each individual unique?*

Cattell, though also a trait theorist, is concerned with the ways in which human beings are all alike. His question: *What are the common elements from which all personalities are compounded?* Once that question is answered, of course, the amount of each element in any individual personality can be assayed.

For *Skinner*, the big questions have to do with learning, and more specifically with learning from experience. *What principles underlie learning by experience?* That is the question Skinner's research program sought to answer. How do the consequences of behavior change behavior? Are there any general principles or laws we can observe?

Bandura's question is similar to Skinner's—not surprising, since both are behaviorists—except that it has to do with learning by observation: *What principles underlie learning by watching?* How does watching someone else's behavior change the observer's behavior? Are there any general principles or laws to be discovered?

The perfectibility of human nature has been the abiding concern of Carl Rogers. For *Rogers,* the key question to be answered is: *What constitutes optimal human development and what conditions foster it?* What are the characteristics of a human being who has become everything that a human being can become? And what events and experiences contribute to growth in this direction?

Maslow's project was more conspicuously ethical. He wanted to know how we should live. The answer, he thought, could be found in human nature itself. *What ethical guide to living can de deduced from human nature?* is the question *Maslow's* theory seeks to answer.

Kelly was impressed by how the pictures of the world that people carry around with them inside their heads either interfere with their adjustment to life or facilitate it. The basic question *Kelly's* theory attempts to answer is: *How do people represent the world to themselves?* Are there any general principles, in the form of postulates and corollaries, that regulate this process of construing?

Table 14–3 summarizes the questions addressed by each of the theorists we have studied. One of the main reasons why all of these theories are so different, and in fact often conflict, is that each theorist was concerned with answering a slightly different question. Just as the concerns of these theorists differ, so the concerns of you, the readers of this book, will differ. Those differences are legitimate. Not everyone is interested in the same thing. The theory that is most meaningful to you will in all probability be the one that addresses the question which has been most personally perplexing for you.

TABLE 14–3

Questions Addressed by Each Theory

Theorist	Question
Freud	How can people gain control of their lives?
Jung	Why the same themes and symbols in widely separated times and places?
Erikson	How does a person answer: Who am I?
Murray	How shall we capture or characterize personality?
Allport	What makes each individual unique?
Cattell	What are the common elements from which all personalities are compounded?
Skinner	What principles underlie learning by experience?
Bandura	What principles underlie learning by observing?
Rogers	What is optimal human development and what conditions foster it?
Maslow	What ethical guide for living can be deduced from human nature?
Kelly	How do people represent the world to themselves?

BASING YOUR CHOICE ON UTILITY

Perhaps you are a practical person who becomes impatient with all this abstract talk about assumptions and theoretical questions. Maybe you are just interested in finding a theory that works. In that case, it makes sense to think of theories as tools, each one specifically adapted to a particular task. You can drive nails with a screwdriver, but it does not work nearly so well as a hammer, the tool that was designed for that job. On the other hand, a screwdriver is unsurpassed for driving screws, because that is the job it was made to do. The same is true of theories. Like the tools in the toolkit, each theory does a certain job best . Some are more useful than others. Just how useful any one of them is, is partly a matter of tastes and preferences, or even of values. Consider, for example, a molding cutter that does nothing more than apply a decorative edge to a piece of stock. It is useful, but perhaps it is not as essential as the saw that is needed to construct the main body of a desk or bureau. Some tools seem slightly more frivolous—luxury options, if you will. But again, let me remind you, that is a question of values.

Having said that, let me cautiously suggest that some of the theories included in this book are generally regarded as being more practical than others. Perhaps the distinction should not be so much between practical and impractical theories as it should be between theories that are applied and theories that are academic. Using that system of classification, the theories that fall under the heading of *applied* are those of Skinner, Bandura, Cattell, Freud, Kelly, and Rogers. Those under the heading of *academic* belong to Maslow, Allport, and Erikson. This is not intended to imply that any of these theories is exclusively applied or academic, only that each emphasizes one more than the other. Jung and Murray are not included under either heading, because they both seem to emphasize applied and academic concerns about equally (see Table 14–4).

TABLE 14–4

Applied Versus Academic Theories

Applied	Academic
Skinner	Maslow
Bandura	Allport
Cattell	Erikson
Freud	
Kelly	
Rogers	

Carrying the tool analogy a step further, the personality theories we have studied can be regarded as tools designed to do one of five different jobs. Many of them are designed, for example, for *clinical* applications. They are particularly helpful in the practice of counseling or psychotherapy. The theories that fall into this category are those of Freud, Bandura, Rogers, Kelly, and perhaps to a somewhat lesser degree, Skinner. There are, however, many different tasks that confront a clinician, and perhaps a further distinction may help in selecting the right tool for the job. Behavioral theories, such as those of Bandura and Skinner, are particularly appropriate for working with clients whose symptoms are rather clearly defined—people who suffer from crippling fears such as **agoraphobia**, for example; or who seem unable to manage addictive behaviors such as drug or alcohol abuse, smoking, gambling, and overeating. Wherever there is a specific target behavior that can changed through some kind of program of training, a behavioral approach is probably the most effective tool to use. In fact, whenever the solution to the problem lies in having the client learn a repertoire of new skills—whenever the problem is one of acquiring know-how—the insights of Skinner and Bandura will be uniquely relevant. The theories of Freud, Rogers, and Kelly, on the other hand, are particularly appropriate for treating clients whose symptoms may be harder to pin down, and who suffer more from what are sometimes referred to as **existential neuroses**. These clients are not lacking so much in know-how as in know-what. They just do not know what to do with their lives. They experience great difficulty in making decisions. They seem to suffer a paralysis of the will. Their fundamental problem may be a pervasive sense of meaninglessness. A more self-reflective, insight-oriented therapy may be more appropriate in these cases. In addition to the theories of Freud, Rogers, and Kelly, those of Jung and Erikson are also relevant to this concern.

In the second place, some theories are expressly designed for use in *personnel* selection. Cattell's theory is the most obvious candidate for this use. Murray too may be included under this heading, although I have not emphasized that aspect of his theory.

Third, some theories are relevant to *educational applications*. They are useful in guiding the design of training programs in business and industry, or in improving teaching techniques in the schools. While none of the

TABLE 14–5

The Job for the Theory

Clinical	Personnel	Educational	Biographical	Policy
Freud	Cattell	Skinner	Murray	Maslow
Bandura	(Murray)	Rogers	Allport	(Skinner)
Rogers		(Bandura)	Erikson	(Rogers)
Kelly			(Freud)	
(Skinner)			(Jung)	
(Jung)				

theorists we have considered has designed his theory exclusively for this application, several have devoted considerable attention to it. They include Skinner, Rogers, and to a lesser extent, Bandura.

Fourth, if your task is *biographical* or historical, there are still other theories that are useful in helping you to understand the lives of individuals and their unique roles in history. Murray, Allport, and Erikson have all designed theories to do this job. Also applicable, although not designed quite so exclusively for this task, are the theories of Freud and Jung.

Fifth, certain theories are more broad and general in their application. They are designed to aid in the formulation of social *policy*. How can we design a better society and upgrade the quality of life for all our citizens? That is the job tackled single-mindedly by Maslow's theory. And though it is not the principle task for which the theories of Skinner and Rogers have been designed, it is a job to which both have applied their theories also.

These five kinds of jobs, and the theories designed for each, are summarized in Table 14–5.

An old saw states that there is nothing more practical than a good theory. Clearly there are no theories that are not useful. What theory is most useful depends on the job that you want to do. And the choice of the job you want to do depends on your personal system of values. The desire to be done with theories and simply to find a tool that works may be an effort to dodge questions of value. It is a dodge that cannot succeed, however, because every technical application of a theory rests upon certain value assumptions and carries with it certain value implications. Whether one buys Maslow's theory or not, it is hard to deny the validity of his observation that psychology, and especially personality psychology, is inextricably intertwined with ethics.

A FINAL WORD

Perhaps you have settled on a favorite theory by now. Maybe you picked one a long time ago, when you first read the chapter devoted to it—a kind of love at first sight. But if you have not decided to buy one brand lock, stock and barrel, do not be dismayed. The majority of students prefer to select components from a number of different theories and to put them together themselves to build their own personalized system. If you want to buy one of the theories from this catalogue complete and as a unit, that is fine. But you should not feel pressured to do so out of a mistaken sense that that is what most people do.

If you do elect to put together your own system by using parts from several different theories, however, you should be alert to the possibility that you may encounter problems of compatibility. The parts may not fit logically together. Their assumptive bases may even be mutually contradictory. Components from various brands of personality theories are not universally interchangeable. Some simply will not plug into each other without damaging the logical consistency of the component. Logical consistency may be the hobgoblin of small minds, yet there is a limit to how much inconsistency you can have and still pretend to have a theory.

Fortunately for those whose concerns are primarily practical and applied, a system that is not theoretically flawless may still work rather well. Despite logical contradictions among the theories from which they derive, practical applications of those theories may often be combined effectively. For example, the treatment program in one hospital unit where patients are suffering from chronic pain syndrome uses diagnostic personality tests based on both the trait and the psychodynamic traditions; hypnosis; psychodynamic psychotherapy; biofeedback; relaxation training; systematic desensitization; and a **token economy**. The theories on which all these diagnostic and therapeutic techniques are based cannot possibly be made logically compatible, yet the patients in this unit regularly get better. Why practices based on contradictory theories should add up to effective therapy is a moot question, but it is something that has been demonstrated too often for us to deny that it can happen. And when it does happen, we cannot help wondering why. Rather than dispensing with our theories, we feel compelled to revise them or develop new ones. The human mind seems to abhor the vacuum of having no theory.

Perhaps this suggests that Kelly's claim is the only thing of which we can be absolutely certain—human beings inevitably hatch theories to explain to themselves and others why things happen as they do. Maybe Kelly is right when he says that we need these systems of constructs to predict and control future events. But whatever the reason, it does seem true that everyone of us cannot avoid formulating some kind of theory, no matter how vaguely articulated, about why people do what they do. Everyone is a personality theorist; it cannot be otherwise. My hope is that this consideration of some of the greatest ideas in personality theory has helped you to become more self-conscious of your own personal constructs; led you to evaluate them, pro and con, in a new light; and provided you with some new options, new components you may not have known were available.

REFERENCES

Giorgi, A. (1970). *Psychology as a human science*. New York: Harper and Row.

Koch, S. (Ed.). (1959, 1962, 1963). *Psychology: A study of a science* (Vols. 1-6). New York: McGraw-Hill.

Koch, S. (1981). The nature and limits of psychological knowledge. *American Psychologist, 36*, 257–269.

GLOSSARY

60 to a column?.

Accommodation   the creation of new concepts and mental categories to classify new stimuli, according to Piaget's theory.

Actuarial prediction   pertaining to the kind of forecasting of risks on the basis of which insurance companies establish their premiums.

Affective   pertaining to the emotions or feelings.

Agoraphobia   fear of open spaces; a behavior disorder in which the patient may be afraid to leave the house, or may be subject to sudden attacks of panic when on the street.

Anal stage   second stage of psychosexual development (1-3 years old), during which instinctual gratification derives from bowel functions.

Analysis   the intellectual operation of breaking things down into their constituent parts for purposes of understanding.

Analytic psychology   the brand name for Jung's theory of personality and technique of psychotherapy.

Anorectic behavior   self-starvation or refusal to eat, which is the primary symptom of persons diagnosed as having the behavior disorder of anorexia nervosa.

Archetype   unconscious collective ideas that motivate behavior and manifest themselves concretely in myths, symbols, and dreams.

Assimilation   the use of existing concepts and mental categories to classify new stimuli, according to Piaget's theory.

Assumption   an assertion taken for granted or accepted without proof.

Atomism   the idea that things must be broken down into their constituent parts in order to be understood.

Autistic   refers to a disorder of infancy or early childhood in which the patient is withdrawn from others, suffers distortions of perception, is intolerant of changes, and may show bizarre motor or speech behavior.

Aversive stimuli   stimuli that people prefer to avoid.

Baseline   term used by behavior modifiers to refer to frequency of emission of target behavior under ordinary conditions, i.e., before any therapeutic intervention.

B-cognition   cognition or knowledge of being, knowledge of the object in and of itself as an end in and of itself; the kind of knowledge conferred by the peak experiences.

326

Cardinal trait   in rare individuals, a trait that so dominates the personality as to push all other traits into the background.

Castration anxiety   irrational fear of having the penis cut off or being otherwise dismembered or mutilated.

Castration wish   desire to cut off someone else's penis or otherwise physically injure him or her, or to diminish his or her power.

Central trait   a characteristic that pervades the entire personality and motivates every aspect of behavior.

Charismatic   capable of inspiring popular enthusiasm or support as a result of unusual qualities of leadership, said in some cases to result from divine inspiration.

Classical conditioning   also called respondent conditioning: Pavlov's dog type of learning in which previously neutral stimulus becomes capable of evoking response through repeated pairing with stimulus that naturally produces that response.

Coefficient of correlation   a measure of the extent to which two or more things that are observed to change, change together.

Cognitive   having to do with the intellect or the rational faculties; processes by which we acquire knowledge.

Compulsion   an act that a person feels irrationally compelled to perform repeatedly and often ritualistically.

Conative   pertaining to the aspect of experience having to do with willing, striving, and effort.

Conditions of worth   requirements or criteria that people set for themselves and on the basis of which they assess their personal value, depending upon whether they meet or fall short of said criteria.

Congruence   Rogers' term for a perfect match between inner feelings and desires and outward actions, with resulting sense of being real or authentic as a person.

Constitutional trait   a trait that derives from one's hereditary endowment.

Constructive alternativism   refers to the fact that events are capable of being construed in more than one way, and hence that an individual may change her or his contructs.

Control group   subjects in an experiment who do not receive the experimental treatment or manipulation.

Correlation matrix   a table of coefficients of correlation among multiple variables, e.g., the correlation between A and B, A and C, B and C, etc.

Culture fair tests   tests that are not biased in favor of any one cultural group.

Cybernetic   concerning the manner in which feedback systems control and regulate behavior.

Dependent variable   responses of subjects in an experiment to the experimental manipulation.

Dialectical   based upon a dialogue of question and answer; or based on the philosophy of Hegel, which emphasized change resulting from the opposition of contradictory forces (thesis and antithesis), whose resolution (synthesis) produces a new thesis.

D-cognition   ordinary knowing, cognition organized by deficiency needs.

Defense mechanism   an unconsciously motivated distortion of reality that we adopt to protect ourselves against the unpleasant experience of anxiety.

Discriminative stimulus   any stimulus, which having been present when a behavior was reinforced, becomes capable of eliciting that behavior; a sign or a signal that reinforcement may be available.

DSM-III   the *Diagnostic and Statistical Manual*, third edition, of the American Psychiatric Association.

Eclectic   choosing what seems best from the theories of others.

Ego   the executive agency of personality which negotiates with the external world of reality and which includes the subjective sense of selfhood.

Ego psychology   a school of neo-Freudian theory that holds that the ego does not operate exclusively in the service of the id, but has energy resources of its own.

Elementalism   the idea that things must be broken down into their constituent parts in order to be understood.

Empathy   process of putting oneself in the place of another and seeing things as she or he does.

Encode   to convert information into a suitable shorthand for easy storage in memory and effective subsequent retrieval.

Enuresis   involuntary urination, bed-wetting, etc.

Environmental-mold trait   a trait that has been learned through interaction with the environment.

Empiricist   the philosophical position that assumes that knowledge is derived, or is to be derived, from experiment or from sensory experience.

Episode   the smallest unit of analysis in Murray's analysis of events—namely, a single creature–environment or need–press interaction.

Erg   a source trait that is motivational and the result of hereditary endowment.

Ethnography   a branch of anthropology that attempts to describe and classify cultures scientifically.

Ethology   that branch of biology which studies animals in their natural habitat.

Etymological root   the linguistic derivation of a word.

Existential   refers to the notion that individuals are absolutely free and must accept responsibility for their actions in an ambiguous and absurd world.

Existential neurosis   a condition in which patients complain of a lack of meaning and direction in their lives, have difficulty making decisions, and feel empty and mechanical.

Extinguished   refers to behavior which once conditioned is now no longer performed.

Extrovert   an outgoing personality type who makes friends easily and appears open, unguarded, and carelessly confident.

Factor analysis   an elaboration of correlational techniques which tries to discover the elemental traits or abilities underlying test responses.

Fixation   failure to grow beyond a given developmental stage.

Fixed interval schedule   reinforcement is delivered after the passage of every interval of n units of time if at least one response has occurred during that time.

Fixed ratio schedule   reinforcement is delivered after every nth response.

Fixed-role therapy   Kelly's brand of psychotherapy in which patients role-play characters who use new and different personal construct systems.

Free association   technique Freud devised for making unconscious processes conscious, wherein the patient lies on a couch and says whatever comes into his or her mind no matter how silly or embarrassing.

Fully functioning person   an individual who is in the process of becoming everything that he or she potentially is, and who consequently reveals the essence of human nature.

Functional analysis   an analysis aimed at studying the consequences of manipulating specific variables.

Genital stage   final and mature stage of psychosexual development (beginning at puberty), during which the focus of instinctual gratification is the genital organs, but in the context of unselfish loving relationships.

Gestalt psychology   a school of psychology that emphasizes the innate organizing tendencies of the mind, and champions an holistic approach to psychology.

Historiography   the interpretation of history

Holism   the assumption that phenomena can only be understood when looked at as a whole, that atomism leads to error.

Hypothetical construct   a force or entity the existence of which is inferred in order to explain an observed phenomenon.

Id   unconscious instinctual mental processes which motivate all behavior.

Identification   assuming the characteristics and behavior of another person in an attempt to appropriate her or his identity.

Independent variable   conditions in an experiment fixed or manipulated by the experimenter in order to study their possible effects.

Individual differences   the study of variations among human beings on measures of various traits and abilities.

Inductive reasoning   reasoning in which generalizations about an entire class of phenomena are based on observation of a part of that class; reasoning from particular to general.

Interactionalism   the theory that both internal traits and external situational factors determine behavior.

Introspection   literally to look within, to observe systematically one's own mental processes.

Introvert   an inhibited, retiring personality type, who prefers solitude and mental reflection, and who tends to shy away from social interaction.

Latency stage   fourth stage of psychosexual development (6-12 years old), during which the instincts lie dormant or are sublimated in academic and athletic pursuits.

Law of parsimony   the principle, accepted by scientists, that the best theory is the simplest theory consonant with all observed data.

Live modeling   a method of behavior therapy based on vicarious conditioning, in which patients observe models engaging in behaviors patients find aversive, but with models coming to no harm.

Longitudinal   refers to a research strategy that studies individuals as they grow and develop over a long period of time.

Long-term memory   permanent memory.

Mandala   any of a varaiety of circular symbols representing the universe or the self, e.g., the zodiac.

Mechanism   the view that natural processes (including perhaps psychological processes) are explicable in terms of the same physical principles that are thought to govern machines.

Metaphysical   concerning the ultimate nature of reality, of what really is real.

Modeling   learning by observing the performance of others, and especially the consequences of that performance.

Multiple personality   a kind of double amnesia wherein one person displays two or more distinct and separate personalities, e.g., as in *The Three Faces of Eve*.

Mutation   genetic alteration producing inheritable change in an organism.

Need   an hypothetical construct inferred to account for the organism's wants and requirements.

Negatively reinforced behavior   behavior that has been learned because it was regularly followed by escape from or disappearance of aversive stimuli.

Neo-Freudian   any of a variety of theories of personality and/or psychotherapy based upon Freud's theory, but sufficiently different as not to be approved by the Psychoanalytic Society.

Neurosis   a pattern of maladaptive behavior characterized by excessive anxiety and/or maladaptive techniques for controlling anxiety.

Normal distribution curve   the bell-shaped line that results when observations of a characteristic such as height or IQ scores in a large population are plotted on a graph.

Obession   an idea that continually intrudes into consciousness, e.g., the tune that keeps running through your head.

Oedipus complex   the bundle of feelings and motives surrounding the three- to six-year-old boy's romantic attachment to his mother, including his desire to do away with his father, and his fear that the father will retaliate by castrating him.

Operant conditioning   process of learning as a result of the consequences following behavior.

Operational definition   the defining of concepts on the basis of procedures or operations, e.g., intelligence may be operationally defined as your score on a given test.

Oral deprivation   failure to get enough sucking and other oral gratification during the first-psychosexual stage of development, resulting in fixation at that stage.

Oral stage   first stage of psychosexual development (0-1 year old), during which instinctual gratification is focused on the mouth.

Ordination   Murray's term for establishing long-term plans and arranging them in order of priority.

Pansexualism   the idea that all behavior is sexually motivated; literally, sex is everywhere.

Paranormal   psychic phenomena, such as extrasensory perception, clairvoyance, mind over matter, etc.

Peak experience   an ecstatic mystical experience, such as occurs in connection with religious exercises, sexual orgasm, philosophical insight, athletic success, observation of art, childbirth, or drug use, and which conveys, according to Maslow, special knowledge.

Penis envy   literally, desire to have a penis or jealousy of those who do; symbolically, desire for stereotypically masculine kinds of power.

Personal construct   a mental pigeonhole or category in a system of classification according to which a person organizes her or his experience in order to predict future occurrences of similar events.

Persona   literally, the mask; figuratively, one's public personality.

Phallic stage   third stage of psychosexual development (3-6 years old), during which the focus of instinctual gratification is the genital organs, and the child first becomes aware of sexuality.

Phenomenological   an approach to psychology that focuses on people's subjective experience of self and world.

Phobia   an irrational fear, i.e., a fear of something most people do not fear, or a much more intense than usual fear of something most people fear only mildly.

Pleasure principle   Freud's theory that people are motivated to maximize pleasure and minimize pain.

Positive reinforcement   any stimulus which, when it follows a response, makes it more probable that that response will be emitted again.

Press   the power that objects in the environment (including other people) have to benefit or to harm a person.

Primary reinforcement   gratification of innate rather than learned needs or drives—food, sex, sleep, etc.

Proactive   self-generated, caused by something within the person rather than by environmental factors.

Proceeding   a unit of analysis in Murray's analysis of events, in which a person does something to an object, or vice versa, actions and reactions follow, and then the action is concluded.

Projective test   a technique for assessing personality in which the subject responds to an ambiguous stimulus by producing a story, drawing, description, or whatever. Inadvertently, subjects reveal some of their personality in their productions.

Prospection   Murray's term for the preliminary phase of planning an action during which one imagines the possible consequences of various plans.

Psychohistory   an interpretation of history or of historical characters in the light of a psychological theory.

Psychological hedonism   the theory that human behavior is motivated by pleasure seeking.

Psychopath   an individual having a personality disorder characterized by antisocial behavior, inability to form deep personal attachments, and very weak conscience.

Purposive behaviorism   the brand name of Edwin Tolman's theory, which emphasized how the attraction of goals directs behavior.

Regression   going backward through developmental stages, thus becoming progressively immature,

Reinforcement   an event that follows a response and strengthens it, making it more likely to be repeated.

Remediation   remedying or correcting developmental defects.

Repertoire   a collection of available behaviors capable of being performed at any given moment.

Replicate   to repeat or do again, especially as in an experiment.

Repression   unconsciously motivated process of keeping unconscious, or making unconscious by forgetting, instinctual urges, feelings, and memories that would create undue anxiety if consciously recognized.

Resistance   point at which a patient free associating in psychoanalysis "draws a blank" and cannot think of any associations.

Rorschach test   a projective test in which the subject interprets ten inkblots, first as whole images, and then with reference to specific parts of each inkblot.

Rotation   a mathematical procedure involved in factor analysis, which affects the number and nature of factors found.

Schedule of reinforcement   the timetable of reinforcement of responses, according to rate or interval.

Scheduling   term used by Murray to refer to the fact that in planning events in one's life, one must arrange one's time and perhaps forego certain activities in favor of others.

Secondary trait   a trait that does not pervade the entire personality and hence manifests itself only under certain circumstances, e.g., musical talent, impatience with machines that do not work.

Self-actualizing person   an individual who is in the process of becoming everything that he or she potentially is, and who consequently reveals the essence of human nature.

Self-reinforcement   compliments or criticism one gives oneself; roughly equivalent to one's conscience.

Sensitization   the process of becoming attentive to or even vigilant about a stimulus.

Sentiment   a source trait that is motivational and was learned.

Serial   Murray's term for an intermittent succession of proceedings, all of which follow the same theme.

Serial program   one of several terms Murray uses to refer to the planning by a person of an entire course of events in his or her life.

Serial thema   a characteristic interaction of need and press that runs through many proceedings.

Sociobiology   a theory of human social behavior recently advanced by biologists, emphasizing the role of genetic factors in producing behaviors that contribute to the survival or extinction of species in the course of evolution.

Solipsism   the theory that only the self can be known with certainty to exist.

Sophistry   false and deceptive reasoning.

Source trait   one of 15 or 20 of the very most elemental building blocks of personality discovered by Cattell through factor analysis.

Sublimation   the process whereby instinctual energies are rechannelled so that substitute gratification is found.

Superego   that aspect of personality which corresponds approximately to the ordinary idea of the conscience, including ideals and principles on the one hand, and guilt induction on the other.

Surface trait   one of a cluster of 40 or so traits discovered by Cattell by calculating what observable traits are highly intercorrelated.

Symbolic modeling   a method of behavior therapy like live modeling except that patients view models on film.

Synthesis   the process of combining elements or constituent parts into a unified whole.

Systematic desensitization   a method of behavior therapy in which the patient is conditioned to associate previously anxiety-producing stimuli with states of relaxation.

Taxonomy   a system of classification.

Token econony   a behavior therapy technique in which subjects are reinforced for performing target behaviors with tokens—poker chips, check marks, or whatever—which can be cashed in later for candy, privileges, or other desired items.

Transference   process that occurs in psychoanalysis when the patient reacts to the analyst as father, mother, or some other emotionally significant person from his or her past.

Unconditional positive regard   non-judgmental acceptance of a person without her or his being required to meet any requirements; acceptance regardless of merit.

Urethral eroticism   the confusion of sexual feelings with the process of urination, so that urination and everything associated with it produces sexual "kicks."

Variable interval schedule   delivery of reinforcement occurs at the end of each time period if at least one response has been emitted, but the length of time periods changes from one period to the next.

Variable ratio schedule   delivery of reinforcement is contingent upon the number of responses, but that number changes after each reinforcement is delivered, e.g., gambling situations.

Vicarious conditioning   the conditioning that may result from observing someone else being conditioned.

Vicarious reinforcement   reinforcement you receive by watching someone else perform a behavior and be reinforced for it.

INDEX

A

Addiction, 196
Adler, A., 60, 121, 271
Aggression, 62, 215-216, 219-220, 224, 276-277
Alexander, F., 117
Allport, F., 140-141
Allport, G., 3, 5, 14, 21, 23, 25, 118, 140-159, 163-164, 292, 312-313, 321-322, 324
Anastasi, A., 175
Anima, 81
Animus, 81
Archetype, 78-85, 88-90
Assumptions, 8-13, 130-131, 316-320, 325
  atomism, elementalism, 12, 314, 319-320
  causality, 9, 130-131, 317
  determinism, 9-10, 53-54, 107-108, 191, 204-209, 235-236, 259, 314, 318
  free will, 9-10, 53-54, 107-108, 204-209, 235-236, 240-241, 259, 318
  good or evil human nature, 11, 319-320
  heredity vs. environment, 11, 80-83, 85, 89-90, 107-108, 182, 191, 232, 319-320
  holism, 12-13, 240-241, 259, 314, 319-320
  irrationality, 10-11, 308-309, 318-320
  linear time, 8-9
  metaphysical, 8-11, 205
  methodological, 11-13, 205
  objectivity, 11-12, 314, 319
  orderliness, 8
  rationality, 10-11, 308-309, 318-320
  subjectivity, 12, 240-241, 259-260, 319
Atomism (*see* Assumption, atomism)
Attentional processes, 218-220
Attitude, 170, 182
Autonomy, 98

B

Bandura, A., 3, 30-31, 182-183, 214-239, 260, 264-265, 312-314, 321-324
Banker, S., 106
Bannister, D., 302-303
Barrett-Lennard, G., 261-262
Basic need, 273-278, 287
Basic trust, 98
Bavelas, J., 303
B-cognition, 282-283
Behavior modification, 31, 54, 183, 188-189, 201-204, 208, 216, 226-227, 235
  experiment, 202-203
Behavioral theory, 182-183, 315-317, 323
Behaviorism, 89, 285
Behavior therapy (*see* Psychotherapy, behavioral)
Benedict, R., 271
Bernheim, H., 41-42
Bias
  cultural, 176
  observer, 22, 30, 131-132
  sample, 23, 121

Photo Credits

†